T0365255

Paradox in the Contrivance of Human Development

Robert Kowalski

iUniverse

PARADOX IN THE CONTRIVANCE OF HUMAN DEVELOPMENT

iUniverse books may be ordered through booksellers or by contacting:

iUniverse LLC
1663 Liberty Drive
Bloomington, IN 47403
www.iuniverse.com
1-800-Authors (1-800-288-4677)

ISBN: 978-1-4917-4035-4 (sc)
ISBN: 978-1-4917-4036-1 (e)

Printed in the United States of America.

iUniverse rev. date: 11/18/2014

This book is dedicated to my wife, children and grandsons, and to three friends who are no longer with us

–Dr. Rod East, Chris Morrice and
Cristina Maria Dib Taxi.

And the end men looked for cometh not,
And a path is there where no man thought:
So hath it fallen here.

Euripides, The Medea

This book is by way of an anthology largely made up of previously published works. As such I would like to acknowledge the generosity of the publishers of the following articles:

With kind permission from Taylor & Francis - www.tandfonline.com

Chapter 1 was originally published as: *Journal of Comparative Social Welfare*. 26 (2-3), 153-164.

Chapter 3 draws on parts of: *World Futures* 61(3), 188 – 198.

Chapter 5, now modified, was originally published as: *Journal of Comparative Social Welfare*. 27 (3), 189-205.

Chapter 7 was originally published as: *World Futures* 69 (2), 75-88.

Inderscience

Chapter 3, now modified, was originally published in: *International Journal of Management Concepts and Philosophy* 2 (2), 168-182.

Elements of Chapter 10 are drawn from parts of: *International Journal of Management Practice* 2 (4), 297 – 305.

With kind permission from Pluto Journals

The first part of Chapter 8 was originally published as: *World Review of Political Economy* 3 (1), 30-42.

With kind permission from Springer Science+Business Media B.V.

Chapter 2 was originally published as: Chapter 10. In Georg Peter & Reuss-Markus Krausse (eds.) *Selbstbeobachtung der modern*

Gesellschaft und die neuen Grenzen des Sozialen. pp. 185-201. Wiesbaden: VS Verlag.

With kind permission from Protosociology

Chapter 4 was originally published in: *Protosociology* 29, 149-171.

Chapter 6 was originally published as: *Protosociology* 30, 286-312.

Parts of Chapter 10 are drawn from: *Protosociology* 20, 390 – 411.

Finally

I am also grateful to Mike Carter for permission to use Figure 4.1; to Dr. Milford Bateman for permission to use Figure 9.1; and to Professor David Ellerman for permission to quote extensively from *Helping People Help Themselves*.

Contents

Acknowledgements

The ideas expressed in these pages have crystalized over twenty years of professional work and academic study. In addition to the authors cited in the text I have been greatly influenced by personal exchanges with a great number of colleagues. Amongst them I would like to thank Professors David Ellerman, Pervaiz Ahmed, Gerhard Preyer, Brij Mohan, and Neil Malcolm for their support at the outset and at key moments along the way. I would also like to thank individuals who have contributed by reading and criticizing earlier drafts of particular sections including Dr. Milford Bateman, Professor Steve Martin, Dr. John Smith and Professor Edward Majewski. In particular I would like to thank Professors Bruce Baker, Marcel Botelho and Steve Bartlett, Dr. Ryszard Kamiński, Inga Kaškelyte and Steve O'Connor without whose sustained, personal support and encouragement the work would have been impossible.

Preface

I have been very fortunate in being able to work in both education and rural development, which has allowed me to interact with people from the widest range of backgrounds and situations, and to be humbled by their extraordinary generosity to me as I have trespassed upon their struggles, their aspirations and their triumphs. I must make it clear from the outset that, in my professional life, I have never been engaged in what I will call Humanitarian Assistance, but have been challenged by the context that is understood to be Development Assistance.

For many years now I have felt the need to share some of my thoughts and perceptions from this experience with a broader audience. As Adam Smith (2006, p.336) noted: "*The desire of being believed, the desire of persuading, of leading, and directing other people, seems to be one of the strongest of all our natural desires.*" Following my retirement from activity in the field and the admonitions of Søren Kierkegaard (Ferré, 1998), I can procrastinate no longer. Of course there are other texts that I should read and other observations that I should make before I set pen to paper, but time is pressing and I must take action today.

My purposes in writing are both to inform and particularly to provoke my fellow professionals who are engaged in the '*Social Welfare*' business, and to put my thinking to the test of collegial criticism. As Sabel and Reddy (2003, p.3) suggested: "*consider what follows not as ... a new cathedral of development thinking, but rather as an offering in the bazaar of collaborative work on a theme that concerns us all.*" To these ends I direct my writing towards advisers and consultants who influence the management activities of '*Social Welfare*', in all of its many guises, through their engagement with governments and civil society organisations, including academics and teachers in institutions of adult education.

By following the approach that Ellerman (1995) came to describe as '*Intellectual Trespassing*', I believe that I have arrived at a contribution that has novelty and value because of the very diverse nature of my reading and the varied directions that my pursuit of self-knowledge has taken as a result of my own practical experiences. These parallel activities of study and action have shaped my particular, idiosyncratic perceptions that, I hope, will represent a fresh synthesis that is both broad in scope and pertinent in content. I hope to make this contribution both challenging and practical. In short I am attempting a very ambitious project: a journey of exploration which, like '*the grand tour*', is less about reaching a final destination than about the impact that the process of travel will have upon the traveller.

My entry point is a concern felt by many, and frequently expressed, that all is not well in the business of Social Welfare (Dichter, 2003; Mohan, 2011).

My subject is management, but management in the context of local and international social development. This, Thomas (2000) has suggested, is qualitatively different from management conducted in other contexts. However, many of the issues that I will explore are pertinent to management wherever it occurs and, as I will show, the context of Social Development does throw up some difficult challenges for managers, consideration of which has important implications for both those development professionals and managers in what Deci (1995, p.158) refers to as: "*one-up positions*" in other contexts that are related to development through having to pursue organisational missions that encompass the achievement of external social impact[1], as well as having to achieve more proximal organisational change.

These differences and similarities are predicated upon what I will argue is a confusion of spheres of organisational activities, which represent hierarchically dissociated management roles, which itself is linked to a confusion of logical typing that generates the very paradoxes that managers have to wrestle with across the board.

Given this situation, I must begin by exploring development to ensure that you, my reader, will be able to recognise the boundaries and overlaps with your own contexts. I will then explore the nature of paradox, from a philosophical perspective, to establish the dimensions of the field that I wish to elaborate. After that I will turn to specific manifestations of paradox in the management and development contexts with sorties into anthropology, sociology and economics, culminating in a deliberation of the phenomena known as double binds. The entire piece will be completed by a consideration of Action Research and Higher Education in the development context, and drawing out a brief set of recommendations.

My chosen style of writing seeks to give due recognition to the authors who have shaped my thinking, from my earliest days, by using their own words to illustrate and elaborate particular points in the unfolding argument. As Dreschler (2004, p.72) explained: "*on such a potentially contentious question there appear[s] to be some safety in borrowed authority.*" This also ensures that my paraphrasing takes the form of selecting passages rather than providing a complete interpretation, a procedure that should enable the reader to judge the extent to which I have grasped the original author's intention. As Yrjö Engeström put it:

---

1 For example Education Institutions at all levels, Social Services, Prisons and Health Services.

An original quotation, when it is not mishandled and mutilated so as to be totally subordinated to the single-minded purpose of the author, represents a ***voice*** *and a* ***language*** *of a researcher other than the author. It represents a dynamism of its own, never perfectly in line with the author's intentions. It allows for a variety of interpretations and associations, not only the ones the author employs in his line of reasoning.* (Engeström, 2007, p.13)

Chapter 1

The Phenomenology of Development

1 Introduction

The concept *development* means different things to different people. For some it links to the process of maturation of the individual human being - physical, psychological and emotional. For others it conjures up images of chemical, physical or biological change, including evolution. In business it refers to an extension into the provision of new or enhanced products or services. A fourth field is that of processes of changes in the capabilities of human communities, whether at a local, regional, national or global[1] scale. It is to this latter understanding that this book specifically addresses itself.

Even within this field of human development there are differences of perception about what is at issue. For many the question "what is *development?*" is best addressed by looking at the historical processes that have resulted in the emergence of the, self-styled, developed countries. For others it is a matter of identifying current deficiencies of the, so-called, developing countries, under the

1 Globalisation?

imperative of modernization and the transfer of technology. For some it is a matter of examining the forces of exploitation that maintain the current imbalances in access to the world's resources with the concomitant scourge of poverty (Rist, 2002).

2 History

The historical processes theme can be seen in those Hegelian and Marxist theories, which suggested a certain teleology leading inextricably towards some pre-ordained destination for humanity (Watts, 1995; Porter, 1995) – ideas that have shaped the socialist theories of development with their own modernization agenda. It is also manifested in the ideas of Toynbee (1974) who recognized a less determinate teleology to history under the influence of the universal principles of '*Challenge and Response*' and '*Increasing Complexity*' that are reminiscent of General Systems Theory (von Bertalanffy, 1968; Rihani, 2002). These ideas are finding their contemporary expression in the works of Jacobs (see the very instructive Jacobs' Ladder described in Ellerman (2005a)) and Diamond (2006). Finally, there is the post-modernist interpretation of human existence (Sachs, 1992), which precludes any sense of the inevitable, which denounces the forces of colonialism and hegemony and validates the possibility of self-determination as the proper manifestation of development.

However, whichever was the correct interpretation of the historical process it was firmly put to one side when the project of *Development*, variously described as *Economic Development, Social Development,* or *Achieving Wellbeing* was announced. When President Truman coined the term *Development* in 1949 (Esteva, 1992) he clearly had in mind an idea that the peoples of the world should aspire to '*catch-up*' with the circumstances prevailing in the United States of America and, in order to achieve that aspiration, a plethora of agencies and interventions were to be initiated and supported for the foreseeable (*sic*) future. Interventionist Modernization was the only game in town, not only because the economic powers of the West signed up to it but because it was also the vision and philosophy behind Soviet development activities in those regions under its domination (Shreeves, 2005).

3 The Modernization project

Modernization was founded on the belief, real or simulated, that human well being was best equated with economic performance, which in turn was best achieved through upgrading the physical infrastructure, through introducing technical innovations and through training the technicians that would support them, led by the state. This programme was always going to be expensive, so International Financial Institutions (IFIs) were founded to manage the various aspects of making the resources available to client states, mostly through the provision of credit. Civil engineering firms, management consultants and technical experts from the developed countries provided their services in return for those credit dollars, often both designing initiatives and interventions as well as implementing them.

Regrettably, the main results of this approach can be characterized as '*white elephants*' and national debt. Indeed, there are many examples of how the process of rural development has not lived up to its promise and our expectations. As Jamieson (1987, p.89) has indicated: "*The enthusiastic hopes... that characterised the early decades of development were being eroded by disappointment, controversy, and most recently, even cynicism and bitterness.*" Hancock (1993, p.190) put it even more strongly: "*...if the only measurable impact of all these decades of development has been to turn tenacious survivors into helpless dependants - then it seems to me to be beyond dispute that aid does not work.*"

Rahman (1993, p.213) noted that the benefits of development have yet to trickled down to the vast majority of people in most '*developing*' countries, and Kaplan (1996, p.ix) echoed this saying: "*after more than 30 years of international development ..., problems of unemployment, housing, human rights, poverty and landlessness are worse than ever.*" The indigenous resources that might have been utilized in the organic, historical process of development were now used to service the resources borrowed to finance a development agenda that was neither indigenous nor organic.

Of course this is only one side of the story and indeed it would be strange if, after so much effort and expenditure, we could show no successes at all. Nevertheless, there remains a genuine concern that development professionals were making significant errors in the way that they pursued interventions, as Severino & Charnoz (2004, p.77) commented: "*The world progresses, and official development assistance contributes to that progression. Yet, development theories and paradigms have failed time and time again.*" In its early forms this interventionist approach to development was undertaken through top-down processes that had been begun under the historical epoch of colonialism (Rist, 2002) – with the main change being that the costs of the initiatives were being placed increasingly upon the backs of the populations of the developing country concerned through the mechanism of financial loans. However, it became clear that a process directed towards the goal of helping a particular section of society or humanity to '*catch-up*' is not really development, but is a manifestation of paternalism that claims to be founded on the basis of "*having an interest in being disinterested*" (Rist, 2002, p.91)[2]. This development is reminiscent of the actions of an American industrialist, described by Jane Addams who said:

> *Like* [Shakespeare's King] *Lear ...Pullman exercised a self-serving benevolence in which he defined the needs of those who were the objects of his benevolence in terms of his own desires and interests.* (Quoted by Ellerman, 2001, p.14).

2 Hereafter referred to as Rist's paradox.

Therefore, it seems evident that *Economic Development* cannot itself be development, although it may be a necessary condition for it.[3]

4 Promotion of Autonomous Development

This failure of *Economic Development* was attributed to an inability to take up and maintain the latest technology and blamed upon the lack of local human capacity. So the next phase in the development of development was characterized by an increasing emphasis on *Technical Assistance*, which fairly quickly took on the mantle of *capacity building* and *institutional strengthening* (Fukuda-Parr, Lopes & Malik, 1999). However, development is also not about making others like ourselves. Paulo Freire recognised this when he stated:

> *the oppressed are not 'marginals', are not men* [sic] *living 'outside' society. They have always been 'inside' – inside the structure that made them 'beings for others'. The solution is not to 'integrate' them into the structure of oppression but to transform the structure so they can become 'beings for themselves'.* (Freire, 1971, p.48)

This kind of thinking ushered in the next and current phase of locally determined agendas underpinned by the donors' interests in social development, which represented a merger of the philosophy of external intervention to achieve modern standards of well-being with the post-modernists' demands for the self-determination of the developing countries and their populations and communities under the banners of democratization and good governance. It also saw a greater emphasis upon the Non-Government sector in service provision and engagement with the private sector.

---

3 But see Easterlin (1974).

In its first whitepaper Department for International Development (DFID), described development as the means of achieving:

> *A global society where everyone can live in peace and security; have a say in how their community is run; and have access to those things we so often take for granted, like clean water, fresh air and the chance to earn a living and bring up healthy, educated children. We want governments to be accountable to their people; obey the rule of law; protect human rights and create opportunities for economic growth.* (DFID, 1997, p.2)

5 Meta-development

In many respects these phases of development practice can be related to the three types of actions itemized by Habermas (Finlayson, 2005). Thus the first approach constituted '*Instrumental Actions*' – actions to achieve specific results, which are founded upon instrumental reasoning, the calculation of the best means to a given end. The second approach constituted '*Strategic Actions*' – actions that involve getting other people to do things as a means to achieving one's own ends. The third and current phase would seem to constitute '*Communicative Actions*' – actions that attempt through discourse to create consensus for establishing a programme of change, but which nevertheless remains contaminated with relicts[4] of the first two approaches.

Thus, what we can observe from this catalogue is the development of development (meta-development) or what may be described as the phenomenology of development (the explication of the process as experienced), which may be both captured and, to some extent, explained by reference to change management processes and, in

4 It would in many ways be just as appropriate to use the word '*relics*' here to capture the sanctity of the associated belief systems.

particular, to a perceptual framework described as a hierarchy of epistemology developed from Neuro-Linguistic Programming (Dilts, Epstein & Dilts, 1991) and presented in Table 1.1.

	Dominant Development Approach	Which relates to →	Hierarchical Epistemological Levels (Dilts, Epstein & Dilts 1991)	
Earliest ↓	Infrastructure and Technology .	→	Environment	Lowest ↓
	Technical Assistance	→	Behaviour	
	Capacity Building and Institutional Strengthening	→	Capability	
	Rules of the Game; Governance	→	Values	
Latest	Cultural change (the whole modernization agenda)	→	Identity	Highest

Table 1.1 The Process of Meta-development

The human societies and communities of developing countries as well as their location within the global economy are complex systems, and achieving systemic change invariably requires changes at different levels. Experience shows that the pursuit of interventions to bring about a more rapid, systemic scale, process has been dogged by a cycle of failure, each successive turn of which has led to interventions then being targeted at the next level up, with more or less the same equivocal results. This may be attributed to the processes of resistance to change lodged in the values and identity of those who are challenged to change. In this way, Clarke (2006, p.12) identified the principle that: "*People do not resist change, but they do resist being changed.*" As a consequence, it is even conceivable that the interventions so far undertaken in the name of development have actually hindered or warped those unforced, historical processes that could have brought about the social, economic and cultural changes that might have allowed the epithet '*developed*' to be applied to those countries that have had to endure them.[5]

However, as Rodrik (2011, p.174) recognized: "*the wait for development to take place on its own could take a very long time*". So, what is the alternative? The Millennium Development Goals, signed up to by nearly two hundred of the world's national governments, represent laudable aspirations for the well-being of large sections of the human population that are currently enduring a miserable, largely unfulfilling and, for many, brief existence. How can we stand aside and wait for history to take its course? As Haq (2000, p. 79) acknowledged, sustaining current levels of poverty is clearly immoral. But what do we understand by Poverty?

6 The Issue of Poverty

As Sahlins (1997, p.19) argued: "*Poverty is not a certain small amount of goods, nor is it just a relation between means and ends; above all, it is a relation between people. Poverty is a social status. As such it is the invention of civilization.*" Indeed, Mohan (2009, p.12) recognized that: "*Poverty is a consequence of politics of hegemonic oppression; it is not the cause of inequality.*" The processes that lead to and maintain poverty (often presented as the antithesis of '*developed*') have been described in relation to issues of the Centre/Periphery interaction (Prebisch, 1985; see Figure 1.1).

5 For an exposition of the losses through opportunity costs see Ellerman (2007, pp. 156-7).

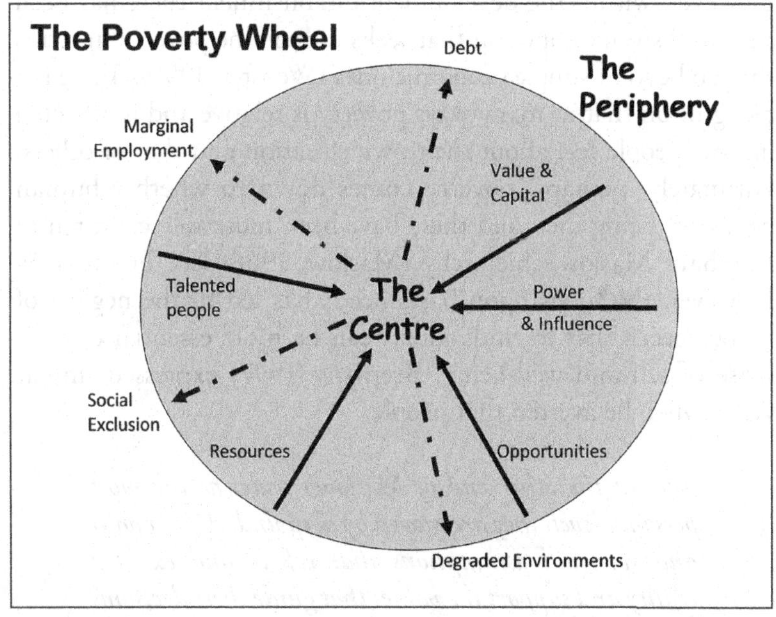
The Poverty Wheel
Debt
The Periphery
Marginal Employment
Value & Capital
Talented people
The Centre
Power & Influence
Social Exclusion
Resources
Opportunities
Degraded Environments

Figure 1.1 The Interaction between the '*poor*' at the periphery and the '*élite*' at the centre.

The terms of exchange and the power structures that govern them draw positive impacts towards those occupying the centre and, conversely, repel negative impacts towards those existing at the periphery – climate change being but the latest evil to be visited upon the vulnerable. The '*Poverty Wheel*' can operate at any level, global; regional; national; local; community or even household, with those holding the central position deriving benefits from exploiting those at the periphery. Thus Western Europe would be at the Centre where Africa would be on the periphery; South Africa at the Centre and Lesotho at the periphery; Johannesburg at the centre and rural Transkei at the periphery; Community élites at the centre and female headed households at the periphery; adults at the centre and the aged and children at the periphery.

However, within the development establishment there has been a ground swell of opinion that seeks to redefine poverty in terms that go beyond simple economic ones (Webster, 1990). There is a recognition that in many ways poverty is relative and is reflected in how people feel about their own situation and that of others. Ultimately, perhaps, poverty comes down to whether human needs are being met, and these have been most ably captured in Abraham Maslow's hierarchy (Maslow, 1968) (see Figure 1.2). However, the focus upon basic needs has led to the neglect of higher needs that for individuals can be more essential to their sense of self and well-being. Beemans (1997) expressed similar views when he averred that people:

> *start at the other end of Maslow's scale: at the most personal level, they are moved by deep underlying moral and spiritual assumptions that reflect and explain reality and support the values that guide their decisions about whether to change or not to change.*

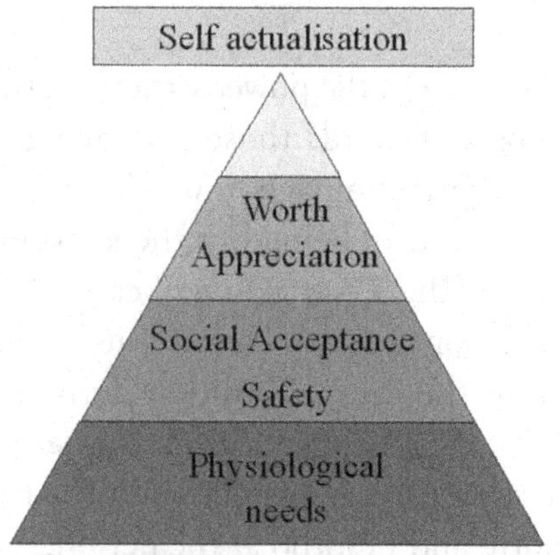
Self actualisation
Worth
Appreciation
Social Acceptance
Safety
Physiological
needs

Figure 1.2: Maslow's hierarchy of the prepotency of needs

Humanitarian assistance in the face of natural and man-made (*sic*) disasters seeks to deal with needs at the lower levels. However, as Ellerman (2005b) points out, there is always a moral hazard in that such aid can act in opposition to needs at the higher levels. This is what Buchanan (1977) refers to as the Samaritan's dilemma by which help creates dependency.

Today we do not speak so much about wealth and poverty but about well-being and livelihoods, that link to health, environment, education and access to decision-making and human rights. Most recently this has been refined into a framework of 5 capital assets (Financial; Natural; Infra-structural; Social; and Human) that both contribute to a position of vulnerability and deprivation and, just as importantly, represent potential resources that can be harnessed and built upon and from which a livelihood can be constructed (first order responses to problems)(Carney, 1998).

In addition, there is a recognition that the economic and social system is underpinned by power structures that ensure the security of those with access to power (Rahman, 1993). The formal structures of laws and regulations and the informal networks of patronage and privilege place those individuals and groups who lack some or all of the 5 capitals at a disadvantage (second order problems). This system of disadvantage is frequently referred to as the '*Poverty Trap*' (see Figure 1.3).

Thus development interventions that seek to address issues of poverty have to engage with the systemic reasons for marginalization within a dynamic environment as well as, or possibly with greater urgency, than dealing with the simple absence of identifiable resource groups.

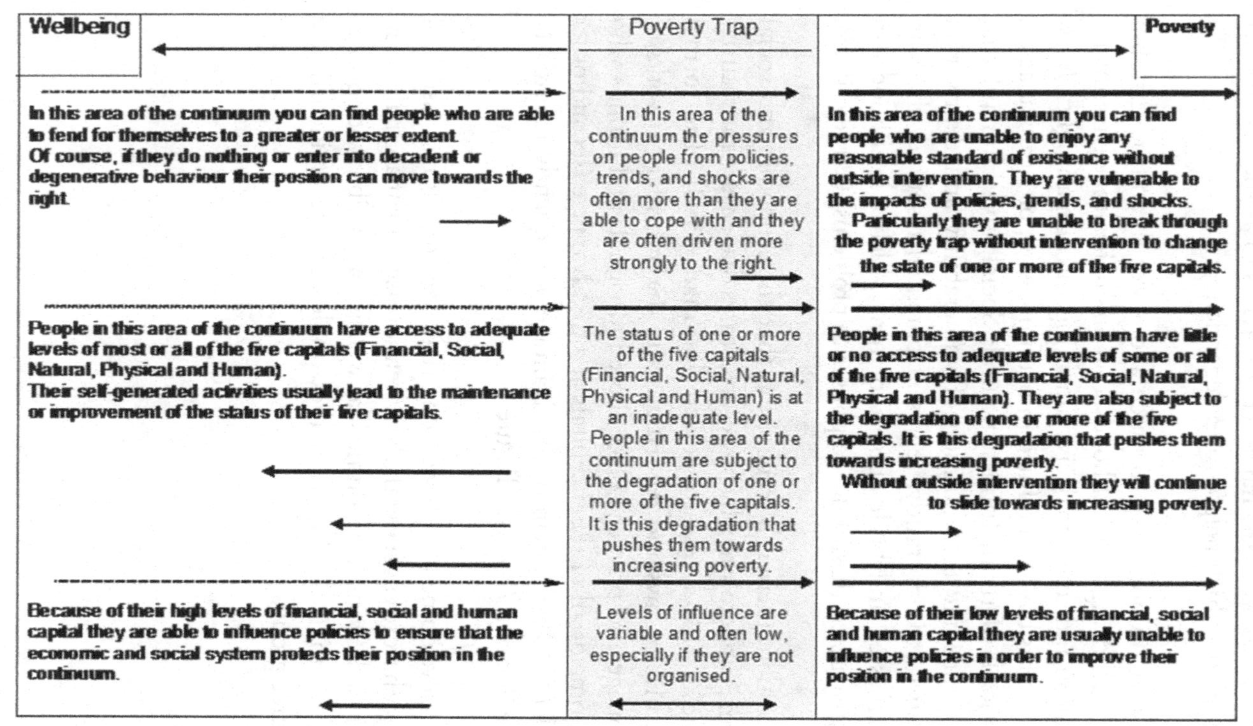
Wellbeing
Poverty Trap
Poverty
In this area of the continuum you can find people who are able to fend for themselves to a greater or lesser extent.
Of course, if they do nothing or enter into decadent or degenerative behaviour their position can move towards the right.
In this area of the continuum the pressures on people from policies, trends, and shocks are often more than they are able to cope with and they are often driven more strongly to the right.
In this area of the continuum you can find people who are unable to enjoy any reasonable standard of existence without outside intervention. They are vulnerable to the impacts of policies, trends, and shocks.
Particularly they are unable to break through the poverty trap without intervention to change the state of one or more of the five capitals.
People in this area of the continuum have access to adequate levels of most or all of the five capitals (Financial, Social, Natural, Physical and Human).
Their self-generated activities usually lead to the maintenance or improvement of the status of their five capitals.
The status of one or more of the five capitals (Financial, Social, Natural, Physical and Human) is at an inadequate level.
People in this area of the continuum are subject to the degradation of one or more of the five capitals.
It is this degradation that pushes them towards increasing poverty.
People in this area of the continuum have little or no access to adequate levels of some or all of the five capitals (Financial, Social, Natural, Physical and Human). They are also subject to the degradation of one or more of the five capitals. It is this degradation that pushes them towards increasing poverty.
Without outside intervention they will continue to slide towards increasing poverty.
Because of their high levels of financial, social and human capital they are able to influence policies to ensure that the economic and social system protects their position in the continuum.
Levels of influence are variable and often low, especially if they are not organised.
Because of their low levels of financial, social and human capital they are usually unable to influence policies in order to improve their position in the continuum.

Figure 1.3. Illustration of the Living Standards Continuum and the Poverty Trap.

7 Development as Managed Change

Confronted by these issues Jamieson (1987) and Uphoff (1996) suggested that *Development* is really *Managed Change* in response to an ever-changing environment. Thus, although the approach to development is still to intervene, professionals and practitioners have been seeking to redefine the nature of the management of such interventions. Indeed, Thomas (2000) has argued that there are three kinds of management pertinent to these considerations: management in development (same management different context); management of development (typical task oriented management but with particular results in mind); and management for development (where the processes of management are part of the results to be achieved – congruent management) – thereby reflecting Habermas' three level hierarchy of action (Finlayson, 2005).

Furthermore, over the last ten years, there has been a noticeable shift in the practices associated with development assistance. As outlined above, where in the nineteen seventies and eighties development was primarily about enacting initiatives (putting in infrastructure and providing technical assistance), by the nineteen nineties and into the new millennium there has been an almost universal '*moving-up*' by the development agencies (donors), eschewing doing in favour of influencing policy and operating through third parties (Wallace, 2000). In many respects this has been driven by the realization that doing is really the domain of the autonomous subject, and thus to do on someone's behalf is to negate autonomy and create dependency.

Ruffer and Lawson (2002) have reviewed in some detail the thinking behind the retreat from projects and towards other aid approaches, particularly budget support, and conclude that, in order to achieve the aspirations of development assistance in achieving autonomous communities, donors are correct in moving away from direct involvement through projects and towards more or less the funding of recipient governments' own programmes.[6]

This moving-up has been accompanied by vociferous espousal of the principles of Partnership, Participation and Capacity Building (Fukuda-Parr, *et al,* 2002). However, we need to be careful of rhetoric, as Crush (1995, p.4) commented: "*what* [development] *says it is doing, and what we believe it to be doing, are simply not what is actually happening.*" All three principles are warmly persuasive of a meritorious approach the implications and demands of which are not spelled out but which are amongst the most difficult undertakings for human social interactions and skills, as Severino and Charnoz (2004, p.87) averred: "*the so-called 'partnership for development', bandied about by the aid community …, is seen as little more than deceitful, rhetorical artfulness.*".

The role of development agencies and their agents (staff, contractors and partners) and their mirror image, the agencies of recipient systems, would seem to be a judicious mixture of direct actions, management of actions, and influencing the choice of actions. The concomitant potential for confusion over who should do what, when and how, captured in Thomas' (2000) 3 types of development management, is the basis and source of many of development's difficulties.

It was, therefore, with a mixture of affirmation and disquiet that I read Ellerman (2002, p.43) writing, in regard to development assistance, that: "*if the doers are to become autonomous, then what is the role of the external helpers? This paradox of supplying help to self-help… is the **fundamental conundrum** of development assistance.*" [emphasis in the original]

At the beginning of the 21st century, why is it that we are still apparently surprised by the paradox of development? Korten

---

6 But see also Hefeker (2006).

(1983, p.220) had long since written that: "[The] *central paradox of social development: [is] the need to exert influence over people for the purpose of building their capacity to control their own lives.*", Gronemeyer (1992 p.64) had acknowledged that: "*Help appears more and more as a conceptually unsuitable means of promoting development.*", Kaplan (1996, p.3) had indicated that: "*We cannot cause development.*" and Pieterse (1999, p.79) had written that, "*The Tao of development means acknowledging paradox as part of development realities: such as the antinomies between … … intervention and autonomy.*"

Why has there been such a resolute avoidance of considering the nature, impact and management of paradox itself in the formulation of fresh responses to the challenge of development? Especially when Seers (1969, p.3) resolved that: "*Since development is far from being achieved at present the need is not, as is generally imagined, to accelerate economic growth …. But to change the nature of the development process.*" or when Kaplan (1996, p. 64) observed, that the development practitioner: "*needs to understand the process of development in order to facilitate the 'stuck' organisation into taking their next step … to a point of greater consciousness and awareness*". Is it that we engage with the problem of development at the wrong level (1st order rather than 2nd order change?) so that, although behaviours change, systemic change is avoided? *Plus ça change plus ça le même chose!*

Let us, therefore, next turn our attention to the nature of paradox in the expectation that it will reveal some understanding of how we can manage paradoxes when we are operating in roles and context which of their nature are paradoxical.

Chapter 2

Paradox and Logical Types

1 Introduction

The value of paradox is that it can be both a means of stimulating creativity and a method of expressing it. Indeed, the greatest use of paradox is in the field of humour where many jokes and capers are made possible only by the sweet confusion that paradox brings. However, the matter of creativity and humour are not the subject of our analysis here, our attention must be placed upon the various manifestations of paradox in the role of management in the context of development. From writers such as Bateson (1972), Laing (1990), Watzlawick (1993), Hofstadter (2000) and Talbot (2005) I became aware that paradox seems at once to be at the very heart of what it means to be human, whilst at the same time being responsible for many of the dysfunctions that beset individuals, enterprises and societies. In order to deal with the paradoxes of management and development we need first and foremost to understand the nature of paradox.

There are a number of synonyms or synonymous expressions that we need to be aware of, for example Antinomy (conflicting authorities or laws), Catch-22 (damned if you do, damned if you don't)(Dichter, 2003), Conundrum (puzzling question), Double edged sword (Cuts both sides), Irony (Baylies, 1995), Gordian Knot (Sabel & Reddy, 2003) and Oxymoron (contradictory terms conjoined). The Oxford Dictionary defines paradox as a '*seemingly contradictory statement that may nonetheless be true*', but Quine (1976, p.1) extended this to: "*a paradox is just any conclusion that at first sounds absurd but that has an argument to sustain it.*" Watzlawick, Bavelas and Jackson (1967, p.187-197) referred to this type as the "*logico-mathematical paradoxes*" in order to distinguish them from paradoxes which result from discrepancies in the structure of thought that they term "*semantic antinomies*". We shall come back to these latter in section 4.

However, in more general usage paradox is associated with descriptions of situations where things don't seem to fit together in practice, or when practice contradicts theory. Nevertheless, it is important to recognise that paradox is not simply a dilemma or difficult choice between scenarios that deny access to the benefits provided by the declined alternative (Talbot, 2005). Although some authors (Handy, 1994; Clegg, Cunha & Cunha, 2002) have treated paradox as predominantly an irreconcilable choice between opposites, it is most useful for us to begin by considering it in its classical form as a tool to challenge our understanding of the nature of reality or as Reagan (1990, p.39) put it: "*Paradoxes are helpful when they serve to dramatize that a formulation is incomplete or inconsistent.*" Paradoxes have been devised within many cultures in the past with this specific intention in mind (for example the use of Zen Buddhist *Koans* – Kubose, 1973; FitzPatrick, 2005). The Greeks, for example Parmenides, used paradoxes as tools to assist them to think through problems of logic. They believed the universe to be logical, and therefore that the presence of apparent paradoxical contradictions represented a sign that our current thinking must be flawed.

Let me illustrate this by means of an example.

2 Zeno's Paradoxes of Motion

Zeno was concerned to explore whether, contrary to appearances, motion is impossible. His ideas on this matter have not come down to us directly, but through the works of others (Aristotle, Plato and Simplicius), but he is purported to have advocated through logic that motion and plurality are impossible (Sorensen, 2003; Tsoukas & Chia, 2002). Of all his arguments the most renowned are four paradoxes:

- The Bisection paradox in which Zeno suggests that there is no motion, because that which moves must first cross to the midpoint before it can traverse the full distance and, *reductio ad absurdum*, to divide each previous division with a midpoint repeatedly in infinite regression until it is clear that even the smallest advance must await the completion of a smaller movement.

- The Achilles and the Tortoise in which the slower Tortoise will never be overtaken by the quicker Achilles, for the pursuer, must first reach the place from which the slower, has last started, so that the slower must inevitably be some distance in front of the pursuer.

- The Flying Arrow which proposes that everything is either at rest or moving. When an object occupies a space equal to itself, then it is always fixed in space in the instant. So a flying arrow is, at any moment, unmoving.

- The Stadium in which Zeno considers two files of athletes, each composed of an equal number of bodies of equal size advancing in opposite directions with equal speed. Thus, if each file has achieved the maximum possible speed then they will move towards each other at twice maximum possible speed.

The first two arguments are usually interpreted as challenges to the idea of continuous motion in infinitely divisible space and time. They differ only in that the first is expressed in terms of absolute motion, whereas the second illustrates that the same argument applies to relative motion. In itself Zeno's point is not paradoxical, it simply indicates that the physical world must be regarded as consisting at some level of finite indivisible entities.

Zeno then suggests, through '*the Flying Arrow*', that if all time is composed of instants, and motion cannot exist in any instant, then motion cannot exist at all. Thus, in any single slice of time there is, apparently, no physical difference between a moving and a non-moving arrow. As Anon (2006, p.3) observed: "*if there is literally no physical difference between a moving and a non-moving arrow in any discrete instant, then how does the arrow "know" from one instant to the next whether it is to move? In other words, how is causality transmitted forward in time through a sequence of instants, in each of which motion does not exist?*"

We arrive at Zeno's paradox proper when the arguments against infinite divisibility are combined with the complementary set of arguments regarding motion itself (The Flying Arrow and The Stadium), which show that a world consisting of finite indivisible entities is also logically impossible, thereby presenting us with the conclusion that physical reality can be neither continuous nor discontinuous. In all four of Zeno's arguments on motion, the implicit point is that if space and time are independent, then logical inconsistencies arise regardless of whether the physical world is continuous or discrete.

Now, and here is the point of my argument, it is worth noting that modern physics has concluded that the classical image of space and time was fundamentally mistaken, and in fact motion would not be possible in a universe constructed according to the classical view. As Bohm (1951) has argued, the theory of special relativity answers Zeno's concern over the lack of an instantaneous difference between a moving and a non-moving arrow by proposing a fundamental re-structuring of the basic way in which space and time interrelate. David Bohm's resolution of the paradox of motion is that special relativity vindicates Zeno's scepticism and intuition about the nature of motion – as Koestler (1967, p.217) declared: "*scientific discovery is paradox resolved.*"

Again, as Anon (2006, p.4) commented: "*We now recognize that position and momentum are incompatible variables, in the sense that an exact determination of either one of them leaves the other completely undetermined.*" According to quantum mechanics, it is unthinkable for an object to have momentum and a definite position at the same time, just as Zeno propounded. The universe does not (and arguably, could not) work the way people thought it did. Therefore, we come to the realisation that common sense can be illogical[1] and is based on a potentially fraudulent, empirical reality, which has often misled us because our experience of reality remains incomplete.

An important example of Rist's paradox is given by Jacques Godbout and Allain Caillé (2000, p.173) who recognised that:

> *This crucial distinction between gift and market stems from a split in the gift-giving act, a split that sacrifices the non-monetary attributes to supply-and-demand and the search for an equivalence between these two elements. By dividing up the act of giving, the mercantile model dooms itself to never being able to account for the gift, just as Zeno's Paradox, in dividing up movement, can never explain how an arrow reaches its target.* (Godbout & Caillé, 2000, p.173)

[1] Indeed, Sorensen (2003, p.145) asserted that "*The nature of common sense is not itself common sense*".

Thus the idea suggested by this example is that paradox can result from a misunderstanding of how reality and our perception actually interact. In this way Douglas Hofstadter challenged us with this *koan*:

> *Two monks were arguing about a flag. One said, 'The flag is moving.' The other said, 'The wind is moving.' The sixth patriarch, Zeno, happened to be passing by. He told them, 'Not the wind, not the flag; mind is moving.'* (Hofstadter, 2000, p.30)

Therefore, it is important to understand the way that paradoxes can be generated through the way we perceive reality, and the way that we represent our perceptions of reality to ourselves and to others.

3 Paradoxes of Perception

These ideas about the way that perception and paradox interact can be further explored through the work of the Dutch graphic artist Maurits Escher (Hofstadter, 2000), whose elegant drawings characteristically contain visual illusions and paradoxes (For example see Figure 2.1).

When confronted by such a picture it is our nature to search for patterns, but the patterns are not '*out there*', rather they are already laid down in us through the physical way our neurology appears to be assembled (Colour range, binocular vision etc.) and its' fixed programming (some fixed ways of perceiving such as those that underpin Adalbert Ames' experiments (Bateson, 2002, p.29-34)), and in the ways that we have become programmed to select and order sense data through our experience (learned patterns).

Figure 2.1 M.C. Escher's "Waterfall" www.mcescher.com

So, what do we see when we look at the *Waterfall*? The picture appears to be made up of parts which are both familiar and sensible but which, when put together, reveal some disturbing discrepancies. Water seems to flow up hill. However, as Bateson (*op.cit.*) observed, we conveniently and pragmatically represent the universe we perceive as made up of parts and wholes, but the way we do it is entirely arbitrary. When we look at precise details - the lines, angles, and shading – they conform very much to our expectations. When we look at the separate portions of the picture – bottom right, bottom left and parts of the centre – they too conform to our anticipated patterns. It is at the next level of assemblage that our reason recoils. The left-central section contains tricks of perspective that reverse the relation between the top and the bottom which, when connected with the other parts, generates misperception.

However, if we regard this drawing as just one amongst a whole set of Escher prints, where the topic or purpose of the drawings is to generate challenges to our perception, then there once more emerges a sense of pattern and conformity (albeit to Escher's pattern rather than to one of our own). Indeed, Wilson (1990, p.115) suggested that: "*Constant reminding ourselves that we do not see with our eyes but with our synergetic eye-brain system working as a whole will produce constant astonishment as we notice, … how much of our perceptions emerge from our preconception.*"

These ideas suggest that the resolution of paradox is not only a matter of finding the logic in reality and adapting our understanding accordingly (as in section 2), but that paradox can be generated though our own choices[2]; by what we choose to focus upon that then becomes the basis of the relationship of interest. As Carr, McAuliffe and MacLachlan (1998, p. 26) recognised: "*what our perceptual system happens to class as 'figure' and 'ground' radically alters what we see and do **not** see.*" Then the next challenge that confronts us is how do we share our perceptions with others in order to validate our notion of reality? We have to take recourse to language and thereby to open the possibility of introducing further forms of illogicality.

4 Semantic Antinomies

Another explanation of the origins of paradox applies to the semantic antinomies of Watzlawick, *et al* (1967) and which has been captured by Ryle (1960, p.11) who said: "*Sometimes thinkers are at loggerheads with one another, not because their propositions do conflict, but because their authors fancy that they conflict.*"

2 Usually unconscious choice.

At the heart of the way we behave is the language we use to describe what we are doing. Postman and Weingartner (1969, p.107) reflected that: "*one of man's most primitive traits is to respond to the symbols he invents as if they are whatever he invented them to symbolise*". Korzybski (1933) cautioned us to be aware of the mismatches between the way we describe the world in words and the real world and pointed out that a map of somewhere is not the same as the terrain it represents, and the word is not the same as the thing named. We encode our experiential reality with words, thus creating our perception of reality. However, our coding has slippage. Chomsky (1957) added the idea that language has both a surface structure and a deep structure causing our utterances necessarily to be an impoverished reflection of how we have represented experience to ourselves, which in turn is only a shadow of whatever was captured by our organs of sense about the actual event itself.

As Richard Bandler and John Grinder averred:

> *This use of language to communicate is actually a special case of the use of language to represent. Communication is, in this way of thinking, the representation to others of our representation to ourselves. In other words, we use language to represent our experience – this is a private process. We then use language to represent our representation of our experience – a social process.* (Bandler & Grinder, 1975, p.38).

They also emphasised the unconscious, almost automatic nature of language when they (*op.cit.*, p.22) said that: "*Language so fills our world that we move through it as a fish swims through water.*"

Using language requires two types of understanding. The first is about the rules of grammar – the syntax. The second is about the meanings of the words, both denotative (socially accepted direct meaning) and connotative (personal associative meaning) – the semantics. One of the basic rules of syntax is the division of utterances into Subject (a noun) and Predicate (the rest) about which there has been much philosophical debate (Strawson, 2004), which cannot be dealt with adequately in these pages.

However, three quotations on the issue are worth consideration, as Gregory Bateson explained:

> *Language continually asserts by the syntax of subject and predicate that 'things' somehow 'have' qualities and attributes. A more precise way of talking would insist that the 'things' are produced, are seen as separate from other 'things', and are made 'real' by their internal relations and by their behaviour in relationship with other things and with the speaker.* (Bateson, 2002, p.57).

Robert Anton Wilson went further in suggesting that our subject-predicate language programmes us to expect '*ishness*' or '*essence*' which he (Wilson, 1990, p.101) explained as: "*the Aristotelian universe assumes an assembly of 'things' with 'essences' or 'spooks' inside them, where modern scientific (or existential) universe assumes a network of structural relationships.*" and Whitehead (1922, p.14) said that: "*The alternate philosophic position must commence with denouncing the whole idea of 'subject qualified by predicate' as a trap set for philosophers by the whole syntax of language.*"

The nub of these arguments is that perception and language draw artificial (though useful) distinctions between parts of our reality, which we label as objects, or nouns, and we down play the processes, or verbs, that underpin the relationships between these apparent objects. We emphasise the subject of the picture rather than the field in which the subject exists and with which it interacts.

Linking back to our earlier discussion of Zeno's paradoxes of motion we can now see that the implications of David Bohm's resolution are quite profound. The idea that there is no real distinction between motion and matter challenges us to look at our language and the way that we use it to describe and to conceptualize reality. The difference between nouns and verbs suddenly becomes less helpful. Fixed states are replaced by processes, and stability and change seem to be attributes of all matter. Indeed, as Hans Vaihinger pointed out:

> *All that is given to consciousness is sensation. By adding a Thing to which sensations are supposed to adhere as attributes, thought commits a very serious error. It hypostasizes*[3] *sensation, which in the last analysis is only a process, as a subsistent attribute, and ascribes this attribute to a thing that either exists only in the complex of sensations itself, or has been simply added by thought to what has been sensed…* (Vaihinger, 1924, p.167).

Gregory Bateson was particularly critical when he said:

> *Professional linguists nowadays may know what's what, but children in school are still taught nonsense. They are told that a 'noun' is the 'name of a person, place or thing', that a 'verb' is 'an action word', and so on. … they are taught … that the way to define something is by what it supposedly is in itself, not by its relation to other things.* (Bateson, 2002, p.15).

This links to a language trap we have, certainly in English, known as *Nominalization*. This is a form of distortion of language by which we turn a process (a verb) into an object (a noun). As Bandler and Grinder (1975, p.33) stated: "*Its effect is to convert the Deep Structure representation of a process into the Surface representation of an event.*" You can detect whether this has happened by a simple test; if you can imagine the object (noun) in a wheelbarrow being pushed down the road - then it is truly an object and no distortion has been made. If you cannot imagine that, then it is a verb in disguise (e.g. management, participation, power, development, knowledge)

3 Treating something that cannot be denoted as if it can.

(O'Connor & Seymour 1993). Indeed, Bhaskar (2002, p. 114) speaks of: "*vast words which pick up some hierarchical structure of discursive acts and give them a name and so make us think of them as entities.*" and, as Searle (1995, p.57) recognised: "*What we think of as social **objects**, such as governments, money, and universities, are in fact just placeholders for patterns of **activities**.*"

A good example of the realisation of the disservice wrought by nominalization was captured by Stacey (2001, p.4) when he wrote that: "*Knowledge is not a 'thing', or a system, but an ephemeral, active process of relating. If one takes this view then no one ..., can own knowledge. Knowledge itself cannot be stored, nor can intellectual capital be measured, and certainly neither of them can be managed.*" and Snowden (2002, p.102) utilized this realization within his argument that: "*knowledge is paradoxically both a <u>thing</u> and a <u>flow</u>; in the second age* [of knowledge management] *we looked for things and in consequence found things, in the third age we look for both in different ways and embrace the consequent paradox.*" Importantly, Weick and Westley (1996, p.441) drew a similar conclusion in regard to learning when they noted that: "*the same word 'learning' refers to both an outcome and a process, giving it a circular, tautological sense, and concealing rather than revealing the dynamics of the process and the exact nature of the outcome.*"

The distortion of nominalization has the effect of denying the possibility of full understanding by implying a fixed state rather than a dynamic process. As O'Connor and Seymour (1993) argued, a verb is a continuingly unfolding process the nature of which is lost if it is nominalized and converted into an immobile noun. One way by which people lose confidence and power is to turn an ongoing process into an event. Or as Illich (1978, p.8) noted: "*we are the witnesses of a barely perceptible transformation in ordinary language: verbs which formerly expressed satisfying actions have been replaced by nouns which name packages designed for passive consumption only*". This coincides with Erich Fromm's observation that:

> *ever more frequently an activity is expressed in terms of having; that is, a noun is used instead of a verb. But to express an activity by to have in connection with a noun is an erroneous use of language, because processes and activities cannot be possessed; they can only be experienced.* (Fromm, 1995, p.47)

This statement also recognises that there is a direction to the way in which languages are evolving, and it is one that is increasing people's dis-empowerment. Again, as Pugh and Hickson (2000, p.187) recorded: "*Weick feels that language could better reflect this constant ambiguous flux by making more use of verbs and less of nouns. Indeed, he urges people to 'stamp out nouns': to think of managing rather than management, of organizing rather than organization.*"

An important response to this challenge, and following on from Korzybski's (1933) earlier attempts, has been the evolution of a precise way of speaking that avoids the mis-representation of reality by avoiding the use of all forms of the words '*is*' or '*to be*' and which is referred to as E-Prime (Bourland, 1949). Robert Anton Wilson explains these moves as follows:

> *The case for using E-Prime rests on the simple proposition that 'ishness' sets the brain into a medieval Aristotelian framework and makes it impossible to understand modern problems and opportunities...... Removing 'ishness' and writing/thinking only and always in operational/ existential language, sets us, conversely, in a modern universe where we can successfully deal with modern issues.* (Wilson, 1990, p.98).

We can see here an echo of Gilbert Ryle's call for us to be aware of, and to avoid the pitfalls associated with the distinction between precise, academic language use and everyday use of similar language forms by lay people, when he said:

> *This apparent conflict is not, then, to be described as a conflict between one theory and another theory, but rather … between a theory and a platitude; between what certain experts have thought out and what every one of us cannot but have learned by experience; between a doctrine and a piece of common knowledge.* (Ryle, 1960, p. 3)

5 Kant's 3rd Antinomy

At this point it will be appropriate to apply these insights to other paradoxes that exercise philosophers and that will be pertinent to our considerations of management and development. Perhaps the most significant of these is the issue of determinism and its manifestation in the tension between free will and necessity, generated by cause and effect, and which is often referred to as Kant's 3rd Antinomy.

This is an ancient paradox set out in the claim, on the one hand, that we act in accordance with our own free will, or as Kant (1964, p.270) stated: "*Causality according to the laws of nature, is not the only causality operating to originate the phenomena of the world.*" versus the claim that everything we do is determined by nature, or: "*everything in the world happens solely according to the laws of nature.*" (Kant, *ibid.*) on the other. Leading us to ask if an agent is ever free to bring about that which otherwise would not occur?

The determinism point of view gives no room for manoeuvre for, as Scruton (2002, p.98) phrased it: "*What I shall do at any future moment is therefore inexorable, given present (and past) conditions. So how can I be free?*" or as Arthur Schopenhauer observed:

> *Every man, being what he is and placed in the circumstances which for the moment obtain … can absolutely never do anything else than just what at that moment he does do. Accordingly, the whole course*

> *of a man's life, in all its incidents great and small, is necessarily pre-determined as the course of a clock.* (Schopenhauer, 1951, p.48).

This in turn lends its weight to, but does not necessarily entail, fatalism and passivity, as Gilbert Ryle portrayed it:

> *We are not exercised by the notorious fact that when the horse has already escaped it is too late to shut the stable door. We are sometimes exercised by the idea that as the horse is either going to escape or not going to escape, to shut the stable door beforehand is either unavailing or unnecessary.* (Ryle, 1960, p.21),

which prompted Emo Phillips to quip: *"I'm not a fatalist, but even if I were, what could I do about it."* (quoted by Dennett, 2003, p.12)

However, the concept of cause and effect itself has been challenged over the years. Ray Billington summarised the doubts that David Hume raised in regard to the whole notion of cause and effect thus: *"Hume maintained that the constant conjunction of events does not imply causality. Experience – our perception of events – may lead us to infer that this is so, but reasoning or reflection may assure us that we are wrong to jump to such conclusions."* (Billington, 1993, p.235).

Peter Munz brought the arguments up to date by reference to Karl Popper's explanation that:

> *we cannot actually observe causal connections. All we can ever see is sequences which may or may not be accidental. ... [Popper] explained that once we have a general law in mind, we can deduce from it, given an initial condition, what the general law predicts would follow as a consequence from the original condition. Given the general law, the initial condition can be seen as the cause, and the consequence as the effect.* (Munz, 2004, p.43).

For a good review of the many issues involved in cause and effect see Lincoln and Guba (1985), and their conclusion, that causality is much overrated, is well argued. However, I am not exercised at this point by the difficulties of identifying THE cause, or whether a cause is local to the effect, or whether a cause must precede an effect, but rather by the apparent necessity of believing that there are causes, and that we can identify them.

It seems that there are three reasons why human beings must believe in cause and effect, and indeed do so. The first is contained in the nature of being an animate organism, which in order to operate effectively in its environment must use sense organs to mediate that interaction. All organs of sense would appear to operate upon a principle of stimulus and response, which is itself an example of cause and effect. Then, as Cook and Campbell (1979, p.28) pointed out: "*humanity's strong and stubborn psychological predispositions to infer causal relations … can be seen as the product of a biological evolution of brain-mind processes, which has resulted in a psychic unity concerning causation.*"

The second reason is that in order to make sense of our environment we must be able to make predictions that are based, as Kant (1964) argued, upon our use of mental frameworks – one of which is cause and effect. As Abel (1976, p.2) commented: "*Causality, for example, is not an inherent attribute of events, but rather provides the form for our cognitive discourse about the world; it is one of our categories of understanding.*"

The third reason is that common sense suggests that the universe can only be rational – which is tantamount to saying that it is lawful, and laws are the outcomes of the repeatable associations of cause and effect that Hume identified as the core nature of such relationships, as Lincoln and Guba (1985, p. 135) put it: "*for laws, to be laws, depend upon causal relationships themselves.*"

Or, as Robert Rosen observed:

> *The idea of Natural Law has two quite separate facets. On the one hand, there is implicit in it a belief that the sequence of events manifested in the external world is not utterly capricious or arbitrary or chaotic, but rather that there exists some relation between them ...: causality. Thus, the first facet of a belief in natural law consists of a belief in a causal order relating events we perceive in the external world. We ... probably could not stay sane, without a belief in causal order.* (Rosen, 1986, p. 37),

Which led Carl Jung to summarise the situation thus:

> *The philosophical principle that underlies our conception of natural law is causality. But if the connection between cause and effect turns out to be only statistically valid and only relatively true, then the causal principle is of only relative use for explaining natural processes and therefore presupposes the existence of one or more other factors which would be necessary for an explanation.* (Jung, 1973, p.5).

So what of free will? Daniel Dennett exposed the challenge of free will when he posited that:

> *Our brains have been designed by natural selection, and all the products of our brains have likewise been designed ... by physical processes in which no exemptions from causality can be observed. How, then, can our inventions, our decisions, our sins and triumphs, be any different from the beautiful but amoral webs of the spiders?* (Dennett, 2003, p. 305),

where the case for free will has been captured by Henry Allison who explained it thus:

> *To take oneself as a rational agent is to assume that one's reason has a practical application or, equivalently,*

> *that one has a will. Moreover, one cannot assume this without already presupposing the idea of freedom, which is why one can act, or take oneself to act, only under this idea. It constitutes, as it were, the form of the thought of oneself as a rational agent.* (Allison, 1997, p.43).

Hence, in turn, we possess a sense and a belief that we are able to choose to initiate or take actions freely. Or, according to Freud (1949, p.87): "*there is within you a deeply rooted belief in psychic freedom and choice.*", although he rejected it. However, Dilman (1999, p.172) averred that: "*To deny free will is to deny the kind of agency which characterizes human beings and their ... mode of existence.*" Indeed, as Dennett (2003, p.13) recognised: "*Free will is real, but it is not a pre-existing feature of our existence, like the law of gravity. It is also not what tradition declares it to be: a God-like power to exempt oneself from the causal fabric of the physical world.*"

The second reason that supports our belief in free will is its necessity in underpinning ethics. If everything is in some way predetermined then how can we accept the concept of '*agency*' and the moral responsibility for our actions? Thus as Haji (2003, p.250) put it: "*If determinism is true, nothing is right, wrong, or obligatory. Hence, the determinist cannot explain to the offender that what he did was legitimately wrong, and then discourage him from performing similar actions in the future.*" But, just as agency requires free will, it also requires that the actions we take will bring about the effects that we seek – for if we cannot intentionally shape events how can we be held to be responsible for them. For, as Roger Scruton observed:

> *It seems that we describe the world in two quite different ways – as the world that contains us, and as the world on which we act. We are part of nature obedient to natural laws. But we also stand back from*

> *nature, and make choices which we believe to be free.* (Scruton, 2002 p.22).

Even philosophers like Adam Smith have fallen into the practice of ambivalence. In his reference to the *'Invisible hand of the market'* (Skinner, 1997) he demonstrated an attachment to determinism, but it had a counterpoint in his demand that entrepreneurs be set free to pursue their individually chosen objectives. Indeed, Sedlacek (2011, p.7) commented more generally that: "*One more paradox is this: A field* [economics] *that* ***believes*** *in the* ***invisible hand of the market*** *wants to be without mysteries.*" Nevertheless, just as causality and determinism seem allowable, so free will in some degree or other is equally allowable, but is this a true conflict? Scruton (2002, p.103) drew attention to this issue when he sought to explain the views of Strawson who: "*suggests that the conflict between freedom and causality is not a conflict in rem, but a conflict between two kinds of attitude: the interpersonal and the scientific.*" Again, Kant (1951, p.116) argued that: "*no genuine contradiction is to be found between the freedom and the natural necessity ascribed to the very same human actions; for [reason] can abandon the concept of nature as little as it can abandon that of freedom.*" and, following Dilman (1999, p.148): "*If we reformulate Kant's dichotomy between 'reason and inclination' into one between 'commitment and mere desire' we would come nearer the truth which Kant was straining after.*"

So we come to the purpose and point of this entire section, and I hope that your patience will be rewarded. The confusion between the two sides in causality and free will is a failure to differentiate between concepts that are at two different levels. According to Kant (1951, p.114): "*the intelligible world contains the ground of the sensible world and therefore also of its laws;*" and as Mischel (1967, p. 617) asserted: "*The explanation of human actions must differ in type from the causal explanations of the physical sciences.*" This is compatibilism. Like Immanuel Kant and David Hume, and more recently Daniel Dennett and Henry Allison, we may conclude that there is a world of difference between the predictable cause and effect of natural laws and the less predictable interaction between living things and their environment (including each other).

Powerfully, Gregory Bateson drew upon the ideas of Carl Jung and made a distinction in the phenomena of cause and effect, saying that there can be a:

> *notion of a dividing line between the world of the living (where distinctions are drawn and difference can be a cause) and the world of non-living billiard balls and galaxies (where force and impacts are the 'causes' of events). These are the two worlds that Jung ... calls creatura (the living) and pleroma (the non-living).* (Bateson, 2002, p. 6-7)

This suggests that we cannot equate the cause and effect of physical nature with the motives and actions of biological organisms. Although, in as much as animals have a physical being they are subject to natural laws, it is clear that in many other respects life is provided with a large variety of alternative responses to unfolding scenarios. Gilbert Ryle took these divisions to another level in respect of the impact of consciousness and reason when he remarked:

> *living things are not merely complex mechanisms; the biological sciences are not mere off-shoots of mechanics. Where there is life there is purposiveness, and where there is sentient, mobile and, especially, conscious and intellectual life there are progressively higher and higher levels or types of purposiveness.* (Ryle, 1960, p.125).

Indeed, Arthur Koestler remarked that:

> *A living organism or social body is not an aggregation of elementary parts or elementary processes; it is an integrated hierarchy of semiautonomous sub-wholes, consisting of sub-sub-wholes, and so on. Thus the functional units on every level of the hierarchy are double-faced ... : they act as whole when facing downwards, as parts when facing upwards.* (Koestler, 1964, p.287).

So we must end this section with a caution that semantic antinomies may also come about because we fail to recognise the hierarchical structures that phenomena fall into. When we talk of matters that are not of the same order we introduce unnecessary confusion into our deliberations. Again, as Gilbert Ryle recognised:

> *competing answers to the same question, though given in different terms, would still be in cognate terms of the same category or set of categories, whereas there could be no competition between answers to different questions, since the terms in which these very questions were posed would themselves be in alien categories.* (Ryle, *op.cit.*, p.9)

This leads us on to consider one last paradox, based upon these differences of level, and the associated occurrence of self-reference.

6 Russell's Paradox and Logical Types

Bertrand Russell expounded another paradox[4] thus:

> *The comprehensive class we are considering, which is to embrace everything, must embrace itself as one of its members. In other words, if there is such a thing*

4 Subsequently known as Russell's paradox.

> *as 'everything', then 'everything' is something, and is a member of the class 'everything'.* (Russell, 1993, p. 136).

He explained this as the class being forced to be a member of itself, a situation not allowable in logic, thus generating a paradox. It is a paradox because two different levels of abstraction, or logical types, are being mixed up, and he (*op.cit.*, p.53) defined types in that: "*we may say that individuals, classes of individuals, relations between individuals, relations between classes, relation of classes to individuals, and so on, are different types.*"

After Zeno, the classical example of a paradox is the liar's paradox, attributed to Epimenides, the Cretan, who is purported to have said, *'All Cretans are liars'.* Confusion arises because if the enunciator himself is a Cretan, then the statement is a lie, and yet if the statement enunciated is a lie then Epimenides, as a Cretan, is impossibly speaking truth, and so on *ad infinitum* (Berman, 1981; Sorensen, 2003). Careful consideration of this example shows that the paradox is generated by the attempt at self-reference. As we saw above, the rule that Russell (1908) applied in logic or mathematics to such a case can be elaborated as '*no class of objects can be a member of itself.*' In the example above the word '*Cretan*' is being used in both the sense of a class (the adjectival boundary for the enunciator of the statement) and as an item within that class (an ethnic group signified by the word *Cretan*). It is the self-reference from a higher logical type to a lower that generates a '*Strange Loop*' (Hofstadter, 2000), and which causes us disconcertion.

Another example might be the following statement: '*I cannot recall a single instance when my memory let me down*', and then there is Groucho Marx' famous aphorism[5] that: '*I don't want to belong to any club that will accept me as a member.*'

---

5 http://www.marx-brothers.org/info/quotes.htm accessed on 22 October 2006.

Furthermore, Yolles (2004) contributed to the explanation of Russell's paradox thus: "*Gödel … showed that any attempts to prove that a logical system is sound (and therefore having validity and truth) will result in a paradox unless reference is made from outside the system.*" Which prompted Beer (1994, p.7) to recognise, in consideration of the paradoxical statement that: "*The barber in this town shaves everyone who does not shave himself. Who shaves the barber?*", that in order to talk about the failings of the language contained in the statement requires the use of language at a different level from that used in the statement itself – which he called Metalanguage. He also said that: "*a metalanguage offers a more embracing perspective than the lower-order language. It does do this – but the whole point is missed:*

A metalanguage is competent
To discuss undecidability
In the language".

And his point is precisely that semantic antinomies are quite often the result of invalid use of language that leads to undecidability that can only be discussed by taking recourse to metalanguage, and by recognising the distinction between language and metalanguage.

As Berman (1981, p. 220) acknowledged, the mathematical axiom that: "*there is a discontinuity between a class and its members, seems trivially obvious, until we discover that human … communication is constantly violating it to generate significant paradoxes.*" This notion, that human communication does not conform to the logic of *the Principles of Mathematics*, is founded upon the recognition that in any act of communication there are three logical levels in operation as follows:

Level one – is the manifest content or message of the communication itself – the denotative meaning.

Level two – is about the relationship between the people in communication as it relates to the manifest content.

Level three – is how the receiver is to discriminate between types of communication at level two.

Let me illustrate this by reference to Édouard Manet's painting *Déjeuner sur l'herbe* (Figure 2.2).

Figure 2.2 Édouard Manet's *Déjeuner sur l'herbe.*

As a piece of art we can see that it works at three levels:

Level 1 - the manifest content of seated figures, basket of fruit, bather, frog, bullfinch, etc.

Level 2 - the way that the viewer can relate to the images presented to them – e.g. literally or metaphorically.

Level 3 - the way that Manet comments upon art within the elements of the painting (the size relative to the subject; the front lighting of the nude; the eye contact of the nude with the viewer; the references to the earlier works of Giorgione/Titian, Raphael, & Michael Angelo) that suggests the way that the viewer is to respond to the painting. Indeed, it is very much the way that this last level operates as a comment on the art of the time that singles out this composition as a great painting.

But a work of art is also a piece of communication between the artist and the viewer, and in this respect it also demonstrates three levels:

Level one is the painting itself, with all the images and forms of presentation.

Level two is the relationship between the artist and the viewer; mediated by the painting (am I here to entertain you; or to amuse you; or to titillate you; or to inform you; or to edify you; or to challenge you?).

Level three is the means whereby the artist is able to signal which response is to be made and thereby signals the nature of the relationship in level two. In this case it is the way that Manet keeps and breaks the prevailing norms of painting that signals to the viewer that the relationship is one of intellectual and moral provocation, and also that Manet was a serious commentator on the nature of the society of which artist and viewer were a part. It is this latter level of comment that marks out for us that, as well as the painting being a great piece of art, the artist was a genius of his time.

Thus the levels two and three contain information about context and information about intention, both of which are referred to as Metacommunication, since it is about the relationship between things not the things themselves. As Berman (1981, p.220) averred, "*all meaningful communication necessarily involves metacommunication - communication about communication – and is therefore constantly generating paradoxes of the Russellian type.*" It is this multi-level nature of human communication that lies at the root of paradoxes being so common.

7 Concluding Remarks

To summarise this chapter, and to look forward to the remainder of the treatise we need to rehearse the types and causes of paradox. The first is the notion that our empirical understanding of reality is simply mistaken. The second is that sense very much depends upon the scale on which we choose to perceive reality. The third is that the language we use to describe and explain reality inevitably oversimplifies things. The fourth is that we seek to treat as equals processes that would be best portrayed as occurring at different levels or logical types, and finally that when confronted by phenomena that are of different logical types our language leads us to generate Strange Loops of self-reference.

When we undertake management roles, particularly where such roles are performed in contexts that require the pursuit of organisational missions that encompass the achievement of external social impact such as development, we are frequently confronted by phenomena that we describe as or others ascribe to paradox (or its synonyms). Now we need to explore such phenomena through the lenses provided by our philosophical appraisals above in the expectation that our understanding and scope of choices of behaviour will be enhanced.

Chapter 3

The Paradoxes of Management

1 Introduction

Argyris (1992, p.39) emphasized the central role of paradox in management theory when he queried: "*If paradoxes are an important phenomenon for administrators, ..., why is it that the prominent theories of administration or organization do not have them as a central focus?*" Indeed, many authors have commented about paradoxes in the context of management (Peters & Waterman, 1982; Handy, 1994; Denison, Hooijberg & Quinn, 1995; de Wit & Meyer, 1999; Lewis, 2000; Wharton 2001; Clegg, *et al.*, 2002). They have often used synonyms such as *contradiction* (Peters & Waterman, 1982; Lewis, 2000) or *dilemma* (Hampden-Turner, 1990) to express the nature of the challenge facing managers, but this has confused the real issue of paradox with the rather more prosaic situation of having to make difficult choices. This confusion is compounded by a lack of distinction between those paradoxes that managers have to deal with, such as simultaneously coping with change and stability (Peters, 1988; Park & Krishnan, 2003) or the tension between individual and team working (Rabey, 2003), and those paradoxes that are embedded in management itself, such as simultaneously providing control and freedom

(Clegg, *et al, op.cit.*) or Harvey's '*Abilene Paradox*' (Harvey, 1988) or Miller's '*Icarus Paradox*', (Miller, 1990). In other words there is a lack of distinction between the management of paradoxes and the paradoxes of management.

Without an understanding of these differences and distinctions it is inevitable that those responses that managers are encouraged to make by various authors seem in themselves to be contradictory. Some have advocated the reconciliation of opposites (see Denison, *et al,* 1995), usually in favour of one of the options apparently on offer. Others have advocated maintaining the paradox to gain benefits from the resulting tensions that are present (see Eisenhardt, 2000; Lewis, *op.cit.*; Clegg, *et al, op.cit.*), and many extol the virtues of managers who are able to 'live' with paradox (see Peters, 1988; Handy, *op.cit.*; Lewis, *op.cit.*). Few have sought to understand the nature of paradox as outlined in the previous chapter, nor to recognize the different causes of paradox as a prelude to improving management itself. As Arthur Schopenhauer recognized: "*The essence of paradoxical thinking 'is not so much to see what no one yet has seen, but to think what nobody yet has thought about that which everybody sees'.*" (Shelton, 1999, p.33).

This chapter seeks to explore paradoxes of management in relation to the causes of paradox outlined in chapter 2, and to offer some guidance on appropriate responses.

2 The Core Paradox

Paradoxes occur at many different levels within the process that we refer to as management. In my view the core paradox of management is contained in its very definition, as Parker Follet described it "*Getting things done by other people.*"[1] and as Waelchli (1989, p.59) capture it: "*Management 'is' responsibility for the work of others.*" This creates the challenge of having responsibility for

1 Quoted in Hannagan (2002, p.5).

achieving objectives whilst being excluded from the possibility of directly doing the job. It is the paradox of having controlling power without the doing power and has been ably described elsewhere (McGregor, 1960; Peters & Waterman, 1982).

This is a paradox of self-reference or recursion[2], one of Hofstadter's '*Tangled Hierarchies*' (Hofstadter, 2000, p.10), which is also represented in the Viable Systems Model (Beer, 1989, p.34) that recognizes that "*any viable system contains, and is contained in, a viable system*". Such recursion leads to management in a hierarchical organization being challenged to serve its appropriate sub-system and not to give way to issues of status for, as Beer (1994, p.317) warns: "*by confusing metasystem with supra-authorities we have almost lost the chance of understanding what to do* [as managers]." Again, and importantly, Seely, Duong and Trites (2000) captured this functional hierarchy in relation to project management in their four level *Dynamic Baseline Model*, where each level has its own ambit of knowledge. The levels are given, from lowest to highest, as *Management by Rules*; *Management by Methods*; *Management by Objectives*; and *Management by Values*, which represent their version of the graded responses to the challenge of getting things done by others. Such grades are also represented as having their respective and different mechanisms for reducing the variety that workers generate with that gradation being brought about by the increasing requirement of an organization to utilize its workers' variety in order to control the variety of its environment (Waelchli, 1989). Raul Espejo put this challenge in the following terms:

> *management, having lower implementation variety than the autonomous units they control, cannot possibly maintain awareness of all that is going on within them; there is a natural 'information gap'. Yet management knows that they are accountable for any loss of control.*

---

2 See section 6 in chapter 2.

> *The information gap often leads to a feeling of discomfort and uncertainty on the part of management ('what is going on down there? How can I tell if they're telling me the truth?') This anxiety to know more leads to increased demands for special reports and the undertaking of more investigations, to keep 'in control'; ... At the very time that autonomous units need more flexibility to respond effectively to their own environmental pressures, managers' behaviour is reducing this flexibility. Because of the law of requisite variety management in the cohesion function cannot win with this type of control strategy.* (Espejo, 2003, p. 19).

Of course, the things that managers are attempting to get others to do are not capricious but are goal directed, thus equating management with providing direction. According to Lincoln and Guba (1985, p.151) the nature of the act of management is such that: "*While we may not be able to produce ..., the precise outcome that we desire, we believe that it is possible to shape affairs in a desired direction*". However, in setting objectives we raise again the paradox of free will and determinism – where determinism can be presented as a chain of cause and effect, and free will represents a first, uncaused cause.[3]

In setting out strategic plans we, as managers, exercise our free will in order to determine (cause and effect) the actions of others. However, to plan is inevitably to subscribe to both sides of Kant's antinomy. In precisely this vein Bendix (1956, quoted in Perrow, 1979, p.60) asked how entrepreneurs could justify the advantage of: "*voluntary action and association for themselves, while imposing upon all subordinates the duty of obedience and the obligation to serve their employers to the best of their ability?*" Thus we believe in cause-and-effect when we treat people as objects to be managed and we believe in free will when we take it upon ourselves to plan

3 See the quotation by Roger Scruton in section 5 of chapter 2.

to change the future. But the first fails because people exercise their own self-determination as subjects and choose their own responses to situations and external initiatives (Hirschman & Bird, 1971)[4]. The second, free will, also fails because of a lack of omniscience on the part of the planners, exemplified in the proverb '*Be careful of what you wish for!*'

Nevertheless, most authors agree that the central role of management takes the form of decision-taking, at a number of levels. These have been variously and synonymously categorized as Strategic, Administrative, and Operating (Ansoff, 1987, p.23), or Normative, Strategic and Practical (Beer 1994, p.437), and Discovering, Choosing and Acting (Stacey, 1992, p.87), and where the prime characterization of a decision is a commitment to future action (Mintzberg, Raisinghani & Théorêt, 1976). However, I prefer to see these categories as the second level of management, subsumed under '*getting things done by others*', and requiring managers to undertake three essential roles – providing direction, control and motivation all of which activities contain their own, inherent paradoxes.

3 The Essential Role of Providing Direction

Providing direction is often seen as synonymous with the process of strategic planning, which is an activity by which, as Dror (1971) stated: "*man in society endeavours to gain mastery over himself and shape his collective future by power of his reason.*" Or again, according to Wildavsky (1973, p. 128), it may be seen as: "*the ability to control the future consequences of present actions…Its purpose is to make the future different from what it would have been without this intervention.*"

---

4 Importantly Ellerman (2005, p.27) has explained this as the limits of agency theory, where external motivators are part of cause-and-effect, and internal motivation is the exercise of free will, culminating in the distinction between passive causality and active causality.

The paradox of management contained in this role is the need to commit to an objective whilst retaining manœuverability. A manager has to show commitment without being committed, as Putz and Raynor (2005, p.48) recognised: "*integral leaders, in a truly Zen-like way, achieve organizational goals by not committing themselves to those goals.*" The difficulties of seeking to propel an organization towards an envisioned state have been emphasized by Stacey (1992) who maintained that it is not possible to know what awaits any innovative system advance and that predicting the future in order to select an appropriate objective would seem to be inherently difficult if not downright impossible. The paradox of management, which relates to setting the future to which the actions of others are to be directed, is contained within the misperception of relative motion. Although not a specific formulation within Zeno's paradoxes of motion (Sorensen, 2003, p.49; chapter 2 section 2), this issue is founded upon the metaphorical translation of change as motion.

Thus an observer (manager) looking forward in time and space establishes a desired future (vision or goal) whose position must be located relative to the observer's current situation, in order to be able to proceed towards it. Whilst it may be clear that the desired future is itself in motion, it must be sufficiently motionless to be locatable as a target. However, since the observer is also in motion (present moment changes) this apparent stability of the desired future may be due to one of two explanations. The first case is that of relative motion i.e. that changes in the location of the desired future are offset by similar changes in location of the present state (relative perspective) – which would imply that projecting the present into the future is probably a sound strategy. The second is that of a phenomenon, which in visual perception is described as parallax, where the more distant an object is the more stationary it seems relative to the motion of the observer or to nearer objects (in the present space and time)[5]. Future events often unfold in

5 The collision of birds with motor vehicles is often ascribed to parallax

catastrophic ways that come as a complete surprise because we were unable to perceive their trajectory. The paradox is that we have no means of knowing whether, in any given situation, we are in case one or case two and in order to proceed we need to discriminate accurately.

Beer (1981, p.12) explained an analogous predicament when he compared the similar types of change that can be experienced at both inflections of a sigmoid growth curve, which both show an apparent upward trend even though the underlying pattern is very different, and the challenge that such discrimination presents to the strategist.

This is also akin to the processes that Bateson (2002) differentiated as *'Feedback'* and *'Calibration'*, which he likened to shooting at a target with a rifle and shooting at a bird in flight with a shotgun, respectively. The importance here is that, in the former case, taking time to refine strategies should improve performance via a process of Ready→Aim→Fire that might be recognised as the *Design School Approach* (Mintzberg, Ahlstrand & Lampel, 1998). Whereas in the latter case it seems more a matter of Ready→Fire→Aim, or more importantly of Ready→Fire→Adjust, that is reminiscent of *Emergent Strategies* and the *Learning Approach* to strategy formation (Mintzberg, *et al, op.cit.*) where any amount of deliberation beyond the most cursory scene setting is an inappropriate delay in gaining the experience that will make adjustment possible.

Nevertheless, managers are expected to provide a direction that will mobilize the troops, or as Wildavsky (1973) argued, in order to affect the future it is necessary to change people's acts to ones they would not in those circumstances normally employ. However, providing the direction is not the management job done, for as Smith (1973, p.197) recognised: "*There is an implicit assumption in*

– the bird simply does not perceive that the car is moving.

most policy studies that once a policy has been formulated the policy will be implemented." which must be resisted at all costs.

But management is seen now as more science than art. As Handy (1994 p.12) noted: "*Manage always did mean 'coping with,' until we purloined the word to mean planning and control.*" Somehow, in the search for greater professionalism (Rittel & Webber, 1973), management has become harder and this hardness seems to come in the form of control. As Waelchli (1989, p.59) put it, in reference to Ashby's *Law of Requisite Variety*: "*management has been the practice of controlling or limiting variety in natural systems, ... so that the remaining natural forces within a system could move it towards man's chosen goals.*"

4 (Planning and) Control

The provision of control is seen as that quintessential management role that delivers the performance of others in the achievement of objectives (Mullins, 2007). Control is often equated with having a plan for, as Mintzberg (1994, p.213) put it: "*to have it on paper is to have it under control.*" Planning is thereby seen as the complimentary procedure that supports and enables control. Again, Waelchli (1989, p.60) recognized that: "*Planning, seen cybernetically, is the selection from the unconstrained set of all possible future states, that one ..., that ... the manager wants to see.*" In other words, in terms of Ashby's *Law of Requisite Variety*, planning is a variety attenuator. According to Koontz (1958, p.48) planning can be regarded as: "*The conscious determination of courses of action designed to accomplish purposes. Planning is, then, deciding.*" Or as Mintzberg (1994, p.9) saw it: "*Planning has been used as a virtual synonym for decision making*".[6]

---

6 Later I will take issue with the synonymous use of the terms decision-making and decision-taking.

The planning process results in the establishment of a plan, which usually sets out the objectives, the actions to be taken, the resources required or available, the indicators by which success will be assessed and feedback loops established, and the attendant risks to success (Davidoff & Reiner, 1973; Faludi, 1973). Resources are then mobilized and actions initiated.

However, the formulation of a plan also carries within it a number of paradoxes. The first of which is the tension between the stability of a fixed programme and the need to retain flexibility. As Adler and Borys (1996, p.79) expressed it: "*Such … situations create an organization design dilemma because the routine parts cannot be managed in a mechanistic, coercive, and bureaucratic way at the same time and for the same employees as the nonroutine parts are managed in an organic and empowering way.*" Managers have to be able to adapt to unfolding situations that may or may not conform to what was predicted. But, as Mintzberg (*op.cit.*, p.184) remarked: "*Flexible planning remains just another oxymoron.*" Indeed, he lamented that in planning adaptability tends to be sacrificed in favour of stability, and yet the planners want their cake and eat it, keeping stability but wishing to be responsive to changes in the external environment.

Managers must finesse this paradox by sticking closely to the plan until it has proved itself to be unworkable – and not a moment longer. It is a talented manager that can display such skill. Beer (2004, p.769) emphasized this when he recognized that: "*only an idiot would actually implement a plan, if that is the product of planning.*" But inevitably, by settling on one course of action, choice precludes following alternative routes. To choose is to close doors as well as to go through them. As Steiner (1979, p.46) recognized: "*Plans are commitments … and thus they limit choice. They tend to reduce initiative in a range of alternatives beyond the plans.*" In this way Mintzberg (*op.cit.*) warned of the conservative nature of planning, and that detailed plans have a tendency to generate resistance to change.

The tensions outlined above have been elaborated into a specific paradox by de Wit and Meyer (1999, p. 104) who drew attention to this particular paradox when they recognized the contradictory nature of strategic planning and went on to name it as the: "*paradox of deliberateness and emergentness*". They maintained that this paradox is embodied in two sides of an apparently irreconcilable dispute between those who believe that it is necessary to articulate intended courses of action as explicit plans and those who: "*doubt the value of plans and focus on the emergence of strategy in the absence of explicit intentions.*" Furthermore, these conflicting parties are considered to hold opposite views about the value of having formal planning systems to generate the plans.

If we take recourse to the views of Gilbert Ryle (quoted in section 4 of chapter 2) regarding the perceptual nature of conflicting ideas, we may be forgiven for thinking that this particular paradox might be a storm in a tea cup. Indeed, it seems likely that what we are dealing with here is a confusion of levels of perception as explained in section 3 of the previous chapter. An analogy from biology that might prove helpful in the reconciliation of these apparently opposing views is the relationship between genotype and phenotype, as explained by Bateson (1972, pp. 346-363). Accordingly, the manifestation of an organism is defined by its genetic programme (genotype) which has been translated into the organism itself under the influence of the environment upon the ontogenic realization of that programme (phenotype).

Thus there are two levels of influence at play in the ontogeny of any organism – the genetic programming (or plan) and its flexible interpretation in the light of the environment (or improvisation). As Bateson (1972) recognized, both the programming and the flexibility are necessary components of a successful process of ontogeny. The degree of latitude permitted to be expressed in the phenotype is itself a genotypically determined characteristic i.e. the plan also lays down the boundaries of the flexibility of its interpretation (the discretion of the implementers, including the obligation to consult).

As Chamberlain (1968, pp.154-5) recognized: "*planned order is not the antithesis of individual freedom but is necessary to it … the issue is not plan or individualism but how much of each.*" In management terms, the plan is both necessary and fundamental. But the discretion that is given to the implementers of the plan is also necessary if the strategy is to become reality. It is the degree of that discretion that defines where in the deliberateness – emergentness continuum any given example is situated, and the degree of its match to circumstance determines whether the paradox is perceived as an obstacle in managing or not.

5 Analysis versus Synthesis

A second paradox of planning is contained in the dichotomy of the process into Analysis and Synthesis.[7] Each of these processes is associated with very different skills and is often given to different kinds of staff to lead and to the separation of the planners from the doers. Indeed Mintzberg (1994, p.324) observed that they may be of two types: "*one being more predisposed to the analysis associated with the left hemisphere* [of the brain], *the other to the synthesis more closely associated with the right hemisphere.*" Moreover, Devons (quoted in Wildavsky, 1971 p.102) drew attention to a paradox generated by such separation when he said that: "*another paradox* [of the planner is] *to have substantial power and be certain that* [one's] *advice would normally be taken, yet … to be absolved from responsibility.*" However, as Mintzberg (*op.cit.*) recognised, there is inevitably a certain rationality within the construction of plans[8] which has analysis, not synthesis, as its essence, and

---

7 This is mirrored by the distinction in the research process between the creation of the initial research questions ("*the context of discovery*") and rigorous data handling ("*the context of justification*") (Lincoln & Guba 1985, p.25).

8 Which we shall explore in chapter 10, section 2.

this accounts for the downplaying of the importance of creative actions within the planning process. Analysis is by its nature substantially backward looking and synthesis looks forward[9], but this emphasis on analysis has the tendency to project the past into the future and to provide conservative options.

It is noteworthy that Roy Bhaskar has explained critical reality as an acceptance that any possible understanding of the world is based upon a combination of what we know and the generative absence of what remains to be known, thus:

> *The rational kernel of dialectic is as a learning or developmental process driven by absence. For instance in science we have a theory which is incomplete in some way, this incompleteness, betokening absence will generate contradictions, inconsistencies, anomalies which will pile up to a point at which they will become unbearable. Then we will have the moment of transcendence to a greater totality and that transcendence to a greater totality will remedy the initial generative absence; and in that remedying of the absence will restore consistency within the theoretical field.* (Bhaskar, 2002, p.38)

Since planning is about analysis of the situation and formulation of a response, the analysis, undertaken by whomsoever, must inevitably be incomplete (generative absence). It is in this latter aspect that we find the true position of the plan. A plan can be no more than an attempt to describe reality and it will always be lacking some aspect of full understanding. As Beer (2004, p.769) recognized: "*If the plan ... is conceived out of a model that assumes complete information, it is mistaken. If it admits to using incomplete information, then obviously more information will start to be available before the ink can dry.*" Therefore, planning should be a dialectical process that moves from one degree of understanding

9 Or indeed laterally!

to another by the incorporation of fresh aspects encountered from the experience of its implementation and which are drawn from what is inevitably only another incomplete part of the generative absence.

In the past professional planners have served the policy makers by providing the expert advice and analysis upon which proposed plans were based. More recently they have come to recognise that other stakeholders have much '*expertise*' to contribute about the generative absence by way of indigenous knowledge and important client perspectives. As a result the role of the planning professionals has shifted towards facilitation of a whole process of participation from which the planning choices and plan emerge. This role requires an entire set of new skills of the professional planners beyond their existing technical know-how (Dagron, 2005).

6 The Process of Decision

Any plan can be seen simply as an agreed set of actions that have been chosen in order to achieve specified objectives, within an overall context. The choice of objectives and actions are the result of a decision that has been taken by a person or persons charged with the responsibility and authority to do so (**Decision-taking**). There are only three ways to take a decision, the first is for a single person to decide by a process of weighing each of the options in relation to all the known issues (a rational decision), or which takes into consideration interests outside of the immediate options (a political or a corrupt or an irrational (sometimes intuitive) decision). The second is for a group of people to go through a similar process and then to cast their vote for the option that they have chosen (intuitively, rationally, politically or corruptly), with the decision going with the majority of votes cast. The third is to place the decision in the hand of chance and through some form of coin tossing, augury, lot drawing or random number generation to discover the choice.

Decision-making, on the other hand, can be a vastly more complicated business. In essence it is a process of identifying the possible options and is made up of a sequence and variety of mechanisms for gaining the information and perspectives that will lead to the formulation of a proposed plan or alternative plans about which the designated authority will take a decision. As Mill (1985, p.77) recognized: "*To refuse a hearing to an opinion because* [the authorities] *are sure that it is false is to assume that* ***their*** *certainty is the same thing as* ***absolute*** *certainty. All silencing of discussion is an assumption of infallibility.*" There are clear benefits to be obtained from bringing about such decision-making as a widely consultative process, and the breadth and depth of the gathering of facts and opinions are determined by the predilection of the decision-taker(s) to obtain a wide view and the time, resources and skill that they have at their disposal for the consultation.

Clearly, systems in which the decision-takers consider themselves to be authorities in the matter of fact and expert opinion or in the art of synthesis acknowledge little distinction between the processes of decision-taking and decision-making (Miller, Hickson & Wilson, 1996). More sensitive decision-takers appreciate the value of collapsing the hierarchy during the exploratory, decision-making process so that the decision that is eventually arrived at can be seen to be transparent and rational, rather than corrupt or covertly political. Where decision-making is a very impoverished process it is not hard to conclude that the decisions taken are likely to be at best intuitive or at worst irrational or corrupt.

It is at this point that the power of the decision-implementers comes to the fore, for no matter how powerful the decision-takers consider themselves to be, it is only once the decision has actually been put into effect that the power of the decision comes into being (Assagioli, 1999). As Hardy and Clegg (1996, p. 624) pointed out: "*because of embodiment, the people hired as labour will retain ultimate discretion over themselves, what they do, and how they do it. Consequently, a potential source of resistance resides in this inescapable and irreducible embodiment of labour power.*" Indeed, as Child (1972) recognized for plans to be implemented it is important to gain the cooperation of those who most closely affect the plan. Thus the essential question at this point is whether the decision shall be executed, and it is here that resistance or reluctance on the part of the implementers can thwart the intentions of the decision-takers.

Mintzberg (1994 p. 42) suggested that "*Deep commitment … is a necessary prerequisite to the successful pursuit of difficult courses of action and [it] … grow[s] out of a sense of ownership of a project*". However, in order to implement the plan the doers need to understand it; to be motivated towards the goal (its purpose and its method) and to have no higher priorities; to be capable of carrying out the necessary actions and to have sufficient resources. The fullest involvement of the implementers in the decision-making process can pay dividends in reducing the amount of coercive force that has to be expended in order to get things done against resistance, and *vice versa*. As Allen Amason recognised:

> *common understanding of the rationale underlying a decision will give the individual team members the ability to act independently but … consistent with the actions of others and … with the spirit of the decision. Commitment … reduces the likelihood that a particular decision will become the target of cynicism or countereffort.* (Amason, 1996, p.125)

In relation to the associated management of consensus in decision-taking, it is important at this point, for us to consider a particular paradox of management, the Abilene Paradox, and to understand how to avoid it.

7 The Abilene Paradox

This was identified by Harvey (1988, p.18) thus: "*The inability to manage agreement is a major source of organization dysfunction.*" and "*It is ultimately the cause of self-defeating, collective deception that leads to self-destructive decisions within organizations.*" (*ibid.*, p.22) The essence of this problem is that groups of people collectively come to choose that alternative course of action which is actually unpalatable to them all in order for individuals not to have to press their own views and thereby upsetting the group cohesion.

Harvey (1988) explained this by way of an analogy to a lynching, in which the following three components are present:

(1) nobody really wants to take part in the hanging;

(2) that each individual takes part because they believe, falsely, that the others want to do so; and

(3) that everyone is afraid that the others will exact some penalty upon them if they do not take part.

In order to make an appropriate response to an *Abilene Paradox* Harvey explained that we must recognize that it is the nature of such paradoxes to be destroyed by the discovery and sharing of the alternative logic that sustains them. As he (*ibid.*, p.19) emphasized, the most important of a variety of reasons that the paradox was avoided was that: "*the group became conscious of the process and did not reach the point of repeating the cycle with greater intensity.*" His recipe for dealing with those behaviours that result from an *Abilene Paradox* is reflected in his comments that: "*the power to destroy the paradox's pernicious influenced comes from confronting and speaking to the underlying reality of the situation, and not from one's hierarchical position within the organization.*" (*ibid.*, p.23)

Importantly it must be noted that the various aspects of the Abilene Paradox described above, and in more detail by Harvey (1988), suggest that it falls within a set of behaviours that characterize people confronted by paradox and are described as '*double binds*' (Bateson, 1979; Kowalski, 2004). These are phenomena that permeate both management and development and will be explained in detail in chapter 10, section 3.

At this point we must notice the similarity of this problem with that which Argyris (1990) has described as '*theory-in-use*', where the various parties within an organization skillfully, but unconsciously, manage their social interactions in such a way as to undermine the outcomes that they would consciously pursue. This is also linked with Amason's (1996, p.128) recognition of the importance of *Team Cognitive Capabilities* and *Team Interaction Processes* and the tensions between *Cognitive* and *Affective* conflicts (Argyris' '*espoused theory*' and '*theory-in-use*', respectively) that result and their impact upon the quality of decisions.[10]

8 Conflict Management

Life and conflict are intertwined. Put two human beings together and conflicts emerge. Please note that violence is not implied by the nominalization – conflict, simply any and all forms of disagreement (For a useful review see Weeks, 1992).

As Thomas (1976) recognised, the way we handle conflicts is governed by two vectors: (i) How much we want our objective (the substance of the conflict) and (ii) How much we value our relationship with the other party (which itself may be based upon our power relationship). This may be illustrated as in Figure 3.1. Therefore, the choices open to us in how we approach a conflict can be considered as follows:

---

[10] Argyris' ideas will be explored at greater length in chapter 4, section 2.

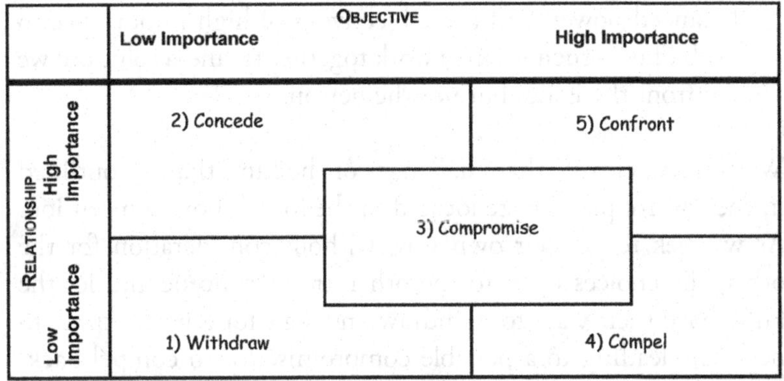
OBJECTIVE
Low Importance
High Importance
RELATIONSHIP
High Importance
Low Importance
2) Concede
5) Confront
3) Compromise
1) Withdraw
4) Compel

Figure 3.1. The conflict matrix (After Kowalski, 2005, based on an idea by Thomas, 1976).

1. If the Objective is not of high immediate importance to us, or we lack the power to insist, and the relationship is also not important to us – then we may put the conflict on hold; we withdraw for the time being.

2. If the Objective is not of high importance to us, or we lack the power to insist, and the relationship is important to us, or the other person is powerful and we dare not offend them – then we give in; we concede more or less graciously, even before we are challenged as in the *Abilene Paradox*.

3. If we need a resolution of the conflict, and are evenly matched with the other in power and determination – then we may engage in give and take; we compromise as the appropriate strategy, though recognising that it will leave neither party satisfied.

4. If the Objective is of high immediate importance to us, or we have the power to insist, and the relationship is also not important to us – then we may get our way; compelling the other person to concede, using ploys, tactics and manipulation.

5. If the relationship is important to both of us, or we have balanced power, and the Objective is of high importance to both of us – then we may work together to find a solution; we confront the issues but not the person.

We can see, clearly, that challenges of the kind that we outlined in the control process are located in the fourth box, compulsion. As we seek to get our own way, without consideration for the other, the choices open to the other are to concede and let the bully have their way; to withdraw and wait for a better time; to negotiate leading to a possible compromise; or to compel back. What does not seem to be in our repertoire is for both parties to move towards confronting their problems. As Harvey (1988, p.24) in discussing his Abilene Paradox recognized: "*Confrontation becomes the process of facing issues squarely, openly, and directly in an effort to discover whether the nature of the underlying collective reality is agreement or conflict.*"

PSYCHOLOGICAL CONSIDERATIONS

As Kowalski (2005) noted, at any moment the behaviour we choose is very much determined by our programming and character, as much as by any rational consideration of the prevailing situation. In that respect it is helpful for our deliberations here if we take recourse to *Transactional Analysis* (TA) (Berne 1966) to enable us to understand that programming. A central concept within the range of programming covered by TA is that of *Life Positions*. This involves our beliefs about ourselves and other people. Sometimes we are happy with ourselves; we like ourselves, but other times we may not. So there are two possible belief systems about self from which to view the world – *'I am okay with me'*, and *'I am not okay with me'*. Similarly we may hold two alternative views of the people around us. So we may feel that *'You are okay with me'* or '*You are not okay with me*'. Ernst (1971) combined these perspectives into a matrix of four possible life positions that he called '*The OK corral*', which is further elaborated in Figure 3.2.

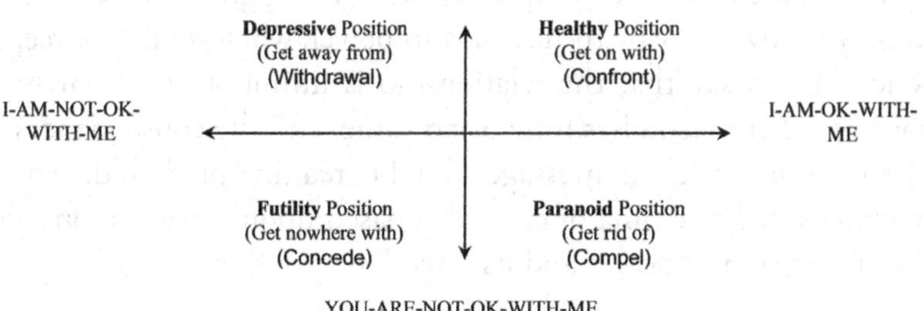
YOU-ARE-OK-WITH-ME
Depressive Position
(Get away from)
(Withdrawal)
Healthy Position
(Get on with)
(Confront)
I-AM-NOT-OK-WITH-ME
I-AM-OK-WITH-ME
Futility Position
(Get nowhere with)
(Concede)
Paranoid Position
(Get rid of)
(Compel)
YOU-ARE-NOT-OK-WITH-ME

Figure 3.2 *The OK corral* (After Kowalski, 2005, from an idea by Ernst, 1971)

When we are in the *Healthy* position we are positive and work well with others. When they are in the *Healthy* position themselves the same holds true. So, rationally we should seek to be in our *Healthy* position and to help others to be in their *Healthy* position. Unfortunately, quite often we are not responding from that location but from one of the other three, possible positions. When that is the case we fall into negative feelings and behaviour and so do other people in a similar case. When we are in the *Paranoid* position, or the *Depressive* position, or the *Futility* position, we encourage others to drop in to one of these less resourceful states too.

There are obvious links between this psychological model of our life position, our psychological resource state, and our behaviour as manifested in our approach to conflict. For example the *Futility* position is linked to *Withdrawal*, the *Depressive* position to concede and the *Paranoid* position to *Compulsion*. The only approach to conflict management that falls within the *Healthy* position is *Confront*. It is the only box in the matrix where we allow ourselves to want our objective and at the same time to allow other people to want their objectives whilst valuing them as human beings and our relationship with them.

Quite simply, these life positions are at the heart of McGregor's X and Y approaches to management (McGregor, 1960). Both parties rightly view the act of compulsion as an act of aggression. Seeking to get your own way by the use of your power, whatever its' source, is actually to say that the relationship is unimportant. That to you the other person has little or no value, and the consequences of projecting such a message can be readily predicted. For managers this dilemma of control is based upon the question of the application of power and its attendant paradox.

THE PARADOX OF POWER

As Dahl (1957, p.201) acknowledged: "*The concept of power is as ancient and ubiquitous as any that social theory can boast.*" but what is it? The essence of the concept has been captured by Greiner and Schein (1989) as that capacity which enables you to influence another person's willingness to accept your ideas or to get others to do what you want. Or as Stacey and Griffin (2005, p.17) acknowledged: "*in relating to each other people cannot do other than both constrain and enable each other at the same time.*". But Foucault has captured another aspect of the nature of power by suggesting that power can only exist where there is resistance (Mills, 2003).

However, we see here another paradox since the more power that has to be exerted in order to coerce compliance, the less powerful one actually is. Or as Hardy and Clegg (1996) recognized, there is a central paradox of power whereby one's power is increased by delegating it to others and, in an oblique reference to the deliberateness-emergentness paradox solution in section 4, they went on to say that: "*the delegation of authority can only proceed by rules; rules necessarily entail discretion; and discretion potentially empowers delegates.*" (*op.cit.*, p.634).

Such a trade-off chimes well with the position of Weber (1947) who stressed the vital role of legitimacy in the exercise of power as authority. Since the exercise of power has cost implications the utilization of authority as a means of overcoming resistance cannot be over stated. Indeed, Hardy and Clegg (*op.cit.*) emphasized the importance of avoiding overt and coercive types of power by utilizing the legitimacy that is afforded by institutions. Indeed, power's most subtle manifestation of manipulation is in setting the boundaries of discourse through what Gramsci (1971) refers to as hegemony, which is the uncritical acceptance of assertions about what constitutes truth made by or on behalf of social elites, such as managers, to establish spontaneous consent to the general direction of a society or institution by that élite.

Of course exercising our power to get our way is most frequently negative in effect because its main point of action is in controlling or limiting the actions of others – which may be referred to as 'power-over' (For a discussion of relational power see Rowlands, 1998). Clegg (1989, p.4) recognised this constitutive conception of power as: "*a locus of will, as a supreme agency to which other wills would bend, as prohibitory; the classic conception of power as zero-sum; in short, power as negation of the power of others.*"

Again, as Robert Chambers observed:

> *Most uppers see their power in zero-sum terms: if they have less, others will have more, and they will be worse off. . . .We talk of 'giving up power' and 'abandoning' it, implying loss, and 'losing' and 'gaining power' implying a zero sum.* (Chambers, 1997 p.205)

However, *power-over* is falsely attractive in nature since, as suggested above, the acquisition of *power-over* is usually accompanied by the need to hand over large quantities of it to others to act '*in one's name*'. Significantly, the more power-over that is brought to bear in a given situation, the more that is required to be applied, or as Ranson, Hinings and Greenwood (1980, p.8) recognized: "*power is most effective when it is unnecessary.*" In addition, *power-over* is also disabling since it creates distance between decision-takers and the impact of their decisions. Indeed, decision-takers are often less powerful than decision-implementers simply because humans lack the ability to control or do everything (omnipotence)[11].

In this respect Neil Long and Manuel Villareal commented that:

> *Even those categorized as 'oppressed' are not utterly passive victims, and may become involved in active resistance. Likewise, the 'powerful' are not in complete control of the stage and the extent to which their power is forged by the so-called 'powerless' should not be underestimated.* (Long & Villareal, 1994 p.50).

Or again, as Pfeffer (1981, p.5) recognized: "*it is interesting that in spite of the considerable degree of power possessed by lower level employees, these employees seldom attempt to exercise their power or to resist the instructions of their managers.*"

Thus exemplifying that *power-over* usually operates against *power-to. Power-to* is characterised by being the energy that people can apply to their actions. Although these actions may have positive or negative impact, the *power-to* element is fundamentally positive-sum in nature. That is, the amount of *power-to* that an individual possesses has no limiting effect upon the *Power-to* of any other individual. Motivation, determination, creativity and enthusiasm are essentially limitless and, if anything, are actually contagious. As such *power-to* is a general good that enables people to achieve their goals (see Uphoff, 1996).

As Kowalski (2005) maintained, in certain circumstances *power-to* can decline below zero in response to *power-over*, and then it takes on a negative, destructive form, leading to increasing resistance, sabotage and ultimately violent opposition. People's motivation,

11 See the Hardy and Clegg quotation in section 6.

determination and enthusiasm are often in inverse proportion to the amount of *power-over* that others hold.

9 Motivation

This returns us conveniently to the third aspect of the management role, motivation, which is linked to the previous two (Providing Direction and Control) by essentially involving the provision of clarity of direction, indicators for tracking success, and confidence to proceed. Once more the planning and the management processes seem to overlap and to go hand-in-hand. Mintzberg (1994, p.15) highlighted the relationship and the importance of clarity when he said that "[Planning] *must be seen, not as decision making, not as strategy making, and certainly not as management, but simply as the effort to formalize parts of them.*"

This aspect of placing the plan in a more public domain has often been propounded as the main reason for planning. Zan (1987, p.193) saw: "*The common characteristic* [of various planning systems as] *the process of rendering things explicit.*" and Sawyer (1983) emphasized the necessity of bringing management processes out of the minds of just the leaders and into group forums for sharing. However, this is also a source of dispute, where the emphasis shifts from direction and control coming out of a plan and towards the importance of the planning process itself. As Steiner and Kunin (1983, p.15) asserted: "*Plans are sometimes useless but the planning process is always indispensable.*" and Wildavsky (1973, p.152) was even more critical in saying: "*Since the end is never in sight* [man] *sanctifies the journey; the process of planning becomes holy.*"

Beer (1979, p.338) was more positive when he wrote that: "*Planning is **not** an activity resulting in products called plans: it is a continuous process, whereby the process itself – namely that of aborting the plans – is the pay-off.*" Indeed, and most importantly, Beer (1979) clearly identified planning as the managerial embodiment of cohesiveness (glue) which is often presented as the primary characteristic of organisation itself. Again, in reference to Ashby's Law, Waelchili (1989, p.66) recognized that: "*One element of motivation, the idea of 'participation', seems to have been a significant precursor to the effective managerial use of variety amplification.*" This perspective, and others, has led to the emphasis on participation that now pervades the accounts of management practice, especially in development (for example see Cooke, 1998). This is presented as a process of discourse that holds all the elements identified by Foucault (1981), and draws upon aspects of power in regard to who is permitted to speak (rarefaction), what can be spoken about (power/knowledge) and who speaks the truth (experts) that involves a variety of parties naming their world. These three mechanisms whereby the influence of power is brought to bear are:

Who can speak – who gains access to voicing their perceptions?

This means that limitations placed upon who can take part (rarefaction) and how various groups are to be represented are set both overtly – by the use of invitations, permissions and recognitions – and covertly – by the restricted availability of information about the process and by the resource implications of taking part in it (attendance and/or opportunity costs) (Dahl 1990).

What is to be spoken about – how is the agenda set? What is not to be considered?

It means that both the opportunity to influence the process through which the subject matter to be considered is decided, and to influence what subject matter will be considered may be restricted before discussions take place (power/knowledge), and thereby places some issues beyond the particular discourse (Lukes, 1974).

Whose opinions count most as the '*truth*'?

It also means that when discussions take place the opinions of some individuals, institutions or organizations are considered to be more '*truthful*' than others e.g. experts versus primary stakeholders or that for some groups their own perceptions must give way to the hegemony of those more powerful voices (Gramsci, 1971).

Thus, to paraphrase Harold Lasswell (Morgan & Welton, 1986), by way of reference to Foucault, in attempting to discover the generative absence in any plan, it is important to ask: *Who can ask about What, by What means, with What language and to What effect?*

Indeed, it seems that the implementers are frequently left out of the planning process. As Worthy (1959, p.78) observed: "*workers are seen as means rather than ends, doers rather than planners or initiators; to be manipulated ... in other interests and for needs other than their own.*" Even when they are engaged they may simply be passive information providers, or as Mintzberg (1994) noted, inputs are increasingly sought by participation, but the final results are still driven from above. However, to be efficacious the implementers have to make sense of the plan and they can only do so in relation to their existing perspective (Porter & Onyach-Olaa, 1999). So it is more efficient and effective for them to participate in planning rather than simply to receive the plan. For we must remember, as Craig and Porter (1997, p.235) recognised: "*They do not fully disengage from their own dreams and ideals, but bring them along on the project journey, and try to realise them within the confined space of the project.*"

Or again, as Paul Marris averred:

> *When those who have power to manipulate changes act as if they only have to explain, and when their explanations are not at once accepted, shrug off opposition as ignorance or prejudice, they express a*

profound contempt for the meaning of lives other than their own. For the reformers have already assimilated these changes to their purposes, and worked out a reformulation which makes sense to them, perhaps through months or years of analysis and debate. If they deny others the chance to do the same, they treat them as puppets dangling by threads of their own conceptions. (Marris, 1975, p. 166).

Now, remembering our role in getting things done by others, it is important to note that in getting them to tackle problems there are two potential approaches. One in which the process is proscribed, which we may term *Algorithmic*, and one where the process is more open ended, which we may describe as *Heuristic*[12]. These are often presented as alternatives, but I believe are better understood as being at different logical levels, *Heuristic* being at a higher level than *Algorithmic*. Waelchli (1989, p.69) identifies much of the early scientific approach to management as the *Algorithmic* model, where the worker is to be encouraged to simply follow instructions – "*The worker's inherent variety is here considered entropic; what management wants is a precise, obedient and tireless low-variety machine.*" This has also been identified as M^c^Gregor's Theory 'X' (M^c^Gregor, 1960).

Modern management science takes a more flexible approach that has been identified as the Heuristic model, where management must seek to utilize the employees' variety in order to counterbalance the variety of the external environment – "*The worker, with shared corporate value system and corporate goals embedded in his soul, and with freedom, even a charge, to act intelligently on those values, has become, in a sense, an extension of management.*" (Waelchli, *op.cit.*).

Fred Waelchli goes on to say that:

---

12 Definitions are provided by Beer (1981, p.53).

> *If management does properly the work of value articulation, and if the worker adopts management's vision of societal change and makes it part of his intellectual and emotional fabric, then the worker has become, in a real sense, management.* (Waelchli, 1989, p.71).

Thus participation, far from being a source of increasing complexity that threatens the managed enterprise, becomes the wellspring of that very variety that will counter the vagaries of the environment within which the enterprise seeks to maintain its viability. In so doing the participants gain a faith and confidence in the rightness of the enterprise and see their role in it recognized.

Thus the final, and most important, aspect of motivation to which we need to give our attention is that of giving confidence in the plan. Karl Weick recounts a story of soldiers lost in a blizzard in the mountains who escape their predicament by using a map that is subsequently shown to be of another region entirely. He goes on to say (Weick, 1990, p.4) that: "*if you're lost any old map will do. For … a map provides a reference point, an anchor and a place to start from, a beginning, which often becomes secondary once an activity gets underway.*" Thereby revealing another paradox, which links back to that of the manager needing to commit without being committed and to the paradox of relative motion, namely that the value of a plan may not be in its accuracy and detail, nor in the level of participation that has gone into the process of analysis and synthesis of the plan, but in the belief that there is sufficient collective understanding of both the current position and future prospects to set forth, which itself stems from the belief that the plan is accurate and clear and has been widely shared (Dalton, 1988).

10 The Icarus Paradox

At this point it is appropriate to turn our attention to those behaviours that have been described by Miller (1993) as the '*Icarus Paradox*' where successful managers turn virtues into vices or as Handy (1994, p.60) put it: "*Business history is littered with the stories of founding fathers who thought that their way was the only way*". These vices are enumerated as the '*focusing trajectory*' encompassing rigid control and obsession with detail; the '*venturing trajectory*' that lures managers into businesses about which they know little or nothing; the '*inventing trajectory*' that siphons off resources into grandiose projects; and the '*decoupling trajectory*' that transforms skilled marketers into bureaucratic producers of fixed offerings (Miller, 1990, p.4).

This clearly relates to the paradox of team work that Rabey (2002) explained as the tension that exists between the individual, who can innovate, and the team, that can incubate innovations and bring them to fruition. This has long been recognised as the challenge of the second curve (Morrison 1996), where it is necessary to let go of the past and take up new opportunities. As Putz and Raynor (2005, p.47) noted: "*the paradoxical requirements of persistent growth demand that senior management simultaneously cope with the needs of potentially disruptive initiatives.*" It requires a very different ambiance to support innovation than to manage the routine business (also see the Adler & Borys, 1996 quotation in section 4 above).

Miller (1993, p.116) emphasized how much the Icarus Paradox is driven by a process of simplification thus: "*Ultimately, a rich and complex organization becomes excessively simple – it turns into a monolithic, narrowly focused version of its former self, converting a formula for success into a path toward failure.*" In this regard Beer (1979, p.17) drew attention to the Pareto curve with its typical point of inflection at the 20%-80% coordinates and the role that it plays in management thinking. To regard the costly[13] and marginally relevant tail of the Pareto curve[14] as a problem that needs to be removed (simplification), he suggests, is a recipe for setting out upon a process of *'eating'* the business through devoting scarce resources in pursuit of control over these *'outlying'* parts of the business and in losing the contribution that they make to the overall business by shutting them down. Once more, we have an indication that parts of the organization must exist that do not conform to the mainstream, but which management must find ways to foster by accepting both the unorthodox contribution that they represent and the impossibility of successfully dispensing with them altogether[15].

11 Frameworks as Models of the Planning Processes

Lincoln and Guba (1985, p.154) recognized that: "*Management thus involves a great deal more than the 'prediction and control' promised by positivistically oriented social scientists.*" Therefore, if we are to understand management behaviour in undertaking a paradoxical responsibility itself fraught with paradox, then there is an underlying need to pull together all of these issues and generate a model of the range of behaviour that constitutes the management role. As Hall (1976 p.13) puts it: "*The purpose of* [a] *model is to enable the user to do a better job in handling the enormous complexities of life.*" Or as Checkland and Scholes (1999, p. 22) describe it, in regard to Soft Systems Methodology: "*an epistemology which can be used to try to understand and intervene usefully in the rich and surprising flux of every day situations*", also speaking of: "*models* [that] *could be compared with real-world action in a problem situation in order to structure a debate about change.*" (*ibid.* p.309). Beer (1989 p.14) drew attention to the process of scientific modelling as a comparison between systems of experience and perception through '*homomorphic mapping*' of

13 In terms of the application of control resources.

14 In the sense that the tail is seldom seen as '*Core Business*'.

15 Throwing the baby out with the bathwater.

elements in the model against elements in empirical experience, deepening from fairly speculative '*Insight*' through some sense of '*Analogy*' to detailed '*Isomorphism*'.

As an attempt to construct an instructive model of management, the basic, hierarchical structure of managing together with its paradoxes, discussed above, can be further explored and explained by reference to a fractal structure[16] as proposed by McWhirter (1999), and which he called the '*Epistemology Grid*'. He bases this fractal structure on a three part pattern of Why; What; and How, repeated at two levels (although there are conceivably more). These are presented in respect of the processes of Managing, cross-referenced to the previously outlined views of *Ansoff (1987), †Beer (1994), °Stacey (1992), and ^Kowalski (2006) in Table 3.1, below.

16 The basic concept of fractals is that they contain a large degree of self-similarity. This means that they contain little copies of themselves repeated at each subsequent level buried deep within the original.

Fractal Level 1	Fractal Level 2	Attendant manager contributions:
Policy† (why?) (Decision-Making^) (Strategic Direction*)	Discovering°	Expertise and Collapsing the Hierarchy
	Choosing°	Transparency, Authority and Responsibility
	Acting°	Devolution, Resourcing, Capacity Building
Planning† (what?) (Decision-Taking^) (Administrative Control*)	Discovering°	Stakeholder Participation
	Choosing°	Feasibility, Transparency and Accountability
	Acting°	Delegation, Resourcing, Capacity Building
Enactment† (how?) (Decision-Implementing^) (Operational Motivation*)	Discovering°	Quality Circles, Reflective Practice
	Choosing°	Day-to-day management, Flexibility
	Acting°	Team Work, Division of Labour, Resource Tracking, Capacity Building

Table 3.1: The Fractal Model of Managing (After Kowalski, 2006, p. 176)

We can describe fractal level 1 as encompassing *Policy* (Decision-Making) that provides strategic direction; *Planning* (Decision-Taking) that provides administrative control; and *Enactment* (Decision-Implementing) that provides operational motivation. Each of these in turn, at fractal level 2, can be seen as involving *Analysis* (Discovering); *Option selection* (Choosing); and *Implementation* (Acting) in respect of the process at fractal Level 1. This is very reminiscent of the *Viable System Model* (Beer, 1989, p.22) which proposes a 5 part model of any system which reproduces the three levels above[17], together with the recognition

[17] Indeed, we can also see in the above pattern the three domains that Yolles (2004, p.746) listed as: "*cognitive or existential, the virtual or organising, and the phenomenal or behavioural.*" and which, not unlike the fractal system above, he placed in a recursive pattern: "*by which*

that such a pattern is recursive: "*systems of increasing complexity are nested within each other like so many Russian dolls or Chinese boxes to produce the whole.*" Culminating in Beer's observation that: "*Any viable system is made up of and is contained in another viable system*". Such recursion was also recognised as pertaining to layers of democratic government by Dahl (1990, p.72) when he suggested that: "*stages of government fitting together rather like the components of a Chinese box are necessary if 'the people' are to 'rule' on matters important to them.*"

Now, unless each of the parts and levels are effectively understood and managed, then the results of any application of knowledge (a decision) will be at best fragmentary, and probably lead to unachieved goals. However, seldom do the protagonists in the entire process have such an overview of what is involved, as Beer (1989, p.24) observed: "*purely hierarchical models of management are useful for little more than apportioning blame.*" Many believe that once *Option Selection* at policy level has been undertaken then implementation would inevitably follow. Within each fractal, at level 2, there is a process of Implementation and, as we have seen above, it is this that is of vital importance in delivering change on the ground.

In relation to the management roles outlined above we can see that the key management responsibility to the overall process (of getting things done by others) is, as Barnard (1928) recognised, communication. As Clarke (2006, p.23) acknowledged: "*the role of management, understood in cybernetic terms is to structure communication linkages between itself, the subsystems within and the 'super systems' without.*" Within the fractal structure presented above the managerial contributions to direction, control and motivation are summarised in the right hand column of Table 3.1.

---

we mean that each of the three domains can, through the local context of its own validity claim about reality, recursively host the set of the three domains." (Yolles, *op.cit.*, p.755).

12 Concluding Remarks

Beer (1966, p.425) has emphasised that: "*Since the normal occupation of management is to be expert in using the practical language of the firm's operations, there is the danger that the management will never speak the metalanguage in which its own structure can be discussed.*" This is one reason why it is important for academics to assist in the development and deployment of this metalanguage of management. However, even in the academic literature about management there is a tendency to use the term paradox in an undisciplined way. In particular there is a noticeable failure to draw a distinction between the paradoxes of management and the management of paradoxes. In line with explanations elsewhere (Bateson, 1979; Beer, 1989; Kowalski, 2004), the paradoxes of management emerge as a result of the confusion of logical types. The fractal model above represents a hierarchical structure of such logical typing that invites confusion by conflation of roles and contamination by trespassing functionaries. Beer (1989, p.28) identified this pathology as: "[Subsystems] *Three and Five can collapse into each other, leaving the critical Five subsystem a mere functionary.*" Leading to: "*when something goes wrong in System Three (or even One)* [Five people promoted from Three] *are likely to dive down into the problem that they understand so well – never to emerge again.*" (Beer, *op.cit.*, p.29)

In my own view, in the management of paradoxes it is important that our response is not to choose one side or the other, nor to merge the '*opposites*', nor indeed to live with the tensions, but to understand logical typing and thereby the nature of the challenges that confront us. The secret of successful management is to recognise those functions that are at a different logical level and those that are not, to know when to collapse the hierarchy for decision-making, when to show and gain commitment (without being committed), when to delegate, when to coach and when to leave the initiative to others. What we must not do is compound the problem by various behaviours that do not acknowledge the interaction between levels and which we shall explore more fully in chapter 10.

Chapter 4

The Paradoxes within Development

1 Introduction

As we saw in chapter 1, Jamieson (1987) and Uphoff (1996) have suggested that *development* is really a process of *managed change* in response to an ever-changing environment. Thus development necessarily suffers from all the paradoxes that bedevil management highlighted in the previous chapter. In addition, many other paradoxical issues that are pertinent to the context of development throw up important implications for both professionals and managers in what Deci (1995, p.158) refers to as: "*one-up positions*" in other contexts that are related to development through having to pursue organisational missions that encompass the achievement of external social impact[18], as well as having to achieve more proximal organisational change. In this regard there seems to be five particular, though related, paradoxes that fall into this category, namely:

---

18 For example Education Institutions at all levels, Social Services, Prisons and Health Services.

1. The core paradox of helping to self-help, where intervening inevitably robs people of their necessary autonomy[1]. As Ellerman (2005b, p.2) recognised: "*the notion of helping people to help themselves is in fact a deep conundrum far more subtle than is realized by the many development agencies*", which leads to the self-sabotage of paternalism in the external promotion of self-efficacy.

2. The paradox of causality whereby agencies of development believe that they can control a process which of its nature is spontaneous and self-organising, and that they alone are free to determine what shall be done whereas their agents and the objects of development have no choice but to act entirely as they are required on pain of punishment i.e. conditionality. Such contradictory beliefs extend to a syndrome of ontological perceptions that lead to the separation of what Argyris (1990) has termed '*theory-in-use*' from '*espoused theory*', which dichotomy contributes to further paradoxical phenomena.

3. The Samaritan's dilemma or moral hazard – founded upon confusing or conflating the acute needs of humanitarian aid and the chronic requirement for development assistance – bound up in the paradox of *The Gift* and Rist's paradox.

4. The epigenic paradox of the individual creating society and society creating the individual – beginning with the call by Paulo Freire (1971) for the oppressed to liberate themselves and ultimately leading to the paradox of democracy and the tragedy of the commons (Hardin, 1968).

5. The paradox of sustainable development – development's dependence upon growth through consumption (captured in the symbol of Ouroboros), Jevons' Paradox (Polimeni &

---

1 Individuals able to learn; able to manage their diet and health; able to adapt to social norms.

Polimeni, 2006) and the inadequacy of the '*better management*' approach to the conservation of resources.

And it is instructive to examine each in more detail before we are able to consider responses to paradoxes in the way that we pursue Development Assistance (DA).

2 The Nature of Development's Core Paradox

As I have remarked before, although it is the external grain of sand which causes a pearl to form, it is the oyster itself which does the making (Kowalski, 1994). In regard to this process of externally stimulating change for development, Korten (1983, p.220) observed that: "*the central paradox of social development:* [is] *the need to exert influence over people for the purpose of building capacity to control their own lives.*" Thus framing the question: how can an external agent of change operate to provide impetus for change without negating the very forces that they are seeking to unleash? In response to which Ellerman (2005b) has provided a wide-ranging exposition and indictment of the nature of the prevailing methodology of DA characterised as helping to self-help, which presents as a self-referential act of meta-communication amounting to '*Let me help you to stand on your own two feet!*'. He refers to this as the helping or fundamental conundrum of development whereby the other person cannot both allow themselves to be helped and at the same time be autonomous. He exemplified this by quoting Jane Addams, who had criticesed the false benevolence of the American industrialist and philanthropist George Pullman[2].

I have been struck by the similarity between these portrayals of DA and another situation described by Paul Watzlawick as follows:

2 See the full quotation in section 3 of chapter 1.

> *In disturbed family interaction we frequently observe that – quite reasonably – the parents expect of their child that he become independent of them and begin to live a life of his own, but that, on the other hand, they interpret any step that their child may make in that direction as a sign of ingratitude, disaffection or even treason. Thus, no matter whether he remains dependent or attempts to become independent, he is wrong and a bad son.* (Watzlawick, 1993, p.109),

which itself is also reminiscent of an earlier observation made by Alexis de Tocqueville that:

> *Above this race of men stands an immense and tutelary power, which takes upon itself alone to secure their gratifications and to watch over their fate…….It would be like the authority of a parent if, like that authority, its object was to prepare men for manhood; but it seeks, on the contrary, to keep them in perpetual childhood.* (de Tocqueville, 2002, pp. 861-2).

Thus presaging the opinion expressed by Eade (1997, p.13) that development interventions that do not improve people's current capability assuredly will increase their vulnerability. Furthermore, Rogers (1993) and Ellerman (2002) drew an analogy between education and development. In both the main basis for saying that teaching and development are similar is presented as the impossibility of performing either task because of the paradoxical relationship between the intention and the act. Gilbert Ryle identified the paradox of teaching when he wrote:

> *How in logic can the teacher dragoon his pupil into thinking for himself, impose initiative upon him, drive him into self-motivation, conscript him into volunteering, enforce originality upon him, or make*

> *him operate spontaneously? The answer is that he cannot.* (Ryle, 1967, p.118).

Unsurprisingly this is also true of health (Tucker, 1996) where responsibility for individual well-being has been usurped by technocrats (in this case doctors) in an instrumental fashion that has led to the emergence of a dominating business interest (the Medico-Pharmaceutical complex) that completes the formation of a public lacking self-help and control over their own lives, and where the main beneficiaries are the capitalist élites who are able to extract value from the system so constructed.[3]

In order to understand what is going on it is helpful to take recourse to the language that is being used. In English the verb '*to develop*' is almost unique in that without modification it can represent the transitive concept of a subject having an impact upon an object (another person) – the professional response to development, '*I develop you*'; or the intransitive concept in which the active subject is also the object – a person is responsible for and able to undertake their own development, '*I develop my skills*'; and thirdly it can encompass the passive, transitive concept of a person being the object of a process that is immanent within the object itself but not under its control as a subject – '*Over time I have developed a taste for sugar.*' As Pieterse (1999, p.79) recognised: "*Development refers both to a **process** (as in 'a society develops') and an **intervention** (as in 'developing a society').*" Recognition of which caused Cowen and Shenton (1996, p.438) to observe that: "*Development defies definition … because of the difficulty of making the intent to develop consistent with immanent development*".

Nevertheless, it is clear that on the one hand the '*professional helper*' uses and justifies their thinking by reference to the

---

3 As Illich (1978, p.79) noted: "*Beyond a certain level of intensity, professional health care, however equitably distributed, will smother health-as-freedom. In this fundamental sense, the care of health is a matter of well-protected liberty.*"

transitive form, whilst on the other the intransitive verb supports the '*doer*' in adopting an internal locus of control. This leads to the means-ends or push and pull debates about intervening in order to stimulate an intransitive action, or as Porter (1995, p.69) observed: "*The transitive and intransitive meanings of development became blurred to the point of obliteration.*"

As discussed in chapter 2, the other linguistic device that is at play is that of turning a verb into a noun (nominalization), which further adds to the blurring of meaning. The development issue most readily identified with nominalization is the paradox of participation (Cleaver, 1999), which is essentially about the tension between means (verbs) - drawing upon stakeholders' self-determination in order to direct development initiatives; and ends (nouns) - whereby stakeholders may be empowered through the establishment of participatory processes to become generally more self-determining. Here, more so than with development itself, there has been an hegemonic struggle over the meaning of the concept '*participation*', which can be represented in a diagram setting out the range of the continuum of meaning and interpretation in terms of four vectors, the locus of decision taking; the type of management activities; the role of the local people; and the outsiders' perception of local people, as in Figure 4.1, below.

As Nelson and Wright (1995) noted, in any organisation there are likely to be a whole variety of meanings of participation and people presume that they are using the same meaning, leaving implicit ideological differences uncontested. Given the range of meanings catered for in Figure 4.1 it is hardly surprising that the word participation holds comfort for everyone.

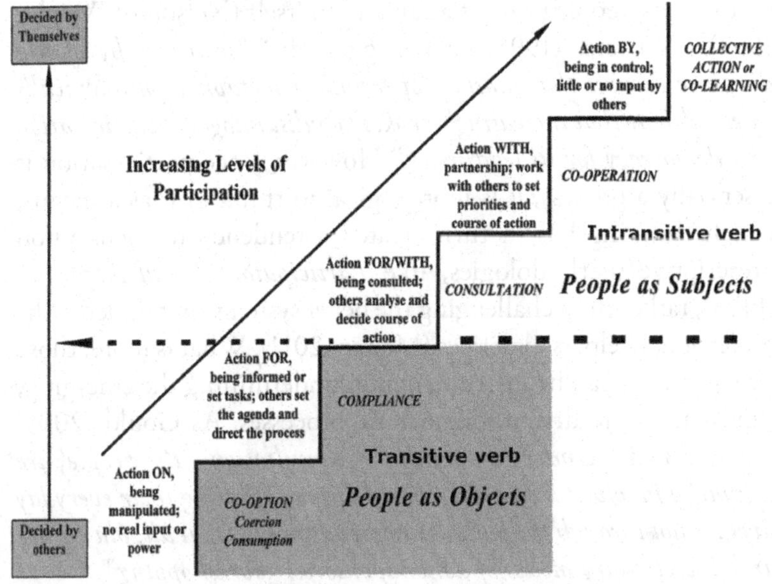
Decided by Themselves
Decided by others
Increasing Levels of Participation
Action BY, being in control; little or no input by others
COLLECTIVE ACTION or CO-LEARNING
Action WITH, partnership; work with others to set priorities and course of action
CO-OPERATION
Intransitive verb
Action FOR/WITH, being consulted; others analyse and decide course of action
CONSULTATION
People as Subjects
Action FOR, being informed or set tasks; others set the agenda and direct the process
COMPLIANCE
Transitive verb
Action ON, being manipulated; no real input or power
CO-OPTION
Coercion
Consumption
People as Objects

Figure 4.1 Hierarchy of Participation (Assembled from ideas presented in Arnstein, 1971; Pimbert & Pretty, 1997; and Wotton, *et al.*, 1994 and with entire acknowledgment to my colleague Mike Carter who drafted an earlier version).

Clearly one of the benefits that people perceive as stemming from participation is the smoother implementation of change (see section 6 in chapter 3). This is often presented as '*participation as means*' which begs the question of the ultimate purpose of the process, captured simply as development.[4] The obfuscation helps to hide the fact that the interest groups concerned do not share a common purpose nor, indeed, wish to elaborate upon their purposes. However, the advocates of participation often emphasise its role in shifting the balance of power between individuals and within societies. Perhaps it is the recognition that participation has the potential to alter such power structures

4 See the quotation of Weick and Westley (1996, p.441) given in chapter 2 section 2, who drew a similar conclusion.

that tempts people to see it as an end in itself (Nelson & Wright, 1995). As Porter (1995, p.93) suggested: "*The hierarchy of this discourse ensures that mastery of technical metaphor paradoxically rules a debate that increasingly evokes populist images of participation and democracy for its legitimacy.*" However, since participation is essentially a process, it is more logical to think of it as a means, which thinking has in turn created a tendency to focus upon prescriptive methodologies, like *Participatory Rural Appraisal* (PRA), rather than challenging the belief systems that underlie the professional helpers' practices (Mohan, 2011). What is more, those very practices can be instrumental in undermining the emerging, legitimate, state driven, democratic processes. As Gould (2005, p.141) noted: "*Under the politics of consultation, 'the people' are primarily involved in major policy decisions affecting their everyday lives ... not through the ballot or referendum but, if at all, via ad hoc and discretionary modes of donor-sponsored 'workshopping'*".

Furthermore, in discussing participation, Dahl (1990) emphasised that there is a '*criterion of economy*' that reduces the scope and effectiveness of participation in decision making. Not everybody can, nor indeed wishes to participate in the making of all decisions, and resource constraints, particularly time, must inevitably limit the extent of participation. In emphasising the desirability of participation as a means professionals need to pay particular note of the paradox that this generates for, as Dahl (*ibid.*) remarked too many speakers talk as if others are willing to take part in making decisions without any consideration of the costs of the time this takes: as if time is not valuable and as if there were no opportunity costs to attending meetings. This '*criterion of economy*' should inform the extent to which people are coerced into participating in development initiatives, where true empowerment would support citizens in being able to choose exactly when not to participate. True freedom of choice comes from informed consent and an ability to resource the choosing, or as Sen (1999, p.17) put it: "*the view of freedom that is being taken here involves both the* ***processes*** *that allow freedom of actions and decisions, and the* *actual* ***opportunities*** *that people have, given their personal and social circumstances*". Both of these freedoms are hard to achieve in externally driven interventions (just about any case involving outsiders), and leads to dilemmas such as whether or not to pay an attendance *per diem* (Smith, 2003).

Thus, although the approach to development is still to intervene, professionals and practitioners have been seeking to redefine the nature of the management of such interventions. Indeed, as we noted in chapter 1 section 7, Thomas (2000) has argued that there are three kinds of management used in development contexts which are pertinent to these considerations: '*management in development*' (same old management approach, just a different context); '*management of development*' (typical task oriented management but with particular kinds of results in mind); and '*management for development*' (where the processes of management model the results to be achieved – congruent, autonomy respecting management) – thereby reflecting Habermas' three level, hierarchy of action (Finlayson, 2005). Thus the first approach constitutes '*Instrumental Actions*' – actions to achieve specific results, which are founded upon instrumental reasoning, the calculation of the best means to a given end. The second approach constitutes '*Strategic Actions*' – actions that involve getting other people to do things as a means to achieving one's own ends. The third would seem to constitute '*Communicative Actions*' – actions that attempt through discourse to create consensus for establishing a programme of change but which, nevertheless, remains contaminated with relicts[5] of the first two approaches.

When you think about it, all situations where there is an external agent of intervention, which is seeking to achieve changes, primarily in behaviour, that relies upon the subtle modification of the internal processing of the subjects themselves, should be

5 It would in many ways be just as appropriate to use the word '*relics*' here to capture the associated devotional belief systems.

moving inexorably to a state of autonomy. As Ellerman (2005b, pp.7-8) recognised: "*All those who make their living in the helping professions are in the paradoxical position of working to eliminate their own jobs.*". Indeed, Mohan (2011, p.154) captured it as: "*The goal of social work, I reiterate, ought to be the end of itself.*"

In a separate elaboration that helps us understand this paradox of heteronomy, Argyris (1990, p.23) argues for another division, that between conscious and unconscious knowing, thus: "*Human beings hold two kinds of theories of action. The first is their espoused theory, which is composed of beliefs, values, and attitudes. The second is their theory-in-use, which is the one they actually use when they act.*" Indeed this follows the views of Scott (1998, p.94) who recognised that: "*As individuals* high *modernists might well hold democratic views about popular sovereignty ... but such convictions are external to, and often at war with their high-modernist convictions*". Thus it is perfectly possible for professionals and practitioners to openly acknowledge and accept the importance of adopting practices that do not undermine self-help, which are autonomy respecting (Ellerman, 2005b), whilst in their daily actions they ride rough shod over the needs and sensitivities of the people[6]. This is often explained as the belief that agents cannot be left to their own devices and assumed to be acting in the interest of their principal (*ibid.*), and that the principal in development is the donor – who pays the piper calls the tune. Fukuda-Parr, *et al* (2002, p.8) also drew attention to this particular paradox when they wrote that: "*the asymmetric donor-recipient relationship* [contains] *the belief that it is possible for donors ultimately to control the process and yet consider the recipients to be equal partners*".

What is clear is that at least the first two of Thomas' traditional approaches of the '*professional helper*' are undertaken from a perspective that places the person or people who are assisted as objects - seeing people as objects in the process and not as subjects

6 A process that Mohan (2005) describes as '*the development delusion*'.

of the process – as *persons* rather than as *beings* – and development as an action done to others (a transitive verb) rather than an action engaged in (an intransitive verb). In a similar respect it is instructive to note that in 1950 Douglas McGregor, in prophetic vein, stated that:

> *Out of all this* [study] *has come the first clear recognition of an inescapable fact: we cannot successfully force people to work for management's objectives. The ancient conception that people do the work of the world only if they are forced to do so by threats or intimidation, or by the camouflaged authoritarian methods of paternalism, has been suffering from a lingering fatal illness for a quarter of a century. I venture the guess that it will be dead in another decade.* (Bennis, 2006, p.xx).

Alas, with notable exceptions, most management continues to approach their task from Theory X assumptions[7] (Ellerman, *op.cit.*). Furthermore such a perspective and its associated practices are made possible because of a continuing adherence to a false theory of the nature of causality[8].

---

7 For an explanation of Theory X see McGregor (1960)

8 Stafford Beer (1986, p.14) noted that: "*We have a theory of causality which, as a matter of fact, was blown to shreds by David Hume hundreds of years ago, but nobody seems to have noticed*"

3 The Paradox of Causality in Development

We treat people in development, or education or health care as objects rather than subjects (Freire, 1971), primarily because we hold a notion of deterministic causality that Tallis (2003, p.202) described as: "*An incorrigible sense of self, unique to humans,* [which] *founds a self-validating sense of (agentive) efficacy.*" that persuades us to relate to living things as objects not realising or understanding that Newtonian physics as a sub-set of a larger reality is applicable only to interactions within the physical world, and then only in limited ways, for as Pieterse (1999, p.70) held *Cartesian* and *Newtonian* premises only hold sway in a limited range of circumstances. Indeed, Hardin (1973, p.67) had averred that: "*The* ***subject-predicate*** *structure of our language makes it all too easy to* [falsely] *assume that the world is composed only of (**one cause)-(one effect**) logical pairings.*" Furthermore, Lincoln and Guba (1985, p.129) noted that: "*The development of interventions … depends on the viability of the concept of causality; interventions (causes) are designed in ways that will eliminate undesirable states of affairs (effects) and/or substitute desirable ones.*" but they did not recognise that design itself is undertaken as if it is an act of free will (an uncaused cause). As Adam Smith recognised:

> *The man of system … seems to imagine that he can arrange the different members of a great society with as much ease as the hand arranges the different pieces upon a chessboard; …* [however] *in the great chess-board of human society, every single piece has a principle of motion of its own, altogether different from that which the legislature might choose to impress upon it.* (Smith, 2006, pp.234-5).

Stacey (1992, p.124) captured this paradox as: "*Practical people, … still adhere to the view that nature follows fixed laws with clockwork precision that makes it foolish to talk about creative natural systems, whereas human systems move in creative ways determined by the purpose and intention of their principal members.*" Indeed, Rom Harré observed that:

> *Instead of a world of passive beings waiting quiescent, independent, and unchanging to receive an external stimulus from another moving body, physicists conceive of a world of permanently interconnected, mutually interacting centres of energy whose native activity is modulated and constrained by other such centres.* (Harré, 1981, p.14).

If this is true of inanimate matter (pleroma), then how much more so is it applicable to the world of living subjects (creatura)? (Bateson & Bateson, 2005). As Scott (1998, p.93) commented: "*One of the great paradoxes of social engineering is that it seems at odds with the experience of modernity generally. Trying to jell a social world, the most striking characteristic of which appears to be flux, seems rather like trying to manage a whirlwind.*" Indeed, Elias (1991, p.62) recognised that: "*The interplay of the actions, purposes and plans of many people is not itself something intended or planned, and is ultimately immune to planning. .... the autonomy of what a person calls "we" is more powerful than the plans and purposes of an individual "I".*"

Irrationally, we extend our naïve notion of causality way beyond what can be empirically demonstrated when we seem to believe that other people are responsible for the way that we feel and, if truth be told, also for the way we act. So, on the one hand we believe that we can cause others to feel and behave and on the other we can feel learned helplessness by ceding control of our internal state and our behaviour to others. Yet, as O'Connor and Seymour (1993) emphasised, if we hold that another is responsible for the way we feel, then we are ascribing to them, as it were, some psychic power that they cannot have and, *vice versa*, you cannot assign to yourself such magical powers over their responses[9]. However, we must recognise, with Stacey and Griffin (2005), that human life is lived in a here and now that is constantly being formed through interaction with others[10].

Furthermore, our sense of self-efficacy (agency) is tantalisingly transitory. As Allison (1997, p.41) put it: "*freedom is an idea … that can never be encountered in possible experience … it is a* ***thought*** *that we bring to the conception of ourselves, insofar as we conceive ourselves as agents*". We seem to be able to make conscious choices between courses of action that are based on knowledge, understanding and a set of ethical beliefs. As Ellerman (2005b, p.41) would have it:

Action = [Range of possible] *Behaviour* + *Motive* ....*(1)*

Yet psychology makes it clear that our conscious awareness of such deliberation before we act is neither necessary (Dennett, 2003) nor sufficient, as Grunwald (2009, p.30) captured it: "*Our impulsive ids overwhelm our logical superegos*".

Moreover, in my own experience, most people still behave as if '*the world*' or '*knowledge*' exists in an absolute form whereby everyone can experience reality in the same way (M^c^Farlane, 2006). Reuben Abel set out an anecdote that tellingly encapsulates the choices of such ontological positioning:

> *There were three baseball umpires, calling balls and strikes. The first one said, I call them as I see them. The second one said, I call them as they are. But the third one declared, until I call them, they ain't nothing. The*

9 O'Connor & Seymour (1993, p.110) importantly noted that: "*With cause and effect patterns* [of thinking] *you become either the victim or the nursemaid of others.*"

10 See the quotation of Stacey & Griffin (2005, p.17) given in chapter 3 section 4.

> *first umpire is a sense datum subjectivist: nothing will persuade him that he may have made a mistake. The second is a rationalist: he declares that he is describing the objective structure of the world. Only the third realizes that sorting out pitched baseballs is a man-made ordering; nothing in the world is objectively a 'ball' or a strike' without an umpire's decision.* (Abel, 1976, p.59)

People may readily concede that each person sees the world differently and yet their subsequent behaviour runs contrary to what one would expect of someone who holds such a belief. This indicates that, at a deeper level, they retain an objectivist conception of reality. This tenure can be seen most prevalently in argument, during which each party seeks unavailingly to convince the other of the '*rightness*' of their view.

Such objectivism also enables people to hold a profound belief in the value of '*expert knowledge*' over '*indigenous knowledge*' (Chambers, 1992), and to value a short-term technical fix before a sustainable, human level solution. But the contrary, constructivist argument runs that we all construct reality in our own minds. Sensory input is built up into unique maps in the mind of each one of us, which Kelly (1955) called *personal constructs*, and all events are perceived through filters of experience and meaning, that provide for none of us to experience the world in the same way. The fable of the blind men and the elephant (A Poem by John Godfrey Saxe (1816-1887)[11]) is an entirely appropriate representation of the constructed nature of reality.

The only sense to be made of such an object lies in the impoverished information our limited senses provide, filtered through what we already know of the world. Or as Thomas Hobbes observed: "*there*

---

[11] For the details of the fable see http://thesanecenter.com/WhatWeBelieve/ElephantParable.htm accessed on 22 August 2011.

is no conception in man's mind, which hath not first been begotten upon the organs of Sense." (Quoted in Berman, 1981, p.181).

Although Berman (1981, p.217), in reference to the ideas of Karl Mannheim, maintained that: "*If ... all knowledge is situation bound, it becomes difficult for any conceptual system ... to argue that it possesses an epistemological superiority over any other such system*", the position of regarding reality as a singularity enables people to force their opinions upon others. Shor (1993, p.28) interpreted Paulo Freire's position on such an approach to education as: "*society* [is] *controlled by an elite which imposes its culture and values as the standard.*" Indeed, Berger and Luckman (1966, p.127), describing the socially constructed nature of reality, recognised that: "*He who has the bigger stick has the better chance of imposing his* [sic] *definitions of reality.*" Leading Chambers (1997, p.76) to warn that: "*All who are powerful are by definition uppers many times over. Others relate to them as lowers. In their daily lives multiple uppers are vulnerable to acquiescence, deference, flattery, and placation. ... ... It becomes easy and tempting for them ... to impose their* [fallacious] *realities and deny those of others.*"

Furthermore, M^c^Niff and Whitehead (2003, p.22) have expounded the idea of personal forms of knowing that are juxtaposed to the traditional, written down *E-theories*, which they described as *I-theory*, which is an individual's belief system generated by a dialectical process of action and reflection: "*theories which are ... tacit forms of knowing, and which emerge in practice as personal forms of acting and knowing*". Which substantiates Freire's concept of emancipation through enabling people to '*name their world*' (Freire, 1971).

Even so, it is also beneficial to take recourse to the distinctions made by Aristotle in respect of knowledge and which have been well elaborated by Carr and Kemmis (1986), and later by Flyvbjerg (2001), namely knowledge as *episteme* (universal, alethic truths); *technē* (know how) associated with the achievement of pre-determined objectives (*poesis*); and *phronesis* (ethical judgment or prudence) associated with living our life (in all its aspects including our professional practice) in the right way (*praxis*)[12]. The traditional development project leads to an emphasis upon *technē* rather than *phronesis* in approaching the practice of the helping professions, as Cleaver (1999, p.598) recognised: "*The project imperative emphasizes meeting practical rather than strategic needs, instrumentality rather than empowerment.*" For, as Carr (2006, p.434) noted: "*Within the dominant culture of modernity, the concepts of **phronesis** and **praxis** have been rendered marginal and now face something approaching total obliteration.*"

This prominence of *poesis* and *technē* has been mirrored in the ascendency of technology above metaphysics. Where technology has been built upon the Aristotelian view of the universe[13]. But, as Scruton (2002, pp.107-8) noted: "*the scientific worldview contains a fatal temptation: it invites us to regard the subject as a myth, and to see the world under one aspect alone, as a world of objects*". This general tendency to reify our world is accompanied by a predisposition to regard all issues as technical problems of objects in the world, rendering *Technical Assistance* synonymous with action for development (O'Connor & Kowalski, 2005). Hence the statement by the International Monetary Fund (IMF) that:

---

12 It is important to note the distinction between **poesis** which is about taking action whose end is known ahead of the practical steps that are taken to achieve it and which is guided by a form of thinking that the Greeks called ***technē*** and that today we would call instrumental or '*means-end*' reasoning and **praxis,** which is a way of acting in the world because its '*end*' – to promote the good life – exists, and can only be achieved, by the very way we act (Carr, 2006), or as Bateson (1972, pp.161-162) captured it: "*We have to find the value of a planned act implicit in and simultaneous with the act itself, not separate from it in the sense that the act would derive its value from reference to a future end or goal.*"

13 See the quotation by Wilson (1990, p.101) given in chapter 2 section 2.

> *IMF technical assistance supports the development of the productive resources of member countries by helping them to effectively manage their economic policy and financial affairs. The IMF helps countries to strengthen their capacity in both human and institutional resources, and to design appropriate macroeconomic, financial, and structural policies.* (IMF, 2011),

Which itself is deeply contradictory since the majority of the desired outcomes listed are heavily dependent upon the application of prudence (or *phronesis*) (Kane & Patapan, 2006) and their achievement is far from being a straightforward matter of following technical recipes. However, it does coincide with an observation made by Biggs and Smith (2003, p.1748) that there is an often repeated theme in development discourse whereby powerful agencies try to '*depoliticize*' their actions and portray them as purely a technical and mechanical issue.

Perhaps the place where all of these considerations come together is the important issue of motivation, since both the notions of free will and controlling others are grounded in the concept of purpose and making meaningful actions (Frankl, 1985). The factors that are considered to motivate people have been separated into two basic categories – those intrinsic to the individual (e.g. Maslow's higher levels (Maslow, 1968); Herzberg's motivator factors (Herzberg, 1974); or M^c^Clelland's motivating needs (M^c^Clelland, 1987)) and those that are extrinsic and supplied by others (e.g. Herzberg's hygiene factors). As promoters of externally generated initiatives we are inexorably drawn towards the use of extrinsic motivators and then we are disappointed by the responses or by the perverse incentives we create. Ellerman (2005b, p.45) noted that: "*external incentives superimposed onto a system involving internal motivation in order to better achieve control will tend to crowd out and atrophy the internal motivation.*" This is particularly noticeable in the attempts to use conditionality in order to bring about or enforce reforms, as DFID (2005, p.6) emphasised: "*conditionality which attempts to 'buy' reform from an unwilling partner has rarely worked*". Again, Ellerman (2005b, p.210) noted that: "*Real reforms beyond the stroke-of-the-pen variety will usually require some 'own reasons' or more intrinsic motivations for successful implementation.*" – and so any process of change that seeks to truly empower people, change attitudes or alter second order factors needs to be indirect and carefully foster intrinsic motivation.

Now, as asserted in the previous section, Argyris (1990, p.23) argues for a division between what we openly maintain to be our rationale[14] and that upon which we unconsciously base our actions. As George Bernard Shaw captured it: "*What a man believes may be ascertained, not from his creed, but from the assumptions on which he habitually acts.*"[15] Accordingly, with Argyris (*op.cit.*) we should recognise that the big problem and challenge is to get people to behave according to how they hold they should behave[16].

---

14 In line with Bateson (2002) a rationale is a tautology or set of axioms which, when mapped onto a description provide us with an explanation.

15 http://www.brainyquote.com/quotes/quotes/g/georgebern101583.html Retrieved September 29, 2011.

16 See Ovid's *Metamorphoses* vii 20 ff: "*I see the right, and I approve it too, Condemn the wrong - and yet the wrong pursue.*" Or St Paul's letter to the Romans Chapter 7 vs 15 & 18-19: "*I do not understand my own actions. For I do not do what I want, but I do the very thing I hate.... I can will what is right but I cannot do it. For I do not do the good I want, but the evil I do not want is what I do.*" The Holy Bible: New Revised Standard Version. Or the observation that:

> *Behaviorists have always known we don't really act like the super rational Homo economicus of the neoclassical-model world. Years of studies of patients who don't take their meds, grownups who have unsafe sex, and other flawed decision makers have chronicled the irrationality of Homo sapiens .... We plan to lose weight, but ooh-a cupcake! We are especially irrational about money; we will pay more for the same thing if we can use a credit card, if we think it's on sale, if it's marketed with photos of attractive women. No wonder we apply for mortgages we can't afford. No wonder our bankers approve them.* (Grunwald, 2009, p.30)

Indeed this follows the views of Sachs (1992, p.1) who felt that it was necessary to: "*deal with development … as a particular cast of mind.*" Therefore, the first step we have to take, as professionals, is to become aware of our *theory-in-use*.

So, if we consider the series of issues traced above, which pertain to the helping enterprises, over which we might have beliefs that could be differentiated in such a way, we can begin to see an entire syndrome of dissonance that would have profound implications for practice (see Table 4.1). It is also important to recognise the vertical linkages between these beliefs as previously elaborated. Thus the view that we can predict events if only we have enough data (Mechanical – Determinism) is very much congruent with *Objectivism* (the belief that there is one reality that we can all come to know), which in turn leads to the ascendancy of expert opinion, to the epistemological view that knowledge is about alethic truths (*episteme*) or instrumental means-ends know-how (*technē*), with the Aristotelian view of a universe of things that have attached qualities and attributes, and to have faith in the merits of the efficacy of carrots and sticks in order to get things done.

Axes of Belief	Theory-in-use	Espoused Theory
1. Causality	→ Predictability Determinism	→ Compatibilism
2. Epistemology	→ Objectivism	→ Constructivism
3. Value of knowledge	→ Expert Knowledge (E-theories)	→ Intrinsic Knowledge (I-theories)
4. Focus of knowledge	→ Knowledge as *Episteme* or *Techne*	→ Knowledge as *Phronesis*
5. Existential position	→ Aristotelian Universe (Reified)	→ Existential Universe (Flux)
6. Source of Motivation	→ Extrinsic Motivation	→ Intrinsic Motivation

Table 4.1 A Syndrome of Dissonance - Conceptual orientations governing the difference between theory and action.

The social enterprise activity that most closely encompasses such a syndrome is the planning of initiatives[17] and, as argued earlier, we believe in our own free will when we take it upon ourselves to plan to change the future and yet we believe in mechanistic, cause-and-effect determinism when we treat people as objects in the development process. But the latter fails because people exercise their own self-determination as subjects and choose their own responses to situations and external initiatives and the former, our free will, also fails because we lack omniscience and cannot predict with certainty what affect our unfolding plans will have (Kowalski, 2007). Nevertheless, experts draw up the plan with only limited input from local stakeholders. The planning approach tends to be distinctly instrumentalist, in contrast to the stance of Stacey and Griffin (2005, pp. 8-9) who emphasised that: "*Design, programs, blueprints and plans exist only insofar as people are taking them up in their local interactions*", and with little regard to *communicative action* that would yield *praxis* rather than *poesis.* Consequently, in the process of implementation, the plan becomes reified (Kowalski, 2007), so that changing it is prohibited, and it is bound up with conditionalities which, though presented as manifestations of good faith, are distinctly coercive in intent (Paloni & Zanardi, 2006). Under these circumstances it is unsurprising that Easterly (2006, p.5) thought that: "*All the hoopla about having the right plan is itself a symptom of the misdirected approach to foreign aid taken by so many in the past and so many still today.*"

Furthermore, the activity of planning in the development process culminates in the methods of accountability that require evidence of cause-and-effect linkages that support attribution but where nevertheless, as Stacey (1992, p. 124) captured it: "*We can claim to have achieved something intentionally only when we can show that there was a connection between the specific action we took and*

17 See the quotations from Dror (1971, p. 105) and Wildavsky (1971, p.101) given in chapter 2 section 2.

the specific state we achieved; ... that what we achieved was not materially affected by chance." Indeed, because of a false notion of causality, attribution, like the *Holy Grail*, is much sought after but very seldom chanced upon.

The overall effect has been the emergence of two, apparently antithetical, reactions to planning (IDS, 2001) – one that advocates the detailing of a plan as a necessary management tool (see for example Dearden & Kowalski, 2003; and Dale, 2004), and another that rejects planning as either a futile diversion (Easterly, 2006) or as a deeply political process that emphasises the power and interests of the donors over and above the needs and interests of the poor and marginalised (see for example Chambers, 1997). This latter response can also be understood as being due in part to the alien nature of planning itself and, to paraphrase Sir John Harvey-Jones, it is not in man's nature to plan; doing is more enjoyable, and when we don't plan failure takes us completely by surprise, denying us the trouble of worrying about it before hand (Jones, 2003, p.4). It is also partly due to the desire to escape the rigours of planning for a more flexible and permissive development environment.

Nevertheless, having accepted the paradoxical nature of the planning process we cannot abandon the need to plan[18]. On the contrary, we have to approach the practice of planning through compliance with those espoused theories (Kowalski, 2007) and as Beer (2004b) advocated, our proper assistance to other people and communities is to help them to be able to plan. Development of its nature must be purposeful, but it must serve the interests of the subjects of the process, i.e. it must begin from a faith in the competence of people to act in their best interests, and it is

[18] Despite Easterly's (2006) protestations, even in searching mode it is necessary to have a plan to underpin the searching behaviour – random walk is a characteristic found only in rudimentary ethology – where you have purpose and choices you will develop a plan even if you don't call it that.

only ethical to take an external lead where such competence has been in some manner demonstrably compromised[19] and not just because the subjects hold a different view of the situation from that of the predominantly Western professionals.

4 The Moral Hazard

It follows, therefore, that our activities in development should be determined by a very clear appreciation of whether the subjects in our interventions are compromised in their competence or not[20]. There is precisely a moral hazard in providing and receiving help that Buchanan (1977) referred to as the 'Samaritan's dilemma' by which help can induce dependency[21]. We must ask ourselves, in the first place, what it was about the situation of the traveller that prompted the Samaritan to intervene? In a study of college students' reactions to emergency cases, Bierhoff and Klein (1990, p. 257) listed five characteristics of circumstances that generated altruistic responses as: "*dangerous situations; rareness of events; few commonalities with other events; unforeseeability of the events; and requirement of instant action*".

If we apply this list to our helping situations then poverty *per se* does not call for the Samaritan's response[22]. Nevertheless, Benedict XVI (2009, section 21) recognised the goal of development as: "*rescuing peoples, first and foremost, from hunger, deprivation, endemic diseases and illiteracy*" which, with the exception of the latter, is largely to equate it with humanitarian assistance in the face of natural and man-made (sic) catastrophes. Indeed, in respect of development assistance, Gronemeyer (1992, p.54) had emphasised that the decision to deploy assistance is not determined by any cry for help but rather by an external assessment that the circumstances

---

19 See also '*altruistic moralism*'.

20 Ellerman (2005b, p.13) captured it as: "*The working assumption is that the condition of needing aid* [is] *externally imposed*".

21 See also Gibson, Andersson, Ostrom & Shivakumar (2005).

22 Neither does it call us to pass by on the other side.

represent a departure from some acceptable norm. But Mohan (2011, p.138) captured with commendable precision the essential distinction between humanitarian assistance and development assistance when he said that: "*A mere posttrauma treatment and counselling simply insults the victims' humanity by overlooking the causes of their tragedies*".

To carry the Samaritan analogy to its ultimate latitude, if the source of his benevolence had been founded in the concept of development rather than humanitarian assistance then we might have expected to see him pursuing improvements in policing or actions to establish alternative livelihoods (for erstwhile robbers) or even upgrading the emergency services. As it was he provided immediate succour and financial support into the future – which is where the moral hazard lay, because there was no mechanism for establishing the boundary of the help[23] - or as Ellerman, 2005b, p.13) recognised: "*Charitable relief in the longer term is an 'undercutting' form of unhelpful help*". Indeed, Esman and Uphoff (1984, p.77) warned: "*Communities, especially poor ones, can benefit from external assistance, but to rely much on it creates a dependency that may prove to be counter productive. The concomitant paternalism is likely to inhibit self-help and even undermine long-standing patterns of community initiative*". As Ellerman (2005b, p.14) explained: "*Eleemosynary aid to relieve the symptoms of poverty may create a* ***moral hazard*** *situation to weaken reform incentives and attenuate efforts for positive developmental change to eliminate poverty*". So, in all those actions of solidarity that spring from our compassionate humanity the collateral creation of dependency needs to be avoided at all costs.

The forgoing leads us to conclude that there is a continuum of contexts of external interventions that runs from the normal organic processes of human development driven by self-interest, the market and the opportunistic/ exploitative system, at one

23 In current parlance he had no exit strategy.

end, through to the alleviation of death and misery through humanitarian aid in the face of natural and man-made (*sic*) disaster requiring immediate action at the other. It is a significant error to think about and treat them all in the same fashion simply because they seem to demand our attention and the donation of resources.

In this latter regard we can benefit from recognising a paradox of giving identified by Godbout and Caillé (2000, p.173), quoted in full in chapter 2 section 2, which underpins Rist's paradox. In regards to our deliberations in chapter 2, this is an important simile that warrants making an extensive review of giving, which will form the focus of the next chapter.

Chapter 5

The Gift – Marcel Mauss and Development Assistance

1 Introduction

From the range of paradoxes of development outlined in previous chapters, there is one in particular, which Berthélemy (2006, p.179) identified, whereby: "*The motives of development assistance have been long disputed in the development finance literature. Discussions have been focussed since the 1970s on the opposition between egoistic behaviour, linking aid to the self-interest of the donors, and altruistic behaviour, relating it to recipient needs and merits.*" which is worthy of exploration since, in many ways, it recapitulates the paradox at the heart of Marcel Mauss' system of *The Gift* (Mauss, 2002).

Now, concern has been expressed over just how little thinking about *The Gift* has influenced sociology, which has led to the misunderstanding that *The Gift* is only relevant in archaic societies. For example Adloff and Mau (2006, p.95) suggested that: "*sociologists have ... paid little heed to forms of social interaction that can be localized neither on the side of self-interest nor on that of morality.*" and again (*ibid.*, p.119): "*Sociology has for too long overlooked the fact that this principle* [of reciprocity] *can be traced back neither to normativist nor utilitarian explanations and nevertheless represents a principle of the construction of modern societies. ... Taking this perspective as a basis opens up a rich field of empirical research into the constitution of modernity.*"

Clearly if sociology in general has not responded adequately, the inescapable corollary is that this deficiency extends into discourses on International Development Assistance (IDA) in that, despite the basis of the whole enterprise being founded upon giving[1], concepts springing from Mauss' *Gift* have not been used in any systematic way to explore and enhance our understanding of IDA.[2] So it is in the spirit of providing input for ongoing social dialogue and social praxis that I offer this chapter, not in the expectation of settling debates but rather in the hope that we might bring a greater appreciation of the varied meaning of what we are doing to our professional practice of development.

2 Key points from theories of *The Gift*

In the first instance, since apparently Mauss' work is not well known, we must rehearse the core and associated theories of *The Gift* before we can use them as a lens through which to examine development practice. In this I will take recourse to a seminal work by Godbout and Caillé (2000) as well as Mauss' original treatise (Mauss, *op.cit.*), together with a leavening from the writings of a number of other authors.

(1) The primary concept is that *The Gift* is not positioned where it is traditionally believed to be. Typically the alternative loci for exchanges of objects are proposed as either a mercantile exchange

---

1 Just note the occurrence of *Gift* words within discourses about Development e.g. Donor, Recipient, Contribution, Beneficiary

2 Indeed, so far I have been able to discover only 3 publications in the literature which make only passing reference to it: Rist (1997), Stirrat & Henkel (1997) and Zaoual (1997).

of equivalent value mediated through calculated self-interest (egoism), or a one-sided passage of value undertaken as normative behaviour (altruism). As such, it has been proposed that for a gift to be a gift it must be freely given with no contamination by personal gain (Derrida, 1994). However, Mauss was adamant that *The Gift* is neither part of an exchange of equivalent value nor an act of disinterested benevolence, as Godbout and Caillé (*op. cit.*) argued, we are encouraged by either/or thinking to adopt a position that hides the truth from us. Thus, Adloff and Mau (2006, p.97) emphasised that: "*The dichotomy of interest and morality is transcended or dissolved by the effect of the gift*" and Jacques Godbout and Allain Caillé explained the accompanying paradox thus:

- It appears that *The Gift* expects no return, that to give a gift is to be disinterested.

- But that any gift system inevitably contains reciprocation. That is what astonished Mauss, and it has been at the centre of studies of *The Gift* ever since.

- Because logic suggests that either *The Gift* is not disinterested or it does not exist.

and "*The essence of the gift, it seemed, was that it was not a gift.*" (Godbout & Caillé, *op.cit.*, p.92).

Mauss (2002, p.4) described *The Gift* as: "*the present generously given even when, in the gesture accompanying the transaction, there is only a polite fiction, … and when really there is obligation and economic self-interest.*" Adloff and Mau (*op.cit.*, p.107) recognised *The Gift* as: "*Being founded on non-equivalence, spontaneity and indebtedness, a gift-based relationship is not explicable by means either of an individually utilitarian or of a normative-holistic approach.*" Indeed, Godbout and Caillé (*ibid.*) captured the true significance of *The Gift* when they suggested that its role is to bridge the gap between the individual and the group.

(2) Furthermore, Mauss emphasised that what is given is seldom of direct use but rather is symbolic of the nature of the relationship it fosters. Consequently the considerations behind *The Gift* are concerned with that symbolism, as he encapsulated it: "*to make a gift of something to someone is to make a present of some part of oneself. ... that one must give back to another person what is really part ... of his nature*" (Mauss, 2002, p.16). This idea had been captured before by Emerson (1983, p. 536) who said: "*it seems heroic to let the petitioner be the judge of his necessity, and to give all that is asked, though at great inconvenience.*" and again: "*The gift, to be true, must be the flowing of the giver unto me, correspondent to my flowing unto him.*" (*ibid.*, p.537) and more recently Benedict XVI (2009, section 6), in respect of charity, said: "*to give the other what is 'his', what is due to him by reason of his being or his acting.*"

(3) In addition, although we associate gift giving with exchanges between members of an extended family (kinship) its real significance is in its support for social interactions between strangers. It cannot be emphasised too strongly that the self-interest in *The Gift* is not in what is given in return, but in the relationship which is opened up. As such it pre-dates the establishment of market relations and, in evolutionary terms, gift giving almost certainly originated in the earliest Hominid societies. Indeed, I adjudge that it is so fundamental to social interactions between strangers that a disposition to give is genetically programmed into human behaviour in much the same way that we have an inherent ability to use language (Pinker, 1994)[3]. As Mauss (2002, p.105) made it clear: "*To trade, the first condition was to be able to lay aside the spear.*" and, as Adloff and Mau (2006, p.97) asserted: an exchange of gifts first brings about that rapport which enables

3 Wright (2001, pp.22-23) noted that: "*a part of human nature, rooted ... in the genes; that natural selection, via the evolution of 'reciprocal altruism', has built into us various impulses which ... are designed for the cool, practical purpose of bringing beneficial exchange.*" Indeed, Benedict XVI (2009, section 34) averred that: "*The human being is made for gift, which expresses and makes present his transcendent dimension.*"

the subsequent pursuit of self-interested exchange by way of trade, for: "*gifts and induced reciprocities are deeply social acts which, though not based on interest, are not disinterested; they establish and perpetuate relations of mutual indebtedness.*" (*ibid.*, p.100). Indeed, Putnam (2000) declared that, like a Golden Rule, reciprocity is embedded in the moral codes behind all civilized life.

(4) The Gift system, and its' associated cycle of reciprocity, is formed by a triple obligation which Bourdieu (1992) listed as the '*obligation to give*', the '*obligation to return a gift*' and the '*obligation to receive*', and he represented the interaction as leading to one of three outcomes: refusal, incapacity to respond or counter gift (*ibid.*). In this way, a gift, though freely given, represents a challenge to the recipient that must involve a response (which includes the possible absence of a counter gift) which, take note, will define the relationship between them from then on. Indeed, at one level the giving of a gift proclaims the desire for a relationship, as Adloff and Mau (*op.cit.*, p.109) stated: "*Gifts are … signs and manifestations of the demand for commitment as an end in itself.*" and it is the interest in such a relationship that is the driving force of the exchange. Again, Godbout and Caillé (2000, p.15) emphasised that: "*the system of the gift is not ... an economic system but the social system concerned with personal relationships.*" and Douglas (2002, p.xi) stated that: "*The cycling gift system is the society.*"

Crucially, in order for a gift to be a righteous act, it must presume an ability on the part of the recipient to participate in such a relationship. As Bourdieu (*op.cit.*, p.100) described it: "*The exchange of honour, … is defined as such ... that is, as implying the possibility of a continuation, a reply, a riposte, a return gift, inasmuch as it contains recognition of the partner to whom, … it accords equality in honour.*" Again Bourdieu (*op.cit.*, p.98) explained it thus: "*the gift may remain unreciprocated, when one obliges an ungrateful person; it may be rejected as an insult, inasmuch as it asserts … the possibility of reciprocity, and therefore of recognition.*" Furthermore, a gift and its obligation to reciprocate may involve different individuals within recognised social groupings, e.g. one family to another or one community to another. Indeed, Mauss (2002, p.6) made it clear that: "*it is not individuals but collectivities that impose obligations of exchange and contract upon each other.*"

Moreover, the riposte must not be immediate but can remain suspended over the relationship as a useful tension that will ultimately have to be released by a response at an appropriate moment for, as Bourdieu (*op.cit.*, p. 105) noted: "*if it is not to constitute an insult, the counter-gift must be deferred and different, because the immediate return of an exactly identical object clearly amounts to a refusal.*" and "*To betray one's haste to be free of an obligation one has incurred, and thus to reveal too overtly one's desire to pay off … gifts received, … is to denounce the initial gift retrospectively as motivated by the intention of obliging one.*" Gouldner (1960, p.175) quoted Seneca in this regard, who held that: "*a person who wants to repay a gift too quickly with a gift in return is an unwilling debtor and an ungrateful person*".

Importantly for our argument Douglas (2002, p.ix) asserted that gifts cannot be considered as free and that: "*What is wrong with the so-called free gift is the donor's intention to be exempt from return gifts … from the recipient. Refusing requital puts the act of giving outside any mutual ties.*"

(5) Next, Godbout and Caillé (2000) recognised the importance of two other systems of exchange that exist in society by maintaining that the system of The Gift is crucial to the proper functioning of the market and the welfare state having personal relationships as its focus, and it takes precedence over both them. Indeed, as Adloff and Mau (2006, p.110) acknowledged: "*reciprocal relations … also accompany or structure all processes of social interaction, including those organized by the state or the market.*" It follows that we need to differentiate the nature of those later phenomena; the market and the welfare state.

As societies changed from hunter-gathering and subsistence agriculture to the production of surpluses and the division of labour so the possibilities of the market emerged. The exchanges became more complicated and the relationships greater in number, shallower and less lasting. The market stands alongside the system of *The Gift* and is more purely about the achievement of self interest in the exchange of objects which have utility value[4], with the concomitant calculation of winning and losing. As Bourdieu (1992, p.115) portrayed it: "*as the relationship becomes more impersonal, … as one moves out from the relation between brothers to that between virtual strangers, so a transaction is less and less likely to be established at all but it can, and increasingly does, become more purely 'economic'.*" Thereby allowing the interested calculation that is present even in the most generous exchange to be more and more openly expressed.

The market system is characterised by three features that differentiate it from *The Gift*; the search for equivalence in the value exchanged; the required immediacy of the reciprocation; and the freedom to be quit of the interaction once the exchange has occurred. Of course the equivalence of the exchange is in no small measure determined by perception and is now facilitated by the medium of money. To those operating within the market system the principle is '*caveat emptor*' and the system encourages amorality. Bourdieu (*op.cit.*, p.115) noted that: "*informants will talk endlessly of the tricks and frauds that are commonplace in the 'big markets', … in exchanges with strangers.*" Godbout and Caillé (2000, p.95) recognised that: "*Time is at the heart of the gift and reciprocity, while elimination of time is at the core of a mercantile relationship.*" and "*the mercantile ideology defends the right to silently terminate a relationship as soon as the benefits derived from it are no longer deemed satisfactory.*" (*op.cit.*, p.51), and summarised the mercantile relationship as: "*an objectivation of the world and of relationships both among people and between people*" (*op.cit.*, p.214).

4 "*Giving in order to acquire*" (Benedict XVI 2009, section 39).

Charitable giving and religious precepts of altruism are frequently caught up in *The Gift* debate. Alms[5] are traditionally targeted at strangers or those at the margins of a community who are perceived as unfortunate victims, deserving of empathetic support[6], and which are portrayed as entirely disinterested, as Stirrat and Henkel (1997, p.72) captured it: "*Unlike the Maussian gift, these gifts are given without thought of return … and there is no obligation on the recipient.*" Nevertheless at this level there are forms of reciprocal benefits that are capable of taking the place of reciprocity by the ultimate recipients (e.g. reward by a deity[7]) (*ibid.*). Indeed when they talked about: "*an obligation to give, not an obligation to maintain a social relationship.*" (*ibid*, p.72) they were overlooking the '*social relationship*' that is created and encouraged between the giver and the charitable NGO intermediary. True Christian charity is quite far removed from modern alms practices, as Benedict XVI (2009, section 2) recognised: "*charity … continues to be misconstrued and emptied of meaning, with the consequent risk of being misinterpreted, detached from ethical living and … undervalued.*" and it is much more aligned with *The Gift* since Christian charity has a three part obligation, as Benedict XVI (*op. cit.*, section 3) emphasised: "*the intellect attains to the natural and supernatural truth of charity: it grasps its meaning as gift, acceptance, and communion.*"

This moral imperative to give has more recently been usurped by the state. Godbout and Caillé (2000, p.51) explained that: "*the development of the welfare state has often been cited as a*

---

5 Mauss (2002, p.22-23) suggests that: "*Alms are the fruits of a moral notion of the gift and of fortune on the one hand, and of a notion of sacrifice, on the other.*" and Benedict XVI (*op.cit.*, section 9) recognised modern charity as: "*Giving through duty*".

6 Bierhoff & Klein (1990, p. 257) list five characteristics of circumstances that generate altruistic responses as: "*dangerous situations; rareness of events; few commonalities with other events; unforeseeability of the events; and requirement of instant action.*"

7 As Mary Douglas (2002, p.xii) noted there is: "*a Vedic principle that sacrifice is a gift that compels the deity to make a return.*"

happy substitute for the gift, one which limits injustice and restores dignity, unlike earlier systems of redistribution grounded in charity." However, on closer inspection it seems that the welfare state has much more in common with the market than with *The Gift*. Where *The Gift* is characterised by spontaneity and generosity, the welfare state is calculating and coercive, as Godbout and Caillé (*op.cit.*, p.60) recognised: "*All the resources that move through state channels got there through constraint. But this is the exact opposite of a voluntary gift – a gift that is imposed* [on the giver] *is not a gift.*" and, please note, Douglas (2002, p.xix) argued that: "*Social democracy's redistributions are legislated for in elected bodies and the sums are drawn from tax revenues. They utterly lack any power mutually to obligate persons in a contest of honour.*"

Indeed, market tenets are often manifested within state systems, for example Godbout and Caillé (*op.cit.*) noted that principles of equality play the same role in the provision of state welfare systems as the search for equivalence does in trade. Indeed they argued that: "*State involvement … tends to transform a disinterested act into unpaid work, thus … bringing about the social deconstruction of the gift by including it in a model of monetary equivalence.*" (*ibid.*, p.59). Or, as Stirrat & Henkel (*op.cit.*, p.74), in the context of International NGOs, commented: "*The pure gifts* [of charity] *become, in the end, the currency of systems of patronage.*"

In summary, the main difference between the system of *The Gift* and the market or the state is that the former is primarily about establishing social relations, whereas the others are essentially about the exchange of utility. Indeed, Godbout and Caillé (*op. cit.*, p.195) were emphatic that *The Gift* stands as a '*metasystem*' to the market and the state, that is it sits at a level above these economic systems and provides the context in which both are able to function. The market is characterised by the ability to: "*owe nothing to anyone, to be able to walk away from a social bond and discharge an obligation just as you change tradesmen when you're not satisfied – this capacity for exit, … is the defining feature of modern freedom ... embodied in the market and echoed in the welfare state.*" (*ibid.*, p.63). They emphasised that the 'producer-intermediary-client model' is equally manifested in both the market and the state and paradoxically both depend upon and seek to destroy *The Gift* relationship, which, as Stirratt and Henkel recognised, has allowed mercantilism to insinuate itself into what would in many respects be an altruistic relationship. Thus: "*in order to compete for* [donor funded] *contracts, NGOs have in effect to work as if they are private companies and adopt modes of operating and even forms of organizational culture that approximate those of the commercial market-oriented world.*" (*op.cit.*, p.70).

(6) On a more contentious point, in developing Mauss' ideas, Godbout and Caillé (2000) argued that the project of modernity itself is antithetical to *The Gift*. They suggested that the ancient system of *The Gift* is enacted in the context of social obligation, and that a core objective of modernity is to free people from encumbering obligations that Bauman (2000, p.13) described as: "*burdening one's bond with mutually binding commitments [that] may prove positively harmful*". Furthermore, they argued that: "*The modern realist refuses to believe in the existence of the gift because the gift is seen as diametrically opposed to material, egoistic self-interest.*" (*op.cit.*, p.7). Indeed, Stirrat and Henkel (*op.cit.*, p.77) supported this view maintaining that *The Gift* is the diametric opposite of the modern world's deeply calculating interactions, and Benedict XVI (2009, section 19) emphasised the same trend: "*As society becomes ever more globalized, it makes us neighbours but does not make us brothers.*" Actually Godbout and Caillé went so far as to maintain that an essential outcome of modernity is the annihilation of the system of *The Gift*, maintaining that dispensing with *The Gift* is the modern mind's idea of Utopia. The end result, they suggested, is: "*The modern individual, pseudo-emancipated from the duty of reciprocity, staggering under the accumulated weight of what she or he receives without making any return,*" (*ibid.*, p.220). In contrast to this attempted eradication, Godbout and Caillé recognised that *The Gift* is resilient and continues even in the most modern

societies, and that, far from being dead or moribund, it is very much thriving and that: "*despite all the reasons to believe in its final and irrevocable disappearance, the gift is everywhere.*" (*op.cit.*, p.11).

(7) Of course, the system of *The Gift* that Mauss describes is not without its drawbacks. The first is contained within the roles of Giver, Recipient, Reciprocator for, as Carr, *et al.* (1998, p.189) captured it: "*How does it **feel** to be an aid 'recipient'?*". Emerson (1983, p.536) averred that: "*It is not the office of a man to receive gifts… We do not quite forgive a giver*", and again: "*It is a very onerous business, this of being served, and the debtor naturally wishes to give you a slap.*" (*ibid.*, p.537).

The whole approach of altruism is dogged by resentment, for example Emerson (*Ibid.*) suggested that: "*all beneficiaries hate all Timons, not at all considering the value of the gift, but looking back to the greater store it was taken from.*" Which chimes precisely with the view expressed by Gergen and Gergen (1971, p.101) that: "*when a state appears to be highly affluent, its aid is less impressive to the* recipient." Importantly, Godbout and Caillé (2000, p.134) identified that implicit in *The Gift* is the strange law of alternation that: "*decrees that it is impossible to give, or to play, except by taking turns.*" But this emphasises the significance of being able to take on each of the three roles and the iniquity of abrogating the role of giver to oneself alone.

Moreover, in describing the learning process Bateson (1972) drew attention to the tripartite system of '*Stimulus-Response-Reinforcement*', and emphasises that the '*Response*' reinforces the provision of the '*Stimulus*' as much as '*Reinforcement*' reinforces the '*Response*'. In the same way we can see that in the tripartite system of *The Gift*, of '*Giving-Receiving-Reciprocating*', '*Receiving*' reinforces '*Giving*', but more importantly '*Reciprocating*' reinforces '*Receiving*'. The absence or impoverishment of the ability to reciprocate impinges on the nature of receiving and impedes the relationship of mutuality that *The Gift* seeks to foster.

Secondly, there is the matter of hierarchy for, as Blau recognised: "*reciprocity … [is] a mechanism for the generation of asymmetries of power.*" (Adloff & Mau, 2006, p.104). Certainly, according to Derrida: "*the aporetic result of A's giving B to C is that A, instead of giving something, has received and C, instead of receiving something, is now in debt.*" (Derrida & Caputo, 1997, p.141) and the recipient may feel that they have been put under some obligation. Furthermore, Adloff and Mau (2006, p.117) observed that: "*the gift … often expresses a … place in a hierarchy and protects [it].*" As Stirrat and Henkel (*op.cit.*, p.73) observed: "*the problem with the pure gift is ... the seeming lack of reciprocity: that the receiver is left in a position of indebtedness and powerlessness.*" In this regard Mauss (2002, p.83) noted that: "*The unreciprocated gift still makes the person who has accepted it inferior, particularly when it has been accepted with no thought of returning it.*" and emphasised that: "*To give is to show one's superiority … . To accept without giving in return, … is to become client and servant,*" (*op.cit.*, p.95). Schoeck (1969, p.21) portrayed this drawback as: "*The more one seeks to deprive the envious man of his ostensible reason for envy by giving him presents … the more one demonstrates one's superiority and stresses how little the gift will be missed.*"

Such inequalities force recipients into other forms of reciprocity, as Adloff and Mau (2006, p.105) captured it: "*The receivers of services fit into a social hierarchy with clear imbalances of power and acknowledge this hierarchy – … as a reciprocal response.*" Thus, although receiving is properly ameliorated by the ability to reciprocate directly in appropriate and generous fashion, in certain circumstances the reciprocity may be directed towards third parties that in some way complete the circle of *The Gift*. Failing these alternatives reciprocity can be achieved by submissive behaviours, giving way in various social settings that communicates to everyone the relative social standings. Indeed, Gergen and Gergen (1974, p. 133) maintained that: "*Aid has so often been used by donors to bend recipients to their will.*"

The third drawback follows on from the second in that in certain circumstances *The Gift* is used precisely to gain hierarchical ascendancy. Mauss (2002) argued that, whilst *The Gift* is a system of exchange that enables and fosters social relationships, it has, nevertheless, the propensity to be expressed as an agonistic relationship that promotes rivalry and destructive forms of behaviour. The clearest manifestation of such agonistic behaviour is '*The Potlatch*', or as Mauss (*op.cit.*, p.7) referred to it: "*the system of total services*", in which everything is effectively caught up in the exchanges. It is quite evident that a system of behaviour based upon the three steps of giving; receiving; and reciprocating, and where the latter is delayed and the scale of its generosity is necessarily greater than the original gift, is a positive feedback system reminiscent of symmetrical schizmogenesis (Bateson, 1972), bringing with it the prospect of armaments' races that can be: "*slowed down by acceptance of complementary themes such as dominance, dependency, admiration,*" (*ibid.*, p.324).

Fourthly there is the way in which a gift is made. Gifts can be deeply patronising, casting recipients willing or not into the role of children or the infirm (Carr, *et al.* 1998). As Godbout and Caillé (2000, p.8) stressed that when the giver, or the way that a gift is proffered, is perceived by the recipient as noxious, then *The Gift* itself is seen to be toxic. Pierre Bourdieu captured it thus:

> *The 'way of giving', the manner, the forms, are what separate a gift from a straight exchange, moral obligation from economic obligation. To 'observe the formalities' is to make the way of behaving and the external forms of the action a practical denial of the content of the action and the potential violence it can conceal.* (Bourdieu, 1992, p.126),

and it is evident that the greater the disparity between the power of the donor and the recipient the greater the likelihood that what

Bourdieu (ibid., p.127) called "*symbolic violence*" will be intended and/or perceived.

(8) A further stumbling block in the path of smooth relations stemming from *The Gift* is the impact of misalignment of the cultural symbolism underpinning an exchange of gifts. Any meeting between strangers has thc propensity to be a collision between different cultures. Karen Sykes exemplified the scale of the challenge in the encounter that occurred between cultures in North America in that: "the *Indians and the early Americans misunderstood who and what they were looking at, as they peered at each other through different viewfinders.*" (Sykes, 2005, p.100). Indeed, Bateson (1972) proffered three alternative outcomes of such collisions; complete fusion of cultures, elimination of one culture or both, or persistence of the cultures in dynamic equilibrium within one community, and it is easy enough to find examples of all three having taken place[8]. Indeed it can be argued that DA is predominantly directed towards the establishment of a universal, Western culture, which Ritzer, 2007) has called '*Grobalization*'[9].

From the stand point of this review, the greatest disparity would seem to be between a culture of *The Gift* and one operating from the perspective of the market. Karen Sykes described the unequal exchanges between the native Americans and the settlers in the case of the acquisition of Manhattan Island in which the settlers probably thought that they had bought the land, in the usual way, whereas the Indians may well have thought that what they had done was to establish peaceful and lasting relations with the Europeans (Sykes, *op.cit.*, p.99). The outcome of the exchange would appear to be a vindication of the observation that: "*to*

8 See reference to this upon a global scale (Pieterse, 2004).

9 For an example see Bateman's (2010) cogently argued critique of the motivation for microfinance to be adopted as the tool for poverty alleviation.

operate within the system of the gift is tantamount to being taken advantage of all the time." (Godbout & Caillé, 2000, p.38).

(9) Because the system of *The Gift* is paradoxical, gift-giving contains deep ambiguities, as Osteen (2002, p.14) emphasised: "*Gifts at once express freedom and create binding obligations, and may be motivated by generosity or calculation, or both.*" So how is one to discern what lies behind a gift? Mauss (2002, p.99), noted that: "*The most ... routine exchanges of ordinary life, like the 'little gifts' that 'bind friendship', presuppose an improvisation, and therefore a constant uncertainty, which ... make all their* ***charm****, and hence all their social efficacy.*" Again, as Adloff and Mau (2006, p.107) stated: "*a gift-based relationship contains irreducible uncertainty, indeterminacy and risk; it tends to remain in a state of structural uncertainty, such that trust can thus be generated.*" Accordingly, for the main purpose of *The Gift* to be fulfilled it seems inescapable that there can be no certainty of motive, of time frame nor of appropriate response. As Sykes (*op.cit.*, p.100) captured it: "*exchanges made to open new relationships open each party to 'more than they bargained for' in the trade.*"

One of the bi-products of paradox, such as that exhibited by *The Gift*, is the creation of double binds (Kowalski, 2004), in which the relationship is important, there are mixed messages, and there is inadequate channels of communication (Bateson, 1972), and we see that as a rule a double bind is more than simply an impossible dilemma or a paradox.

Indeed, we can see these characteristics manifested in *The Gift*, for it is always and entirely about important relationships conducted in situations of ambiguous intent. As Godbout and Caillé (2000, p.187) pointed out: "*There is an active and conscious refusal of explicitness on both sides, a hypocrisy that is dual and symmetrical and so, logically, absurd and with no foundation.*" and there are strong prohibitions that prevent reference to obligation – i.e. *The Gift* must be freely given, but the closer we are to a contract, with everything explicit, the less free we are not to reciprocate damaging the quality of the underlying relationship. Indeed they were clear that hiding what is actually happening is necessary so that the goods that circulate embody the bond of obligation, and yet this cannot be spoken about openly without demonstrating that the inherent message of trust and relationship have not been taken up. Furthermore, this encryption, this strategic obfuscation, requires effort as Bourdieu (1992,) recognised, the effort needed to hide the implicit purpose of the exchange of gifts is as great and as important as the effort that goes into the gift giving act itself.

With enforced spontaneity, time delays, disparity between words and actions and above all the imperative of workable social relations, it is clear that circumstances of *The Gift* contain all the necessary ingredients for double binds, with all the positive and negative possibilities they encompass (Bateson, 1972).

3 International Development Assistance from the point of view of *The Gift*?

Armed with the insights provided through the anthropology and sociology outlined above it is possible to identify a number of points of contact with the practices of development assistance and their contexts:

A. Modernization Agenda:

As Escobar (2004, p.15) noted: "*Development was the name given to the strategy of modernization.*" So we may conceive of development as a sub-strand within the overall essay of modernity. Indeed, Pieterse (1999, p.70) had commented that: "*development is applied modernity, all the contradictions of modernity are reproduced within development as dramatically unresolved tensions.*" In particular the modernity project is fissured by a paradox – the two realms that it seeks to separate – and thereby dispense with the system of *The Gift* – cannot be separated. Interest and disinterest are like matter and motion (Bohm, 1951). As such, along with particle physics (Kowalski, 2012a), Jacques Godbout and Allain Caillé related the nature of the relationship between gift and market to that between position and motion contained in Zeno's paradoxes, as exemplified in the quotation in chapter 2 section 2.

Because IDA is thus embedded in the modernity project so donors both act from a position in which *The Gift* system is downplayed and which seeks to annihilate its existence whilst illogically being entirely dependent upon the relationships at both state and personal levels that only the system of *The Gift* can provide, for as Gergen and Gergen (1971, p.90) recognised: "*most States will not even accept initial overtures for aid from a country that does not otherwise maintain friendly relations.*" and "*Assistance programmes do not exist apart from the relationships among the participants.*" (*ibid.*, p.88). What is clear is that the Western cultural agenda underpinning IDA is strongly influenced by a market approach to exchanges (even of Humanitarian Assistance) that places great store on the formalization of the exchange, on the importance of delivering value to the donor, and on the short term nature of the commitment. As such it cannot foster those positive attributes of *The Gift*, in particular the trust, the spontaneity and the mutuality that focuses upon the nature and characteristics of the other party in the exchange.

B. Impact of Cultural Mismatch:

Sykes (2005, p.110), in discussing cultural collisions, asked: "*Is it dangerous to assume in all colonial encounters that the persons involved share a belief in the primacy of homo economicus, of the rationalist economic person?*" The values that underpin mercantile exchange are determined as much by the influence of power as intrinsic worth[10]. Indeed, Granovetter (1985: 483) had maintained

[10] For example it seems likely that the exchange rates determined at the arrival of the first European traders were in part set by the cultural disconnect between a predominantly mercantile system and a gift based

that: "*the level of embeddedness of economic behavior is lower in non-market societies than it is claimed by substantivists and development theorists, and it has changed less with 'modernization' than they believe;*" but he also argued that this degree of embeddedness has been and continues to be greater than the theories of formalists and economists would suggest. Furthermore, Carr, *et al.* (1998, p. 158) acknowledged that: "*hosts may find themselves being pulled and pushed in **differing** directions, say by a foreign system of working, … versus a 'traditional' system of social conduct and moral obligations*". For again, it is clear that in IDA the protagonists' greater acceptance of the basic premise of modernity and indeed immersion in it, on the one hand, and the probability of the recipients' cultural adherence to *The Gift,* since recipients inevitably operate within a culture that still accepts its legitimacy[11], on the other, must provide very different '*view finders*' through which to perceive any given situation and respond to it.

So we may infer that the system of *The Gift* is part and parcel of those cultural misunderstandings that Hofstede (1984) highlighted. Under these circumstances misperceptions are inevitable in regard to issues such as parsimony, calculation, individualism, blunt speaking and corruption.

---

one, and continue to have an impact on North – South exchanges today.

11 Since by definition it logically follows that the less developed a society the less modern it is and therefore the greater the likelihood that more elements of the system of *the Gift* are maintained, both at a social and personal level. As Rist (2002, p.233) noted: "*what can one say of societies of the South, where reciprocity systems operate much more extensively* [than in the North]". Or as N'Dione, *et al.* (1997, p.371) maintained: "*Many African societies still live according to the model of reciprocity. 'I receive, therefore I exist. I give, therefore I am respected.'*"

C. The incompatibility of agendas and the alternatives:

There are three agendas at play in the IDA business – 1) gaining working relationships to promote good will and a willingness to deal – as in *The Gift* between strangers; 2) promoting systemic development to support economic growth, international trade and national policy agendas – as in the market system of pursuing self-interest; and 3) combating the impacts of natural and manmade (*sic*) disasters and alleviating extremes of poverty[12] – as in humanitarian assistance and the state system of social redress. From all the foregoing it becomes perfectly clear that these purposes are incompatible if pursued through one, mixed approach. For, as Gergen and Gergen (1974, p.125) observed: "*Aid may also be used to secure … favourable economic concessions, political influence, protection of business investments, and military bases*" and they follow it with an understated footnote: "*These various aims may not be mutually facilitative.*" If aid is used to buy influence it risks being resented or rejected on the one hand or to do damage to the self-esteem (self-efficacy)[13] necessary for authentic development on the other (Gergen & Gergen, 1971).

Now, as Hagen (2006, p.267) maintained: "*the history of foreign aid relations might be read as a continual search by the donors to … maximize the returns to their funds as judged by them, with recipients trying to make sure that their spending priorities … prevail.*" which sounds like a straightforward description of a market exchange. However, confusion of approach has long been present, as Gergen and Gergen (*op.cit.*, p.87) affirmed: "*Donor States have long been aware that technical assistance can be employed as an instrument of*

12 Benedict XVI (2009, section 21) recognised the goal of development as: "*rescuing peoples, first and foremost, from hunger, deprivation, endemic diseases and illiteracy.*" which is largely to equate it with Humanitarian Assistance, and is in contrast with his earlier statement (section 20) that it is: "*the establishment of authentic fraternity.*"

13 As Bierhoff & Klein (1990, p.259) observed: "*The recipient wants to prevent the conclusion that he was unable to master his fate.*"

statecraft, and that political outcomes can be secured with what are ostensibly economic gifts." Whereas Benedict XVI (2009, section 58) clearly asserted that: "*Economic aid, in order to be true to its purpose, must not pursue secondary objectives.*"

A market approach to IDA is contractually explicit and linked to immediate exchange of value. It is cold and calculating of interests and it justifies a variety of behaviours, for example Gergen and Gergen (*op.cit*, p.92) note that: "*Several aid personnel mentioned modes of deception which enable their agencies to retain control while appearing to give it away at the same time.*" Moreover, Stirrat and Henkel (1997, p.75-76), in the context of International NGOs, commented that: "*there is still an asymmetry between givers and receivers, and he who pays the piper not only calls the tune but attempts to make sure that it is performed.*" Thus a market approach is manifested in conditionality and, as Ellerman (2005b) noted, conditionalities are not only ineffective, they also sabotage the objective of autonomous development. The only way to operate within a market based approach is to conform to the desires of the donor – to recognise their power and status in the hierarchy, to subjugate oneself, with all the bad feelings that this entails.

The proffered alternative is humanitarian assistance (HA) – systems that seek to deal with disasters, from whatever causes, or to redress the extremes of disadvantage generated by capitalism and the market (Herbert, 1991), often characterized as charity, altruism, moral imperative, and the good Samaritan. But there is precisely a moral hazard in such aid that we have identified as the '*Samaritan's dilemma*' by which help creates dependency, which in turn links to Say's Law applied to DA, where: "*the presence of the offer of aid then* ***creates*** *a new scenario where the problematic situations are partly incentivized by the aid offer. The order of causality is reversed.*" (Ellerman, *op.cit.*, p.113).

The attempts to channel resources through erstwhile charitable conduits fare little better. As Stirrat and Henkel (*op.cit.*) noted, the channelling of resources to a Southern NGO from its Northern partner is not the disinterested act that it would at first seem but is frequently accompanied by suspicion and hard bargaining. Furthermore, it is clear that: "*the development gift is no longer a free gift but the object of calculated systems of exchange and negotiation.*" (*ibid.*, p.77) once again blurring the distinction between alms and the market.

As a result of this indiscipline and mishmash of approaches, no-one can be sure whether any particular transaction falls under the rules of *The Gift*, the market or formalized alms. The consequences of such inconsistency and ambiguity are deeply damaging for relationships, and for the achievement of sustainable well-being, on the one hand, and for those dubious practices of economic development, whether concealment, advantage taking, manipulation, procrastination, fungibility of resources, rent seeking, or outright corruption, on the other.

D. Gift-driven Double Binds in Development:

The inconsistency and ambiguity associated with *The Gift*, when coupled with relationships of power based upon reward and punishment, are fertile grounds for double binds. It is not that the difficulties posed by the impossible choices of a paradox are damaging, though they are, but that double binds are particularly potent because the paradox is felt at two levels. Double binds are part of *The Gift* system itself for, as Fukuda-Parr, *et al.* noted (quoted in chapter 4 section 2), the relationship between recipients and donors is conducted under the professed belief that it is between equal partners even though the donors require to be in ultimate control. The main dangers are contained in the inability to withdraw and the inability to comment upon the inconsistency.

4 How taking a gift approach might work:

There are a number of aspects of the practice of International Development Assistance that might be modified as a result of the understanding provided by Marcel Mauss' observations. The most important amongst them is the need to recognize the difference between development, humanitarian aid and relationship management, and I make bold to put forward some suggestions of how we might approach the challenge.

A. Deal with the dis-interest agenda:

Some time ago Gergen and Gergen (1971, p.102) noted that DA given from one state to another has as its fundamental purpose the enhancement of the power and welfare of the donor, and in many ways this continues to the present day (Wang, 1999; Schaefer & Kim, 2013). However, if, as Offerman (2002, p.1424) observed: "*deviations from selfish behaviour are driven by assessments about the negative or positive intentions of other players.*" it seems that, like Dale Carnegie (1936), if we are genuinely to pursue the national interest of gaining influence with strangers then only an approach through *The Gift* will work. Any contamination of that system by naked or covert self-interested agendas negates the relationship building. Thus a first suggestion is for the separation of the three agendas into relationship building; humanitarian assistance; and development assistance, mirrored by a separation of the agencies that pursue them.

This places *The Gift* as the primary role and the system of behaviour for the Ministry of Foreign Affairs (or equivalent), whose proper agenda is building the relational platform upon which other agencies can operate. Such an approach will act as a call to: "*outdo one another in showing honour*"[14] and model the sorts of gratuitousness of fraternity that will challenge others to respond

---

14 St Paul's Epistle to the Romans chapter 12 v 10

in kind[15]. The features of *The Gift* will be exhibited strongly in that what is given will match both the recipient and the giver in regard to their nature and character. Gifts will be spontaneous and generous without exceeding the ability of the recipient to reciprocate appropriately, remembering the caution that if a relationship is one way, and without motive or interest then it is no relationship at all (Godbout & Caillé, 2000). The gifts will tend to be physical and cultural objects and opportunities. This would not preclude them from being targeted towards disadvantaged groups. Furthermore, in order to deal with the fact that the rigidity and inflexibility of the aid chain means that there is no mechanism whereby DA can be reciprocated (Carr, *et al.*, 1998) means must be found to enable the recipient country to reciprocate, observing the same terms as the giver, i.e. access to equivalent groups in the giver's country should be available to the recipient when their turn at giving arises. Under *The Gift* give what is needed, and ensure that it genuinely does match the recipient; give of yourself by way of commitment and preparedness to take on the obligations of *The Gift*; give without preconditions but only to those with whom you are comfortable.

B. Dealing with altruism:

The most dangerous of gifts are those in response to dire need[16]. In the face of disaster our humanity demands that we respond. As Ellerman (2007, p.153) pointed out, the cry that '*Children are dying*!' is about HA, not development *per se*. However, the combined problems of the moral hazard and Say's Law, on the one hand, and the temptation to attach conditions to the aid provided that address donor interests, on the other, make such aid more problematic that it ought to be. Thus one suggestion that addresses this might be to channel HA solely through multilateral agencies

15 This will be vital if the levels of co-operation envisaged by Jeffrey Sachs (2009) are to be attained.

16 See for example, the list presented by Benedict XVI (2009, section 21) quoted in chapter 4 section 4.

(e.g. the UN; EU; INGOs), which would remove any taint of self-interest (Gergen & Gergen, 1971).[17] Such agencies would operate much as the welfare state systems operate at national level, but would require enhanced oversight to ensure that instances of HA were not crowding out local self-help (Ellerman, 2005b), that they provided value for money to the tax-payers of the donor countries, and that they took into consideration true opportunity costs (Ellerman, 2007).

Again, remembering that: "*Only a god can receive without ever having to reciprocate.*" (Godbout & Caillé, 2000, p. 41) and taking note of comments by Carr, *et al.* (1998) and Bierhoff and Klein (1990) regarding the importance of reciprocity, it is important to build into this HA system opportunities to contribute, according to one's means. Thus the humanitarian assistance system proposed might take on the form of a mutual insurance fund to which nations could openly subscribe what they could afford and draw upon, at need, and that could become part of a state's disaster management planning. In must be noted that the ability to take part in HA, as a donor, should be perceived as a desirable outcome of the process of development.

C. Separating Development Assistance from Humanitarian Assistance:

When assistance is received through the system of *The Gift* it is ameliorated by the overwhelming nature of the need at that instant, on the one hand, and a presumed ability to reciprocate such assistance once normality has been restored, on the other. However, development doesn't hold this urgency[18] nor require reciprocation by the beneficiaries in the future. Furthermore, Ellerman (2007) recognised that there has been a tendency for aid agencies, in the face of the difficulty of achieving development,

---

17 Paul VI (1967, sections 51 & 52) made a clear call and argument for the establishment of a world fund.

18 Other than the imperative to disperse funds!

to re-align their activities under the banner of poverty reduction, which I have argued is more about HA, whilst all the while maintaining the fiction that it is still DA. However, development is an undertaking that is neither rescuing nor gift giving but is rather about the engagement in an active process of social change that has rewards for both the donor and the recipient. Again, Ellerman (*op.cit.*, p.153) recognised that: "*Genuine development assistance … is a slow, subtle and painstaking process.*"

Bearing this in mind, and drawing upon ideas from *The Gift*, it seems clear that bilaterally and multilaterally supported development initiatives could be undertaken through a market approach by distinctive, designated agencies and with explicit, transparent contracts and conditions, and in which the nature of the reciprocity is laid out, with the prospect of: "*opportunity to **pass on** benefit, by helping a third party.*" (Carr, *et al.* 1998, p.196). Or to reciprocate in kind, as Adloff and Mau (2006, p.115) recognised: "*the services of the general public establish a relationship of debt which demands activities of redress from the debtor which are co-operative and conform to norms*". Under these circumstances the aid can be tied in any way that the partners see fit. Both sides are able to pursue their interests, negotiate and manipulate as necessary and withdraw at any point should the situation dictate.

However, this should be accompanied by measures to avoid the temptation of dressing up DA as some form of disinterested and benevolent practice, particularly by using erroneous language (O'Connor & Kowalski, 2005), but rather to make explicit the market based and potentially exploitative nature of the relationship. Indeed, one problem that has contributed to the rise of heavily indebtedness has been a failure on the part of citizens to distinguish between aid that is a grant and aid that is a loan, incurring the need to service the debt and to pay it back. Under these circumstances there is no possibility of holding the government to account, as Easterly (2006, p.148) noted: "*The big problem ... is that the principal is the rich-country politician and not the real customers, the poor in poor countries*".

This proposed, final separation of the different exchange agendas is not advanced in order to give naked self-interest unbridled dominion over the development process but is advocated in order to encourage transparency and to provide no fig leaves of altruism to obscure the need to make real progress towards social justice. The adoption of a market based approach to DA would also allow a more open realignment of mercantile value systems through initiatives like Corporate Social Responsibility, Tri-sector Partnerships, Fair Trade and Stewardship Certification schemes, on the one hand, and the rule of law and rights based approaches to improvements in governance, on the other.

D. Dealing with donor hubris:

Pieterse (1999, p.79) observed that: "*One of the core problems of development is its pretentiousness, the insurmountable arrogance of intervening in other people's lives.*" and Mohan (2007) discusses the challenge of the hubris of donors, which inevitably arises from the superior position of giving. The triple role of *The Gift* normally precludes superiority, particularly as it acts against the core purpose of fostering relationships. The market, likewise, is characterized by an exchange of equal value and seldom encourages superiority, although power relations ultimately dictate the terms of the exchange. Somehow it is the disparity that benevolence conveys to the relationship that fosters a sense of self-righteousness that Freire (1971, p.35), quoting Erich Fromm, attributed to sadistic tendencies: "*The pleasure in complete domination over another person ... is the very essence of the sadistic drive.*" and which is incongruent in relationships founded upon democracy and positive unconditional regard. Indeed it is instructive to note the words of St Ambrose: "*You are not making a gift of what is yours to the poor man, but you are giving him back what is his. You have been appropriating things that are meant to be for the common use of everyone. The earth belongs to everyone, not to the rich.*" (Paul VI, section 23).

Nevertheless, there is a way to counteract hubris. This is by giving voice to the recipient role by countenancing Dalyell's (2000), call to provide a '*thorn in the flesh*' of the rulers (in his case the executive branch of government). His thoughts echo: A wise Roman emperor receiving the adoration of his people after a triumph was always accompanied by a slave who whispered in his ear '*remember Caesar, thou art mortal*'.[19] Indeed, this theme was taken up by Ellerman (2001, p.29) when he proposed that: "*devil's advocacy might not only be tolerated but fostered in a development agency functioning as an open learning organization*". There is a strong case to be made that this particular aspect of giving voice to balance the asymmetrical donor-recipient relationship is actually a matter of applying good governance. It also goes straight to the heart of double binds. As such the appointment of an Ombudsman for development (Kowalski, 2004) within all donor agencies to whom any stakeholder can go to seek redress might be an appropriate step to take.

E. Utilise the Potlatch:

An aspect of Mauss' study that encompasses pridefulness is the Potlatch. This is a social system that establishes status through extravagant hosting of events; through the provision of sumptuous gifts; and on occasion the actual destruction of wealth in a cycle of outperforming rivals. Now Peter Kropotkin observed that:

> *Men who have acquired wealth very often do not find in it the expected satisfaction. Others begin to feel that, whatever economists may say about wealth being the reward of capacity, their own reward is exaggerated. … they try to find an outcome for that deeply human need*

[19] Carr, *et al.* (1998, p.28) also refer to this practice.

> *by giving their fortune, or their forces, to something which, in their opinion, will promote general welfare.* (Kropotkin, 2010, p.153)

Thus it seems to me that, in an era of super-rich individuals, society should encourage philanthropy of an extreme kind, even as a means to lavishly display their wealth, and promote the emergence amongst the wealthy of something akin to the Potlatch.[20] We could further stimulate them to engage in a '*contest of honour*' with each other to see who can give the greatest events and gifts e.g. feasts; cultural events; clinics; schools; hospitals; universities; prizes for achievement in entrepreneurship etc. – the recipients of which could be communities in the developing world as well as the most marginalised sections of developed countries, and the environment.

---

20 See Tom Leonard in New York 12:34AM BST 05 Aug 2010 http://www.telegraph.co.uk/news/worldnews/7927500/American-billionaires-pledge-fortunes-to-charity.html Accessed on 8/10/2010 See also the recent phenomenon of the '*ice-bucket challenge*'. www.besttimepass.net/ice-bucket-challenge/ Accessed on 26/08/2014

Chapter 6

The Paradoxes of Social Development

1 Introduction

In addition to those considerations surrounding the moral hazard of receiving aid there is also a corresponding hazard for the giver. When the helper has an interest in finding opportunities to be helpful it can generate imprudent behaviour leading to increases in the number of cases necessitating assistance, a manifestation of Say's Law applied to development assistance[21], In fact the development professionals are also caught in a double bind that is this moral hazard in reverse – because, like the recipients of DA, they are themselves dependent upon the continuing dependence of the recipient, for if the recipient were to become truly independent – capable of self-help – then the '*external*' helper would no longer be necessary. The helpers cannot withdraw from helping, particularly since they have an imperative to '*get money out the door*', nor can they comment upon the paradox to which they are party (Tendler, 1975; Kowalski, 2004). The fable

21 See David Ellerman's quotation in chapter 5 section 3C.

of the emperor's new suit of clothes[1] is entirely the nature of this double bind in which professionals find themselves.

Thus we should recognise that the dependence of donor staff and agents and all the other ways in which the developed world is dependent upon the recipients of DA is not included in the analyses of the prevailing situation – and largely remains '*outside*' the deliberations of what can be done to improve the existing state of affairs. This involves the misperception of development professionals that they are external to and detached from the system that they are analysing or into which they are designing interventions. Indeed, Koestler (1967, p.245) emphasised that: "*It is a paradox as old as Achilles and the Tortoise, that the experiencing subject can never fully become the object of* [their] *experience*"[2] and conversely that they can never exclude themselves from their role in creating the world they observe.

Moreover, this leads to a complicated relationship that Ralph Stacey explained as:

> *the agency-structure debate … refers to the freedom of the individual to act and denotes those causes of human action to be found in the individual. Structure refers to the causes of human actions to be found in society, institutions, organizations and groups. Social structure is defined as the pattern of recurring relations between people in their ongoing dealings with each other,* (Stacey, 2001, p.42).

Which highlights the next seeming paradox of development wherein individuals are inextricable tangled up in the social systems that they both inhabit and co-create causing them

1 A tale by Hans Christian Andersen http://www.andersen.sdu.dk/vaerk/hersholt/TheEmperorsNewClothes_e.html accessed on 22 January 2012.

2 See also Roger Scruton's quotation in chapter 2 section 5.

inevitably to be less free and self-efficacious than they imagine or indeed than is imputed to them (Hayek, 2007), and which has been termed the *Epigenic Paradox* (Kowalski, 2010).

2 The Epigenic Paradox - The Structural Paradox of Individual and Society

All the protagonists of development are caught up in this entanglement of epigenesis (Kowalski, 2007)[3]. As Stacey (2001, p.101) noted, human action is dependent upon history, modified by the current circumstance, so that we can only start our journey from where we find ourselves. In addition to the agents of the donors (of whatever persuasion) being unable to think themselves into the parameters of their own analyses, the objects of development are also unwittingly enmeshed in their own circumstances. As Rodrik (2011, p.172) remarked: "*Telling poor countries in Africa or Latin America that they should set their sights on the institutions of the United States or Sweden is like telling them that the only way to develop is to become developed.*" Indeed, Lewis (1964, p. xxiv), in his seminal study of poverty in Mexico, noted that: "[poverty] *has a structure, a rationale, and defence mechanisms without which the poor could hardly carry on. In short, it is a way of life, remarkably stable and persistent, passed down from generation to generation*", which he termed a '*culture of poverty*'. To be sure, Freire (1971, p.48) had also recognised this encompassing structure of oppression[4] and Seabrook (1988, p.168) captured what it is to be marginalised in a society that has been constructed by and for others when he noted that: "*the poor do not inhabit a separate culture from the rich: they must live in the same world that has been contrived for the benefit of those with money.*"

---

3 Epigenesis here follows Bateson's definition (Bateson, 2002), namely Becoming (from the Greek word *genesis*) by building upon (from the Greek word *epi*) what already exists.

4 See Paulo Freire's quotation in chapter 1 section 4.

Furthermore, Paulo Freire had posited: "*the absolute necessity that the oppressed be self-emancipated rather than 'led' on the basis of struggles around their immediate interests by an avant-garde of revolutionary intellectuals.*" (Aronowitz, 1993, p.15), which appears to run contrary to the earlier expressed views of Kant (1991, p.55) who had maintained that: "*There is more chance of an entire public enlightening itself. This is indeed almost inevitable, if only the public is left in freedom. For there will always be a few who think for themselves, even among those appointed as guardians of the common mass.*", which Cole (2005, p.47) reaffirmed when he said that: "*Development theorists have to assume an activist role, facilitating people's awareness of the evolving social parameters of their experience, as a step towards people's participation in the social control of their existence in order to realize their particular potentials: praxis.*"

It is noteworthy that Clegg (1989, p.95) has also drawn attention to: "*the tension … between a conception of* [the] *real interests* [of others] *and the possibility of our knowledge of them.*" as a basic inconsistency in Marxism. Leading Aronowitz (1993, p.16), to highlight the challenge of: "*the antinomy of populism and vanguardism*" in reference to the contradiction between Freirian theory and the experience that actions for development have been largely initiated by sympathetic (*sic*) representatives of the '*oppressors*' rather than the '*oppressed*' themselves. Furthermore, Rahnema (1992 p.125) commented on this tension when he wrote that: "[There is a] *necessity for 'progressive' groups of non-alienated intellectuals to transcend their class interests and to engage in conscientization exercises.*" Indeed, Benton (1981, p.162) had alluded to a '*paradox of emancipation*' that ensures that if emancipation is to be achieved then it cannot be self-emancipation.[5] Again, Rahnema (1992, p.125) highlighted the dangers that emerge from such a paradox by warning that frequently: "[Such] *Agents of change … have tried to use conscientization or participatory methods, simply as new and more subtle forms of manipulation.*"

---

5 But see the suffragette movement.

This brings us to the need to consider this, perhaps, most perplexing paradox of development that of the primacy of the individual agent or the social structure, which is linked to those issues of free will and agency discussed in chapter 4. Sheldrake (1988, p.58) referred to it as: "*the paradox of all material forms. The form is in one sense united with matter, but the form aspect and the material aspect are also separable.*" Indeed, Hodgson (2007) captured such a core paradox when he noted that one central problem of social theory is the relationship between individual agency and social structure and explained it as: "*institutions are simultaneously both objective structures 'out there', and subjective springs of human agency 'in the human head'. Institutions are in this respect like Klein bottles: the subjective 'inside' is simultaneously the objective 'outside'.*" (*ibid*., p.108).

This opens an enormous subject that has engaged the minds of so many people more versed in these matters than am I. Nevertheless, it is such an important issue in the development discourse that I feel compelled to explore it, albeit briefly and idiosyncratically.

Accordingly, Ollman (1993) had asked:

- how can people make their own history and yet also be made by it?
- how do we both have free will and yet be conditioned? and
- how can the future be both open and necessary?

Furthermore, Bauman (2000, p.30) had observed that: "*Society* [is] *shaping the individuality of its members, and the individuals* [are] *forming society out of their life actions while pursuing strategies plausible and feasible within the socially woven web of their dependencies.*" Such concepts led Cole (2005, p.49) to ask: "*Which comes first: the (human) egg or the (social) chicken? Each is the condition and effect of the other in a perpetual process of evolution of what potentially is*".[6]

When Archer (1995, p.72) explained that: "*This is the human condition, to be born into a social context (of language, beliefs and organization) which was not of our making.*" she was capturing a conundrum that others had commented on before, for example Einstein (1998) had asserted that the individual operates in so many ways by themselves, and yet they depend so much upon society — in their physical, intellectual, and emotional existence — that it is not possible to imagine them, or indeed to understand them, outside a framework that is society. In fact, May (1974, p.226) had declared that: "*Continually through human history and through the life-span of each one of us, there goes on this dialectical process between individual and society, person and group, man and community … It is a dynamic relationship in which each pole exists by virtue of the other pole*".

So, how can we understand this manifestation of recursive self-reference that is at the very core of the human social condition? Within structuration theory Anthony Giddens saw actors and structures as two sides of the same coin with neither having ontological priority over the other (Craib, 1992). Whereas critical realists conceive of structure as an emergent property of the interactions of individuals, and therefore at a higher logical level (Bhaskar, 2002). Nonetheless Ralph Stacey and Douglas Griffin sought to rule out the confusion of different logical levels as an explanation of the epigenic paradox when they averred that:

> *there is no notion of individuals at one level and social structures at another. Individual minds/selves paradoxically form the social while being formed by the social at the same time… … human reality is*

6 Indeed Korten (2006, p.152) made a similar observation that: "*if the wise state is a product of a wise citizenry, and a wise citizenry is the product of a wise state, which comes first?*"

> *the temporally iterated interaction between human bodies so that any concept of a whole is an imaginative construct arising in that interaction, giving a sense of unity, coherence and continuity to experience.* (Stacey & Griffin, 2005, p.15)

It is noteworthy that they (*ibid.*, p.16.) had recognized that: "*A social object … does not exist as a thing (physical object) but as a generalized tendency on the part of large numbers of people to act in similar ways in similar situations.*" Indeed, Bhaskar (2002, p.114) has argued that: "*of course there is social structure, but it is a property of a series of human acts. It is not an entity*".

Such considerations led Stacey (2001, p.173) to take recourse to the role of time in generating the paradox by suggesting that: "*It is in th*[e] *living present that the future is perpetually being constructed…. The forming present.. signif*[ies] *the time structure of forming while being formed at the same time as the inclusion of the past and the future in the experience of the present.*" which, in reference to the role of time in a bell circuit (see Figure 6.1), Bateson (2002, p.55) had similarly explained as: "*The **if… then** of causality* [of the bell circuit] *contains time, but the **if… then** of logic is timeless. It follows that logic is an incomplete model of causality.*"

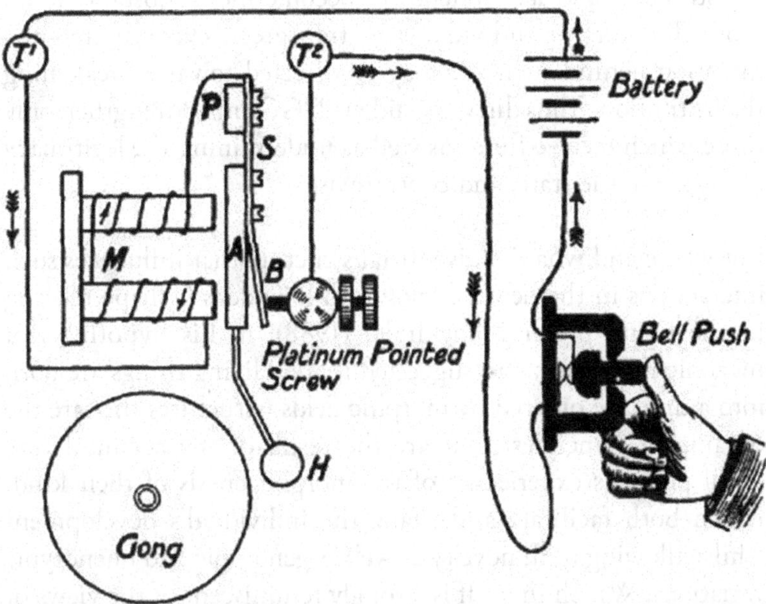
T¹
T²
Battery
P
S
M
A
B
Bell Push
Platinum Pointed
Screw
H
Gong

Figure 6.1 A Simple Bell Circuit (when the Bell Push is closed the current flows and armature A is attracted by the magnet M and breaks the connection at B, removing the attraction and restoring the circuit, etc. resulting in the vibration of the hammer H). The magnetism in the circuit is transient and comes and goes with the flow of current, as a result of its absence or presence.

Thus an agent is momentarily able to act in ways that maintain the social structures (institutions, organizations, conventions[7]) or that call their existence into question, but then has been and is subject to the influence of those very social structures. Furthermore, the nature of this relationship between the individual and the emergent social structure contains the possibility of another paradoxical dimension, for as Searle (1995) recognised, every time that an institution is used becomes a new expression of the user's commitment to the institution, which affirmation helps

7 Which, in development terms, are frequently referred to as Policies, Institutions and Processes (PIPs) (Carney, 1998).

the structure and its influence to become more substantial and more difficult for individuals to transgress, even though the intention behind such use may be directed towards weakening the institution. Thus directing aid via NGOs may strengthen only those which receive funds as well as undermining the legitimacy of organs of the state, and contrariwise.

But where and what is this virtual structure that influences such interactions in the here and now and how does it shape relating in the living present? Sheldrake (1988), in his hypothesis of morphic resonance, had suggested that all living things are born into a universe ordered by morphic fields (structures that are the organising principles) that are the result of the accumulation of all previous experiences of the morphogenesis of their kind, which both facilitate and shape the individual's development whilst allowing both novelty as well as genotypic and phenotypic variations. Which in itself is strongly reminiscent of the views of Giddens (1982, p.35) who spoke of: "*recursively organized rules and resources*" and structure which: "*exists only in a virtual way, as memory traces and as the instantiation of rules in the situated activities of agents*" (Giddens, 1989, p.256), that left human beings to be both constrained by their circumstances, as well as being a reflection of, and a reaction to them (Hodgson, 2007, p.103).

Thus, Stacey (2001, p.43) related that: "*Closely linked to the ideas of social structure, institutions and organizations are the notions of habits, customs, traditions, routines, mores, values, cultures, paradigms, beliefs, missions and visions. These are all ideas about the repetitive, enduring, shared practices of people in their ongoing dealings with each other in institutional life.*" Moreover, Mohan (2011, p.10) had recognised that '*culture*' is simply a pattern of learned behaviours that we inherit and pass on to posterity. Indeed, Hodgson (2007, p.106) emphasised that: "*institutions work only because the rules involved are embedded in prevalent habits of thought and behaviour.*" Furthermore, it must be noted that Bateson (1972, p.170) had also declared that: "*The events stream is mediated to* [individuals] *through language, art, technology, and other cultural media which are structured at every point by tramlines of apperceptive habit.*"

But, like Zeno's flying arrow (Kowalski, 2012), the question arises as to how habits are carried forward in time to influence the interactions of individuals in the living present? We are familiar with the idea of programmed behaviour leading to repetition of patterns (Stewart & Joines, 1987) but what and where are these programmes or scripts? Again, Sheldrake's morphic fields (Sheldrake, 1988) have been put forward as a replacement for the traditional hypothesis that memory is contained within the structure or chemistry of the brain, which Stacey (2001, pp.96-97) had captured as: "*The shift here is from a notion of past experience being more or less accurately recorded and placed in storage, to past experience shaping current relating processes in the living present with its ever-present spontaneous potential for transformation.*" This interpretation also fortuitously encompasses Karl Jung's ideas of archetypes and the collective unconscious (Storr, 1998). As a matter of note Sheldrake (1988, pp. 242-243) has maintained that: "*as children grow up they come under the influence of various social morphic fields, and tune in to many of the chreodes*[8] *of the culture*".

Hence it seems that we are thrust into a world that has been constructed by cycles of human existence that will shape us to operate within a set of circumstances in largely predetermined ways before we have much opportunity to realise that it has happened, let alone to resist it. Indeed, the essence of the critical realists' argument is that children are born into systems of signs and symbols, or language, that already exist as past rules and relationships that are being reproduced in the here and now by the individual family into which an infant is born (Stacey, 2001).

---

8 A chreode is a pathway of change within a morphic field established by use – a cow path (Fritz, 1994)

Or as Hodgson (2007, p.104) noted: "*for any particular actor, social structure **always exists prior** to their engagement with the world.*" Indeed, Georg Wilhelm Friedrich Hegel's view was that the individual and subject are only given meaning by the social institutions in and through which each person achieves social identity through interdependence and reciprocated recognition (Stacey, 2003). To be sure, Bateson (1972, p.170) had commented that: "*We are not concerned with a hypothetical isolated individual in contact with an impersonal events stream, but rather with real individuals who have complex emotional patterns of relationship with other individuals*". So, we surface as individuals who have been subjected to programming of which we are not particularly aware (which Bateson (1972) called Learning II) and we are already set in '*paths of least resistance*' (Fritz, 1994) framed by habits, cultural norms, and identity (individuality). As Yolles (2004, pp. 737-738) noted: "*Although people can consciously act to change their social and economic circumstances, critical inquirers recognise that their ability to do so is constrained by various forms of social, cultural and political domination.*"

3 Identity and labelling

Now, identity would appear to be where agency emerges as the being that both experiences and contributes to the shape of the social world, of which poverty and injustice are a feature. However, identity is yet another nominalization, as Stacey (2001, p.168) emphasised: "*Identity … is not a thing but a process, continuously reproduced and potentially transformed in the living present.*" by interaction with others, which is to say it is a relationship. Although, as Bateson (2002, p.44) recognised: "*In the transmission of human culture, people always attempt to replicate, to pass on to the next generation the skills and values of the parents; but the attempt always and inevitably fails because cultural transmission is geared to learning*", in many ways our future is laid down for us through our temperament and personality, largely determined by our experiences during earliest childhood. Indeed, as Stewart and

Joines (1987, p.101) noted: "*From a child's earliest days, her parents are giving her messages, on the basis of which she forms conclusions about herself, others and the world. These* ***script messages*** *are non-verbal as well as verbal. They form the framework in response to which the child's main script decisions are made.*" So we learn who we are by the responses we receive from significant adults. Fromm (1995) recognised this when he maintained that most people do not gain a sense of self-worth through their own conviction but because they receive the approval of others. Furthermore, Ellerman (2001, p.6) has alluded to the rarity of our ability to gain mastery over this process of enculturation when he wrote that: "*an individual's self-identity (including the larger social units with which the person identifies) are typically not open to intentional and deliberate choice. One chooses according to who one is, but one does not directly choose who one is.*", which runs counter to what Albert Camus called '*the freedom to be*' that is fundamental to an ability to engage in a lifelong psychic exertion to achieve authenticity (Dixon, 2009).

The essence of human existence is that we experience life through our interaction with others. As Vanaerschot (1993) observed, everyone at some point experiences the need to have their existence confirmed by others and Gaylin (1993, p.181) averred more strongly that: "*The human condition, by its very nature, is totally and completely interpersonal.*" Indeed, Immanuel Kant, Martin Buber, and Emmanuel Levinas, amongst others, define human existence on the basis of individuals meeting with other individuals, entirely through which the notion that '*I exist*' is generated (Sedlacek, 2011). Significantly Benedict XVI (2009, section 53) suggested that: "*the human creature is defined through interpersonal relations. The more authentically he or she lives these relations, the more his or her own personal identity matures. It is not by isolation that man establishes his worth, but by placing himself in relation with others.*"

Moreover, within development and social work, in addition to the question of how the marginalized are able to strive against those prevailing social structures (PIPs) in which they are immersed, which in many ways determine their social standing, there is a substantial issue regarding the impact that the protagonists can have on the marginalized through the practice of labelling and its accompanying stereotyping. We label people for the sake of convenience and, as Goffman (1968, p.11), in his seminal work on stigma, maintained: "*Society establishes the means of categorizing persons and the complement of attributes felt to be ordinary and natural for members of each of these categories.*" and that: "*The routines of social intercourse in established settings allow us to deal with anticipated others without special attention or thought.*" (Goffman, *op.cit.*, p.12). Concomitantly, in our dealings with others, we are frequently unaware about how we are categorizing or labelling them or indeed of the impact that such labelling is having upon them. Moreover, Apple (2001, p.261) had noted that: "*Labels too often function to confer a lesser status on those labelled. They create categories of deviance that have an essentializing quality to them.*" Indeed, Bauman (2001, p.119) argued that: "*to be poor in a rich society entails having the status of a social anomaly and being deprived of control over one's collective representation and identity*;"

As Goffman (*op.cit.*, p.24) pointed out, the stigmatized are acutely aware of their failings and this sense of inferiority means that they can experience some chronic feelings of the worst sort of insecurity, which in turn can create anxiety and perhaps even something worse. Indeed, Bauman, (2000, p.67) maintained that: "*Imperfections of* ***your*** *body are* ***your*** *guilt and* ***your*** *shame.*" and subsequently (Bauman, 2013, p.55) spoke of: "*the salt of reprobation is rubbed into the open wound of misery.*" Furthermore Decimus Iunius Iuvenalis had noted that: "*Bitter poverty has no harder pang than that it makes men ridiculous*"[9] and so, for the

9 Juvenal - Satire III line 152. *Nil habet infelix paupertas durius in se, quam quod ridiculos homines facit.*

subjects of development, being given and/or accepting a label is to be avoided if at all possible.

Thus the marginalized are induced to hide the manifestations of stigma on a daily basis. For, as Goffman (1968, p.57) noted: "*The issue is ... managing information about his failing. To display or not display; to tell or not to tell; to let on or not to let on; to lie or not to lie; and in each case, to whom, how, when and where.*"[10] In addition to the long list of disabilities and deviants, this dilemma can be seen amongst illiterates, women, ethnic groups, in HIV positives, in the unemployed, the homeless and in people who are simply labelled as '*the poor*'. This management of stigma is further complicated by the imposed requirement to respond to one's situation and to interact with the agents of '*benevolence*' and yet avoid giving endorsement thereby to the labelling bestowed by those significant others. As Illich (1978, p.50) argued: "*what counts is the professional's authority to define a person as a client, to determine that person's need, and to hand that person a prescription which defines this new social role.*" It can be deeply damaging to self-esteem to have to refer to yourself in pejorative terms conferred by the superior power. The stigma and its label become a source of discomfort in a relationship and damage the quality of communication about the substantive issues. Furthermore, the acceptance of the label by both parties leads to another double bind that ensnares the subjects and protagonists of development interventions for, as Goffman (*op.cit.*, p.148-149) noted, any reciprocal adjustment and approval between two individuals, such as that required by a partnership, can be upset entirely if one of the partners accepts in full the seeming offer that the other is perceived to have made for every '*positive*' relationship is conducted under unspoken promises of consideration and help such that the relationship would be damaged if these offers were actually taken up, and the '*junior*' partner is precluded from

10 Which may also in part account for the conventionally low take up rates of means tested benefits.

commenting upon any shortfalls in the demeanour unaffectedly accorded to them (Carr, *et al*, 1998; O'Connor & Kowalski, 2005; Eriksson Baaz, 2005)[11].

The question then becomes where is the locus of control? Appeals for self-determination are fine, but the marginalised are constantly being labelled by others and have to respond through those labels and, given their relative social status, are encouraged to believe them and accept the discredited status of their humanity which the stigma signifies (Rahman, 1993). This in turn can be manifested in inferiority complexes, learned helplessness and fatalism on the part of the marginalized[12], and as a tendency to patronize and infantilize them by the agents of welfare and development (Carr, *et al*, 1998). How can such a relationship form the basis for actions to bring about change that relies substantially upon a change of capability of the marginalized? Which is tantamount to asking how any individual or group can break out of a social structure that has been responsible for establishing their character, their perceptive field and the terms of their social exchanges? We are all products of the societies that have nurtured us, and before we can reshape those societies we have the challenge of overcoming the restrictions that such upbringing has imposed upon us. For example, Sen (1999, p.284) recognised that a child who is denied access to elementary schooling not only is deprived as a youngster but carries this disadvantage through rest of their life.[13]

---

11 Creating the conditions for a double bind.

12 Or indeed that whole syndrome that Oscar Lewis (1964) characterized as a '*Culture of Poverty*'.

13 But contrast this with John Dryden's observation that: "*By education most have been misled; So they believe, because they were so bred. The priest continues what the nurse began, And thus the child imposes on the man.*" (Dryden, 1742, p.63).

4 Agents and change

Although, as Cole (2005) has suggested, societies can only develop because individuals choose to act differently, as, with an evolving understanding of their existence, their social purpose changes. Indeed, he subsequently maintained that: "*The dynamic of the development process being individuals' frustration at being denied the opportunity to realize their emergent potentials, by social forces beyond their control.*" (Cole, 2006, p.343), which Beckhard (1969) had summarised as:

Change will occur when: D x V x F > R ....(2)

Where *D* is dissatisfaction with the current situation (Avoidance motivation) [14]
V is a vision of what is possible as an alternative (Attraction motivation)
F is the perceived feasibility of the first steps necessary to move towards that alternative
R is resistance to change

Nevertheless, the question remains - how can the individual come to influence those social structures so that they can be of and for themselves? For as Wolfgang von Goethe, Friedrich von Schiller, Alexander von Humboldt and Friedrich Hölderlin maintained, a truly self-directed life would require that the uniqueness of each person should permeate and determine all of their actions and products (Hinchman, 1996).

An insight may be garnered from vocational education, in respect of which Lave and Wenger (1991) introduced a concept of '*legitimate peripheral participation*' whereby individuals are permitted to attach themselves to a coterie of practitioners, first as observers and then gradually joining in until they become

---

14 Which Edgar Schein (1996) refers to as '*Disconfirmation*'.

proficient themselves. This may be more familiar as a process of formal apprenticeship, but its relationship to socialization in general can be appreciated in Lave and Wenger's statement that: "*children are, after all, quintessentially legitimate peripheral participants in adult social worlds*" (*ibid*., p.32). Clearly, before you can begin to contribute to shaping your community you have to attain a sufficient standing to achieve influence. However, Kant (1991, p.54) had emphasised that: "*enlightenment is man's emergence from his self-incurred immaturity. Immaturity is man's inability to make use of his understanding without the guidance of another*". But the guidance of another, imprinted in childhood, is an inevitable, subliminal leitmotif accompanying all our subsequent actions. Indeed, as Santos (1999, p.39) captured it: "*how is it possible to make silence speak without having it necessarily speak the hegemonic language that would have it speak?*"

Furthermore, a practitioner in any particular field must learn the manner of thought of their discipline. They must apply themselves assiduously, thereby making the patterns of thought in that field second nature (Ellerman, 1995). Only once a person has been admitted into the ranks of mastery are they permitted to venture criticism, always recognising, with Ellerman (*op.cit*., p.30), that: "*Societies do not promote to positions of status and influence those individuals who are likely to attack the foundations of the society. And any individuals who aspire to positions of status and influence are unlikely to harbour 'unsound' opinions.*" Thus a rite of passage process contributes to the crossing of a boundary that then permits the person to effect changes. However, this is precisely the situation where the individual is constrained by their socialization within the existing structures of thought and behaviour, as Damrosch (2006, p.39) noted: "[apprenticeship] *subtly reinforces social as well as intellectual conformity*". Indeed, Ellerman (*op.cit*., p.1) recognised that: "*If there are shortcomings, limitations, or mistakes involved in the defining thought patterns of the field, it is unlikely that a normal practitioner would escape them … Mastery of the mistaken thought patterns is part of what counts for proficiency and expertise.*" Beer (2004a, p.789) went further in suggesting that socialization of this kind brings about a process of triage[15] in which the middle socio-economic groupings mistakenly side with the preservation of the *status quo*, which really benefits just the élite and then in the short term only. Leading Bauman, (2000, pp.17-18) to suggest that: "*people may be incompetent judges of their own plight, and must be ... guided, to experience the need to be 'objectively' free and to muster the courage and determination to fight for it.*"

When you add onto this the various processes whereby individuals in groups come to behave other than they would if left to their own devices, which Cooke (2001, p.103) listed as: risky shift, the Abilene paradox[16], group think and coercive persuasion, as well as what Jürgens Habermas captured as the *Weltanschauungen* or ideologies[17] that distort people's ability to reach an unbiased consensus (Servaes, 1996; Finlayson, 2005), then it becomes an even more challenging prospect for the voice of the marginalised to authentically shape their life-world. As Long (2004, p.30) noted: "*much depends on whether one can adjust one's point of view and line of work to fit in with current dominant development discourse.*"

Furthermore, there are dangers to which change agents are subjected, such as those noted by Machiavelli (2005, p.22) who long ago had recognised that: "*there is nothing more difficult to execute, nor more dubious of success, nor more dangerous to administer, than to introduce new political orders. For the one who introduces them has as his enemies all those who profit from the old order, and he has only lukewarm defenders in all those who might profit from the new order.*" Moreover, Watzlawick, *et al.* (1967, p.

---

15 Triage comes from the French verb 'trier' to sort – and here is not to be confused with its subsequent association with disaster management.

16 see chapter 3, section 7.

17 "*ideologies are functional false beliefs, which ... serve to shore up certain social institutions and the relations of domination they support.*" (Finlayson, 2005, p.11)

213) maintained that: "*A person in* [such] *a double bind situation is therefore likely to find himself punished … for correct perceptions, and defined as 'bad' or 'mad' for even insinuating that there be a discrepancy between what he does see and what he 'should' see.*" Indeed Scruton (2002, p.114) emphasised that: "*social order is a precarious thing, which cannot be sustained by law alone. Internal and external threats to it can be deterred only if people have the mettle to resist them – the force of character, the emotional equilibrium and the live human sympathies that will prompt them to persist in a cause, to make sacrifices, and to commit themselves to others.*" Therefore, to be an indigenous change agent from amongst the marginalised is an almost impossibly demanding mission requiring, as it does, both high levels of self-confidence, a thickness of skin and a steely resolve.

5 Autonomy and self-determination

Now, it is apparent from a number of writers that the concept of development has come to be bound up with that of the promotion of autonomy, whether this is captured in Pope Paul VIth's expression as: "*artisans of their destiny*" (Paul VI, 1967, section 65); or in Hirschman's phrase: "*progress in problem solving*" (Hirschman, 1973, p.240); or in Korten's theme of: "*building their capacity to control their own lives*" (Korten, 1983, p.220); or in Sen's representation that: "*Development can be seen … as a process of expanding the real freedoms that people enjoy*" (Sen, 1999, p.3); or, as Ellerman (2005b, p.104) emphatically pronounced: "*Long-term economic and social transformation grows, in the last analysis, out of autonomous activity.*" But it is unclear whether these views of autonomy are for individuals, or institutions or communities or any permutation thereof. Indeed, the nominalization that is '*autonomy*' is another instance of the vagueness of language that serves to persuade but not to clarify.

What does seem clear is that human social behaviour is manifested in a hierarchy like a set of Chinese boxes ranging from the individual through households to communities, states and ultimately to global institutions such as the United Nations, the Catholic Church or Green Peace. As Beer (1994, p. 115) recognised: "*every system demands a metasystem; and therefore a second metasystem will be identified beyond that. There is no logical end to the chain,*" Importantly Arthur Koestler asserted that: "*The members of a hierarchy, like the Roman god Janus, all have two faces looking in opposite directions: the face turned towards the subordinate levels is that of a self-contained whole; the face turned upward towards the apex, that of a dependent part.*" and, furthermore, that: "*Every holon*[18] *has a dual tendency to preserve and assert its individuality as a quasi-autonomous whole; and to function as an integrated part of an (existing or evolving) larger whole. This polarity between the Self-Assertive (S-A) and Integrative (INT) tendencies is inherent in the concept of hierarchic order.*" (Koestler, 1967, p.385).

The balanced interplay between the self-interested pursuits of the individual and the integrative requirements of the higher social order is by no means guaranteed. Hardin (1968, p.1244) was rightly sceptical of placing faith in Adam Smith's invisible hand and its concomitant: "*tendency to assume that decisions reached individually will, in fact, be the best decisions for an entire society.*" On the contrary: "*we are locked into a system of "fouling our own nest," so long as we behave only as independent, rational, free-enterprisers.*" (Hardin, 1968, p. 1245). Indeed, a hierarchical structure is a most enduring characteristic of human societies which is invariably based upon a monopoly of power and wealth by an élite group and a contemporaneous struggle by the rest of the population for justice (Rihani, 2002), which has presented every level of social holon

18 Holons are functional units within a hierarchical system. According to Koestler (1964, p.287): "*A living organism or social body is not an aggregation of elementary parts or elementary processes; it is an integrated hierarchy of semiautonomous sub-wholes, consisting of sub-sub-wholes, and so on. Thus the functional units on every level of the hierarchy are double-faced as it were: they act as whole when facing downwards, as parts when facing upwards.*"

with the challenge of determining what for it constitutes social justice and how to bring it about. Beer (1994, p.317) very cogently explained the topsy-turvy nature of elitism when he averred that: "*the failure of metasystems in society is due to their conception as higher authorities which cannot conceivably exert that authority in a free society.*" Indeed Hayek (2007, p.71) maintained that there is a: "*fundamental principle that in the ordering of our affairs we should make as much use as possible of the spontaneous forces of society, and resort as little as possible to coercion,*".

This begins to put an entirely different gloss upon the idea of autonomy or freedom, for as Beer (2004a, p.778) emphasised: "*Autonomy turns out to mean the maximum discretionary action for the part, short of threatening the integrity of the whole. This is a non-emotive definition of a very emotive term: freedom.*" and Bauman (2000, p.40) had observed that: "'*Society' always stood in an ambiguous relation to individual autonomy: it was, simultaneously, its enemy and its* ***sine qua non*** *condition.*" Indeed, as Pressfield (2002, p.37) reported: "*The paradox* [of freedom] *seems to be, as Socrates demonstrated long ago, that the truly free individual is free only to the extent of his own self-mastery. While those who will not govern themselves are condemned to find masters to govern them.*" always remembering with Bauman, (2000, p.36) that: "*The 'citizen' is a person inclined to seek her or his own welfare through the well-being of the city – while the individual tends to be lukewarm, sceptical or wary about 'common cause', 'common good', 'good society' or 'just society'.*" Or as Hinchman (1996, p.488) had observed: "*Kant had presumed, … the literal meaning of autonomy: obedience to a self-imposed law.*" which suggests an internal locus of control, which reins in the pursuit of our individual interests and appetites, that is variously referred to as conscience or responsibility or sense of civic duty. This is the integrative tendency of the holon towards the higher level, not to be confused with identification in which the individual is taken over by the group.[19] Thus, in an ideal

19 "*Integration in a social hierarchy preserves the personal identity and*

society, which possesses such '*hierarchic awareness*', every holon on every level would be conscious both of its rights as a whole and its duties as a part (Koestler 1967).

However, Hinchman (1996, p.489) had noted that: "*Hegel initiated a transformation that has led to our seeing the autonomous individual as a peculiar kind of historical fiction, one that later became a vehicle of Western cultural imperialism.*" The culture referred to being free market, liberal capitalism that emphasises individualism above all else whilst crying crocodile tears when confronted with the results of unbridled human appetite, that Epstein (2009, 121) described as: "*an operant civil religion of personal responsibility, an ethos of neglect and abandonment in denial of compassion, fairness, or adequacy*". Indeed, in 1949 President Truman had announced, with no irony intended, that: "*Democracy alone can supply the vitalizing force to stir peoples of the world into triumphant action, not only against their human oppressor, but also against their ancient enemies – hunger, misery, and despair.*" (quoted in Rist, 2002, p.72). Indeed, DFID set out one of the objectives of UK DA to be the widespread fostering of the values of civil liberties and democracy, the rule of law and good governance, and to encourage the growth of a vigorous and assured civil society (Francis, 2002).

6 Democracy considered

So the concept of a '*developed*' country is presented more and more as synonymous with a '*democratic*' country, and '*development*' has been in many ways supplanted by '*democratization*'. But, as Mohan (2007, p.94) noted: "*democratization is both a euphemism and synonym for Westernization,*" and Korten (2006, p. 153) emphasised that the ideals of liberal democracy articulated by John Locke: "*gave primacy to protecting the natural property rights of the individual*" and have been taken up and supported

---

responsibility of its holons: identification, while it lasts, implies a partial or total surrender of both." Koestler (1967, p.283).

enthusiastically by the enfranchised élites because they: "*lent a patina of democracy to their privilege.*" Throughout the emergence and establishment of current democratic practices societies have been divided between the enfranchised and the disenfranchised which, as Korten (2006, p.146) pointed out, required: "*a moral justification for denying the humanity and right of participation of the disenfranchised by exaggerating the virtues of the former and the vices of the latter*". The only possible excuse for such a policy of disenfranchisement would be a devotion to support every individual as they negotiate a route to bring them to a sufficient state of consciousness that would lift them all into the ranks of the enfranchised (*ibid.*). Furthermore, as Mohan (2011, p.177) observed: "*development without democracy is a farce; democracy without development is hollow.*" The response to these shortcomings within our poverty of culture has become the proselytization of democracy but in a most impoverished form. Indeed, Dahl (2000, p.38) has enunciated five opportunities which are the criteria that authenticate a democratic process as:

1. to participate effectively
2. to have an equal vote in decision taking
3. to have access to education and information
4. to exercise final control over the agenda
5. to include all adults

which, if they are not yet present, should at least inform policies for social development. That they do not feature more strongly in driving social change can be put down to the resistance of oligarchs to the extension of full citizenship (Plato, 1993) based upon their need to preserve free market capitalism. Nevertheless it is evident that we live in self-congratulatory democracies where, as a universal principle, all are proclaimed to be equally free. Yet we must justify imposing inferior rights upon some people; otherwise those functional economic inequalities that sustain our economic system would be threatened (Hann & Hart, 2011). However, these inequalities are not publicly advocated but rather achieved and sustained covertly, whether by constitutional exclusion[20], issuing false prospectuses[21], gerrymandering, electoral dirty tricks or illegal vote rigging. But note that this resistance to democracy also extends beyond the political arena into employment relations and corporate governance where the oligarchs hold unfettered and unaccountable sway[22]. It seems clear that the capitalist premise is that '*democracy*' should only be a thing for the public sphere while enterprises are private (Ellerman, 2010). The plutocrats then use those employment arenas to gain power to subvert the public one.

However, we must recognise that democracy is a complex set of arrangements that is far more than simply holding elections (Easterly, 2006). Indeed, Crick (2002, p.5) suggested that: "*there is democracy as a principle or doctrine of government; there is democracy as a set of institutional arrangements or constitutional devices; and there is democracy as a type of behaviour (say the antithesis of both deference and unsociability).*" Moreover, Lasch (1996, p.86) recognised that: "*democracy has to stand for something more demanding than enlightened self-interest, 'openness,' and toleration.*" Furthermore, even when democracy is openly espoused, inescapably government and social institutions result from the interactions of individual people who, if they do not authentically exhibit democratic behaviour, undermine or negate the democratic policies and arrangements that are publicly advocated, which espousal is then perceived as just so much hypocrisy (Brunsson, 1989).

In just this way, because of our imperfect democracy's support for the ascendancy of individual property rights that is the

---

20 Including non-proportional voting systems such as first-past-the-post.

21 Including unequal access to the media for the competing points of view.

22 "*The employment contract transfers and alienates the right to control the employee's actions within the scope of the contract to the employer who then exercises that right in his or her own name, not in the name of the employees.*" (Ellerman,1995, p.32) – so much for the inalienable right to self-determination.

cornerstone of the Western, exploitative, predatory culture, in the words of Roy (1999, p.10) democracy: "*has become little more than a hollow word, a pretty shell, emptied of all content or meaning*". As Dahl (2000, p.173) recognised: "*when we look closely,* [we discover] *that* [market capitalism] *has two faces. Like the emblem of the Greek god Janus, they face in opposite directions. One, a friendly face, points towards democracy. The other, a hostile face points the other way.*" Which is supported by Dani Rodrik's more recent conclusion that free markets are incompatible with democracy and that: "*the cost to society from individual freedom is too high.*" (Rodrik, 2011 p.120). With deep irony Ellerman (1995, p.5) noted that: "*Orthodoxy is blessed with the Happy Consciousness that liberal capitalism has no basic structural violations of human rights and that, far from violating the principles of private property and democracy, it is based upon those principles.*" Indeed there is something deeply incongruous about the protestations of Western leaders regarding their adherence to the cultural values of freedom (including free markets and property rights) and democracy (predominantly the inalienable right to self-determination). Particularly when the current, Western dominated, global culture is manifestly culpable in the lack of peace, the many deprivations that people suffer, the lack of social justice and in the immediate existential threats to humanity (Korten, 2006) not because of its espousal of democracy but because it actually places the provision of Robert Dahl's five opportunities that authenticate a democratic society in the wings rather than giving them centre stage.

In the absence of full democracy what we inevitably have are effectively oligarchies of one sort or another[23], the justification for which is frequently based upon an argument that Dahl (2000, p. 27) refers to as: "*the minority of superior competence*"[24], otherwise

23 Traditionally aristocracy, but currently including plutocracy or stratocracy or theocracy or indeed trapezocracy.

24 I am reminded of a passage from Joseph Conrad's *Heart of Darkness* (p.7,): "*The conquest of the earth, which mostly means the taking it away from those who have a different complexion or slightly flatter noses than*

as the rule of the technocrat, which in the development process, is represented by the external intervention of '*expert*', paternalistic agencies and manifested in the domination of *technē* over *phronesis* described in chapter 4, enthusiasm for which must be curbed by reference to a comment made by Illich (1978, p.79) that: "*the professional definition of rights can extinguish liberties and establish a tyranny that smothers people underneath their rights.*" and Margaret Mead's observation (quoted in Bateson, 1972, p. 160) that: "*if we go on defining ends as separate from means **and** apply the social sciences as crudely instrumental means, using the recipes of science to manipulate people, we arrive at a totalitarian rather than a democratic system of life.*"

Indeed, as Mohan (2011) acknowledged, the original enlightenment project was the emancipation of humanity to achieve its true vocation, that was itself a return to the ideas of Socrates, Plato and Aristotle who: "*were … less concerned with securing individual rights than with solving the puzzle of how a society might best … appoint wise leaders of a mature moral consciousness who would guide the society to achievement of its higher-order possibilities.*" (Korten, 2006, p.147)[25]. However, this has become side-tracked into a less noble undertaking that Epstein (2009, p.121) termed: "*a woeful degradation of both human grandeur and civilization's promise*" – the pursuit of individual gratification for members of an élite coterie that Korten (2006) characterised as '*Cloud Minders*', who keep their distance from the lifestyles of the vast majority of human beings[26]. In this way, wealthy people increasingly seek to

---

ourselves, is not a pretty thing when you look into it too much. What redeems it is the idea only. An idea at the back of it:"

25 Although Douthwaite (1999, p.169) speculated that for the technocentrist: "*Perhaps we are not meant to try to work towards an appealing possible future. Such a course implies interference with the self-regulating free market.*" And Hayek (2007) who was adamant that such an approach spells the end of liberty.

26 An increasingly prevalent dystopian theme that appears in Hollywood productions.

cloister themselves from the rest of society (Gray, 1998), use their wealth to secure services for themselves privately, and deny the extension of those amenities as public services to everyone else by using their political sway (Diamond, 2006). In my opinion, nothing more clearly exemplifies this capitulation of the agenda for human realization to the forces of individualism within international development than the observation of: "*the relocation of ethical/political discourse from the frame of the 'just society' to that of 'human rights'.*" (Bauman, 2000, p.29). Significantly, Gray (*op. cit.*, p.109) had maintained that: "*Rights have little authority or content in the absence of a common ethical life.*"

Thus, in the tension between the self-assertive force of the individual and the demands of the integrative force of the social emerges the true paradox of democracy[27] – in the face of alternative social configurations (e.g. an ochlocracy) a democracy can only be sustained by the willingness of individuals to forego their individual interest in favour of the group interest, even to their readiness to lay down their lives to sustain the freedom of others – i.e. altruism. Bauman (2001, p.5) had recognised that: "*We cannot be human without both security and freedom; but we cannot have both at the same time and both in quantities which we find fully satisfactory.*" as seen in the erosion of civil liberties by legislation aimed at curbing acts of terrorism. Indeed, Benjamin Franklyn had observed that: "*Those who would give up essential liberty to purchase a little temporary safety deserve neither liberty nor safety.*" (quoted in Hayek, 2007, p.156).

---

27 Not to be confused with: "*The paradox* [of democracy] *is that the majority may vote to abolish democracy*" (Easterly 2006, p.106), which is really a special case of the general tyranny of minorities by a majority. Which Dahl (1990, p.16), had countered by proposing that: "*If I also want to respect the right of others to their personal choices, if, therefore, I accept them as my political equals, there seem to be at least three possibilities* [of offsetting the tyranny of the majority]: *Mutual Guarantees, Consensual Associations, Autonomous Decisions.*"

The failure of societies to rise to this challenge of the paradox of democracy is captured in the concept of the tragedy of the commons[28], which Garrett Hardin described in the following terms:

> *the rational herdsman concludes that the only sensible course ... is to add another animal to his herd. And another; and another... But this is the conclusion reached by ... every rational herdsman sharing a commons. Therein is the tragedy. Each man is locked into a system that compels him to increase his herd without limit - in a world that is limited. Ruin is the destination toward which all men rush, each pursuing his own best interest in a society that believes in the freedom of the commons. Freedom in a commons brings ruin to all.* (Hardin, 1968, p.1244).

Thus we have seen grazing commons joined by open water fisheries, by deforestation, by depredation of endangered species and by environmental pollution[29]; and the list is likely to be extended soon by the exhaustion of petroleum deposits, climate change and the demise of the welfare state (Hardin, 1973; Morrow & Hull, 1996). In response to which Chambers (1997) has called for what he refers to as *'responsible consumption'* and the altruism of putting the first last. However, Hardin (1973, p.188) has objected to any notion that voluntary abstention in a commons is practical since: "*Nonconscience has a selective advantage over conscience.*", or as Dietz (2005, p.211) put it: "*Altruists do poorly, egoists do well, so in the long run altruists are gone from the market,*" which will inevitably

---

28 As Dietz (2005, p.209) reflected: "*The Prisoner's dilemma, the coordination problem, the undersupply of public goods, the problem of collective action, social traps, shirking, free riders, and moral hazard are all labels for permutations of this problem,*"

29 "*the environment, once a common good available to everybody without considerable contrasts, has become a rare good of which – the polluters – take possession to the detriment of others*" (quoted in Latouche 2003, p.7).

undermine any system that relies upon self-restraint[30], and Korten (2006, p.35) noted that in our winner-take-all culture: "*The high stakes create a powerful incentive to win by any means and exert a strong downward pressure on ethical standards*". Furthermore, Hardin (1968, p.1246) is quite clear that to appeal to people's better nature is actually unethical, because: "*When we use the word responsibility in the absence of substantial sanctions are we not trying to browbeat a free man in a commons into acting against his own interest?*" Indeed, Garrett Hardin surmised that:

> *Sooner or later, consciously or subconsciously, he senses that he has received two communications, and that they are contradictory: (i) (intended communication) "If you don't do as we ask, we will openly condemn you for not acting like a responsible citizen"; (ii) (the unintended communication) "If you do behave as we ask, we will secretly condemn you for a simpleton who can be shamed into standing aside while the rest of us exploit the commons.*" (Hardin, *op.cit.*, p.1246) [31]

This led him (*ibid.*, p.1247) to advocate that the solution is for every commons to be underpinned by a system of governance of resources founded upon coercion: "*mutual coercion, mutually agreed upon by the majority of the people affected.*" so that with the power to consume comes the unrelieved consequences of being accountable and the conclusion that we must bring power and responsibility together once more, within the community (Hardin, 1973).

---

30 I am reminded at this point of the words of Thrasymachus: "*You fool, Socrates, don't you see? In any and every situation, a moral person is worse off than an immoral one. Suppose, for instance, that they're doing some business together, which involves one of them entering into association with the other: by the time the association is dissolved, you'll never find the moral person up on the immoral one – he'll be worse off.*" (Plato, 1994, p.26).

31 Which are the basic conditions for a double bind, all that remains to be added is the injunction not to comment upon the contradiction.

Nevertheless, things may not be quite so clear cut. On the one hand there is the difficulty of devising systems of coercion. According to Hardin (1968) rights of access might be allocated on the basis of:

- wealth, by auctioning quotas.
- merit, as defined by some agreed-upon standards, such as means testing.
- by lottery.
- a first-come, first-served basis, administered to long queues.

But he considered them all to be objectionable. To which can be added the issue of oversight of the enforcement of any processes and regulations with the age old *reductio ad absurdum* of '*Quis custodiet ipsos custodies?*' and the creation of rent seeking opportunities; the more numerous the laws, the more corrupt the republic[32]. On the other hand, and in contrast to Mohan's (2011, p.58) remark that: "*From Wall Street to Rwanda, the gluttony of greed and gloom has produced a widespread dysfunctionality that thwarts all democratic institutions.*", we must take note of William Easterly's assertion that spoliation of the weak by the strong doesn't happen as often as the prisoners' dilemma would suggest, even in the absence of police surveillance (Easterly, 2006). Moreover, Orr (2004, p.169) has also commented that: "*Evidence shows that we are in fact considerably more public spirited than we have been led to believe,*" and Latouche's (2003, p.3) observation that: "*the experts tear their hair out when they meet herders who really do not see the need to increase their flocks beyond what is necessary, just to make money.*" which must give us some grounds for optimism that there is some part of the human population that holds values that are in line with the humanization agenda (either consciously or not) that Mohan (2011) has called Enlightenment II.

32 "*corruptisima republica plurimae leges*" Publius Cornelius Tacitus, Anals III 27.

However, because in general we lack the maturity to govern ourselves but abdicate government to our representatives, who themselves are dependent upon pleasing us; we have created a self-referential, paradoxical relationship that cannot take a systemic view of what is truly in our collective interests. The current failure to achieve authentic democracy has resulted in a political system that is bound to the principle of expediency and, as Bateson (1972) recognised, such expediency can never provide long-term solutions. Furthermore, Diamond (2006, p.496) has drawn attention to the sleight of mouth that is the American dream in that: "*no one in First World governments is willing to acknowledge the dream's impossibility: the unsustainability of a world in which the Third World's large population were to reach and maintain current First World living standards.*" which has generated and impels the current development agenda that is termed '*Sustainable Development*'.

Chapter 7

Sense and Sustainability

1 Introduction

According to a Royal Society report (2012) the *per capita* material consumption of the richest parts of the world is far above a level that can be sustained for 7 billion or more, which is a reiteration of Jared Diamond's earlier observation that the promotion of the American dream is a gross pretence (Diamond, 2006). The sleight of mouth of western leaders that suggests otherwise has generated and impels the current development agenda that is termed '*sustainable development*'. As intellectuals we are call to identify and elaborate the underlying roots of such problems and to expose the nature of dominant discourses that are in error (Harvey, 2011).

The Millennium Ecosystem Assessment (MEA), instigated by the United Nations, has taken the ecological pulse of the planet, and the results so far point to obstacles to sustainability that are almost insurmountable unless drastic changes are implemented in human activities in the very near future (Keil, 2007). So, when they reported in 2005 that:

> *Nearly two thirds of the services provided by nature to humankind are found to be in decline worldwide. In effect, the benefits reaped from our engineering of the planet have been achieved by running down natural capital assets. In many cases, it is literally a matter of living on borrowed time. By using up supplies of fresh groundwater faster than they can be recharged, for example, we are depleting assets at the expense of our children. The cost is already being felt, but often by people far away from those enjoying the benefits of natural services.* (MEA, 2005, p.5)

we should be inclined to accept that a tragedy, which will have the severest consequences for the human species, really is unfolding and that our attempts to achieve a lasting balance with nature are not yet succeeding. Measures that are intended to bring us into closer harmony with our life support systems (Lipietz, 1995; Diamond, 2006; Speth & Haas, 2006) seem to be at odds with the dominant set of values of free market capitalism and its associated acquisitive materialism (Krueger & Agyeman, 2005). Hirschman (1992) was even more critical, maintaining that capitalism, in convincing everyone that morality and public spirit can be dispensed with, and that the universal pursuit of self-interest is all that is needed for satisfactory performance, will undermine its own viability. Indeed, the present world economic system is grotesquely unsustainable and it seems impossible for a sustainable world to emerge and be maintained via the workings of an unconfined, undirected market system (Douthwaite, 1999). Furthermore, we need to take cognisance of the second contradiction of capitalism, which O'Connor (1998, p.245) defined as: "*individual capitals attempt to defend or restore profits by cutting or externalizing costs, the unintended effect is to reduce the 'productivity' of the conditions of production*".

The consequence of continuing with our current practices is to obtain a temporary and unsustainable subsidy that supports current consumption at the expense of generations to come (Korten, 2006). The conclusion seems inescapable, we affluent people can no longer justify advancing our own self-interests at the expense of the interests of others and that the ever-increasing consumption of scarce resources, the amassing of consumer durables, and the fabricated need for services, does not constitute the freedom that we crave (Beer 2004b; Diamond, 2006).

Furthermore, the policy response of advocating that development should be sustainable, which was captured in the Brundtland Commission's definition as: "*development that meets the needs and aspirations of the present without compromising the ability to meet those of the future.*" (World Commission on Environment and Development, 1987, p.40), is fundamentally defective. This is in part due to the definition's ambiguity, which was a result of trying to please all sides (Meppen & Gill, 1998), and substantially due to the conflation of the concepts of sustainability and development, which belong to essentially incommensurable worlds, thereby creating an oxymoron (Visvanathan, 1991). In addition, the purpose of adding '*sustainable*' to '*development*', it is argued (Latouche, 2003), is not to bring '*development*' again for discussion but only to add to it a superficial ecological component. Indeed, some maintain that '*sustainable development*' has become the motto of the day primarily to sustain development itself, rather than to sustain nature or culture (Esteva & Prakash, 1998). Instead, with Mohan (2011), we must avoid simply invoking the oxymoron and demand that a more sophisticated account of the ends that it is intended to serve be given.

In this respect there continues to be a worldwide struggle to determine how '*sustainable development*' will be defined (O'Connor, 1998) which means that '*sustainability*' is clearly not an ecological and economic question but rather is an ideological and political one. Indeed, Meppem and Bourke (1999) concluded that sustainable development creates both images of revolt against wasteful and polluting capitalism and of technology modulating excess and allowing '*business as usual*'. Indeed Orr (2004) maintained that before we can know what sustainability means we first have to decide what we wish to sustain and how we propose to do it. Furthermore, Buckingham (2007) had echoed this arguing that the concept of '*sustainability*' is unhelpful in shaping a vision of an environmental and social future because it makes the assumption that what we have at present is what we need to secure.

Indeed, there have emerged two divergent constructions of sustainability, as Krueger and Agyeman (2005) noted, that of strong/hard sustainability versus weak/soft sustainability, where strong/hard seems much more conservative, advocating holding onto the status quo – sustaining what is, and weak/soft is more pragmatic in that it recognises that situations are dynamic and that change may be necessary to provide adaptation that will ensure survival. This is a manifestation of the ancient paradox of the co-existence of stability and change where systems must be subject to both dampening negative feedback (autopoesis) and learning processes.

2 Dimensions of the Challenge

Nevertheless, as Buckingham (2007) commented, one positive thing that emerges from the term '*sustainability*' is the recognition that the economic, social, and environmental are inextricably linked. In fact, Krueger and Gibbs (2007) had observed that sustainability is not supposed to be a monopod but a tripod. Unfortunately this has often been portrayed using a Venn diagram of three overlapping circles which implies that there are genuine areas of mutual interest (Yates, 2012). However, these three dimensions are by no means necessarily pillars or areas of overlapping interest – they may be better perceived as vectors of tension (see Figure 7.1) which, depending upon whether they are appropriately balanced, determine that the edifice will stand or not. Which Gibbs and Krueger (2007) identified as a summons to fully recognise the interdependency of social justice, economic well-being, and environmental stewardship. The three vectors are: A. between the economic and the social, representing the relative social justice of resource distribution ultimately influencing disposable income levels that could be directed towards nutrition, health, and education; B. between the social and the environmental, representing the differential access to the commons and the concomitant '*footprint*' impact upon the carrying capacity; and C. between the economic and the environmental representing trade-offs between growth and pollution and resources to be devoted to ameliorating damage and developing technologies.

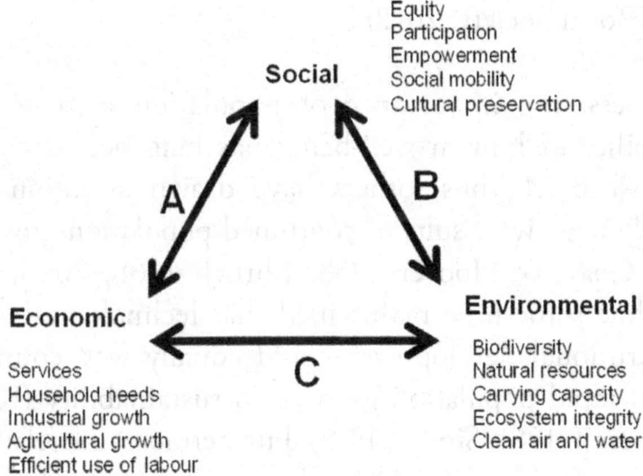
Social
Equity
Participation
Empowerment
Social mobility
Cultural preservation
A
B
Economic
Services
Household needs
Industrial growth
Agricultural growth
Efficient use of labour
C
Environmental
Biodiversity
Natural resources
Carrying capacity
Ecosystem integrity
Clean air and water

Figure 7.1 The three dimensions of the Sustainable Development argument; where: A. is about Equity; B. is about Loading; and C. is about Viability.

Alternatively, Speth and Haas (2006) identified ten major environmental challenges which they maintained are the end result of human impact, and used the customary equation:

$$I = P \times A \times T \quad (1)$$

Where: I = Environmental impact, P = Population, A = Affluence, T = Technology (Holdren & Ehrlich, 1974).

to analyse their root causes. There is no doubt that the main contributor to impact is ***Population***, but the equation has the benefit of demonstrating the role that *affluence* plays, as well as emphasising the importance of *technology* in offering hope for reducing environmental damage. But the equation may be criticised for not providing for other drivers of environmental changes such as policy, institutions and the complexity of social factors (Turner, 1996). Indeed it may be too simplistic, may treat the variables as being independent of each other, and not allow for non-linearities, thresholds and feedbacks in environmental systems (Royal Society, 2012).

Nevertheless, the importance of population increase to the sustainability of human well-being has long been recognised. Indeed, since Malthus, others have drawn attention to the potentially negative results of continued population growth (for example Coale & Hoover 1958; Ehrlich 1968, 2008; Turner 2009) while some have maintained that technological advance and institutional development could equally well counter the impact of rapid population growth on sustainability (Kuznets, 1967; Boserup, 1981; Simon, 1981). Furthermore, the relationship between consumption and population is not straightforward. Every person must consume a minimum amount to survive. Therefore, each additional person will necessarily result in an increase in total consumption. If individual consumption is constant, each person added to the population would increase total consumption by the same amount; but consumption is not constant, neither over time nor between richer and poorer elements of a population (Royal Society, 2012).

So it would seem that some form of limitation of population growth is urgently required, but the population problem is not amenable to a technical solution (Hardin, 1968). Indeed, King and Elliot (1997, p.1441) have characterised our continuing plight as the '*Hardinian taboo*' whereby we refuse to consider or discuss population control thereby preventing ourselves from having to deal with the problem adequately (Butler, 2004). Which, we should note, is a classic sign of the probable presence of a double bind (Kowalski, 2004).

The role of ***Affluence*** is also ambivalent. The liberal answer to poverty was growth which would provide the resources to raise incomes yet, paradoxically, growth is responsible for the voracious use of natural resources and the spoliation of the environment (Bell, 1970). Besides, growth frequently becomes a substitute for equality of income and as long as there is growth there is hope, which makes large differences of income tolerable (Wallich, 1972). Furthermore, higher income inevitably leads to higher consumption, so the factors that drive income may also drive consumption (Royal Society, 2012) and indeed higher income seems not to lead to satiation but, according to the Easterlin paradox, any increase in output makes for an escalation in aspiration and thus the expected positive impact on welfare is undermined (Easterlin, 1974). Indeed, it may be argued that the thing which the individual really wants is not the satisfaction of the wants they had but more and better wants (Stigler, 1987). To be sure, the affluence that we see all around us, and which the advertising industry constantly beams into our homes, is a spur to our own increasing aspirations, acquisitions and attainments. Thus, the absolute and relative poverty of nations generates an irresistible push for growth at all costs, including environmental ones (Speth & Haas, 2006).

Thus we arrive at the final term – ***Technology*** – which is likewise deeply ambivalent. There is no doubt that technology has fuelled development, providing for population growth, increasing longevity and a richer life style in respect of comfort, variety, education, travel and leisure activities. Nevertheless it is this same technological progress that has enabled humanity to damage so many of the world's life support systems, on the one hand, and to begin to provide solutions to these problems on the other. For example, our use of many metals has become more efficient, the costs of resource extraction has fallen by enlarge, and the energy needed to generate electricity has declined (Buckminster Fuller, 1981; O'Connor, 1998). However, in this latter respect we should be aware of another paradox whereby increased energy efficiency actually results in increased energy demand (Polimeni & Polimeni, 2006) where improvements in efficiency lead not to savings, but to the expansion of consumption to take up the '*slack*', which is referred to as Jevons' paradox. Indeed, advances in technology simply increase our ability to do things (Diamond, 2006) requiring more technology to ameliorate the impact, which results in a perpetual technology chase– a manifestation of the Achilles and the tortoise paradox! (Kowalski, 2012a).

As Kowalski (2012b) argued, modernism is fundamentally about *technē* – technology, to such an extent that our culture can be characterised as technocentric. This view point influences our attitude to sustainable development since it is easy to procrastinate over tackling any problem as technocentrism maintains that no unsustainability has become sufficiently serious to require an immediate remedy as there almost certainly is a marvellous innovation waiting in the wings that will provide a cheap solution overnight (Douthwaite, 1999). Indeed, the dominant environmental policy option by default is '*technofix*' largely because it appeals to the uncontested values of the dominant sustainability narratives (Meppen & Bourke, 1999), notwithstanding the fact that the dominant scientific/economic discourse has played a full part in generating the environmental problems we face. Therefore, to rely on these same ways of thinking to define and initiate sustainable practices may be an '*unsustainable*' practice in its own right. Which reasserts the notion that the sustainable development problem is not one that can be solved by technology alone, but will require changes in social organization beyond the current scope of market capitalism. Furthermore, the market fails to guide technology towards good environmental choices and governments have done little to correct poor market signals. Characteristically, once a technology has gained a certain level of deployment, it attains a resilience of its own against alternative products (Speth & Haas, 2006). Nevertheless, sustainable development, under the umbrella of technological innovation, holds sway as the key to business as usual, as most developed states continue to prioritize entrepreneurialism and a largely neoliberal agenda over concern for sustainability (Gibbs & Krueger, 2007). Indeed, this continuation of flawed thinking is exemplified by a statement from the World Bank (1989, p. 44) that: "*to ensure sustainable growth, the future strategy will need to emphasize both sound environmental management and human resource development. … … Properly managed, renewable natural resources can last forever.*" which places faith in management and doesn't speak about non-renewables at all.

Ouroboros, a snake devouring its own tail, is a symbol that signifies death and rebirth; the annual cycle; and the importance of self-sufficiency. Indeed in this latter regard it emphasises that in a closed system indefinite material growth is impossible. Now, although we are not in a completely closed system in that the entropy of the sun constantly emits energy that life on earth, through processes of syntropy, captures and uses to support increases of all kinds (See Buckminster Fuller 1981, p.276), the system is nevertheless subject to the limiting factors of non-renewable components of growth (tap and sink - otherwise known as the commons). Technological innovations may enable us to harvest a greater proportion of the sun's energy and to use non-renewables more efficiently, but the continuing demand for finite resources for growth and to meet the requirements of such technological innovations must eventually impose a limit. There is no way to satisfy economic equations that simply have no solutions, because they are not founded in planetary homeostasis. Indubitably, the universal spread of Western-style consumption is impossible, because the Earth's resources are finite. (Beer, 2004b).

Ultimately conservation is not a technical question of how to achieve our self-interest with the lowest environmental impacts but is rather about morality – what should we want – with minor technical details (Orr, 2004).

3 A Response

To present the solution to the problem of our relationship with our environment as '*sustainable development*', and to argue that that is simply a matter of improving our ability to manage resources more efficiently and effectively is, at the very least, disingenuous. As a solution '*sustainability*' merely suspends the crisis and defers the real terms of conflict between the environment and economic development for another day (Meppen & Bourke, 1999). Inescapably, once one accepts that resources are limited, one has to have a means of sharing the right to use those resources not only among the present population but also with future generations, who can make no claim to use them through today's free-market mechanisms (Douthwaite, 1999). Thus sustainability must entail foregoing something today so that it may be enjoyed in the future. Regrettably, although most people agree that the situation is serious, few seem willing to forego anything in order to solve this problem (Orr, 2004), thereby raising the necessity of establishing who is going to bear the brunt of the abstinence, which currently in so many ways and largely by default are the poor. Indeed, the link to social justice goes deeper, for our relationship with nature is bad because our relationships with each other are already bad (Lipietz, 1995; Benedict XVI, 2009). Such a situation has been presented as the manifestation of what has been labelled a '*culture of 'no-where-near-enough-life-support*'' (Buckminster Fuller, 1981), a '*culture of empire*' (Korten, 2006), and a '*poverty of culture*' (Mohan, 2011), which is the unpromising framework within which we must struggle to establish a resolution.

The theme that, for me, emerges most strongly from consideration of these paradoxes of sustainability is that of the part-to-whole relationship. It is Zeno's arrow once more where we are misled into thinking the individual is separate from society, and society from environment. We are lured into noun (and pronoun) thinking instead of thinking about relationships and verbs (Kowalski 2012a). The proposed hierarchy is individual: society: ecology such that individual autonomy is tempered by the needs of society, and the autonomy of society (including global society) must be tempered by the needs of the world ecological system – if we are to have viable systems (Beer, 1994). Hence the enduring logic of Orr's (2004, p.9) statement that: "*It makes far better sense to reshape ourselves to fit a finite planet than to attempt to reshape the planet to fit our infinite wants*", as opposed to the hubris of modernity that accepts no limits, that is always beyond – beyond morality, beyond tragedy, beyond culture (Bell, 1970).

The importance of this hierarchical linkage is reflected in the concept of the metasystem, of something that is greater or beyond the parochial human condition. When Edward De Bono suggests that without the metasystem a person would act according to their own personal systems, which might be founded on impulse, self-indulgence or immediate gratification, whereas the metasystem lies outside the individual and overrides these considerations in favour of society and a longer time base (Yolles, 2004). Furthermore, De Bono (1990) himself had commented that it is this metasystem which tells them that such behaviour will not be in their best interests in the long term nor in the best interests of society as a whole. Indeed it is the obstinate insistence on the importance of the self/other boundary that should be seen as a principle characteristic of western culture (Holdstock, 1993). Thus we must question the extent to which the problems of development and sustainability are products of the masculine, materialistic, individualistic western culture (Korten, 2006) that has spawned capitalism and from which the majority of development interventions are initiated.

Consequently, it seems, Western '*experts*' come to lead the development enterprise because they have those characteristics and because the society from which they come is epitomized as '*developed*'. Special privilege has been given in development discourse to projects and the professionals that lead them, which seem so essential for successful implementation locally of the global task of development that they are the most commonly invoked conditions placed on '*aiding*' development (Porter, 1995). Nevertheless this should not be taken as evidence that Western development professionals know how to achieve that condition since there is no evidence that the so-called development of the West has in any way been facilitated by the employment of either (Easterly, 2006; Reinert, 2012).

Indeed, in contrast, the benevolence at the centre of the development delusion is not only a false benevolence but it is deeply damaging, and reflects the poverty of culture that is a manifestation of sub-clinical paranoia (Kowalski, 2011), which suggests that the state of the world calls contemporary society to seriously review a way of life that is prone to hedonism and consumerism, regardless of their detrimental consequences (Benedict XVI, 2009).

But who is to facilitate the way forward? Historically, successful autocrats have recognized almost by instinct that their power depends on their creation of a culture that evokes fear, alienation, and learned helplessness, that compels the individual to rely on the autocrat's protection (Korten, 2006) which echoed the sentiment that for the money-makers and their economists there is a game of making money with money by exploiting the general world's assumptions that there is a fundamental inadequacy of human life support (Buckminster Fuller, 1981). Furthermore, the difficulty is heighten by the observation that, by enlarge, it is the most unscrupulous who are motivated to obtain absolute power (Korten, 2006) and corruption and illegality are evident in the conduct of the economic and political class in developed countries, as well as in poor ones (Benedict XVI, 2009).

4 Prospects

So we need to take stock of our current prospects for overcoming the environmental challenges that we have reviewed. In this regard Diamond (2006, p.421) considered those opportunities that societies miss for getting a grip on environmental degradation, and listed a sequence of four: One, failure to anticipate a problem before the problem actually arrives; Two, failure to perceive the problem when it does arrive; Three, failure even to try to address it; Four, they may not succeed in solving it.

But we note on the one hand, as Kovel (2002, p.21) lamented, that: "*humanity is not just the perpetrator of the crisis: it is its victim as well. And among the signs of our victimization is the incapacity to contend with the crisis or even to become conscious of it.*" Then, on the other, the MEA (2005, p.5) has commented that: "*In the streets of a crowded city, in the aisles of a giant supermarket, or on the floor of a gleaming electronics factory, the biological state of Earth's rivers, forests, and mountains may seem a remote concern.*" and then, for example, Žižek (2002, p.35) has confessed that: "*I know very well (that things are deadly serious, that what is at stake is our very survival), but just the same I don't really believe, ... and that is why I continue to act as if ecology is of no lasting consequence for my everyday life*".

As if these signs were not discouraging enough it seems that we also sabotage our responses and are immobilized by deliberation (Keil, 2007). Vested interests seek to delay initiation of those measures that might rescue us by maintaining that there is no crisis or if there is then it is not the product of human activity, when prudence (*phronesis*) would suggest at the very least universally adopting and applying the '*Precautionary Principle*' of 1) preventative anticipation; 2) proportionality of response; and 3) relocating the '*Burden of Proof*' (Speth & Haas, 2006), recognising that leaving a large margin for error is smart over the long haul (Orr, 2004).

Furthermore, we have a tendency to deal with issues in a piecemeal fashion, and myriads of policy measures are employed while the gulf between reality and our objectives widens (Mohan, 2011). Similarly the approach to environmental protection has also failed to take a holistic and systemic approach. Even when targets are agreed they are seldom attained. We lack the drive to see our resolutions carried through – like St. Augustine's '*Give me chastity and continence, but not yet.*' we procrastinate.

This is a result of a paradox of leadership, where individuals must provide impetus to collective actions for the maintenance and enhancement of the metasystems (society and environment), but note not for the direct or exclusive benefit of the individuals who lead, as Beer (1994, p112) maintained: "*the raison d'être of the metasystem is given in logic; it is not necessarily anything to do with hierarchy of status*". Thus in an authentic democracy there can be no self-promoting leaders since all would be equal and, in any pragmatic facsimile we might construct, the leaders would take a facilitative rather than a directive approach, serving what is seeking to emerge (Senge, *et al.*, 2005). Please note also that in the old leadership paradigm there was always a tension between being in the vanguard and being in touch with and responsive to the mood of the troops (Sigelman, Sigelman, & Walkosz, 1992).

The Royal Society in its report has recommended that:

> *Regulation of the many commons that concern all humanity must be achieved by high level negotiations that do not fall back exclusively on appeals to "my nation's interests". Beyond the very short term, the real interests of nations lie in solving global problems in an equitable fashion, not just in each struggling to stay ahead. Implementation requires farsighted leaders who are able to convince voters at home that the conclusions are necessary and just and serve their long-term interests.* (Royal Society, 2012, p.105)

Indeed, if we reflect on the lack of impact of the World Summit for Sustainable Development in Johannesburg, it seems that leadership the world over has failed to rise to the challenge of sustainability, despite the fact that most of the leaders who attended have a higher education degree from the world's most prestigious universities (Martin & Jucker, 2005). So, we must ask why is it that the people who contribute most to exploiting poor communities and the Earth's ecosystems are holders of BAs, MScs and PhDs? (Orr, 2004) Why is the seeming ignorance of our politicians of how the world works as a living system so widespread? Why is it that our leaders so rarely demonstrate respect for the biosphere, wisdom and precaution, or the capacity to challenge unethical actions? And on a par with those concerns, what hope is there for the emergence of such leadership? (Martin & Jucker, *op.cit.*, p.21)

Therefore, we must advocate that curricula that are attuned to sustainability issues, particularly ethics and systems thinking, are at the very heart of our education systems. But more than this, our educational institutions must demonstrate congruence with the values that sustainability requires. In this way they can help to create societies and workforces more sensitive to sustainability agendas, and to produce political and business leaders with earth-literacy appropriate to the challenges of the twenty-first century (Martin & Jucker, *op.cit.*). However, we need to go much further in order to protect nature. It is not enough to provide economic incentives or deterrents, nor to generate an appropriate education. These are important steps, but the decisive issue is the overall moral tenor of society. (Benedict XVI, 2009).

Indeed, we must remember that the crisis we face is principally one of mind, perception, and values (Orr, 2004) and Lipietz (1995) has identified four cornerstones of such a value set as:-

- ***Solidarity*** : which is not just '*equality of opportunity*', but rather a matter of each person being given opportunities at all times. Benedict XVI (2009, section 20) identified this as '*Authentic fraternity*'. It is through altruism that we manifestly integrate the self/other paradox.

- ***Autonomy:*** where in every situation there is the possibility of being in control of the consequences of one's activities. True autonomy means the part having limited discretion over its actions short of jeopardising the integrity of the whole. This is a non-emotive definition of freedom (Beer, 2004a).

- **Ecological responsibility***:* which involves sometimes limiting one's own needs, and always choosing the means to fulfil them which allows for the interests of the biosphere and the rights of future generations. In our use of the environment, Benedict XVI (2009) argues that we have a responsibility towards the poor, towards future generations and towards humanity as a whole.

- **Democracy**: systematically taking into account the opinions and aspirations of everyone on the range of problems concerning their existence, and vigorously searching for a peaceful and creative solution to contradictions which thus emerge between different priorities. Indeed, identity and inclusion can be achieved with greater levels of influence through the processes of democracy (equity), devolution (subsidiarity) and participation (praxis). It is not individuals or genes that survive, but systems of interacting individuals and resources, which for our current purposes means social systems and culture. If we do not find room for other peoples, other cultures and interests other than our own, then we place our collective survival at the gravest risk (Kowalski, 2005). Indeed, we need new initiatives that embody principles learned from other cultures, from other philosophies, and from other methodologies (Beer, 2004b). We need a kind of thinking that supports full emancipation operating within social systems that are accountable to all their stakeholders as well as for their ecosystems. Not to achieve a fair balance between individual and collective interests is a recipe for instability and major breakdowns (Espejo, 2004).

5 Concluding Remarks

Finally, we can return to the part-to-whole relationship for consideration of what Stafford Beer referred to as the problem of '*decidability*', which is captured in the hierarchical relationship between the values and the structure of one level being set by the logically higher system, such that one cannot discuss the nature of a system in its own language, but only in a higher order language (Beer, 1994). For all intents and purposes, and contrary to expectations, that higher language in the matter of society and environment is not science but ethics. Indeed it seems clear that we need to focus our effort on the constitution of societies and organisations that recognise the difference between individuals and citizens (Espejo, 2004), fostering those sentiments that balance individualism with social cohesion and environmental responsibility.

The ultimate challenge is a shift of mind-set that helps us to see that paradox is a symptom of our lack of understanding – of our current misinterpretation, that what is required is not to abandon *technē* but to put greater emphasis upon *phronesis* and to recognise that we must find an authentic approach to democracy as the most promising way to provide a future for humanity. Ego driven self-interest based upon sub-clinical paranoia is not sustainable and we must develop alternatives to it.

Chapter 8

Paradoxes in Economic Approaches to Development

1 Introduction

We have seen that the undertaking that is international development falters in the face of paradoxes associated with social engineering, on the one hand, and environmental sustainability on the other. But there is a third aspect in which we are seeking to change the human condition by changing human behaviour, namely the economic dimension, which we must also consider, albeit to a limited extent given what is after all an extensive literature. However, even a cursory glance at what is available suggests that there are both a number of significant, fundamental, systemic issues as well as some emergent concerns limited to the processes of development itself.

In the former category, and very much contrary to our expectations, we find that both capitalism itself and the substance that is inextricably affiliated with economics, that is money, turn out to be far from reliable as regards definition and logical consistency. In the latter category, we find misgivings about such things as cultural alignment, debt, micro-credit, targeting and indices of progress, consideration of which will form the content of chapter 9.

2 The Capitalist Dilemma

When in 1949 President Truman adopted the term *development* (Esteva, 1992) it was very much to the economic dimension of development that he was referring. More recently, with the ascendancy of neoliberal thinking and policies[1], this has taken the form of proselytizing and expanding free-market capitalism, under the slogan that '*a rising tide will lift all boats*' (Harvey, 2011). However, as Harvey (*op.cit.*, p.120) maintained: "*The saga of capitalism is full of paradoxes, even as most forms of social theory – economic theory in particular – abstract entirely from considerations of them.*"

In this regard there are a number of such paradoxes that we should reflect on as we seek to tackle the issues of poverty and marginalization from an economic perspective, always bearing in mind Brij Mohan's contention that poverty is more a political, than an economic, phenomenon (Gil, 2011). Following the observation that development thinkers had not given sufficient attention to Marcel Mauss' *The Gift* (Kowalski, 2011a), it seems that some of the most fundamental issues at the heart of capitalism are also absent from general macro-economics' curricula. As Shutt (1999, p.198) recognised: "*Amid so many signs that the existing world … order is becoming unsustainable, it is remarkable that there is so little overt questioning of its ideological basis.*" and still departments of economics in universities around the world continue to give precedence to neoclassical theory (Söderbaum, 2012).

However, a very brief review of some of capitalism's basic assumptions suggests that the system that has prevailed in the

1 Rodrik (2011, p.77) speaks of: "*Free market economics* [being] *in the ascendancy, producing what has been variously called the Washington Consensus, market fundamentalism, or neoliberalism.*"

West for scarcely 200 years is actually a glorified Ponzi scheme that operates to the benefit of very few individuals rather than the mass of the people who, as in the children's game, from time to time find that they are lacking a chair when the music stops. Indeed, John Maynard Keynes had recognised that if there is one unmistakable characteristic of capitalism it is the tendency to produce stagnation and depressions hand-in-hand with financial collapses (Minsky, 2008, p.11). In capitalism, like the Ponzi scheme, pyramid selling, or the chain letter, there is an initial appeal to greed and the prospect that everyone will do nicely if we all hold our nerve (remember Roosevelt's aphorism that: "*the only thing we have to fear is fear itself*"[2]), followed by blatant coercion to keep it going at all costs (typified by bailing out the banks because they are too big to fail!), and ending in inevitable collapse, with a host of people losing their shirts, many their livelihoods and some of the most vulnerable their lives (Harvey, 2011).

Indeed, the failed promise of free-market capitalism has been captured by Shutt (2005, p.101), when he remarked that in recent times capitalism has proved totally unable to provide economic security to any but a shrinking fraction of the population and Gray (1998, p.105) who maintained that: "*The dogma that free markets are the most effective means of wealth creation touches the world's actually existing capitalisms at virtually no point.*" In particular it is the paradox referred to as Marx' first contradiction of capitalism (O'Connor, 1998) that should be the starting point for a critical assessment of the wisdom of evangelizing the *Washington Consensus* as a means of bringing about development.

3 The First Contradiction of Capitalism

When I was a boy I was struck by a particular passage in *Genesis* 4 v.17 where Cain, the son of the first man, Adam, after being exiled for murdering his brother, took a wife. I just couldn't escape

---

2 Inaugural address, March 1933.

from the question – where did this woman come from? Thus at the heart of some of our most fundamental mythologies can lurk discomforting discrepancies.

So, in similar vein, Karl Marx, in *Das Kapital,* drew attention to a very simple yet far reaching logical inconsistency at the heart of the capitalist system that Flank (2007, p.30) paraphrased as:

Total value (of commodities) = C + V + S … … … … … (1).

Where C = Total costs of production – machinery, premises, depreciation and raw materials (constant capital),
V = Total labour wages and benefits (variable capital), and
S = Total surplus value appropriated by the capitalist (both profit and the capitalists' own 'use-value' necessary to sustain them in their lives).

Or as Polanyi (1998, p.146) maintained: "*This forms the circulation of money. The managers are at its heart: they squirt the money into every particle of the social body in payment of its contribution to production – and they receive it back again from all these quarters in return for the sale of finished products.*"

Now it seems self-evident that the value of commodities is only realised when they are sold, and yet neither the wages of labour nor the use-value of the capitalists, nor indeed a combination of the two are sufficient to cover in full the price required to exchange for the total commodities. As Sklar (1992, p.166) noted: "*production capacity continuously out ran effective market demand*". Or as Harvey (2011, p.107) expressed it: "*the total wage bill is always less than the total capital in circulation, so the purchase of the wage goods that sustain daily life … is never sufficient for the profitable sale of total output.*" So who buys the remainder? Where does the extra demand that is necessary to purchase the surplus product of labour come from? (O'Connor, 1998)

Indeed, David Harvey had asked:

> *where does the purchasing power to buy all these products* [and services] *come from? There must be … an extra amount of money that somebody holds somewhere to facilitate the purchase. If not, there is a lack of effective demand, … . What is called a crisis of 'under-consumption' results when there is not enough effective demand to absorb the commodities produced.* (Harvey 2011, p.107).

When I put this conundrum to my economist colleagues they frequently take recourse to micro-economics – the labourers don't have to buy their own production. As my Grandmother used to say: '*You can't make a living out of taking in your own washing*'! The workers invariably produce commodities which are exchanged for the commodities of other enterprises, through the medium of money, and in this circulation everyone gets satisfied. The labourers are paid, the putative owners of the materials of production (land, mines, water bodies) are paid, the capitalist get their profit, over and above their original stake, for re-investment and the accumulation of assets. Prices are driven down by investment in technology and increases in productivity. And yet the implications of equation (1), like Cain's wife, won't go away[3]. Indeed, I am reminded of an anecdote that captures the gist of the argument: -

> The CEO of a multinational car manufacturer was showing the general secretary of the trade union around a new, fully robotized plant. As they watched the sterile and highly active machines the CEO

3 Even if we take the step to a system where labour hires capital rather than the current situation of capital hiring labour (Ellerman, 2010), the implications of the equation are by no means overcome – although the likelihood is that the surplus that accrues to labour will be used to generate current demand.

> quipped: "*You sure are going to have a hell of a job unionizing this lot.*" The Trade Unionist sighed and retorted: "*Yes, but it pales into insignificance alongside the difficulty you are going to have selling them cars!*" (also reported by Flank, 2007).

Of course the short-term resolution of this paradox of demand, like Gregory Bateson's bell switch (Bateson, 2002), requires the inclusion of time in equation (1). The initial act of production both supplied commodities and created demand for others[4]. Capitalism was able to get started by investing value that had been accumulated under feudalism[5]. It was then able to circumvent the continuing challenge of the 1st contradiction either by geographical expansion into parts of the world that were, as yet, non-capitalist (through imperialism, colonialism and globalization of free trade); and/or by inducing governments to print money (quantitative easing); and then, most recently favoured, by generating current demand through appropriating the future productivity of labour and using anticipated capital gains on assets to collateralise borrowing (debt and the extension of credit – taking the waiting out of wanting). However, none of these actions are solutions to the paradox in the long run. Globalization is bringing about an end to the supply of any substantial, non-capitalist societies; printing money generates inflation; and using credit means plundering today the current demand of some unspecified time in the future leaving an increased deficiency of demand to occur then, and which future time is proving to be sooner rather than later[6].

---

4 A manifestation of Say's Law, see David Ellerman's quotation in chapter 5 section 3C.

5 As Harvey (2011, p.47) noted: "*The original accumulation of capital during medieval times in Europe entailed violence, predation, thievery, fraud and robbery. Through these extra-legal means, pirates, priests and merchants, supplemented by the usurers, assembled enough initial 'money power' to begin to circulate money systematically as capital.*"

6 As Shutt (2005, p.38) observed: "*while consumption may be stimulated beyond the level of disposable income by reducing the cost of credit, this can only be done by 'borrowing consumption from the future'*" and such

Nonetheless, we must also recognise that there is the small matter of the economic system represented by equation (1) not being a closed system in actuality. Indeed, the beneficence of nature[7] means that a certain level of sustenance is provided *gratis*[8]. But that beneficence does not justifiably extend to non-renewable resources of tap and sink (Hardin, 1968). In fact, under equation (1), we are treating as externalities many things that should really be accounted costs of production (constant capital). Thus forests, open water fisheries, soil fertility, biodiversity, ecosystem services that counter anthropogenic impacts, and geological energy reserves are all being despoiled at little present cost to the capitalist. However, it is important to remember that, as Harvey (2011, p.67) maintained: "*Capital has ... to produce the conditions for its own continued expansion in advance of that expansion.*" and that not only does capitalism have problems in delivering the social conditions for productive labour (e.g. by failing to invest in training or infrastructure) it also destroys the natural conditions necessary for production in what O'Connor (1998, p.159) has termed '*The second contradiction of capitalism*' and which occurs as capital brings about the limitation to its own expansion because through its self-centredness it alienates the workforce, degrades their ability to be creative and productive, and destroys the environment (both natural and '*urban*') upon which future productive ability relies. Notwithstanding, the instabilities that have been outlined above are not to be confused with those generated by competition driving profits down, or lack of market intelligence leading to oversupply, and/or the disproportionalities between the sector producing '*wage goods*' and that producing '*means of produc-*

an: "*artificial boost to demand is bound to be matched by a subsequent downturn.*"

7 Karl Marx speaks of: "*Surplus-value appear*[ing] *as a gift of nature*" (Dobb, 1973, p.40).

8 Grieve (2012, p.138) speaks of: "*manna from heaven or flotsam picked up on the beach of a desert island.*"

tion'. Indeed, during the first half of the last century such crises tended to occur just about every ten years or so (Fulcher, 2004), and are often presented as the inevitable manifestation of the '*business cycle*' (Kalecki, 2009). These minor and more localised crises (*sic*) are at a lower logical level than the systemic inconsistencies of the 1st and 2nd contradictions, and in many ways have been seen as actually helpful in keeping the dynamism of capitalism at peak performance (Schumpeter, 2010). By comparison the crises generated at the systemic level are veritable *tsunamis* and, due predominantly to what may be called the capitalist imperative, are of ever increasing potency[9].

4 The Capitalist Imperative

Thus the instability that is the legacy of the '*demand*' problem of the 1st contradiction is further compounded by the constant appropriation of 'surplus' by the capitalists, which Shutt (2005, p. 33) characterized as: "*the contradictory dynamics of what Karl Marx identified as 'capital accumulation*" which is contained in the term '*total surplus value*' from equation (1). This is substantially the Marxist '*exchange-value*', the maximization of which is the *raison d'être* of capitalist production. However, this term in the equation can only expand at the expense of overall demand, and yet the micro-economic imperative is always both to expand profits extracted and to direct those profits to investment opportunities that will yield the greatest profits in the future. Thus there is a conundrum for capital as it seeks to expand production to exploit labour – by extending the working day/week, or by the application of technology, or by driving wages down or any combination thereof – that Harvey (2011, p.45) has dubbed: "*the capital surplus absorption problem*", which can be described as the constant search for profitable new investment outlets which, although successful in the short run, can only tend to make the on-going problem

[9] Hudson (2012) goes to some length to explain the inevitable predation of the production of economies by the logic of the geometrical growth of savings put out to compound interest.

of keeping up the overall level of profit worse, as it inexorably contributes to the accumulation of capital on which further returns must be found. (Shutt, *op.cit.*).

As Lenny Flank explained it, according to Marx' notation, the capitalist imperative is:

$$M \rightarrow C \rightarrow M' \quad \ldots\ldots\ldots\ldots\ldots\ldots \quad (2)$$

"*Where M is the original capital invested in production, C is the exchange-value which is produced, and M' (pronounced "M-prime") is the money resulting from the sale of this exchange-value.*" and most importantly: "*the aim of the capitalist is to increase the value of M' and to make the difference between M and M' as large as possible.* (Flank, 2007, p.25).

Contrary to Friedrich Hayek's assertion that: "*we strive for money, it is because it offers us the widest choice in enjoying the fruits of our efforts.*" (Hayek, 2007, p.125), Joseph Schumpeter had commented that: "*the pedestrian view [is] that it is the accumulation of capital per se that propels the capitalist engine*" (quoted in Reinert, 2012, p.3) and Shimshon Bichler and Jonathan Nitzan have argued that money has transcended its basic exchange function and has become the measure of another commodity, capital that:

> *is not a narrow economic entity, but a symbolic quantification of power. Capital is not absolute, it is relative. It has little to do with utility or abstract labour, and it extends far beyond machines and production lines. Most broadly, it represents the organized power of dominant capital groups to create the order of – or creorder – their society.* (Bichler & Nitzan, 2012b, p.65)

– the appetite for acquisition of which is, for some people, insatiable.[10]

The inescapable truth is that the need constantly to find ways to expand at a compound rate, and which forces capitalism to reinvest in order to survive, is as much a treadmill for the capitalist as the constant exhortation to be more productive is for the worker (Harvey, 2011). Indeed, Shutt (1999, p.73) argued that: "*the refusal to allow the value of assets to fall imposes an intensifying need to make them 'sweat' even in the face of chronic economic stagnation.*"[11] Furthermore, Harvey (2011, p.130) maintained most specifically that: "*the survival of capitalism in the long run depends on the capacity to achieve 3 per cent compound growth.*" Then, that growth of the monopolist's surplus value precipitates a different kind of crisis as the profitable ways to reinvest it become oversubscribed. Thus echoing Harry Shutt's earlier observation that: "*the inevitable consequence of maintaining a high return on the capital stock as a whole is that yet more investible funds will be generated for which outlets must be found.*" (Shutt, 1999, p.111) and of course the longer the game goes on the larger the sums involved become as the historic surpluses of pre-capitalist societies are inexorably garnered into the hands of the capitalists (Bichler & Nitzan, 2012a). But also note that those sums are held in ever fewer fortunes as the most aggressive and successful capitalists gobble up their weakest brethren [12].

---

10 As Chremelos says in Aristophanes' *Plutos* (lines 189-193): "*Give a man a sum of thirteen talents and all the more he hungers for sixteen. Give him sixteen and he must needs have forty, or life's not worth living, so he says.*"

11 Thus Stiglitz (2010, p.349) noted that a significant factor in the 2008 crisis was that: "*many [on Wall Street] said they 'had' to take on more risk to get the earnings that they had previously had.*"

12 It reminds me of nothing so much as the locust swarms that wreak such havoc, each individual locust being propelled by the possibility of being cannibalised by those around it (Hansen, Buhl, Bazazi, Simpson & Sword, 2011).

If the surplus is not reinvested, but simply held until appropriate opportunities arise then the self-referential equation (1) comes back to bite. This is what Keynes called the '*liquidity trap*' – the more people or banks or corporations hang onto money rather than spend it, the more certain that effective demand will collapse and the less reinvestment in production will be profitable (Harvey, 2011)[13], and this will lead to a fall in economic growth which he argued needed to be countered by government spending.

Now, whilst it is true that the surpluses are seldom accumulated as a pile of money, but are exchanged for assets and thereby find their way back into the economy, nevertheless there is a tendency for them to fuel speculative bubbles by inflating asset prices rather than to generate true value in the productive part of the economy (Hudson, 2011). As we have seen historically, investment in trade had to give way to investment in production in order to continue to expand the necessary level of return of surplus until we reached the accumulation of such sums that production itself could not absorb them sufficiently profitably. At this point new financially based outlets had to be invented and vigorously pursued, including sovereign debt, and sub-prime mortgages.

Furthermore, because of the first and second contradictions, the availability of profitable investment opportunities cannot grow at the same pace as capital accumulates. The result of which, as Fulcher (2004, p.p.117) noted, has been that: "*While one response to declining profitability of production was to search for cheaper labour abroad, another was, as* [Giovanni] *Arrighi has argued, to shift capital from investment in production to speculation in shares, currencies, and derivatives.*" which has proved to be nothing less than high risk gambling, and thence the slide into criminal endeavours was almost unavoidable. As Fulcher (*op.cit.*, p.124) observed: "*The true*

13 This is also referred to as the '*Paradox of Thrift*'.

capitalist is motivated by the amoral accumulation of money and this frequently drives particular individuals to bend or break the rules."[14]

The usual outcomes are periodic crises that are the forcible rebalancing of the system. Thus Harvey (2011, p.71) commented that: "*Crises are, as it were, the irrational rationalisers of an always unstable capitalism.*" Importantly, according to the economic law of supply and demand, as capital expands faster than do the opportunities to employ it profitably the cost (value) of the capital should fall. However, as we have seen for other aspects of capitalism above, it is remarkable that economists have given so little attention to the tendency of demand for capital to fall (Shutt, 1999). The end result, as Harvey (*op.cit.*) explained, is that if growth does not resume, then the over-accumulated capital must be devalued or destroyed. He went on to recognise that: "*The irrational way to do this in the past has been through the destruction of the achievements of preceding eras by way of war, the devaluation of assets, the degradation of productive capacity, abandonment and other forms of 'creative destruction*'" (Harvey, *op.cit.*, p.215).

However, as Harvey (*op.cit.*, p.246) also reminded us: "*A crisis, after all, is nothing less than a massive phase of dispossessions of assets.*" and, unfortunately for the labourers and the petit bourgeoisie, the grand capitalist *rentiers* are sure as hell not going to allow themselves to be the ones who get dispossessed![15] They use their wealth and the power it confers to ensure that as far as possible their assets remain intact – after all what would be the point of all their activities in garnering wealth if the result was simply the value of that wealth being adjusted downward? Again, Shutt

---

14 The list of recent transgressors seems long indeed:- Enron, Worldcom, Barings' Nick Leeson, Bernie Madoff and Allen Stanford, and the unfolding Libor scandal, to highlight but a few.

15 As Harvey (2011, p.226) advocated: "*It will in any case require that the capitalists willingly give up some of their individual wealth and power to save capitalism from itself. Historically they have always fiercely resisted doing that.*"

(2001, p.58) noted the ruling élite's determination never to accept that: "*market forces should be allowed to assert themselves in a way that could seriously threaten the élite's own wealth, above all by letting the growing surplus of capital be reflected in its devaluation on financial markets*".

Thus inflation, often caused by printing money, is squeezed out of an economy by exporting it (price of raw materials not keeping pace with price of manufactured goods) or by increasing the cost of borrowing (interest rates).[16] The credit crunch, when it comes, is transferred to the taxpayer via the state as the lender-of-last-resort. Finally the system operates to create reserves of wealth outside the major capitalists' fortunes through a process of embourgeoisement (Gray, 1998), which generates people with domestic property, savings and pension funds that can be mulct at need, since they are ill-prepared and ill-placed to protect its value when the inevitable, next, systemic level, financial crisis hits[17]. Part of this unpreparedness is the taking at face value of the substance through which market exchanges of value are mediated, as it were.

5 Money

As has been argued in earlier chapters, the endeavour that is development is inextricably linked with the project of modernization. One aspect of which is the promotion of the market approach to exchanges, which are themselves characterised by the search for equivalence in the value exchanged; the required immediacy of the reciprocation; and the freedom to be quit of the interaction once the exchange has occurred (Flank, 2007). Now,

---

16 Note that when interest rates are high those who borrow (usually those who don't have money) have to pay more and those who lend (by definition those who have money) receive more – see *Luke* 19, v. 26.

17 As Ferguson (2008, p.122) observed: "*Time and again, this* [crash] *process has been accompanied by skulduggery, as unscrupulous insiders have sought to profit at the expense of naïve neophytes.*"

Bauer (1991, p.3) argued that: "*The activities of traders set in motion and maintain the process by which participation in the exchange economy replaces subsistence production.*" Moreover, the subsequent and inevitable replacement of barter with an intermediary object is often presented as the origin of money. Indeed, Minsky (2008, p.8) noted that: "*Money is introduced in the standard theory as an efficient device for eliminating the need for a double coincidence of wants to exist in order for trade to take place.*" Whereas Polanyi (1998, p.140) maintained that: "*money [functions] as a medium of expression for subjective, delicate and complex desires,*" emphasising its role in communication at a systemic level.

This process of monetization has itself been driven in part by the process of urbanization. Indeed, money is substantially an urban phenomenon because its substitution in exchange is indispensable in centres of population where the sheer number of encounters precludes finding a precise match of exchange needs, as Simmel (1997, p.176) recognised: "*The metropolis has always been the seat of the money economy. Here the multiplicity and concentration of economic exchange gives an importance to the means of exchange which the scantiness of rural commerce would not have allowed.*" To which we can add that throughout the European empires in the South, the expansion of the money economy has been promoted originally as a colonial mechanism for control of rural productivity through authorities demanding that taxes be paid in money rather than in kind (Galbraith, 1979). Thus money and development would appear to have been inextricably, almost systemically, linked from earliest times, for the purpose of creating stable and productive circumstances for the extraction of value.

As a consequence we can hardly proceed in our pursuit of understanding without trying to secure an appreciation of this phenomenon called money if we are to have any sort of grasp of its impact upon the processes of human development. However, as we shall see, to answer what is money? is no straightforward undertaking, nor one that can be addressed fully in the limited space herein available[18]. So once more I must seek your indulgence as I make an idiosyncratic appraisal of money theory as it relates to the processes of development.

For a long time, and for most purposes, money was seen simply as that intermediate component in trade outlined above. Indeed, according to Anderson (2009 p.9), in Jean-Baptiste Say's view, money: "*served primarily as a medium of exchange, and was not identified as a store of wealth. Like Adam Smith, Say believed that money was not wealth, but rather a means to allow wealth (goods) to be exchanged in the marketplace*". Furthermore, the earliest form that money took was quite commonly gold or silver. In this regard Niall Ferguson maintained that:

> *Money, it is conventional to argue, is a medium of exchange, which has the advantage of eliminating inefficiencies of barter; a unit of account, which facilitates valuation and calculation; and a store of value, which allows economic transactions to be conducted over long periods as well as geographical distances.*[19] [Therefore], *money has to be available, affordable, durable, fungible, portable and reliable. Because they fulfil most of these criteria, metals such as gold, silver and bronze were for millennia regarded as the ideal monetary raw material.* (Ferguson, 2008, pp.24-25)

Moreover, Adam Smith had long since observed that:

> *men seem at last to have been determined by irresistible reasons to give the preference, for this employment [as*

---

18 As Ingham (2004, pp.4-5) lamented: "*Perhaps the greatest paradox is that such a commonplace as money should give rise to so much bewilderment, controversy and, it must be said, error. It is not well understood.*"

19 Which is to imply that these functions are not mutually incompatible, an assumption that has to be questioned.

> *specie], to metals above every other commodity. Metals can not only be kept with little loss, be divided into any number of parts, as by fusion those parts can easily be reunited again; a quality which no other equally durable commodities possess, and which more than any other quality renders them fit to be the instrument of commerce and circulation.* (Smith, 1999a, p.127)

This is often referred to as the '*metalist theory*' of the origin of money and, although it seems that metal was at first just used on its own (e.g. hack-silver), it was not long before coins were minted in a way that guaranteed the weight of the metal without recourse to scales. Then, because of debasement, the new form of fiat money emerged, as Mellor (2010, p.80) observed: "*Given the varying amount of precious metal in coins, the only guarantee of the worth of the coin came from the authority behind the minting.*", which fiat was made possible by the acceptance of the coins for payment of tax. Finally, it was a small step from fiat money as coins to paper money supported by gold deposits and the authority of the state[20].

The next innovation, the separation of the bullion held from the money issued, seems inevitable. As Searle (1995, p.43) noted: "*A stroke of genius occurred when somebody figured out that we can increase the supply of money simply by issuing more certificates than we have gold. As long as the certificates … have a collectively imposed function that continues to be collectively accepted, the certificates are, as they say, good as gold.*" In this way the medieval shortages of precious metals, which had held back economic expansion in Europe, were overcome by printing money and extending credit.

20 For example, British bank notes exhibit the phrase: '**I promise to pay the bearer on demand the sum of …**' and it is signed, not by the Monarch, nor by the Chancellor of the Exchequer (the government) but by the Chief Cashier '**for the Governor and Company of the Bank of England**'.

However, clearly there is more to money than just being a means of exchange (Dichter (2007a). Indeed, we have come to invest more meaning in money than its superficial functionality would warrant.[21] Moreover, Searle (1995, p.47) recognised that: "[People] *need not think, 'We are collectively imposing a value on something that we do not regard as valuable because of its purely physical features,' even though that is exactly what they are doing.*" and tellingly Ferguson (2008, p.31) averred that: "*money is not metal. It is trust inscribed*". For us money has pretty well become a medium in which we live, like water is for fish, and as such we seldom give it the consideration that it deserves. Nevertheless it is astonishing to encounter the contention as expressed by Ingham (2004, p.8) that: "*mainstream economics cannot provide a satisfactory explanation of money's existence and functions; that is to say, orthodox economics has failed to* ***specify*** *the nature of money*"!

Therefore, let us look once more at Marx' notation:

$$M \rightarrow C \rightarrow M' \ldots\ldots\ldots\ldots\ldots\ldots (2)$$

It seems self-evident that the difference between M′ and M is reflected in the added value that labour brings to commodities and services (C), so that the increase in money (M to M′) really is an expression of its labour, or human time content. This led Smith (1999a, p.133) to maintain that: "*The value of any commodity … to the person who possesses it, and who means … to exchange it for other commodities, is equal to the quantity of labour which it enables him to … command. Labour, therefore, is the real measure of the exchangeable value of all commodities.*" and for Flank (2007) to argue that all commodities take their value from the labour that produces them and, therefore, can be viewed as '*solidified labor*'. Furthermore, as Harvey (2011, p.114) observed: "*The underlying problem lies in the contradictions of the money form itself, most easily*

21 Following Postman & Weingartner's observation quoted in chapter 2, section 4.

understood when the monetary system has a clear metallic base. … gold, then represents the value of all forms of social labour, the particular (concrete and tangible) represents the universal (abstract), and private persons can command unlimited social power."

Thus in a very fundamental way money may be considered to represent work, both work already performed and thc promise of work stored for future release[22]. It is noteworthy that Ingham (2004, p.12) has argued that: "*Regardless of any **form** it might take, money is essentially a provisional 'promise' to pay, … Money is a social credit and debt denominated in a money of account.*" thus also emphasising the two-way facing nature of the claim therein represented and which leads to the importance of double entry book keeping since no amount of money can be said to exist without the simultaneous existence of a debt that only it can discharge.

Importantly, Say (1971, p.72) recognised that: "[The merchant, the manufacturer, the cultivator] *all studiously avoid burthening themselves with more money than is sufficient for current use.*" and (*op.cit.*, p.110) furthermore that: "*No act of saving subtracts in the least from consumption, provided the thing saved be re-invested or restored to productive employment.*" So that, as Say (*op.cit.*, pp.71-72) maintained: "*Money distributed through the whole mechanism of human industry, like the oil that greases the wheels of complex machinery, gives the requisite ease and facility to its movements. But gold and silver are not productive unless employed by industry: they are like the oil in a machine remaining in a state of inaction.*" But, like the oil sump in a machine, it may be argued that such pools of temporarily, motionless money (savings) are both necessary and unavoidable. In contradiction of Say's admonition, Harvey (2011, p.111) suggested that: "*there is no compelling rule that says*

22 I wonder if we would so willingly take on debt if we had to issue a promissory note to the effect: "*I promise to provide the bearer with x hours of my labour*" – perhaps we would quickly recognise debt peonage for what it is.

that the conversion of commodities into money must immediately be followed by the conversion of money back into commodities." Indeed, the savings that accrue from production may take many forms, for example compulsory subtractions from wages as pension contributions (e.g. FICA[23]); surplus wages remaining after labour's use-value has been covered; as well as the capitalist's profit. The question then remains, are there sufficient opportunities for investing this money in further productive work that will expand the delivery of fresh goods and services?

6 Finance

This leads us to the traditional view of the role of banking. People bring their savings for which they currently can find no suitable outlet and deposit them in a bank and on which they subsequently receive interest payments. The banker puts such smaller sums together as necessary and finds investment opportunities where entrepreneurs are constrained by lack of capital and lends them the money at a rate of interest greater than that remitted to the savers. The entrepreneur uses the capital to expand production which generates a sufficient profit to service the loan as well as to pay it back when its term is up (amortization). The banker makes an income from the difference in the interest rates (arbitrage) which is an appropriate recompense for their time, expertise and risk. The only requirement is that the bank retains sufficient money (often as bullion) in its vault to meet any reasonable requirement of depositors for access to their liquidity[24].

Simultaneously, the belief prevails that money can only be minted by a central bank backed by a store of gold or foreign exchange. Indeed, Häring (2013, p.4) noted that the public has:

---

23 Under the US Federal Insurance Contributions Act (FICA) a % of earned income up to an annual limit must be paid into Social Security, and an additional, smaller % must be paid into Medicare.

24 More recently this has been manifested as the regulatory requirement to hold funds on deposit with the Central Bank.

"*the impression that only the Government via a government owned and controlled central bank issues money, and only for the benefit of the government.*" However, the shifting form that money has taken means that virtually anybody can create money out of nothing as long as that money will eventually receive the acceptance and backing of the state and its taxpayers as lender-of-last-resort (Mellor, 2010). Furthermore, Galbraith (1976, p.24) declared that: "*the process by which banks create money is so simple that the mind is repelled. Where something so important is involved, a deeper mystery seems only decent.*" This brings us to the idea that the notation (2) applied to money as itself a commodity has been shortened to become:

$$M \rightarrow M' \ldots\ldots\ldots\ldots\ldots\ldots\ldots\ldots (3)$$ [25]

which is tantamount to saying that something can come from nothing, as there is no longer a step that adds value, and thereby emphasising the metamorphosis, ecdysis and severance of finance money from industrial money[26]. To which separation may be added the observation that experience suggests that much less money can be made from producing new goods and service than through speculating on rising prices of items already produced (Reinert, 2013, p.63), which has led the capitalist imperative to opt for asset price inflation, particularly of real estate, and the associated capital gains as the most profitable outlet for the

25 But note that Rossi (2007, p.13) held that money couldn't itself be a commodity because: "*infinite recursivity makes this measurement* [the value of money] *logically impossible.*" and Adam Smith (1999a, p.136) had stated: "*But as a measure of quantity, such as the natural foot, fathom, or handful, which is continually varying in its own quantity, can never be an accurate measure of the quantity of other things; so a commodity* [money] *which is itself continually varying, can never be an accurate measure of the value of other commodities.*"

26 Furthermore, we must note with Reinert (2013, p.68) that: "*Understanding financial crises requires a terminology that distinguishes the financial economy from the real economy.*" which recalls the idea of a meta-language – and once again that language would seem to be ethics.

investment of surplus rather than production (Hudson, 2011), which is in effect a Ponzi scheme[27]. However, economists have traditionally not made this important distinction, as Erik Reinert observed:

> *Ricardo's economic system failed to distinguish between the monetary (financial) sphere of the economy and the real economy of goods and services ...* [failing to] *distinguish between making money in a way that increases the size of the economic pie (**good greed**) and making money in a way that reduces the size of the economic pie (**bad greed**).* (Reinert, 2013, p.59)

This distortion of the relationship between what counts for money and its underpinning by economic production is exemplified by the observation that: "*M3, the preferred definition of money of the European Central bank is 11 times larger than the sum of currency in circulation and reserves of commercial banks at the central bank, i.e. base money.*" (Häring, 2013, p.8). Indeed, there is no longer any necessary link between deposits into banks and their extending of credit. Again, Häring (*op.cit.*, p.11) noted that: "*A banking system that creates deposits in the process of lending does not have to wait for deposits to come in, in order to intermediate them.*" No indeed, it just issues money out of thin air (nothingness) and immediately begins to collect interest on it (literally money for nothing), in the happy expectation that the state will underwrite any liabilities thereby created. Moreover, most money no longer takes physical form, but is simply a magnetic trace on a computer server. It no longer matters what the form is as long as it can function as money (Searle, 1995). So that now we have a situation where money can move at the speed of light, leading Hudson (2011) to observe that finance capital is more transitory than land and capital tied up in plant, and is certainly more mobile than labour. Paradoxically,

---

[27] Effectively a Ponzi scheme is an attempt by large numbers of people to get rich by taking on debt on a large scale, a paradoxical position with remarkably serious consequences.

it may be noted that governments can only hope to keep capital investments in place by convincing capitalists that they are free to withdraw it whenever they like (Bauman, 2000) and they are forced to do this by inappropriately placing finance and its needs at the pinnacle of policy (Hudson, 2011).

7 Functionality

Furthermore, much of current economic theory, and in particular micro-economics, seeks to draw our attention away from more fundamental issues. As Michael Hudson observed:

> *Wolfgang Drechsler has quipped, mathematics has helped enthrone irrelevance as methodology. The key aspect of the mathematization of economics has been its logical necessity of stripping away what the new economic orthodoxy sought to exclude from the classical curriculum: the socially sensitive study of wealth, how it is acquired, and how its distribution (indeed, its polarization) affects social development.* (Hudson, 2010, p.5).

Nevertheless, what seems clear to me is that the concept of the market and its fundamental exchange of objects of value (commodities, raw materials and money), despite the perception that trade involves a precise-to-the-cent price to which both parties agree (Sedlacek, 2011), is not, nor indeed never can have been, an exchange of equal or even equivalent value. As Beckert (2011, p.46) noted: "*If markets were perfect, marginal utility would equal marginal costs and the incentive to produce for the market would vanish.*" Trade would not have developed if, for example, the fur pelts that the North American natives gave to Europeans for their iron tools could only be re-exchanged for those same axe heads and knives on return to the Eastern trading posts. Indeed, nobody I know goes to the market with a view to obtaining an equivalence[28]. On the contrary everyone is looking for a bargain. The only thing that makes the market work is **a perception** by both sides in the exchange that either **they** have obtained more value than they have provided or else that circumstances have coerced them into an exchange that, whilst not of clear advantage to them, nevertheless has enabled them to obtain what they need, with the promise that next time the boot may be on the other foot.

When this market exchange is applied to the employment process it leads to the enduring class struggle that, at the very least, fosters the widely touted attitude that '*they pretend to pay us and we pretend to work*'. This is an outcome that is the antithesis of those truly fulfilling, positive proclivities and human generative actions and which is responsible not just for the alienation of the labourer from the products of their labour, but also for the abdication of the owners and managers from any responsibility for the direct and indirect products and consequences of their enterprises.[29]

The next step is, perhaps, equally surprising in that it is part of the nature of money that it helps to obscure the inequities of the market. Following in the footsteps of Adam Smith and Sergio Rossi, Mellor (2010, p.81) emphasised that: "*Money value is … less certain than even an arbitrary measure such as an inch. Once an inch is chosen as a unit of measurement it stays constant whereas money … can never be assumed to be constant no matter what it is made of.*" Indeed, Mirowski (1991, p.580) commented that: "*the overriding problem of all market-oriented societies is to find some means to maintain the working fiction of a monetary invariant so that debt contracts … may be written in terms of the unit at different dates.*" In other words we are dealing with something variable, but we are self-deceived into treating it as if it is constant. Economists and accountants need to be able to mathematize value and, since

---

28 Although please note that many of my friends and colleagues are subscribing to '*Fair Trade*' opportunities.

29 I have in mind such enterprises as those that produce things like cigarettes, refined sugar, anti-personnel mines and cement.

money is easily counted, it quickly gets taken up as the measure of all things (Handy, 1994). As Searle (1995, p.33) recognised: "*for social facts, the attitude that we take towards the phenomenon is partly constitutive of the phenomenon.*" We believe that money is what it does because in some recursive way it is necessary to accept that it can do this in order for it to be able to function as money.

Nevertheless, and contrary to our earlier definition (Ferguson, 2008), it is clear that money should not be a unit of account, and certainly is not one which facilitates valuation and calculation with any precision[30]. As Kindleberger (1996, p.48) lamented: "*the problem of 'money' is that it is an elusive construct, difficult to pin down and to fix in some desired quantity for the economy*". Furthermore, as a store of value, which maintains over long periods as well as geographical distances, it is a non-starter. It is this very imprecision that allows parties to deceive themselves and others about what is really happening[31] – particularly when the money is in its virtual or digital form. Indeed, the challenge which this presents for governance, was recognised by Ferguson (*op.cit.*, p.59) when he averred that: "*The difficulty of pegging currencies to a single commodity based standard, or indeed to one another, is that policymakers are then forced to choose between free capital movements and an independent national monetary policy. They cannot have both.*" A conclusion that Dani Rodrik also shared, for he observed that: "*how difficult it is to tame finance, an industry which is both the lifeline of all modern economies and the gravest threat to their stability.*" (Rodrik, 2011, p.127).

---

30 As Bichler & Nitzan (2012b, pp.70-71) noted: "*Economics, they say, has its own fundamental quantities: the fundamental quantity of the liberal universe is the util, and the fundamental quantity of the Marxist necessary abstract labour.*" But are such concepts used by many economists today?

31 For example, income tax is charged on bank account interest in the UK even when such interest rates are below the rate of inflation (i.e. when *de facto* the value of the money in the account has actually fallen).

Thirdly, this inequity in the basic exchange process of the market, unlike that of *The Gift* which follows the principle of gratuitousness (Benedict XVI, 2009) being generous and spontaneous[32], is mean spirited and selfish, which are just those attributes that call forth the darker archetypes of Jungian psychology and manifest them in a process of arbitrage – coldly and calculatingly seeking personal advantage at the expense of the other. The sole purpose of which becomes the acquisition of the means of exchange because of its associated social and political attributes. Furthermore, because of its apparent limitlessness, money, and the desire to command the social power it confers, provides considerable social and political incentives to want more of it (Harvey, 2011). It then seems inevitable that such arbitrage would become ever more sophisticated, metamorphosing into operations such as banking (making income on the difference between the interest paid to savers and that charged to borrowers), currency exchange (making income on the difference between rates at which other forms of money are bought or sold)[33], and thence into the operations of the commodities, bond and stock markets, derivatives, hedge funds and speculative manipulation of supply and demand to corner markets and inflate prices, such as that of bread that precipitated the French Revolution (Reinert, 2013).

Fourthly, because money is primarily an abstract concept – a social construct, and, as Searle (1995, p.35) observed: "*This suggests what I think is true, that social facts in general, and institutional facts especially, are hierarchically structured.*", therefore, like commodities it exists at a '*higher order*' than food or water or oxygen, its nature is relational. As Mellor (2010, p.81) recognised: "*Money, whatever its form, is a social construction not a natural form. However as a social form it represents power.*" Now, for organisms all natural substances have optimum quantities and, as Bateson

32 See the account of the widow's mite - Mark 12, vs.41-44 and Luke 21, vs.1-4.

33 See Jesus' actions and sentiments when driving the money changers from the Temple, Mark 11, vs.15-17.

and Bateson (2005, p.85) maintained: "*in biology everything becomes toxic beyond some optimal point.*". But money is different because, although it has a physical form, its real significance is in influencing social interactions. So whereas it cannot, through excess, poison the biological agent, in terms of quantity it can, and does poison sociological systems. Because it is a social construct it has morphed from its initial existence as a medium of exchange into being a mechanism for storing and releasing value and thence into a mechanism for self-aggrandizement and the acquisition of power (Bichler & Nitzan, 2012a). As Flank (2007, p.100) noted: "*the share of wealth which goes to the workers tends to shrink in comparison with the share of wealth that goes to the capitalist. Thus … … no matter how much the workers receive, the bosses receive still more.*" In this form money is schizmogenic[34], both in terms of positive feedback on acquisition (avarice) and on other people's responses (envy; resentment), leading to a typical arms' race or chain reaction. Indeed, Bauman (2013, p.39) commented that: "*an increase in 'total wealth' goes hand in hand with a deepening of social inequality.*" Yet, because of Daniel Bernoulli's '*St. Petersburg Paradox*'[35] (Sorensen, 2003), any increase in wealth of the rich is inevitably less appreciated by them, dollar for dollar, than it would be by the least well off. Furthermore, as Hann and Hart (2011, p.104) recognised: "*Becoming closer and more unequal at the same time is an explosive combination.*" An example from development is the destructive, schizmogenic effect of pay differentials between expatriates and local staff on projects, even though one reason for pay disparity is the different value of the same units of money in their respective cultures (Carr, *et al.*, 1998; Eriksson Baaz, 2005). Furthermore, I have argued that if individual acquisitiveness is a schizmogenic trait that contributes to '*complementary differentiation*' (Bateson 1972, p.68) then it could be argued that all current forms of social welfare are simply actions that are undertaken in order to reduce the tensions within

34 It brings about social divisions.

35 Each new dollar tends to have less influence on one's welfare than the preceding dollar.

the prevailing system rather than to bring about any meaningful transformation (Kowalski, 2011b, p.749).

Finally, George Simmel said that: "*money is the concrete symbol of our human potential to make universal society.*" (quoted in Hann & Hart 2011, p.97), which is perversely manifest in the emergence of plutocracy from the promise of democracy. As Harvey (2011, p.115-116) noted: "*When the credit bubble bursts, which it inevitably must, then the whole economy plunges into a downward spiral ... and it is at this point that capitalism has to create external power in order to save itself from its own internal contradictions.*" Leading Hudson (2011) to argue that what should be obvious to everyone is that, irrespective of whatever political arrangements are in place, the credit system becomes the *de facto* planning system. Thus we see that as the FIRE[36] sector becomes ever more dominant within the global economic system so the totalitarian tendency that Hayek (2007) warned about also becomes more apparent. As the bubble economies wreak their inevitable debt peonage impact upon populations more people are disempowered through the fear of foreclosure and bankruptcy[37] and national policy is subject to scrutiny and approval by the IMF – or indeed by the bond markets.

8 Concluding remarks

It seems that we are ready to accept any explanation for the current crises of our civilization except that the present state of the world may be because our myopic pursuit of some of our most cherished ideals has led to results utterly different from those which we had expected (Hayek, *op.cit.*). Free-market liberal capitalism under the rule of law has not produced even the limited liberties for the mass of humanity that Hayek envisaged, not because liberalism cannot deliver liberty but because the balance of power has never

36 Finance, Insurance and Real Estate – FIRE.

37 See the emergence of the '*precariat*' (Standing, 2011).

enfranchised the vast majority of human beings to formulate the laws that would restrain the predatory and avaricious natures of the small minority of people who have insatiable appetites for the power of wealth and who are not content merely to compete but also demand to set the terms of the game in their own favour. As Bichler and Nitzan (2012b, p.77) maintained: "*private ownership is wholly and only an institution of exclusion, and institutional exclusion is a matter of organized power.*" Thus most laws have been established by the wealthy to protect themselves and their rights over possessions which have arguably been acquired by nefarious means in the first instance[38].

Even though this unjust system is clearly bound for collapse sooner or later under the terms of the 1st and 2nd contradictions the plutocrats seem determined not to face the obvious and permit the search for an alternative. This, it may be argued, is because capitalism is a confidence trick and so *'confidence'* rather than rationality is everything. Now, one aspect of a double bind is the absolute injunction not to comment upon the mismatch between perception and accepted reality (Kowalski, 2004). Thus, for example, Shutt (2005, p.118) noted former Chairman of the Federal Reserve, Alan Greenspan's: "*inability to bring the* [financial] *situation under control without precipitating precisely the market meltdown he had earlier sought to avert.*" which is characteristic of the double bind that is modern economic management.

---

38 See Honoré de Balzac in Le Père Goriot. – "*Behind every fortune is a crime.*" Or again, as Say (1971, p.113) observed: "*The savings of a rich contractor, of a swindler or cheat, of a royal favourite, saturated with grants, pensions, and unmerited emoluments, are actual accumulations of capital, and are sometimes made with facility enough. But the values thus amassed by a privileged few, are, in reality, the product of the labour, capital, and land, of numbers, who might themselves have made the saving, and turned it to their own account, but for the spoliation of injustice, fraud, or violence.*"

Furthermore, Shutt (2005, p.103) had recognised that: "*it is still possible … for the ruling elite to exclude from the main channels of public debate any discussion of radical alternatives to the status quo which might call into question the fundamental assumptions of the self-regulated capitalist profits system.*" as Ramonet (1997, p.181) remonstrated: "*Constant repetition, in all the media, of this* [capitalist] *catechism by almost all politicians, from right to left, gives it such an intimidating force that it stifles all attempts at free thinking and makes it very difficult to resist this new obscurantism.*" Indeed, this prohibition is no better exemplified than by Fulcher (2004, p.126) who wrote just before the most serious financial crisis in seventy years struck, that: "*If there were a viable alternative to capitalism, the current symptoms of crisis might be more serious.*" and, with no irony intended, that: "*The search for an alternative **to** capitalism is fruitless in a world where capitalism has become utterly dominant, and no final crisis is in sight or, short of some ecological catastrophe, even really conceivable.*"[39] Perhaps even more tellingly in 2005 the IMF believed that "*Short of a major and devastating geopolitical incident undermining, in a significant way, consumer confidence, and hence financial asset valuation, it is hard to see where systemic threats could come from in the short term*" (quoted in Nolan, 2008, p.65). Regrettably, It seems to be taking far longer than we might have imagined to free ourselves from *Homo economicus*, and the idea that our sole motivation is and should be individual self-interest (Hann & Hart, 2011).

So, the ship is seriously taking in water and rapidly requires to be reconstructed whilst embarked upon a sea of troubles if all the gains of liberty and prosperity are to be salvaged and carried safely into a future where they can be most equitably enjoyed. To say so is not utopian as some have disparaged but as Mohan (2011, p.172) recognised: "*post-industrial society has failed to reconstruct itself and its deconstruction, howsoever utopian it may look, rests*

---

39 Well I guess if you can ignore the 1st and 2nd contradictions this might well be believable!

on reinventing [a] *social contract that will synergize global forces towards a second Enlightenment –* ***Enlightenment II.***" In contrast, to accept that the system we have is the best we can do seems to be dystopian and myopic in the extreme.

However, as a response to this challenge it is difficult to conceive of a situation where central, coercive, collective planning stands much hope of delivering both liberty and prosperity. As Hayek (2007, p.71) maintained: "*The fundamental principle that in the ordering of our affairs we should make as much use as possible of the spontaneous forces of society, and resort as little as possible to coercion*" seems common sense. Having said that, it is also necessary to recognise that there is a world of difference between liberty and license[40]. It seems clear that both Adam Smith, in *The Theory of Moral Sentiments,* and Friedrich Hayek, in *The Road to Serfdom*, held that there is such a necessary thing as society and that it is constructed from the actions of individuals, but emerges in an organic way as a self-organising system. It is noteworthy that Stafford Beer has defined freedom and autonomy in similar terms[41]. Thus, as Raul Espejo argued:

> *the ethical/political discourse of collectivists was that of a "just society", and of individualists was that of individual "human rights" ..., we need at present a participatory discourse focused more precisely on the constitution of fair societies that recognise individuals with rights and responsibilities, that is of societies and organisations that recognise the difference between individuals and citizens.* (Espejo, 2004, p.676)

Suggesting that a sustainable future for any human society will only be built on a sense of civic membership, always remembering, with Bauman[42] (2000), the proper orientation of the '*citizen*'.

---

40 Liberty = Freedom + Reason ; License = Freedom + Appetite

41 See the quotation from Beer (2004) in chapter 6, section 6.

42 See the quotation from Bauman (2000) in chapter 6, section 6.

Furthermore, neither Adam Smith nor Friedrich Hayek were advocates of big business nor of unrestrained *laissez faire*. Indeed, Hayek (2007, p.205) maintained that: "*A state which allows such enormous aggregations of power to grow up cannot afford to let this power rest entirely in private control.*" But how are we to maintain the dynamism of the free-market and yet limit the accumulation of wealth and power in the hands of a few?

Central to any response to such a question is an appreciation that what we are participating in is fundamentally a two-way **exchange**. This dualistic interaction does not require nor indeed warrant that there be a winner and a loser. On the contrary, when individual restraint is the order of the day there are considerable social benefits. As we saw in chapter 6, the epigenic paradox requires a resolution that is both in the interest of society and, in a recursive way, is also of benefit to the individual concerned. Similarly, in the matter of economics, Count Pietro Verri of Milan held that: "*Because the private interest of each individual, when it coincides with the public interests, is always the safest guarantor of public happiness.*" (quoted in Reinert (2013, p.62)). Thus, short of a general return to *The Gift*, we must encourage individuals to pursue equity and society must reward contribution by explaining the nature of exchange as a zero-sum activity in which for someone to be unrestrainedly rich it is necessary for others to be poor.

In the first instance, as Harvey (2011, p.110) observed: "*Capitalist personal consumption, it turns out, is a very weak source of effective demand.*" which suggests that one key element of a solution must be an encouragement of the rich to spend. However, this should not be limited to increasing the scale of their use-value dispensations, nor to expenditure from which their business enterprises will substantially benefit. On the contrary, as has been argued in chapter 5, section 4E, we should be encouraging the wealthy to take up philanthropic acts akin to '*the Potlatch*'.

At the same time, as Bichler and Nitzan (2012b, p.79) recognised: "*capitalists are driven not to maximize profit, but to 'beat the average' and 'exceed the normal rate of return'. Their entire existence is conditioned by the need to outperform, by the imperative to achieve not absolute accumulation, but differential accumulation.*" Thus, as long as we create a '*level playing field*' it should be possible to put in placc any suitable regulation provided that it applies to all intents and purposes upon a global scale. Of course, as Hayek (2007, p.231) maintained, for there to be a global applicability: "*there must be a power which can restrain the different nations from action harmful to their neighbors, a set of rules which defines what a state may do, and an authority capable of enforcing these rules.*"

Furthermore, the operation of the 2nd contradiction of capitalism means that the combination of the power of capitalist production relations and the impact of productive processes leads to self-destruction by impairing rather than developing their own necessary conditions (O'Connor, 1998). This means that the state, in its broadest sense, must be active in the provision of those necessary though otherwise neglected, conditions of production, which the individual capitalists will not take it upon themselves to provide. Again this would need to take the form of a universal levy on all enterprises to pay for infrastructure, education and legal systems from which all would benefit. This would prevent a general race to the bottom (Korten, 1996) by setting minimum standards for social and environmental protection. But it will need considerable international co-operation and political courage to initiate such a scheme.[43]

In conclusion, it is hard to deny that capitalism, in its current formulation, is not a suitable basis for development. As Gray (1998, p.14) recognised, careful scrutiny: "*illuminates even more clearly the hubris of seeking to transplant worldwide a social institution that has figured only briefly in the history of one strand*

---

43 See the lack of enthusiasm for a *Tobin tax* in the recent financial crisis.

of capitalism". Furthermore, its inherent instabilities create additional vulnerability for the already marginalized poor. If, as it seems, development seeks the embourgeoisement of substantial sections of the population then it is imperative that we put in place protections that ensure that their capital is not easily expropriated by the powerful in times of economic crisis. Furthermore, capitalism undermines the conditions for its own continuance (2nd contradiction) threatening not only production but also those very biological systems upon which our life support is based. The growth imperative creates incentives to devise increasingly risky sources of investment, including driving the general population into debt. Finally, the power relations that currently permeate the structures of global capitalism are inimical to democracy and good governance, and *vice versa* (Rodrik, 2011; Elsner, 2012). Despite the contention that you can have capitalism without democracy but you cannot have democracy without capitalism (Balcerowicz, 2013), the real deal is to get the capitalists to behave responsibly as good citizens and to see their interests as coincident with those of society and not *vice versa*.

Chapter 9

Emergent Paradoxes in Economic Approaches to Development

1 Introduction

In keeping with the previous chapter, it seems that we are misled both in terms of the viability of the capitalist enterprise, the nature of the medium of exchange, and the competence of economists and academics to provide a theoretical framework (*technē* & *phronesis*) that will allow the management of both the global and local economies. Therefore, seeking to achieve economic development by fostering the adoption of liberal capitalism as a reflection of the perceived success of Western societies might at best provide more of the world's population with a cash wage whilst drawing them into the ambit of exploitation. Certainly it would seem that we are proselytizing a way of doing things that promotes the interest of a small élite who have the good fortune to be well placed to seize their opportunity[44], that is highly unstable, leading to bouts of significant dispossession, and which despoils the natural capital upon which everyone depends, but particularly the poor. In doing

44 See the histories of the majority of Russian oligarchs.

so well-meaning interventions have often resulted in the exact opposite of what was intended[1].

2 Debt and the Moral Hazard

It is important at this point to mention a strange phenomenon that seems to run counter to those very same economic principles of the free-market and which has been designated as the *Lucas Paradox*. The orthodox economic view is that the mobility of capital should allow global savings to be invested where there is greatest return, thereby channeling resources to their most productive uses, and raising economic growth (Rodrik, 2011). Thus, because of the effect of the law of diminishing returns on capital investment one would expect such investment to be drawn towards localities where the current level of capital per worker is low, with the prospect of higher rates of return, and thereby stimulating growth and development. However, Lucas (1990) drew attention to the fact that developing countries experience underinvestment in relation to their supposed potential, the Lucas paradox, which is usually ascribed to a lack of institutions that secure investment[2]. Nothing exemplifies this lack of credible institutions in *Heavily Indebted Poor Countries* (HIPC), than the '*capital flight*' of their ostensible kleptocracies' ill-gotten gains into Western investment opportunities rather than into local ones[3]. As Hancock (1993, p.181) characterized it: "*public money levied in taxes from the poor of the rich countries is transferred in the form of 'foreign aid' to the rich in the poor countries; the rich in the poor countries then hand it back for safe-keeping to the rich in the rich countries.*" One can only wonder what the development impact

1 For example the IMF's structural adjustment programmes.

2 For example, Alfaro, Kalemli-Ozcan & Volosovych (2005, p.11) noted that: "*there is a 'cluster of institutions', including constraints on government expropriation, independent judiciary, property rights enforcement, and institutions providing equal rights and ensuring civil liberties, that are important to encourage investment and growth.*"

3 sometimes referred to as the home bias puzzle.

might have been if the miscreants had simply been prevented from re-exporting those funds? But this hasn't prevented the analysts from arguing that the paucity of development is a result of the shortage of capital to invest and advocating the expansion of indebtedness.

Now, as has been noted in chapter 8, one way that capitalism has dealt with its internal inconsistencies has been to loot the future productivity of labour through the mechanism of debt. Thus, as things stand today we have sovereign debt, whereby states, both developed and developing, owe vast sums, and private debt, incurred by individuals to meet necessity and extravagance, conjointly spiraling towards the stratosphere under the immutability of compound interest (Hudson, 2011). As Sedlacek (2011, p.227) remarked: "*Perhaps our era will go down in history as the Debt Age.*" In such circumstances it is unsurprising, therefore, to find that banks, IFIs and governments have doggedly lent unprecedented amounts of finance in an unavailing attempt to bring about the development that should lift populations out of mass poverty.

However, as Hudson (2011, p.24) noted: "*Most loans are not invested in tangible capital formation that increase the borrower's revenue and hence debt-paying capacity. … the problem lies in the inexorable mathematics of compound interest. What needs to be examined is how to cope with the inherent tendency of debts to multiply in excess of the economy's ability to pay.*" The inevitable result is a capital flow to the *rentiers* of the developed world from the HIPCs which is greater than the amount of aid that they receive, which suggests that they would most probably have been in a superior economic position if the loans had not been taken on in the first place.

Furthermore, it is important to remember that European capitalism was made possible by the establishment of a number of mechanisms that protect the entrepreneur from risk by handing it off to others to absorb. Accordingly, one way to organize the economy to induce growth may be by internalizing the benefits and externalizing the costs of doing business and thereby to raise the rate of return to the private sector at the expense of imposing costs on other groups (North, 1981). Indeed, a variety of institutions to protect individuals from bearing the full consequences of their actions have been developed over the course of time, which Chang (2000, p.776) listed as: "*limited liability, central banking (and other lender-of-last-resort facilities), insurance, and the underwriting of risky ventures by the government*". This suite forms what has been epitomised as the moral hazard that underpins Western capitalism.

Indeed, Shutt, (2005, p.93) drew attention to: "*the principle of limited liability which has been regarded as the bedrock of capitalist enterprise*" which constitutes a moral hazard that most recently has encouraged financial institutions to avoid the negative consequences of having made bad loans by using *Chapter 11* bankruptcy regulations to prolong the existence of unviable enterprises (which Shutt (*op.cit.*, p.25) referred to as '*zombie companies*') thereby perpetuating excess capacity in opposition to market forces. Importantly, Rodrik (2011, p.237) also concluded that: "[Markets] *depend on the stabilizing functions that lenders-of-last-resort and countercyclical fiscal policy provide.*" Thus supporting a view that Keynsianism, though often seen as a remedy for the business cycle, can itself bring about moral hazard and decadence, as Shutt (*op.cit.*, p.20) argued: "*by drawing private enterprise into ... dependence on public subsidy,* [Keynesianism] *may well ... have set capitalism on a path to decline from which it may never be able to recover.*"

Moreover, Adam Smith had long ago warned against '*merchants and master manufacturers*' because they: "*have generally an interest to deceive and even to oppress the public*" (Smith, 1999a, p.359). Indeed, Hann and Hart (2011, p.146) had criticised: "*the paradox that, while capitalists celebrate the risks of competition in their self-promoting ideologies, they will do everything in their power to avoid it in practice.*" This is the converse face of the moral hazard of capitalist systems, which in a self-referential way, tempts its beneficiaries to use their political clout to maintain and extend its scope. Without doubt, the private sector spends substantial sums of money in order to obtain legislation that allows it to engage in a variety of nefarious practices (Stiglitz, 2010). Thus big business, predominantly in the FIRE sector, shields itself from the consequences of the market by promoting deregulation and the expansion of bailouts, which Rodrik (2011, p.125) characterized as a: "*quite corrupting effect on politics and institutions*" exemplified by: "*the subprime mortgage meltdown, which demonstrated finance's remarkable ability to undermine governance*". All this comes about from the widespread, self-serving, media-supported identification of private corporate interests with the public interest (Shutt, 2005), ultimately underpinned by the threat that '*if we go down we'll take you all down with us!*' and the whole sorry business (*sic*) of corporate welfare. Indeed Sedlacek (2011, p.135) asked: "*Why did the most indebted banks and companies, which did not compete very well, receive the largest forgiveness?*" Unashamedly, the problem of the moral hazard is greater today than it has ever been (Stiglitz, *op.cit.*).

Thus, the banks began their lending to sovereign governments encouraged by the knowledge that they themselves were secured by the system against the consequences of imprudent behavior. As Stiglitz (*op.cit.*, p.7) commented: "*the seeming mispricing and misjudging of risk was based on a smart bet: they believed that if troubles arose, the Federal Reserve and the Treasury would bail them out, and they were right.*" The way that this played out in the 1980's has been well described by Susan George who characterised her indictment of the banks as '*the debt boomerang*' (George, 1992). Their irresponsible and self-interested[4] lending fuelled this earlier debt crisis in the first place and they then offloaded the undesirable

---

4 Through a system of perversely incentivised bonus schemes.

consequences onto the taxpayers of the developed counties whilst leaving the populations of the HIPCs still owing the sums for which the banks had been largely reimbursed[5]. Indeed George (*op.cit.*, p.65) commented that: "*the tax authorities have set up mechanisms enabling banks to treat third world debts as 'losses' for tax purposes,* ***without any requirement to reduce the debt of the debtor countries***" (emphasis in the original).

But we do well to remind ourselves that natural law asserts that debts and contracts cannot be pursued legitimately at the cost of innocent lives. As the judge, Balthazar (aka: Portia), in Act IV scene 1 of Shakespeare's *The Merchant of Venice*, expounds the law:

> *A pound of that same merchant's flesh is thine:*
> *And you must cut this flesh from off his breast – the law allows it…*
> *This bond doth give thee here no jot of blood; the words expressly are, a pound of flesh: take then thy bond, but in the cutting it, if thou dost shed one drop of christian blood, thy lands and goods are… confiscate.*

Thus it seems a gross violation of natural justice to exact debt service payments and amortization without regard for the consequent impact upon human survival, and particularly that of the most vulnerable who had no part in incurring the debt in the first place.

In addition, whilst observing this process unfold the recipient governments also learnt about this phenomenon of the moral

[5] It is to be noted that in the 2008 financial crash the various sovereign states stepped forward to rescue the banks from the consequences of bad lending. They did not remove the indebtedness of those who had taken up unsustainable mortgages, largely on the grounds that to do so would be to generate a moral hazard for borrowers (Stiglitz, 2010). Compare this with the Parable of the Unforgiving Servant (Matthew 18 vs. 23-35).

hazard and as a result came to trust that, in their turn, either the banks or the IFIs would take care of their debt problems in the same way. Therefore, loans from national and international public agencies came to be used to pay back the banks, rather than funding '*development*' or providing for human welfare (George, *op.cit.*). Indeed, what possible incentive to repay such debts did the borrowers have when they saw the debts regularly restructured or forgiven (Easterly, 2006). This is a manifestation of the moral hazard of the Samaritan's dilemma discussed in section 4 of chapter 4, which brought about circumstances that led Berthélemy (2006, p.184) to assert that: "*According to this* [defensive lending] *argument, donors may be locked in a 'debt game', in which they have to provide new resources to highly indebted countries simply to avoid that these debtors fall in arrears.*" Indeed, despite donors' efforts to clothe their aid in conditionalities, the IFIs through inability or unwillingness fail to enforce their own conditions when borrowers do not comply with them thereby reinforcing the perception that when the chips are down their bluff can be called (Santiso, 2003), which is a manifestation of the double binding nature of the two-way facing moral hazard embedded in the use of debt as a means of promoting development. Indeed, Herbert Spencer had long ago maintained that: "[t]*he ultimate result of shielding man from the effects of folly is to people the world with fools*" (quoted in Kindleberger, 1996, p. 146), which presumably was not the intention behind aid.

Then we must ask ourselves who pays for such reckless lending to corrupt regimes (Santiso, *op.cit.*)? and the answer invariably proves to be either the poor of the borrower country or the taxpayers of the lender country, removing any need for prudence on the part of the lending institutions or that of the borrowing government's officials. Thus I would argue that the loans should either have been underwritten by the personal fortunes of the élites who sign the contracts or else the repayments and servicing should not have been pursued until the economic development that the loans were designed to bring about had begun to yield significant improvements in Gross Domestic Product (GDP)[6], or some other, more appropriate measure.

Of course, we should recognize that the contradictory nature of the business of lending out other people's money (banking) should encourage us to regard it with suspicion. It is quite clear that a fundamental rule of prudent banking is that money should only be lent to people who can demonstrate that, in a fundamental sense, they don't need it - most often manifested in the provision of collateral to underpin the loan[7]. Furthermore, as Rodrik (2011, p.124) noted: "*It was a running joke during the 1930's that foreign finance is like an umbrella which a man is allowed to borrow, but must return as soon as it starts to rain.*" This is in part in the nature of usury[8] where investment is not made on the basis of taking a stake in the enterprise nor as a personal transaction between the owner of the capital and its borrower circumscribed by social relations and the conventions of *The Gift*, but upon the ability of the lender to be quit of any social responsibility towards the debtor. We can observe that the only way that governments can hope to keep capital in place is to convince its' owners, beyond any reasonable doubt, that they can move it away at short notice or indeed with no notice at all (Bauman, 2000) and they do this by inappropriately placing finance and its needs at the pinnacle of policy (Hudson, 2011).

---

6 In much the same way that student loans operate in the UK, repayments not kicking in until a certain income level is reached.

7 Of course the pledging of land – often the family's only source of livelihood – against debt taken on in desperation is another matter entirely.

8 I contend that usury is not simply a matter of lending to extract high interest rates but is as much about the distancing of the lender from the borrower, which is a further manifestation of globalization. It is also fundamentally similar to the extractive nature of the *rentier* class approach to a free lunch captured by Hudson (2012).

This conundrum of lending at interest has also been given force historically by both a moral and legal aversion to usury as a gross exploitation of the poor. For example, *Exodus* 22 vs 25-27:

> *If you lend money to my people, to the poor among you, you shall not deal with them as a creditor; you shall not exact interest from them. If you take your neighbour's cloak in pawn, you shall restore it before the sun goes down; for it may be his only clothing to use as cover;*

and the *Holy Qur'an* 2 vs 275 & 276:

> *Those that live on usury shall rise up before God like men whom Satan had demented by his touch... God has ... made usury unlawful.*
> *If your debtor be in straits, grant him a delay until he can discharge his debt; but if you waive the sum as alms it will be better for you.*

and the concept of sabbatical debt forgiveness set out in the *Torah: D'varim* 15.

Furthermore, in the historical conflict between money lent out for interest and money invested in production, the optimistic predictions of many early economists, like Henri de Saint-Simon, Adam Smith and Karl Marx, that industrial finance would gain, once and for all, the upper hand in this struggle have in recent years been shown to have been entirely premature, and they would have considered our current path of development as a financial dystopia (Hudson, *op.cit.*).

Finally, we must consider a further dimension of debt in that one outcome of the ascendency of large capitalist holdings would be the emergence of a totalitarian system, through their moral hazard opportunity to manipulate political processes. For example, Bichler and Nitzan (2012, figure 17) drew attention to the relationship between the concentration of wealth and power in the USA and the degree of violence meted out to the general populous, as proxied by the size of the prison population. Furthermore, Hayek (2007, p.175) had identified a particular symptom of that trend towards repression in those: "*words whose meaning has been changed into their opposites to make them serve as instruments of totalitarian propaganda.*" which is so reminiscent of the upshot of the construction of '*Newspeak*' in George Orwell's *Nineteen Eighty-Four*, where, in chapter 5, Syme comments that: "*It's a beautiful thing, the destruction of words. ... It isn't only the synonyms; there are also the antonyms. ... A word contains its opposite in itself.*" Echoing again the passage from chapter 6 of Louis Carrol's *Through the Looking Glass*:

> *"When **I** use a word," Humpty Dumpty said, in rather a scornful tone, "it means just what I choose it to mean—neither more nor less".*

Moreover, Hayek (*op.cit.*) observed that: "*Gradually, as this process continues, the whole language becomes despoiled, and words become empty shells deprived of any definite meaning, as capable of denoting one thing as its opposite and used solely for the emotional associations which still adhere to them.*" Remarkably, in just this way the financial system has down played the word '*debt*', with all its negative connotations, in favour of the much more positive and forward looking '*credit*'. How could you overcome the reluctance built up over generations to fall into debt, which in times gone by could lead to dispossession, imprisonment, servitude and penury? Why not reframe it as credit and suggest that it is everybody's birthright to consume now and to worry about payment tomorrow, and for goodness sake never ask yourself in whose interest such a set of behaviours and beliefs operates!

3 Cultural and Capability Misalignment

Certainly the accumulation of capital looking for suitable opportunities for investment, particularly after the oil crisis of 1973, provided the impetus and justification for using loans and sovereign debt as the mechanism for development. Nevertheless, the successful application of borrowing to development under capitalism requires that the funds borrowed are devoted to fostering the necessary preconditions for business expansion in a very disciplined way, which itself requires a particular type of leadership.

Now, a number of authors have drawn attention to the difficulties created by the cultural gap between donors, their agents and the recipients of DA (Biggs & Smith, 2003; Carr, *et al.,* 1998; Eriksson Baaz, 2005; Kowalski, 2004, 2011; O'Connor & Kowalski, 2005). Rather than rehearse those arguments I would like to explore another dimension of that problem. As recounted above, free-market capitalism is a fairly modern development of Western culture which until very recently was only deeply manifested amongst European states and their colonial progeny. Notwithstanding, there is currently a substantial part of those populations that neither think entrepreneurially nor behave in terms of capital accumulation and exchange-value (Kowalski & Kamiński, 1999). Indeed, Dichter (2007b, p.181) noted that: "*one would see quickly and clearly how few people in the world are entrepreneurial.*" Even the professional classes (teachers, doctors, lawyers) are not particularly entrepreneurial and if they have wealth it has usually been set aside against retirement (i.e. it is really deferred use-value). So we can safely infer that the societies of so called developing countries are even less well stocked with people who have their eye on exchange-value and a business approach to affairs[9]. Such pre-capitalist societies function around use-value and surpluses that become the use-value of feudal over-lords and

[9] See Julius Nyerere's observations quoted in Rist (1997, p.130, n.24).

merchants (Hilton, 2006), at one level, and the system of *the Gift* at another (Kowalski, 2011). As Beckert (2011, p.51) noted: "*The traditional **habitus** of the peasant clashes with the rational **habitus** demanded by capitalist society.*"

The Victorian writer and social commentator, Charles Dickens, in chapter 12 of *David Copperfield*, captured the thought processes of the majority of people in such a society in the character of Mr Micawber who lamented that: "*Annual income twenty pounds, annual expenditure nineteen nineteen six, result happiness. Annual income twenty pounds, annual expenditure twenty pounds ought and six, result misery.*" But a capitalist would be miserable if all they made was the odd sixpence!

In a poor country any increase in income is simply exposed to the necessities of daily consumption. Such living on the edge of survival, it has been argued, engenders a rational response to intolerable circumstances characterised as '*accommodation*' (Galbraith, 1979), which leaves little prospect or appetite for capital accumulation. The Irish playwright and socialist thinker, George Bernard Shaw, in Act II of *Pygmalion*, caricatured the situation in the response of Lisa's dustman father when soliciting £5 from his daughter's '*benefactor*', Professor Higgins, as follows:

DUSTMAN. Not me, Governor, so help me I won't. Don't you be afraid that I'll save it and spare it and live idle on it. There won't be a penny of it left by Monday: I'll have to go to work same as if I'd never had it. It won't pauperize me, you bet. Just one good spree for myself and the missus, giving pleasure to ourselves and employment to others, and satisfaction to you to think it's not been throwed away. You couldn't spend it better.

PROF. HIGGINS. This is irresistible. Let's give him ten. [He offers two notes to the dustman].

DUSTMAN. No, Governor. She wouldn't have the heart to spend ten; and perhaps I shouldn't neither. Ten pounds is a lot of money: it makes a man feel prudent like; and then goodbye to happiness. You give me what I ask you, Governor: not a penny more, and not a penny less.

Indeed, most people, operating in the use-value part of the economy when given some funds will spend them upon current needs or invest it in social capital via the operation of *The Gift* – which is what they would do with any form of windfall. As Dichter (2007b, p.186) noted: "*In the 19th century, withdrawals from the wide array of financial systems for the poor – were for medical crises, burials, plots of land, retirement, wedding expenses and so on,*" which is precisely the consumer-orientation that seems to be the current nature of the bulk of borrowing by today's poor (Ellerman, 2007).

Clearly, it takes a particular cast of mind that would borrow money just to invest in making more money. Certainly, Allen (2007, p.53) drew an important distinction between: "*owners of income generating activities* [who] *tend to maximize drawings from their enterprises and minimize the amount of money that is reinvested*" on the one hand and the: "*owners of small- and medium-scale enterprises ... who tend to minimize the amount of drawings from the business and reinvest for growth.*", on the other, arguing that it is both circumstance and disposition that determines the approach that is taken.

Moreover, in my experience political leadership does not necessarily involve having a capitalist disposition, nor indeed any business acumen (Kowalski & Kamiński, 1999), and this is even more accurate of the mindset of the bureaucrat who is most widely characterized as being risk averse. Thus it is almost inevitable that most people with leadership roles in developing countries have not been of this business-like way of thinking (Hettne, 1995) and are quite probably culturally and mentally embedded in a pre-capitalist, *Gift* economy of which they might naturally see themselves as the rightful, key beneficiaries[10].

Of course the whole development enterprise involves two sides, with the donor staff and agents being the mirror image, as it were, of the local protagonists. Once again we see that business acumen and an entrepreneurial spirit are not the prime characteristics on the donor side either, with a loading that normally leans towards the bureaucrat, planner (Easterly, 2006). As Reinhardt (2006, p.297) noted: "*Individuals in these* [aid] *agencies make funding decisions in light of their own incentives*", and Hefeker (2006, p.247) stated that: "*the internal career structures makes officers in those agencies mainly interested in distributing as much money as possible*". Thus we should not be surprised if the handling of International Aid, particularly in the form of loans and Direct Budget Support is not undertaken in a way that most effectively and efficiently leads to economic and/or social development. Moreover, governments and financial institutions themselves need desperately to believe that in the end debts will be repayable out of the extra output generated by the loan itself or else by a subsequent rise in the overall level of economic activity (Shutt, 1999), which requires, one would have thought, the presentation of at least a fairly reasonable business case for the investment backed up by a strategic plan.

Furthermore, setting aside humanitarian assistance, development is about the parallel emergence of systems of governance, media, infrastructure and a healthy and educated citizenry. Indeed, Reinert (2012) has argued for the importance of a simultaneous shift from primary production to value-adding enterprises. As David Harvey had noted, in Europe:

---

[10] Ellerman (2010, p.697) speaks of: "*This idea that 'rulership' is part of capital ownership has become so widely accepted that it could be called the 'fundamental myth' of the capitalist system*", but the converse may also be true, that '*rulership*' demands the ownership of capital – that becoming wealthy is a natural entitlement of our rulers!

> *a nascent capitalist class had to build its alternative social forms at first on the basis of the technologies, social relations, administrative systems, mental conceptions, production systems, relations to nature and patterns of daily life as these had long been constituted under the preceding feudal order.* (Harvey, 2011, p.135)

The same is true today for developing countries. Consequently Rodrik (2011, pp.172-173) observed that: "*Telling poor countries in Africa or Latin America that they should set their sights on the institutions of the United States or Sweden is like telling them that the only way to develop is to become developed.*" Importantly, Harvey (*ibid.*) emphasized that: "*It took co-evolution and uneven development in the different spheres*" and did not happen overnight, nor by importing ready-made systems, thus echoing Hirschman's call for unbalanced development (Hirschman,1992). Indeed, we must note David Ellerman's observation (see the quotation in chapter 5 section 4C) that real DA cannot be rushed.

Finally we must add to these observations the self-sabotage brought about by an IFI agenda that seeks to reduce the scale of the recipient state whilst being entirely dependent upon the capacity of that very state both to implement changes and then sustainably to enforce them. Indeed, the promotion of the rule-of-law appears to dominate the neo-liberal paradigm that also advocates a drastic reduction in the prerogatives of the state, apparently oblivious to the fact that to strengthen the rule of law requires a stronger state capable of exercising legal control over its territory effectively (Santiso, 2003). Moreover, Baylies (1995, p.325) had observed that: "*the instrument charged with ensuring adoption of economic reform* [the civil service] *was subject to weakening by* [structural] *reform measures.*" Furthermore, Lerner (2009, p.42) had concluded that: "*virtually every hub of cutting-edge entrepreneurial activity in the world today has its origins in proactive government intervention*."[11] Thus we see that the chosen approach has been to promote a route to development which in many ways is the antithesis of the organic process that the putative developed economies have experienced in their own development. The primary effect of which has been to plunge countries in Africa, parts of Asia and Latin America into substantial sovereign debt, often to build unsustainable structures (physical and social) without a clear economic or business case having been made.

4 Micro-finance and Embourgeoisement

Given the foregoing, it is hardly surprising that the chosen nostrum for furthering the development of nation states – credit – should be promoted as the local panacea for propelling individuals and communities out of poverty. Although the US government sponsored a number of microcredit programs in Latin America in the 1970s, the '*discovery*' and expansion of micro-credit is mostly attributed to Dr Muhammad Yunus and his pioneering work in Bangladesh with the Grameen Bank (founded in 1983) and with whom he shared the Nobel Peace Prize in 2006 (Bateman, 2010). That micro-credit was taken up with such trenchancy by donors can be attributed to a number of factors other than the assumed economic and poverty reduction impact. The first is that it was seen to be very much a self-help process which might avoid the problem of dependency. The second is that simplistic economic theory suggested that lending small sums to the poor could generate significant returns that have the potential to cover the recurrent costs of MicroFinance Institutions (MFI). Thirdly, just as with sovereign debt, many of the lenders had a vested interest in pushing loans as a result of the expansion of capital holdings needing profitable outlets. As Harper (2007, p.258) suggested: "*Loans are about transferring 'our' money to the poor, which is*

---

11 As Kowalski & Kamiński (1999, p.58) maintained: "*the involvement of local government remains an absolute necessity for creating and sustain BDS under the circumstances that prevail in Poland.*"

intrinsically more attractive than enabling them to accumulate their own money more safely and accessibly."

However, in a seminal critique, Bateman (2010, p. 28) drew attention to a fundamental disconnect in microfinance that is: "*a very awkward problem for the microfinance industry: almost all of the basic assumptions that underpin the microfinance model today are wrong.*" This is almost certainly an outcome of the attempt to reconcile the dissonant motives of assistance, contained in the rhetoric, and exploitation, embedded in the practice[12]. Moreover, the sub-text of development is arguably the embourgeoisement of the masses, as Bateman (*op.cit.*, p.39) captured it: "*social mobilization and state activism helped a large section of the working class in the developed countries to become 'embourgeoisified'*;" However, this is often not what has occurred in developing countries in practice, as Harvey (2011, p.146) observed: "*The purported aim* [of microcredit] *is to permit the population to raise themselves out of poverty and join the merry business of capital accumulation. Some succeed, but for the rest it means debt peonage.*" Furthermore, it is inevitably some of the poorest borrowers who become worse off as a result of taking micro-enterprise credit (Johnson & Rogaly, 1997). Thus another panacea for development again exposes the most vulnerable groups to high risks. Indeed, Wilson (2007, p.106) went so far as to claim that: "*Our power to set people back through debt and shame was far greater than our power to bring them forward.*"

Moreover, David Ellerman had argued that:

> *the microfinance programmes installed by aid agencies and NGOs are not simply falling short of their hype (most observers agree on that) but are yet another faddish form of unhelpful help, an anti-development intervention*

---

12 Morduch (2000, p.618) spoke of: "*the schism between rhetoric and action – and between financially-minded donors and socially-minded programs*".

> *that produces a short-run benefit but may misdirect and undermine sustainable development and poverty reduction in the longer run.* (Ellerman, 2007, p. 159)

and Duvendack, *et al.* (2011, p.75), in a far ranging review, concluded that: "*it remains unclear under what circumstances, and for whom, microfinance has been and could be of real, rather than imagined, benefit to poor people.*"

Microfinance has been sold to development professionals and the wider community on the basis of a package of claims about drawing people out of poverty, empowering women, mobilizing social solidarity and sustainability but, as Morduch (2000, p.620) maintained: "*the claims are often heard together, and they form a core set of ideas. Each is rooted in the experience of some programs in some places and at some times. But as general propositions they each rest on problematic logical extrapolations, inappropriate assumptions, or misleading evidence.*" Moreover, microfinance would appear to be a false prospectus because the concept is based upon faulty economic principles which fly in the face of what economists already clearly appreciated (Bateman & Chang, 2012).

Firstly, the cost of entry into an enterprise means that: "*for all enterprise sectors there remains an identifiable minimum efficient scale of production*" (*ibid.*). Thus microcredit, it is argued, cannot support the sort of enterprise that would be economic and sustainable, but on the contrary: "*only the most simple and unsophisticated microenterprises … very simple trading, retail and service operations, with perhaps some very small production-based operations that can add value very quickly.*" (Bateman, 2010, p.94) are possible. The overall effect, like the *Morgenthau Plan*, is to de-industrialize the economy through focusing what finance is available in these simple sectors of the market[13].

---

13 For an explanation of this plan see Reinert (2006, p.65).

Secondly, as Chang (2011, p.164) acknowledged, there is the fallacy of composition in that just because some people can succeed with a particular business is no guarantee that everyone can succeed with it. Since the range of opportunity for local microenterprises is restricted by local demand and the limited scope of the would-be entrepreneurs the predominant outcomes of microcredit are '*bandwagons*'[14]. Again, for sub-Saharan Africa, Amsden (2012, p.127) had lamented that: "*with fast population growth and sky-high rates of unemployment and underemployment, the hardiest entrepreneur cannot open a small business because other small entrepreneurs are already exploiting the same idea and making a loss.*" Bateman (2010) explained how this works by reference to Figure 9.1.

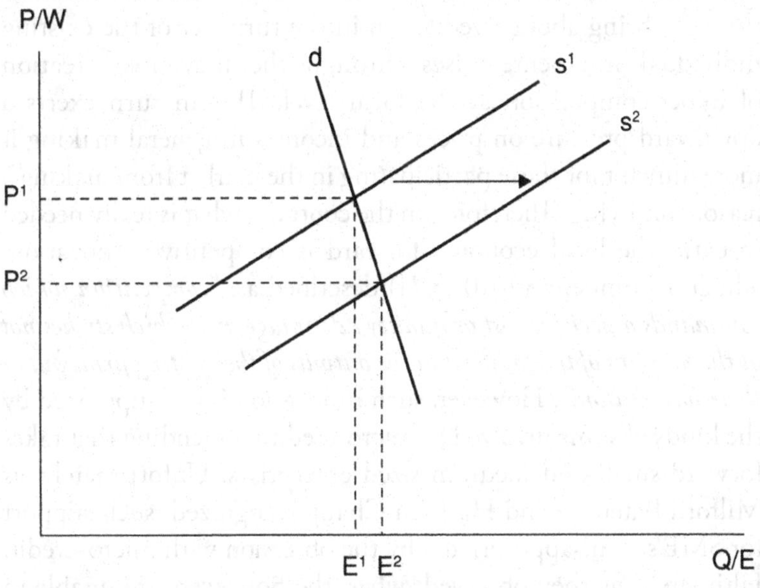

P/W
d
s1
s2
P1
P2
E1 E2
Q/E

Figure 9.1 The supply and demand curves for increasing numbers of microenterprises (after Bateman, 2010, p.65).

14 An example would be renting the use of mobile phones.

When the supply S^1 prevails without external intervention of micro-credit and the quantity of goods or services offered is at level E^1 this produces a price structure at P^1. With the expansion of entrants into the market as a consequence of being given a micro-loan the supply also increases to E^2 which, because demand doesn't expand at the same rate, drives the price down to the new level P^2 making the viability of the pre-existing enterprises and the newcomers less likely.

Moreover, Bateman and Chang (2012) argued that proliferation of microenterprises induced by the availability of microfinance does not necessarily raise the total volume of turnover but rather redistributes amongst those participating in that market the volume of demand which already existed. The end result of this is to bring about a reduction in the turnover of the existing individual microenterprises through the inevitable creation of hyper-competition at the local level. This in turn exerts a downward pressure on prices and incomes in general making it more difficult for those participating in the market from making a reasonable living. Therefore, on the contrary, what is really needed to carry the local economy forward is competitive innovation, which Schumpeter (2010, p.74) described as: "*competition which commands a decisive cost or quality advantage and which strikes not at the margins of the profits and the outputs of the existing firms but at their foundations*". However, such innovation is not supported by the kinds of sums involved in micro-credit, but lending that takes forward small and medium sized enterprises. Unfortunately, as Milford Bateman and Ha-Joon Chang recognized, such support for SME's is misappropriated by the obsession with micro-credit. Ultimately, as they observed, when the borrowers are unable to make repayments the absence of limited liability, the foundation stone of capitalist enterprise in the developed world: "*means the poor lose not just their already minimal income flow, but also any additional assets, savings and land … Social networks and reputational capital are also lost.*" (Bateman & Chang, *op.cit.*, p.23)

Thirdly, as we saw in section 3 above, Dichter (2007b, p.180) held that: "*we began to see poor borrowers use their loans for what the industry has come to call 'consumption smoothing*'", which is to say that the availability of small loans, ostensibly to support micro-enterprise initiation or expansion, tends to be drawn away (fungibility) and into addressing current expenditure needs. Now, it is a very different prospect to lend for consumption rather than for business development. As Adam Smith observed:

> *The stock which is lent at interest is always considered as a capital by the lender. … The borrower may use it either as a capital, or as a stock reserved for immediate consumption. … If he uses it as a stock reserved for immediate consumption, he acts the part of the prodigal, … The man who borrows in order to spend will soon be ruined, and he who lends to him will generally have occasion to repent his folly.* (Smith, 1999a, p.450)

Moreover, as we have seen for sovereign debt, the temptation to take out a loan for consumption in the first instance and then to take further loans primarily to cover the interest and capital repayment on previous loans can be almost irresistible for poor people on the cusp of destitution (Hudson, 2011). Then, when you add to this a system of perverse incentives for the staff of MFIs to make loans, you quickly arrive at what Bateman and Chang (2012, p.27) described as a situation where: "*Both providers and recipients within microfinance are thus automatically stimulated into excessive supply and demand respectively*[15], *thereby providing the fuel for the inevitable 'microfinance bubble*'", a local manifestation of neo-liberalism which is the equivalent of the international sub-prime mortgage fiasco of 2008.

Fourthly, although one of the basic lessons in elementary economics is the principle of '*diminishing marginal returns*', which maintains

15 In cybernetics parlance this is positive feedback and it leads to run away.

that enterprises with relatively little capital should be able to earn higher returns on subsequent investments than those with relatively more capital (Armendáriz & Morduch, 2007), it seems that the Lucas Paradox (discussed in section 2, above) applies equally to individuals as it does to the economies of nation states. Thus, the poorest people are by definition those who could most do with credit but can make the least use of it (Dichter, 2006). Indeed, Armendáriz and Morduch (*op.cit.*), explained that the poor have lower marginal returns despite currently deploying little capital because of the different status of those complementary requirements, which they also lack, and which yield greater returns for the wealthier entrepreneur because of their ability to take full advantage of opportunities as a consequence of their enhanced human and social capitals.

However, in all this enthusiasm to get people into debt we have forgotten the normal process of evolution of enterprises in Western economies. As Bauer (1991, p.43) commented: "*To have capital is the result of economic achievement, not its precondition*", and that it is the ability to save and manage a cash flow that tended to be a precursor to enterprise development. Again, Allen (2007, p.52) observed that: "*the very poor react more powerfully to financial services that build and protect assets than they do to the chance to take on debt.*" When a loan is sought it is most likely to be from family members in the first instance. Indeed, Thomas Dichter noted, because of the unpredictability surrounding loans, that:

> *the* [borrower's] *preference seems to be for self-financing or informal financing, or … both together. Because a loan from a friend or a relative is based partly on a social connection, the entrepreneur gains a hedge since he knows the arrangement is 'softer', more 'patient', more risk-tolerant, and less return-driven than a formal loan.* (Dichter, 2007b, p.184)

which is heavily redolent of the influence of a *Gift* culture rather than that of the market. Nevertheless, and in contradistinction, despite the fact that MFIs' customers need savings and insurance far more urgently than credit and loans they still continue to focus their efforts upon the provision of the latter (Harper, 2007).

Indeed, in relation to the Catholic Relief Services' (CRS) involvement in providing microfinance, Wilson (2007, p.98) lamented that: "*Perversely, the subsidies never travelled to the poor in the form of low interest rates, great service or social impact, but stayed within the confines of our partner microfinance institutions,*". Indubitably, MicroFinance Institutions not only respond to the Ponzi-style dynamics by making inappropriate loans but, as Bateman (2010, pp.41-42) observed: "*Microfinance analysts accept that in practice, however, most MFIs now work with the less poor, and even with the moderately wealthy.*" and that: "*in some countries the middle classes (who make the least risky and most profitable clients) actually benefit the most from the increased supply of microfinance.*" What is more Kim Wilson went on to report that, in the view of Father Paul: "*We* [CRS] *are not reaching the far-flung hamlets. The need for assistance is greatest there.*" (Wilson *op.cit.*, p.102).

5 Ability to Benefit and Targeting Aid

As we saw in the previous section, there is both a curve of diminishing marginal utility as the development effort rises, as Fan and Chan-Kang (2004, p. 431) observed for parts of Africa: "*as investments continue to increase in these favored areas, their marginal returns have begun to decline*". Indeed, studies showed that the larger the existing level of aid, the smaller was the additional growth benefit from any additional amount of aid (Easterly, 2006). Then, at lower levels of input the Lucas Paradox generates an initially asymptotic curve of marginal utility where there is such a lack of ability to respond that at first the development return on effort is hard to see. Or, as Dichter (2006), observed, there is a paradox of microfinance in that the poorest people are badly placed to do much productive with credit, and those who are able to make something of it are those who don't really need it, but rather could use larger amounts on different types of credit terms. For all kinds of development circumstances such combinations generate an overall sigmoid curve (see Figure 9.2).

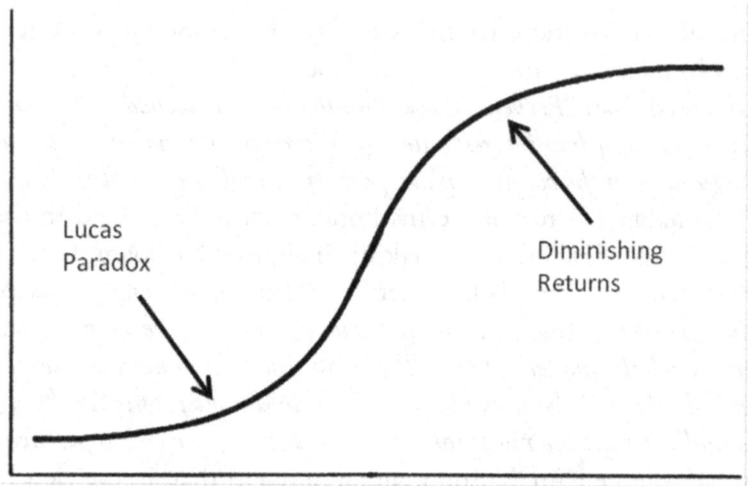
Lucas
Paradox
Diminishing
Returns

Figure 9.2 The Sigmoid Curve of Return on Investment Combining the *Lucas Paradox* and *Diminishing Marginal Returns*

The inadequacy of the ability to respond can be a result of debilitated human capital (e.g. health, education or self-confidence), or social capital (e.g. trades-unions, co-operatives, or mutual funds), or indeed a dearth of those policies, institutions or processes (Carney, 1998) that nurture and support human enterprise. Furthermore, because there are perverse incentives for those in authority to keep their citizens in poverty, as Bauer (1991, p.47) had maintained: "*Paradoxically, aid allocated on the basis of per capita incomes rewards policies of impoverishment*", there is often no momentum for improvement. Moreover, as Collier and Dollar (2002, p.1484) observed in this latter regard: "*There will be a threshold of policy below which even the first dollar of aid is not sufficiently productive in terms of poverty reduction* [to warrant allocating it]." Thus we find that the sigmoid curve is at the heart of the problem of targeting aid at the poorest of the poor, which indeed is where most people mistakenly imagine it to be currently directed.

Now, for the donors of resources for development, whether they are local charities, governments or international organizations of one sort or another, a major consideration is the scale of response relative to the outlay – which may be termed its marginal utility. For, as Collier and Dollar (2001, p.1793) argued: "*world governments ... should give aid up to the point at which the marginal cost of poverty reduction equals its marginal utility to a representative taxpayer.*" Furthermore, even though donors face a complex challenge when targeting aid, it is clear that, as Nunnenkamp and Thiele (2006, p.1200) have insisted: "*need and local conditions should have a larger say on aid allocation if the fight against poverty is taken seriously.*" But the former criterion leads into the first part of the sigmoid curve where development returns on investment are small, whilst the second criterion shifts us into the second part where the beneficiaries are not quite as impoverished as we might wish recipients of aid to be.

This conundrum can be more easily appreciated if we transform the sigmoid curve of figure 9.2 into the gradient of development impact against ability to respond (marginalization), which then appears as a bell shaped curve (see Figure 9.3).

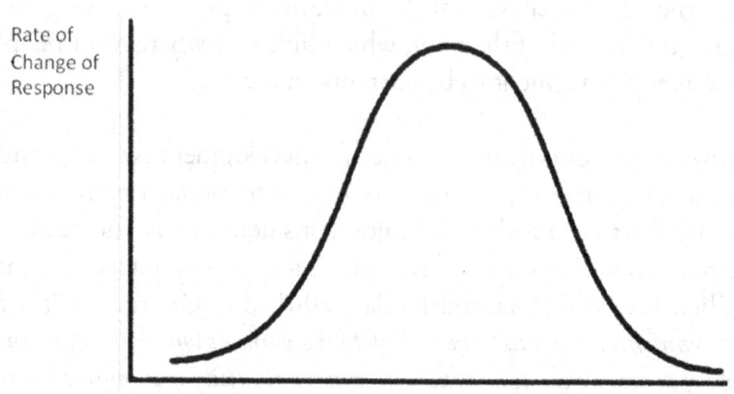
Rate of
Change of
Response
Ability to Respond→

Figure 9.3 The Change in the Rate of Response to Increasing Investment

Thus the greatest development impact of aid resources would occur where the curve is at its highpoint, suggesting that this is the situation of most efficient application. Indeed, the implications of such an approach are quite familiar to helping practitioners. Teachers know from experience that their limited resources are inevitably directed towards the median class ability, even though the most needy students tend to be left further behind as a consequence (Gillborn & Youdell, 2000). Similarly, health professionals frequently have to operate a system of triage in situations where limited resources have to be target to those most likely to benefit (Iserson & Moskop, 2007; Moskop & Iserson, 2007). Indeed, on the surface this would appear to be simply a manifestation of the concept of utility, which is captured in Jeremy Bentham's fundamental axiom that '*it is the greatest happiness of the greatest number that is the measure of right and wrong*' (Burns, 2005). Moreover, in rural development, similar features have been observed, as Galbraith (1979, p.65) noted: "*The most effective work of these* [extension] *agencies was with a minority of farmers, and it was noticed, not without some sense of guilt and failure, that these were usually the most progressive and prosperous, the ones who seemed least to need help.*" Which accords with Everett Rogers and Floyd

Shoemaker's classical representation of extension take up (Rogers & Shoemaker, 1971, p.182). Indeed, extension agents now believe that, despite their best intentions, an agent may simply be unable to help the farmers most in need of assistance (van den Ban & Hawkins, 1996).

Studies of aid allocation record similar phenomena, leading some authors to advocate targeting aid at precisely those circumstances where '*the poor*' are most able to respond. Indeed, on whole the developing world has a good chance of meeting the overall goals of poverty reduction, but the real achievements are and will continue to be concentrated in Asia, while there remains little progress in Sub-Saharan Africa (Collier & Dollar 2001), particularly as major conflicts draw efforts and resources away. Furthermore, Rainer Thiele, Peter Nunnenkamp and Axel Dreher concluded that:

> *the current focus on substantially increasing aid in order to turn the tide and try achieving the MDGs misses an important point. Unless the targeting of aid is improved, higher aid will not have the desired effects. At the same time, it should be stressed that better targeting is just a necessary, but not a sufficient, condition for more effective aid.* (Thiele, Nunnenkamp & Dreher, 2007, p.21)

However, this discussion raises yet again the question of just what is development and how the international community should approach it. Now, Clarke (2006, p.5) advocated that there is a need: "*for a new humanitarian orientation that transcend*[s] *the artificial dichotomy between emergency relief and development, which donors* [can] *expediently use to simplify their allocation of aid budgets.*" whilst it is evident from discussions in earlier chapters that HA differs in significant respects from DA and hence should warrant such a separate approach. Therefore, it seems that a more strategic approach that seeks to understand the *Lucas paradox* and target resources could pay dividends. In this respect, and following a modified '*Boston Box*' approach, Figure 9.4 sets out a typology that could prove useful in identifying the appropriate, strategic mix of approaches for any given situation. However, as Talbot (2005) cautions, the use of either/or categorisations tend to downplay those very paradoxes and contradictions which are actually pervasive of human systems. Indeed, although it seems obvious that to reach as many of the poor as possible would require that more effort goes towards low cost objectives with high benefits, and that little effort goes to objectives where costs are high relative to the benefits, it would demand an acceptance that doing more on one goal implies doing less on another – but, as Easterly (2006, p.164) noted: "*politicians and bureaucrats are terrified of the word 'tradeoff'*".

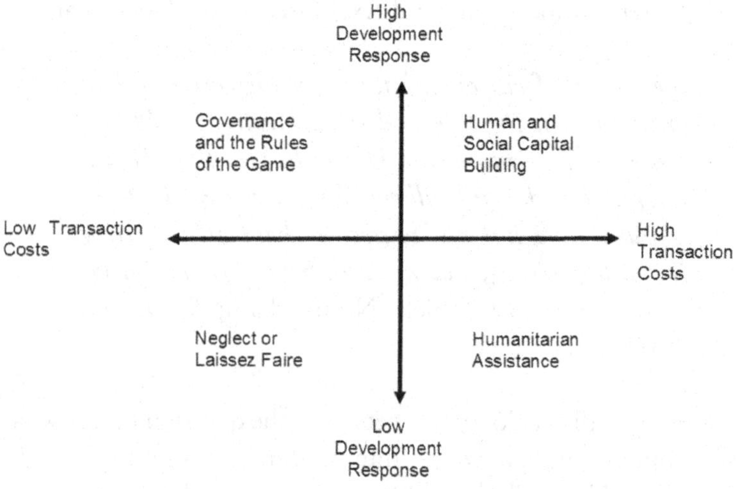
High Development Response
Governance and the Rules of the Game
Human and Social Capital Building
Low Transaction Costs
High Transaction Costs
Neglect or Laissez Faire
Humanitarian Assistance
Low Development Response

Figure 9.4 The Strategic Challenge of Development.

Furthermore, we must take into account that cumulatively, Foreign Direct Investment (FDI) is by far the largest source of external capital flow for all developing countries taken together. In particular, FDI is larger than multilateral and bilateral development assistance put together (Sullivan & Warner, 2004), which must lead us to question whether such capital flows are inside or outside of the managed, intentional process of development. While such capitalistic investment processes, as outlined in chapter 8, are clearly substantially responsible for the putative development of the first world, they were not undertaken with such a purpose in mind. Indeed, the technological, economic, cultural and social changes which those investment processes brought about were primarily a result of self-interested actions, as in Adam Smith's lasting imagery, "*By directing that industry in such a manner as its produce may be of greatest value, he intends only his own gain, and he is in this, as in many other cases, led by an invisible hand to promote an end which was no part of his intention.*" (Smith, 1999b, p.32).

In addition, as we saw in the previous chapter, business has to create in advance the conditions necessary for its own continued expansion if the free-market is to be the engine of development (Harvey, 2011). However, as O'Connor (1998) argued, on the contrary, capitalistic enterprises inevitably undermine their own viability by destroying the very systems upon which they depend (the 2nd contradiction of capitalism[16]), driven by the capitalist imperative. In such systems we see not only the clean air and water that most enterprises require, but also the raw materials (from mines, fields, forests and seas) as well as the physical infrastructure of transport and communications, the social infrastructure of housing and transport for the workers, and the human capital of the health, skills and capabilities of the workforce. Thus not only is there an enlightened self-interest case for business corporations to engage in the provision of these services there is an ethical case for responsible behaviour in the stewardship of this broadly defined nature as well.

16 O'Connor (1998, p.245) stated that: "*the second contradiction states that when individual capitals attempt to defend or restore profits by cutting or externalizing costs, the unintended effect is to reduce the 'productivity' of the conditions of production.*".

6 Corporate Social Responsibility

Some time ago Donaldson (1982, p.42) had asked: "*If General Motors holds society responsible for providing the condition of its existence, then for what does society hold General Motors responsible? What are the terms of the social contract?*" The momentum for the private sector's involvement in development has been gathering ever since. Indeed, Rory Sullivan and Michael Warner reported that:

> *The recent World Summit on Sustainable Development (Rio+10) held in Johannesburg clearly placed the corporate sector at the centre of international efforts to reduce poverty. … the overwhelming sense was of a concept that had been wholeheartedly embraced but where little consideration had been given to what that concept could mean in practice, or how it could be taken up to scale.* (Sullivan & Warner, 2004, p.12).

Moreover, Warhurst (2005, p.152) observed that: "*Society is increasingly expecting global business to work in partnership with others to solve the numerous humanitarian crises and endemic problems facing the world*" and the term '*partnership*' has become a central canon for addressing hunger, poverty and inequality (Contu & Girei, 2013). As James Mayers and Sonja Vermeulen, in the context of the forestry industry, noted:

> *Partnerships refer to the range of relationships and agreements that are actively entered into, on the expectation of benefit, by two or more parties … a very wide spectrum of deals, contracts and informal arrangements between companies and communities, which are mainly a means to share risk between the two parties, with third parties playing important supportive roles.* (Mayers & Vermeulen, 2002, p.24)

This has led to the promotion of Corporate Social Responsibility (CSR), which the Commission of the European Communities (2001, p.6) described as: "*a concept whereby companies integrate social and environmental concerns in their business operations and in their interaction with their stakeholders on a voluntary basis*" and which requires that the firm engages in actions that further some social good beyond the interests of the firm and any requirements of the law (McWilliams, Siegel & Wright, 2006).

Furthermore, such social investment or community development programmes have been implemented through a variety of mechanisms, which Sullivan and Warner (2004, p.17) listed as: "*outsourcing to consultants; … company-led local foundations or trust funds; and … in-house community development or corporate social responsibility teams.*" Whereas the former methodologies drew upon experiences from mainstream development, the last is seen as something different. In many ways CSR has been portrayed as the coming of age of the private sector where firms are able to work with Civil Society rather than in spite of it, to mutual advantage.

Although the motivation for CSR might be the desire to enhance the effectiveness and efficiency of development efforts (Brinkerhoff, 2002), there are benefits for business, as Warhurst (*op.cit.*, p.166) noted: "*opportunities can also be identified – opportunities to enhance value, create new markets and attract new customers and become the preferred business partner and employer of choice.*" Importantly, Howard Shultz and Orin Smith stated that, from their own perspective:

> *Consumers are demanding more than 'product' from their favorite brands. Employees are choosing to work for companies with strong values. Shareholders are more inclined to invest in businesses with outstanding corporate reputations. Quite simply, being socially responsible is not only the right thing to do; it can*

> *distinguish a company from its industry peers.* (Shultz & Smith 2001, p.3)

Which echoes an observation that CSR actions are not about philanthropy or social impact *per se*, but that: "*They are more about … being a responsible citizen.*" (Warhurst, 2005, p.162). Indeed, businesses are also being required to reflect on their risks strategically, taking into consideration wider aspects of ethical, social and political risk that might affect their '*license to operate*' (Warhurst, *op.cit.*).

Amongst the commercially desirable outcomes for CSR Warhurst (*op.cit.*, p.165) listed: "*to facilitate greater stability and economic opportunities to employees, business partners, host governments, community neighbours and shareholders.*" and that these can occur as a result of: "*making profit, paying taxes, engaging in productive business-to-business relationships and following strategies of expansion and growth combined with business values that emphasise social responsibility, good governance and sound and fair employer-employee relations.*" Thus, Hamman and Acutt (2003, p.256) summarized the '*business case*' for CSR as: "*a more responsible, strategic approach to environmental management, labour relations and community development* [which] *should lead to better relationships and improved reputation, and hence greater profits*".

However, Craig Smith (2003, *abstract*) in making the case for persuading companies to take CSR seriously stressed that: "*an individual firm must assess the extent to which the general business case for CSR applies to its specific circumstances.*" and Hillman and Keim (2001, p.136) maintained that: "*The use of a firm's resources always has an opportunity cost. Implementing a social issue participation strategy appears to come at the cost of forgone opportunities to increase shareholder value.*" and that: "*Evidence here suggests the two dimensions of corporate social performance - stakeholder management and social issue participation - have opposing relationships to financial performance.*" Which implies that, from a commercial perspective, no firm can afford to ignore the bottom-line consequences of the range of CSR options open to them.

In addition, there is a CRS paradox whereby it is precisely those large corporations which contribute to social and environmental harm that are considered by promoters of CSR to be key partners in efforts to manage those negative impacts (Hamman & Acutt, 2003). Moreover, under normal circumstances the roles and interests of business and NGOs appear to be in conflict and, as Murphy and Coleman (2000, p.212) emphasised: "*The paradox of business-civil society partnership is inevitable given that it brings together the apparently competing agendas of business and NGOs.*" Indeed, there is an inescapable divergence in the approach of these two sides to community issues, as O'Connor (1998, p.238) had noted: "*For reformist Greens, … the problem is* ***how to remake capital in ways consistent with the sustainability of nature****…. But … corporations construct the problem of the environment in a way that is the polar opposite…, namely, the problem of* ***how to remake nature in ways that are consistent with sustainable profitability and capital accumulation****.*" Moreover, supporters of CSR: "*assume a win-win world and do not recognise intractable conflict between corporate interests and those of civil society. At most, conflict is seen as a process issue, an outcome of paradoxes which should be managed carefully.*" (Bendell, 2000c, p.250)

The end result is often seen to be partnerships that don't live up to their promise (Crewe & Harrison, 1998; Contu & Girei (2013). Nevertheless, Eriksson Baaz (2005, p. 8) cautioned: "*That the partnership policy is poorly reflected in practice cannot be taken as the pretext for a conspiracy – that partnership was never intended.*" As Bendell (2000b, p.97) warned: "*The reality we need to remind ourselves of is one where not everything that is right to do pays, and not everything that pays is right to do.*" Indeed, all things considered, it seems fairly obvious that the very nature of the commercial world dictates that responses to the inherent dilemma of partnership must always come down on the side of business interests.

The entire enterprise that is CSR has been called into question as an inappropriate concern for commerce. Certainly, Milton Friedman upheld that:

> *there is one and only one social responsibility of business—to use its resources and engage in activities designed to increase its profits so long as it stays within the rules of the game, which is to say, engages in open and free competition, without deception or fraud.* (Friedman, 1962, pp.60-61.)

Others have challenged the case upon other lines. Indeed, it has been argued that the practice of CSR does not in truth signifying a change in business culture or ethics, but is rather a reflection of the weaknesses of capitalism in the face of global social movements and the spread of democratic values (Sklair & Miller 2010) that has been termed '*accommodation*'. Moreover, Hamman and Acutt (2003, p.258) maintained that: "*business may be making only partial, superficial or image-related changes to give the impression that it is accommodating social interests.*" [17]

Furthermore, Hamman and Acutt (*op.cit.*, p.259) drew attention to a crucial, related strategy of '*legitimation*' whereby: "*the CSR discourse is characterised by considering private companies as given and immutable economic agents, on whose enlightened self-interest the well-being of… neighbouring communities depends. The possibility of alternative economic structures … is seldom considered, much less significant structural elements of the economy*". The very presence of CSR thereby strengthens the position of the corporation

[17] if not actually spilling over into practices that are referred to as '*greenwashing*' (Ramus & Montiel, 2005; Parguel, Benoît-Moreau, & Larceneux, 2011).

over communities in decision taking by seeming to represent a concession that is in fact no such thing.

Indeed, Leslie Sklair and David Miller maintained that:

> *CSR is … intertwined with the overall strategies of the corporations to resist regulation and to ensure 'voluntary' outcomes. ... One of the key functions of CSR is to enable further deregulation by pointing to the involvement of business in ethical and sustainable activities and indicating that 'multi-stakeholder dialogue' with civil society obviates the need for binding regulation and opens up opportunities for corporate involvement in the public sector and thus increasingly in social policy.* (Sklair & Miller, 2010, p.491).

Similarly, Hamman and Acutt (*op.cit.*, p.257) saw: "*partnerships or voluntary initiatives as an attempt to pre-empt and preclude 'corporate accountability' or compliance with state-sponsored regulations and standards*", and Harvey (2011, p.69) noted that: "*The WTO agreements, for example, codify 'good behaviour' for the states that have signed up … in such a way as to favour the freedoms of corporations to do business without excessive state regulation or interference.*"

Furthermore, such deregulation and liberalisation, Newell (2000, p.32) warned, will: "*heighten pressures to lower environmental standards. The freedom of mobile transnational capital to locate where environmental regulations are weakest is one of the more vocal of a spectrum of concerns about the negative impacts of globalisation.*" which chimes all too closely with the observation that, for business at large, the stakes generated by competition are too strong an incentive to win and inevitably create a downward pressure on ethical standards (Korten, 2006). As Harvey (2011, p.71) noted: "*individual capitalists, working in their own short-term interests and impelled by the coercive laws of competition, are perpetually tempted to take the position of* ***après moi le deluge*** *with respect to both the labourer and the soil.*"

Contrariwise, Rodrik (2011, p.211) maintained that: "*Improving large corporations' social and environmental performance would spur emulation by other, smaller firms. It would alleviate the widespread concern that international competition creates a race to the bottom in labor and environmental standards at the expense of social inclusion at home.*" This is often enacted as '*stakeholder management*' where the business interest is seen as gaining a '*social license to operate*'. Indeed, companies extract enormous public relations benefits in conveying the impression that the private sector is taking its responsibilities to society seriously by publicizing a limited supply of examples of '*best practice*' (Hamman & Acutt, 2003). However, daily practice for the majority of firms would seem to be otherwise. For example, Korten (2006, p.51) drew attention to: "*a wave of exposés in 2002 and 2003 of pervasive corruption at the highest levels of corporate and governmental power [which] suggested that many of our most powerful institutions are in the hands of ethically challenged human beings.*" Indeed, branded items have been produced by subcontractors at factories in South-east Asia which were discovered not only to violate domestic labour laws but also the much trumpeted codes of conduct of the brand owner (Sklair & Miller, 2010) [18].

Indeed, in spite of an endless stream of commission reports and legally binding conventions (Stockholm, Brandt, Brundtland, Rio, Johannesburg, *etc.*) we are no nearer finding solutions to poverty, conflict, human rights abuses and ecological degradation (Murphy & Coleman, 2000). Moreover, there already exists an *International Framework of Human Rights for Business* which, if business were really heart set on CSR, could be adhered to tomorrow as '*norms*' for responsible practice, but which is only gradually being developed into sets of national laws, codes of conduct and voluntary initiatives (Warhurst, 2005).

18 See also the short-lived publicity surrounding the clothing factory disaster in 2013 in Dhaka, Bangladesh.

Furthermore, an *Ethical Trading Initiative* has been established which aims to persuade companies to implement codes of conduct that embody internationally agreed labour standards and human rights in the workplace and to use best practice monitoring and independent verification methods (Murphy & Coleman, *op.cit.*). Indeed, the question we need to ask ourselves has to be: if the private sector is in any significant way wedded to the concept of CSR, or Corporate Citizenship, why would such an initiative be necessary when enlightened self-interest and ethics should already have propelled these firms into the forefront of compliance with these international regulations?[19] Yet, whilst there are clear arguments and standards being articulated by governments and civil society, for the private sector it is business as usual until somebody forces them to comply. Companies are not only dragging their feet but are lobbying strongly to keep regulation at arm's length.[20]

Realistically, the imperative of capitalism to compete precludes any voluntary restraint or indeed incentive to comply with non-statutory guidelines[21]. As Friedman (1970, p.2) noted: "*What does it mean to say that the corporate executive has a 'social responsibility' in his capacity as businessman? If this statement is not pure rhetoric, it must mean that he is to act in some way that is not in the interest of his employers.*" The leopard cannot change its spots nor act contrary to its nature. Indeed, we must argue that, if truth be told, it is unethical to ask anyone to act against their own interests and agree with Hardin (1973, pp.129-130) that: "*a system that depends only on conscience rewards the conscienceless. … … Seeing the counterproductive results of voluntary compliance with guidelines, we finally admit the necessity of coercion for all*".

---

19 If you truly hold ethical values you don't need regulations – St. Paul's letter to the Galatians 5, v. 18.

20 Certainly, Barque (1993, p.164) maintained that the: "*free market is not an effective instrument for raising up a civilisation founded on and governed by ethical values*".

21 As Hardin (1973, p.121) put it: "*rational men are helpless to behave otherwise*".

Moreover, as UNRISD (1995, p. 19) recognised: "*international business cannot be expected to author their own regulation: this is the job of good governance.*" and it can be argued that the current emphases on voluntarism and CSR are misguided, as they forestall the need to build new democratic mechanisms to control the market and hold its institutions to account (Bendell, 2000c). Indeed, contrary to the assertion that CSR would permit the private sector to take on some of the functions that states are finding increasingly difficult to finance and carry out, as in public health and environmental protection, which in turn would narrow the governance gap between international markets and national governments (Rodrik, 2011)[22], Bendell (2000c, p.247) argued that: "*A **subject** of a **resolution** who is also the **agent** making that choice between norms is neither a **subject** nor an **agent**, and the system is not a **regulatory framework**. Consequently the concept of industry self-regulation is a contradiction.*"

At this point I feel that it is interesting to note that, in the development of Management Theory associated with effective team working (Williams, 1996), a number of group resources have been identified that are considered necessary to enable the most effective performance. These are:

ENERGY
CONTROL
INFLUENCE
EXPERTISE

And it is instructive to relate these to the wider organization of human affairs where the concept of Holism seeks to place the commonwealth of the people between the supporting natural environment, which is becoming increasingly fragile and

22 Note that lack of finance can be attributed, at least in part, to companies pursuing ethically questionable policies of tax avoidance.

requiring the utmost good husbandry, and the three partners of a functioning society – namely:

Community
Government
Enterprise

(Pieterse, 1999)

Now, Community contributes largely Influence, Government contributes largely Control, Enterprise contributes largely Energy and all to some extend can contribute Expertise. Indeed, Jem Bendell observed that:

> *Governments' primary concern is with a political system focusing on the creation of rules that can be enforced through coercive means such as the police and courts. Businesses' primary concern is with economic systems where owners are in control and people are induced to do what the organisation desires through monetary rewards. In contrast NGOs focus on social systems and networks based on values and beliefs; they derive their power from their ability to speak to tradition, community benefit and values.* (Bendell, 2000a, p.17)

If we can get a reasonable adherence to the provision of their resource, and if each partner supports the others in the performance of their roles then we could bring about a high performing system. Clearly each is mutually dependent upon the others and should respect their complimentary contributions. Members of the government and administration are also private citizens, as are the owners, managers and workers in business and industry, and should be encouraged to channel their influence democratically through Civil Society. The people, on whom each depends as voters or clients and customers, are also dependent upon the stability and wealth that are generated by government and enterprise respectively. All are entirely dependent upon the natural environment to support life.

Thus a proper manifestation of CSR should be a determination to act within the regulatory framework set down by government and to eschew corruption in all its manifestations, including the exertion of undue influence upon the regulatory process. Indeed, it has been argued that if companies lobbied for heightened regulation, particularly internationally, it would raise the common standard of practice and ensure greater benefit for all (Bendell, 2000c). Governments should concentrate their efforts upon regulating for the protection of the environment, the establishment of reasonable working conditions, health and education, infrastructure and, most importantly, providing a regulatory and fiscal framework that constitutes a level playing field for all players in a given market segment. It is not for them to set prices but to ensure the proper working of the market. Civil Society's role then becomes one of monitoring the private sector's compliance with the regulations, government's even-handed enforcement of the rules and lobbying for the interests of the various constituents of a pluralistic society, whether through trades unions, chambers of commerce, professional bodies, consumer groups, single issue NGOs, *etc.*. Again, it may be argued that, since legal regulation is under pressure of resourcing and, as discussed above, self-regulation is irreconcilable, then regulation by civil society is a valid model for modern business-NGO relations (Bendell, *op.cit.*).

In the meanwhile, as is true for more general development efforts, it is necessary to be able to appraise CSR activity and in a way that it is readily understood, and can be evaluated by third parties (Aras & Crowther, 2009). Of course, this measurement and reporting on a company's performance should encompass economic prosperity, social justice and environmental quality, and the *Global Reporting Initiative* (GRI) attempts to do so in respect of: "*human rights, social development, labour standards, product responsibility, environmental protection and financial and ethical efficiency.*" (Warhurst, 2005, p.154).

7 Measuring Well-being

The real question, therefore, seems to be how to measure what state a person or a nation is in and whether it suffices i.e. their well-being. Perhaps for that reason the place to start such an exploration is in the distinction between the concepts of economy and eudemony. The concept of economy is rooted in the art of the management of the household (Cruz, Stahel & Max-Neef, 2009), which, for nations, over the years has become conflated with the idea of Gross Domestic Product (GDP), which is an accounting of all the measurable, money-based transactions that take place within the boundaries of a state over the course of a year. Indeed, GDP has become generally recognised and utilised as **the** indicator of economic progress. It has been and continues to be widely used as the foremost register of a nation's well-being by interested parties of all persuasions from economists, to policymakers, international agencies as well as the media (Talberth, Cobb & Slattery, 2007). However, Beer (2004a, p.780) lamented that: "*The first variety attenuation which ran quite counter to British viability was the creed of greed itself. Never before had the great majority of Britons been persuaded that the only criterion which matters is wealth, or that money alone is its measure.*"

In this respect, GDP is very much a blunt instrument even for such a limited task. Indeed, there has been growing criticism of its shortcomings. For example, it is widely recognised that per capita GDP can be rising on average even when the majority of people not only feel that they are worse off, but are actually worse off (Stiglitz, 2010). Furthermore, the previously mentioned separation of the production economy from the financial one is clearly apparent in the growth of GDP being far outstripped by the expansion of banking assets for many economies (Peetz & Genreith, 2011). As Sedlacek (2011, p.86) objected: "*what sense do GDP growth statistics make in a situation with a several times larger deficit in its background? What sense does it make to measure riches if I have borrowed to acquire them?*" Then there is the fact that GDP can be increased by ill-being as much as by transactions that have a positive impact. For example environmental pollution can be counted as a double contribution to GDP since we tally it when toxic chemicals are manufactured and again when we clean them up (Talberth, *et al.*, 2007). Furthermore, Latouche (2003, p.4) remarked that: "*A happy person, notes Hervé Martin, does not take anti-depressants, does not consult psychiatrists, does not attempt suicide, does not shatter shop windows, does not spend the day shopping for things as expensive as they are unnecessary*", and Sedlacek (*op.cit.*, p.187) echoed Bernard Mandeville's long-standing argument that: "*vice is a multiplier of effective demand, which becomes a driver for the economy.*"[23] Indeed, political economy is built on the contradictory logic of the desire of accumulation as a precondition for the functioning of capitalism and desire as the origin of misery and vice which are part of the 2nd contradiction (Watts, 1995), and which seldom features in economic theory. As Orr (2004, p.62) observed: "*The dependence of the economy on sin is a phenomenon infrequently studied by economists.*"

Importantly, GDP doesn't take account of the destruction of natural, social and human capital, nor take account of the true value or the depreciation of natural (and other) assets (Coyle, 2011) which are not paid for by the capitalist enterprises. Indeed, a lot of growth has been achieved in this way, which should be seen as a form of borrowing from the future which is more pernicious because the debts thus generated are by no means obvious causing Stiglitz (2010, p.284) to comment that: *We are leaving future generations poorer as a result, but our GDP indicator doesn't reflect this.*"

---

[23] See Bernard Mandeville's notorious *Fable of the bees: or, Private Vices, Publick Benefits*; and Reinert (2013).

Furthermore, taking an approach that concentrates upon GDP as a metric of well-being has a distorting influence upon current perceptions of what is important, which Bauman (2013, p.54) captured, with characteristic percipience, when he noted that: "***the road to happiness travels through shopping****; the sum total of the nation's shopping activity is the prime and least fallible measure of society's happiness*".

Thus we are drawn to conclude that economic welfare is only a very small part and a poor indicator of human welfare[24] and, with Hayek (2007, p.101), to recognise that: "*The welfare and the happiness of millions cannot be measured on a single scale of less and more. The welfare of a people, … depends on a great many things that can be provided in an infinite variety of combinations.*" Indeed, Sen (1999, p.14) argued that: "*An adequate conception of development must go much beyond the accumulation of wealth and the growth of gross national product and other income-related variables. Without ignoring the importance of economic growth, we must look well beyond it.*" which should lead us, with Stafford Beer, to ask:

> *Then what is the metric? … In this case Sir Charles* [Goodeve] *explained that it must be some complicated image of well-being; and he chose to call that by the entirely suitable Greek word 'eudemony'. This is one of the Greek words for happiness, though it comes nearer to meaning prosperity than ecstasy.* (Beer, 1994, p.167).

Thus, this requirement, to find an alternative way of measuring and then comparing, the state of human well-being, has led to the emergence of a number of alternatives, of which a small number are worth mentioning. The first was developed by the UNDP (1990) under the guidance of Mahbub ul Haq and Amartya Sen and termed the Human Development Index (HDI) (Haq, 2000;

---

24 See Scitovsky (1976) and Luke 12, v. 15 – *a man's life consists not in the abundance of the things which he possesses.* v. 23 – *The life is more than meat and the body more than raiment.*

Sen 1999). According to Eric Neumayer the major goal of the HDI:

> *was to focus attention away from income towards a more comprehensive measure of human development. UNDP ... proposed to treat income as only one out of three factors — the other ones currently being life expectancy at birth as a proxy for health achievement and adult literacy together with educational enrolment as a proxy for educational attainment.* (Neumayer, 2001, p.101)

However, whilst the HDI did raise the profile of composite development indicators, its ability to replace GDP as a discriminatory indicator of development has been challenged. Indeed Mark McGillivray concluded that:

(a) *the composition of the index is flawed as it is significantly and positively correlated with each of its component variables individually;*

(b) *as a consequence, assessing intercountry development levels on any one of these variables yields similar results to those that the index itself yields, and more profoundly;*

(c) *with the exception of a minority of country groups, the index largely provides us with little more information regarding intercountry development levels than the more traditional indicator, GNP per capita, alone provides.* (McGillivray, 1991, p. 1467)

Nevertheless, the HDI remains the basis of the UNDP's Human Development Report, albeit in a modified form which itself has received similar criticism (Ravalion, 2012).

The second is a triad; the Index of Sustainable Economic Welfare (ISEW) (Daly & Cobb, 1989), the Genuine Progress Indicator (GPI) (Hamilton, 1999) and a Sustainable Net Benefit Index

(SNBI) (Lawn, 2003). These are often viewed as interchangeable since they are attempts to develop composite indicators of well-being that take into account many of the short-comings of GDP and emphasise sustainability issues and include a number of social and environmental benefits and costs that invariably escape market valuation (Lawn, *op.cit.*). Furthermore they have been used to identify a '*threshold hypothesis*' that holds that for every society there seems to be a stage during which economic growth brings an improvement in the average quality of life, but only up to a threshold point beyond which, if economic growth continues, the quality of life may actually begin to worsen (Max-Neef, 1995, p.117). If such a notion proves to be well founded then the suspicion arises that any benefits of adhering to neoliberal principles may prove to deliver only short term benefits (*ibid.* p.118) contributing another criticism of the *Washington Consensus.*

Thirdly, in searching for a metric of well-being in order to explore its role in the epidemiology of HIV, John Clarke also took recourse to the concept of eudemony, noting that:

> *Beer's development of an algedonic metering system to monitor and track changes in social 'eudemony' (Aristotle's term for well-being) in Chile in the early 70's provides the structure for computing the Eudemony Index, and Max-Neefs concept of nine universal, fundamental human needs (subsistence, protection, affection, creation, participation, idleness, identity, understanding and freedom) provide the content.* (Clarke, 2006, p.3)

Which has led to the development of the wheel of fundamental human needs (see Max-Neef, 1991) as an instrument for measuring well-being in a participatory way.

In actual fact, in relation to our observations in chapter 8, section 5, as Beer (1994, p.170) concluded: "*Cost-benefit analysis converts eudemony into money, which is fine for so long as the money-metric obeys the rules of mensuration: to be additive, to be linear, to be so formulated as to make sense of a maximizing objective function.* [But] *For all the reasons I have given, money fails to be the metric we need.*" Thus, with the ascendancy of the financial economy what constitutes human development is more difficult to square with the values of the Enlightenment and the progressive liberalism of the 19th century philosophers and economists, and challenges us to review and reassert those ideas.

8 Concluding Remarks

As Sheth (1997, p.332) observed: "*The combined impact of [the market] on the poorest of the poor is that they are not entitled to become full wage-earners in the economy or fully fledged citizens in the polity.*" It seems incontrovertible that, in order to make your way in the world, you need to produce something that can be exchanged (or given) in return for those things that you require for your own maintenance and development. Indeed, Rodrik (2010, p.137) argued that: "*The proximate cause of poverty is low productivity. Poor people are poor because their labour enables them to produce too little to adequately feed and house themselves, let alone provide for other needs such as health and education.*" which is not unlike the observation that Say's Law is an assertion about what permits people to purchase in the marketplace, wherein purchasing power is about actual production, which is to say that consumption equals production (Anderson, 2009).

This coincides with the observation made by Amsden (2012, p.120) that: "*Despite championing the cause of poor people around the world and dramatizing the human condition, the United Nation's Millennium Development Goals make no mention of employment generation as a means to battle poverty; there is silence on using economic policies — employment, fiscal industrial, monetary and trade — to create more industries that could provide additional jobs above the subsistence level.*" Thus the actions that could bring about development would seem to be any that will establish the individual's or community's ability to produce value.

Nevertheless, we prefer to take short cuts in the process of development and, under the influence of the moral hazard, seek to avoid the long term relationships that are the hallmark of successful human communities. On the one hand this is manifested in the usury that generates debt amongst states and individuals rather than the proper partnership that would be based upon investment and shared risks, and on the other by financial provision for consumption rather than measures that would either generate the means of production or the conditions necessary for production. The provision of Humanitarian Assistance to keep body and soul together must be accompanied by initiatives that enhance the production of value, but also by governance measures that provide for the poor to produce and save in security.

Furthermore, the proper functioning of the market requires that competition be released. But it is important that, with Joseph Schumpeter, we recognise that:

> *it is not that kind of [price] competition which counts but the competition from the new commodity, the new technology, the new source of supply, the new type of organization ... - competition which commands a decisive cost or quality advantage and which strikes not at the margins of the profits and the outputs of the existing firms but at their foundations and their very lives.* (Schumpeter, 2010, p.74),

Which requires the state to provide appropriate support for research and development. Moreover, the expansion of technology in the production process leads to the displacement of labour and, as O'Connor (1998, p.240) observed: "*Fewer workers, technicians, and others in the labor process produce more, hence, by definition, are able to consume less, absent a deflation of prices.*" which in turn leads to the division of society into the capitalists, an élite group of highly skilled workers, a pool of unskilled labourers and the remainder, which divisions and their schizmogenetic impacts need to be managed by a judicious mix of support for SME's[25]; redistributive, progressive taxation; and substantial programs of education and skills training.

The involvement and balanced development of the three sectors, whose interdependence is founded upon mutual respect for what each brings to the undertaking, is another necessary ingredient. If unscrupulous companies are not going to be allowed simply to exploit uneven playing fields of poor wages, unacceptable working conditions, absent environmental regulation, and weak legal enforcement, then everybody has to sign up to ensuring that governance works for the people, led by civil society and supported by ethical CSR.

Finally, as John Kenneth Galbraith noted:

> *Present also was the thought that the success of both fiscal and monetary policy depended not on superior wisdom but on superior technique. This, all will know by now, has never been so. Were it the happy case, the economic problem would have been solved long since, for in all fields of endeavour good technicians abound.* (Galbraith, 1976, p.345)

Furthermore, Kane and Patapan (2006, p.711) argued that: "*Prudence is the preeminent virtue of active life and therefore of politics and government.*" Thus our present preoccupation with the development of *technē* must give way to a concentration on *phronesis*, particularly as it applies to the management of economics and governance as a route to human well-being.

---

25 Small and Micro-Enterprises.

Chapter 10

Penultimate Essays – Details for *Poesis* and *Praxis*

1 Introduction

Before we can draw matters to a close there are a few issues that should be addressed, for the sake of completeness. The first is a piece of *technē* with which I have wrestled for twenty five years, which has received bad press and vilification throughout, and yet which I have found of enormous help in a wide range of contexts and agencies. Then I want to visit the issue of double binds and examine their extensive occurrence in the practices of development.

2 Logical Frameworks

Over the years and in the foregoing chapters and arguments I have maintained the necessity of planning and the importance of doing it well (Dearden & Kowalski, 2003). Following Alfred Korzybski's aphorism that '*the map is not the territory*' (quoted in Schein, Kahane and Scharmer, 2001, p.11), we must recognise that any plan can only be an approximate description of reality and proposed actions. Furthermore, despite this onus to have a plan[1], the process of planning proves to be more important than the plan produced. The reification of planning and the confusion of the plan with reality are both a result of the paradox of control (Streatfield, 2001) and a source of further paradoxes and double binds.

Now, the planning tool of choice for many development agencies is the Logical Framework (logframe) and, though disliked by many as the embodiment of Western determinism and hegemony (IDS, 2001), should be seen as just a series of questions, which if answered, and frequently re-asked, will enhance the prospects of success for any undertaking, whether paid for by OPM (other people's money) or MOM (my own money) (Dichter, 2003). Table 10.1 sets out those questions in the familiar (*sic*) 4x4 matrix.

The whole framework represents a putative understanding of the context and need for change, but should not be seen as a definitive statement of determined commitment to that and only that understanding. That the logframe is disliked and misused by many professionals is, in my opinion, a tribute to their aversion to doing some serious thinking and to applying themselves with discipline to a fundamental requirement of their chosen employment. Their excuse can be traced to similar traits in their political masters, who are seldom committed to details (Brunsson, 1989), and to the many authors and trainers who have added confusion rather than clarity to the use of logframes (Dale, 2004).

---

1 Al-Bazzaz & Grinyer (1981, p.165) noted a tendency for formalized planning to be forced upon subsidiaries and lamented that "*higher organizations impose a level of formality on this lower level which they are not prepared to operate themselves.*" This is entirely to miss the point of planning and is unprofessional. Supervisors must take their own planning seriously.

Objectives	Indicators	Evidence	Conditions
Goal: What impact on the lives of the poor are we contributing to?	What changes do we expect to see?	How will evidence of these changes be collected and by whom?	What will make this impact sustainable?
Purpose: What change are we seeking to effect?	What measurable outcomes will this bring about?	How will evidence of these outcomes be collected and by whom?	What conditions are necessary for the impact to be achieved?
Outputs: What do we need to put in place or upgrade in order to bring about that change?	What performances do we expect to improve that will take us towards the change we desire? And to what degree?	How will evidence of these improved performances be collected and by whom?	What conditions are necessary for the change to be achieved once the outputs are in place?
Activities: What will be done to put in place or upgrade the things that are required, listed above?	What do we expect to happen on the way to putting them in place?	How will evidence of these achievements be collected and by whom?	What conditions are necessary for our actions to bring about those things?

Table 10.1. The Sixteen Questions of the Logical Framework

Of course, the argument put forward by Dichter (2003) that the logframe has been designed and imposed by the '*helpers*' when it is properly a tool of the '*doers*', and that this draws the '*helpers*' into inappropriate doing, is well made, but it is not an argument against the logframe's utility for the legitimate '*doers*'. To those who maintain their antipathy I ask: if not a logframe then what? A simple demand for donors to hand over the money, and leave us to do the job is clearly a non-starter (Dichter, 2003).

Furthermore, if the framework is just a matter of asking questions then why is it so deeply disliked? The questions themselves are fairly non-contentious and are capable of being translated into language appropriate for any context, so the problem cannot be with the tool itself. Like any other tool in the hands of the unwary or manipulative (Wield, 1999), the logframe can prove to be deeply damaging because of the way that professionals ask the questions and because of the way that they treat the answers. The imposition of a requirement to use the logframe, although well intentioned, is often counterproductive unless it has been supported by capacity building measures (Kowalski & Kaškelyte, 2005).

Ultimately this all comes down to the exercise of power, particularly that manifested in decision-taking, as discussed in section 6 of chapter 3, and the impatience to get on with things. What we are doing when we set out a logframe is simply to seek to make the answers to its questions as comprehensive, as transparent and as shared as we can (Kowalski, 2006) and this has to be the core message of the planning process itself. As Stafford Beer cautioned:

> *we can do no more than foster the planning potential in other people or in disadvantaged nations and communities. To offer them methodologies of planning that do not work is cynical and insulting – but these are the only planning methodologies that we have discovered. To offer them a plan content that defines progress in our terms uses a false measure of eudemony expressed within an alien entelechy.* (Beer, 2004, p.820)

Of course the answer to any question may not be instantly to hand, nor fully comprehensive, nor indeed universally accepted. This emphasizes the importance of being able to live with ambiguity, and to manage consensus during the process of analysis, formulation of the plan and, most importantly, during the subsequent modification of the plan throughout implementation. Our focus should be to think strategically, rather than to complete prescribed lists or apply predetermined categories (Goldsmith, 1996). Similarly, Amabile (1983) stressed that champions of change should have the ability to hold options open for a long time and to suspend judgment.

Nevertheless, although looking forward many futures are possible only one will come to be the actual future. When we plan, therefore, we are setting our sights on one desired future and taking steps to eliminate all the other possible futures. There may not be just one possible path to that actual future – but there should be one best path (efficient, aesthetically pleasing etc.). Therefore, we can perceive a number of potential paths of action, some of which will lead to the desired future, some will not and, of those that will, there will be better and worse paths, but for each we will, with hindsight, eventually be able to answer fully the sixteen questions.

Now, let us take as our point of reference the ideas of Plato who introduced us to the notion of ideal '*forms*' for everything (see Ferré, 1998 p.28-40), and to which actual examples can be related as imperfect copies. In respect of Plato's forms, therefore, we can assert that if our aspired future is possible then there must be an '*ideal*' plan that will deliver it – whether we know which it is or not, whether we care to imagine what it might be or not.

Then we may suppose that for every initiative there must be a '*perfect*' Logical Framework in some ethereal space and it follows that we may expect to be able to produce variants of imperfect plans, and that no version that we produce is capable of being the '*perfect*' logframe. It also follows that, even if we do not produce a physically manifested logframe for an initiative, at the very least a virtual one must exist within the unconscious of the protagonists of the initiative. I say this because a logframe is simply and only the answers to those sixteen questions about the purpose, actions and environment of the initiative. It follows that, since those questions necessarily exist, the answers themselves must exist and, if not explicitly recorded, be either tacit, implicit and/or peculiar to the individual protagonists (i.e. contested).

When the designers produce a logframe of doubtful quality (one that is illogical, or incomplete or lacking clarity (Gasper,

1999)) they are challenging the implementers of the initiative to produce a better one of their own – that is they are requiring **the implementers** to invest the intellectual effort of making sense of the inadequate logframe in front of them. A good team of implementers (in partnership) will be capable of overcoming a poor logframe by devising their own sense. However, they may or may not produce a physical entity that facilitates explicitness, transparency and sharing – a key benefit of the planning process. If indeed they do not then they will need to be very good communicators, and if they do, then they may feel obliged to keep their 'local' plan 'in-house' because its status outside (with the donor, say) might be contentious and its existence bring about sanctions. Where the implementers are unable to formulate and communicate an adequate logframe, either their own or a good '*official*' one, then the initiative will almost certainly founder in conflict and confusion.

Now, we must also consider the impact of having an '*official*' logframe of doubtful quality, upon other aspects of the DA process. For the implementers and the donor's administrators the first issue is reporting. If the logframe is of poor quality then this will make the job of supervision and its mirror image – reporting, very difficult[2]. With a lack of clarity, logic and/or completeness the supervisor will be constantly in need of reassurance that all is well by asking for extended narrative in reports and by focusing on Activities rather than Outputs or Outcomes (Indicators at Purpose level).

The implementer will be struggling to force the activities and achievements that are coming from the '*virtual*' or '*in-house*'

[2] I well remember, whilst coordinating a project in Latin America, at the end of the Inception phase sending to the donor's supervisor a redrafted logframe for ratification. In the meanwhile a first quarterly report fell due and was demanded. I asked if I could report to the new logframe and was told: "No, report to the old one", after all even though obsolete it was the official one!

version into the Procrustean bed that is the inadequate sense to be made of the official framework. The end result is to double the work of everyone involved without adding to the effectiveness of the initiative[3]. Of course, the next step in the aid process is an even greater challenge for an inadequate logframe. The need for donor accountability to the institutions that fund them (for example DFID's accountability to the Treasury via the *Public Service Agreement*) raises the profile of '*Performance Reporting*', a process that is reliant upon being able to score objectively the success of initiatives in a way that can be externally audited. Such scoring can only be on the basis of the verifiable achievement of the objectives of the initiative as set out in the indicators that form part of the logframe. At this point the need for quality plans becomes overwhelming.

For all these reasons it is desirable and a good investment of effort to produce a detailed and shared plan for every initiative, and the logframe is as good a format as any other. I set out in Box 10.1 below some guidelines that I hope will aid the production of more workable plans whether at Policy, Programme, or Project level, bearing in mind the caution advanced by Biggs and Smith (2003) that advocates of manuals and new approaches can get over enthusiastic about the logic and good sense of what they propose, but which may well not be driven by nor meeting the needs of the end users of such new management techniques. Of course, as indicated earlier in this section, the absence of demand for such tools may very well be due to the desire of implementers to be given a free hand to '*get on with things*' – a possible explanation

---

3 I have vivid memories of being invited in to an IFI to help sort out difficulties they were having in relating to their development donors which turned out to be entirely the result of the particular programme being devoid of OUTPUTS, which no one involved from either side had until then recognised. As a consequence, the donors had only been able to inquire about ACTIVITIES, which the IFI in turn perceived as them wishing to interfere in day-to-day management details!

of the failure to learn lessons that Biggs and Smith (*op.cit.*) also lament.

A further point that is often raised is the perception that changing the logframe after it has been agreed is undesirable, difficult or even prohibited. This perception is really a relic of the days of the 'blueprint' or infrastructure projects, when design could be undertaken once, at the outset, by experts and pretty much guaranteed to last to completion. It is far better to produce a good logframe and to update it as the initiative progresses, using an unchangeable PURPOSE to maintain focus[4]. With the advent of '*process*' projects that rely for their effectiveness upon the responses of human beings it has become evident that we are dealing with a qualitatively different approach to the implementation of initiatives, which in many respects is akin to rebuilding the ship whilst at sea.

---

[4] If the PURPOSE needs to change then we are talking about effectively beginning a new initiative.

Box 10.1 Guidelines for Completing a Logical Framework

1. Ensure that there is only one PURPOSE. It is the heart of the plan and should capture the *raison d'être* of the initiative. Always remember that the INDICATORS' box exists for you to explain the PURPOSE in greater detail, which may mean using two or more quite different traits to capture what the change may involve.
2. OUTPUTS are the deliverables of the plan. They should be things – so expressed as nouns – that will continue to exist for some appropriate time after the initiative has been undertaken. They are effectively the initiative's *Terms of Reference*.
3. There are six categories from which potential OUTPUTS can be identified, as follows:
   - ✧ **Human Capacity** (specific people able to do specific tasks or roles)
   - ✧ **Infrastructure** (From big structures like Ports, and Hospitals, to plant, like Water and Sanitation hardware, through to small items, like Tools and Equipment).
   - ✧ **Systems** (processors, such as Committees or Boards, and procedures – providing things like communication systems, reporting systems, accounting systems, appraisal systems).
   - ✧ **Materials** (From documents like Guidelines or Regulations, to publications like Pamphlets or Handbooks, through to Webpages and Blogs).
   - ✧ **Knowledge** (Specifically information and understanding that no-one has at the outset, like Baseline data, Statistics, Analyses, Recommendations or Piloted approaches).
   - ✧ **Awareness or buy-in** (less specific groups or types of people or stakeholders whose support or acquiescence is necessary to the initiative).
4. INDICATORS are the detail of the plan, and should be SMART. According to cause and effect logic, they can only exist once the objective to which they relate has been achieved. Consequently they should fall chronologically between one level of the logframe and the next,[5] and they should not just be the completion of ACTIVITIES at that level, nor indeed a summary of the Activity Based Budget (helpful though that might be).
5. The EVIDENCE column is a chance to think about issues like exactly who is going to be responsible for collecting it? This should not be relegated to a responsibility for the review and evaluation teams. Often such deliberation leads to the identification of more capacity building actions and to the allocation of an adequate budget for monitoring.
6. The CONDITIONS column is an opportunity to undertake a thorough going risk analysis and should be concerned, in the end, with only those residual risks once mitigatory actions have been included with the other ACTIVITIES.
7. Do not say the same thing more than once in different boxes. Each box is an opportunity to explore and communicate about an important issue – so use it!

These guidelines should be followed through an iterative process of several cycles of deliberation with stakeholders that leaves decision-taking to the very end of the design phase, and which is highly participatory and focuses upon exploration and communication.

In the final analysis what defines a '*good logframe*' is one which truly helps stakeholders to make sense of the initiative and which facilitates implementation.

Remember that no plan survives first contact with the enemy – so be prepared to make changes during implementation, always bearing in mind that such changes must also be subject to exploration and communication. It also requires quick response times from supervisors (ATD)!

Finally, don't put the logframe in the file – put it up on the office wall on large A1 sheets, and celebrate achievements graphically, chorally, terpsichoreally and gustatorally.

---

5 The extent of muddled thinking is exemplified by Biggs & Smith (2003, pp.1752-1753) who, in recording that: "*the project's midterm review resulted in just such changes in parts of the project's culture: first, many of the old* ***output*** *indicators were dropped and there were collegiate*

We must recognise that, for the planners, the process of analysis involves taking a viewpoint of a situation that is off the timeline, in the third, dissociated position - looking on (for a fuller explanation see O'Connor & Seymour 1993, pp.141-144)[6], whereas the implementers are necessarily on the timeline itself, being fully associated with unfolding events and necessarily engaged in the living present. Therefore they '*know*' the situation in very different ways and have interests in the logframe that are poles apart; the planners are interested in and accountable at the top levels and the implementers the bottom. They need to come together to share their experience of the initiative, as events unfold. Therefore, it is necessary to recognise that the logframe must be capable of modification and that we must have a supervisory process that recognises this.

Synoptically, I would suggest that we have a concept note stage, where the top two rows of the framework are available, that this is followed by a design and/or inception phase where the third row is partially completed and a rudimentary fourth row is added, to be followed by several stopping-points on the road to completion, where *Outputs* can be added (or taken away) and *Activities* (and their associated indicators, evidence base and conditions) emerge and are enacted or discarded as they prove to be both necessary and sufficient to achieve the desired forward progress (see Figure 10.1).

---

discussions to agree a limited number of time-bound output-to-purpose indicators;" provide evidence that, in this instance, nobody had realised that the old output indicators were erroneous and that more suitable ones were absent. Like so many situations I have encountered the protagonists were in conflict, not because of culture, but because of illogical thinking. Straighten that out and in my experience peace breaks out on all sides as double binds fall away.

6 Ellerman (2005b, p.219) speaks of being in a helicopter hovering above the maze.

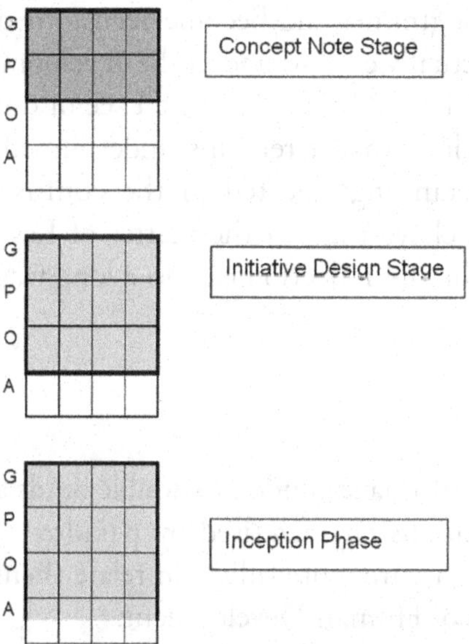
G
P
O
A
Concept Note Stage
G
P
O
A
Initiative Design Stage
G
P
O
A
Inception Phase

Figure 10.1 The three phases of initiative development and their associated logframes.

Such stopping points should be established within the initiative memorandum and it must be explicitly agreed that the fundamental question to be asked at such junctures is *How does the logframe need to be adjusted?*

In conclusion I would say that the importance of planning remains undiminished but that, given the paradoxical nature of the process, the necessary skills within the donor, recipient government, civil society and contractor communities to facilitate their design, implementation and updating will require substantial strengthening to enable them to produce adequate, though necessarily imperfect logframes[7]. Experience attests that when

7 If only to avoid the *Tendler effect* of agencies getting involved in designing projects for their own programmes and where, according to Ellerman (2005b, p.125): "*the organizational imperative to take responsibility for the "product" crowds out the ownership of the clients and leads to passivity and dependency.*"

people sense the utility of logframes and become accustomed to using them then they are actually empowered in the development process (Kowalski & Kaskelyte, 2005). The more I see of donor behaviour the more I conclude that it remains underpinned by some profound misunderstandings located in the confusions discussed above. I firmly believe that, in the matter of Logical Frameworks, a little thought and reflection can go a long way to making everyone's life easier.

3 Double binds

At various points in my thesis I have alluded to double binds and their emergence from situations characterised by paradox. It is now time to elucidate their nature more fully and relate them to the processes and practices of Human Development.

As King Henry VIII says in Act I of William Nicholson's *Katherine Howard*:

> *I want you to kiss me, Kate, but I'll not ask it. As soon as the words are out of my mouth they become commands. So I don't ask you to kiss me. I don't ask for your kindness. Here I stand, not asking. You shall do as you please.* (Nicholson, 1999, p.28)

I think we can all sympathise with Henry's state of affairs (*sic*). True love cannot be commanded, just as Ellerman (2005b, p. 2) noted: "*You cannot force a person to act spontaneously. You cannot externally supply motivation to a person to act on his or her own motivation.*" and Dewey (1916, p.26) had pointed out that: "*while we can shut a man up in a penitentiary we cannot make him penitent*". Yet, perversely this appears not to prevent us from trying.

Examples of paradoxical challenges abound, from the classic trap of '*Have you stopped beating your wife yet?*' to more artful ones like '*Be happy*!' (Watzlawick 1993). Robin Lakoff provides careful insight into how women are double binded into gender inequities thus:

> *the command that society gives to the young of both sexes might be ...: 'Gain respect by speaking like other members of your sex'. For the boy, ... that order, constraining as it is, is not paradoxical: if he speaks (and generally behaves) as men in his culture are supposed to, he generally gains people's respect. But whichever course the woman takes – to speak women's language or not to – she will not be respected. So she cannot carry out the order.* (Quoted in Jamieson 1995, p.13).

Kathleen Jamieson also said that:

> *Binds draw their power from their capacity to simplify complexity. Faced with a complicated situation or behaviour, the human tendency is to split apart ... its elements. So we contrast good and bad, strong and weak, for and against, true and false, and in so doing assume that a person can't be both at once – or somewhere in between. ... when this tendency drives us to see life's options or the choices available to women as polarities and irreconcilable opposites, those differences become troublesome.* (Jamieson, *op.cit*., p.5)

But, even though people quite often refer to such examples as double binds, it is not clear that they have fully understood the real magnitude of the issue in hand. Jamieson (*op.cit*., p.13) described a double bind as: *"a rhetorical construct that posits two and only two alternatives, one or both penalizing the person being offered them"*. But contrast this with the detailed description provided by Bateson (1972), who listed the following three characteristics of a double bind situation:

1. The individual is involved in an intense relationship in which they feel that it is vitally important that they discriminate accurately about the sort of message which the other is communicating in order to respond appropriately.

2. And, they find themselves in a situation in which the other is expressing two levels of message and one of these contradicts the other.

3. And, they are unable to comment about this contradiction in order to adjust their discernment of which of the messages to respond to, i.e., they cannot make a metacommunicative assertion,

and we see that, as a rule, a double bind is more than simply an impossible dilemma or a paradox. Furthermore, James Lawley maintained that:

> *The common expression 'damned if you do, and damned if you don't' is not a double bind because there is only one level of bind (whatever she does she's damned). For it to be a double bind requires a further bind at a higher level precluding escape from the primary bind,* (Lawley, 2000, p.33),

thereby emphasising the proper intensity of double binds, taking them to another level beyond simple paradox. It is not that the difficulties posed by the seemingly impossible choices of a paradox are damaging, though they are, but that double binds are particularly potent because the paradox is felt at two levels. The first is the paradox itself, and the second involves a further bind that prohibits making a choice about or resolving the first paradox. According to Paul Watzlawick, Janet Bavelas and Don Jackson:

> *even though the message is logically meaningless, it is a pragmatic reality: he cannot* ***not*** *react to it, but neither can he react to it appropriately (nonparadoxically), for the message itself is paradoxical. This situation is frequently compounded by the ... prohibition to show any awareness of the contradiction or the real issues involved.* [emphasis in the original] (Watzlawick, *et al.*, 1967, p.212).

In addition to the interdiction against realising that a paradox is occurring, Berman (1981, p. 228) drew attention to another difficulty or dimension of the double bind, in that: "*The crucial element* [that makes a double bind] *is not being able to leave the field, or point out the contradiction*", which is noteworthy in view of Albert Hirschman's argument that: "*there are two polar opposite ways to respond to deterioration in the quality of a relationship ... namely exit (walk away) or voice (try to fix it)*" (Ellerman, 2005b, p.10). However, in development the doer is frequently unable to take recourse to either, placing them in an irreconcilable position that can only be characterised as a double bind.

Being regularly exposed to such situations impacts negatively upon the psychology of even the most robust, as Goleman (1998, p.154) pointed out: "*the repeated experience of* [contradictory] *messages ... that is, messages which are impossible to comply with – creates a warp in the recipient's habitual mode of perceiving.*" In the same vein, Jamieson (1995) concurs with Bateson and his colleagues that responses to a double bind include '*helplessness, fear, exasperation, and rage*' and notes that other scientists have found that in so-called '*normal individuals*', double binds increased expressed anxiety as well. So, for example, we should find in William Easterly's observation that: "*the aid agencies drive the recipient governments and their own frontline workers insane when they declare each objective to be priority number one.*" (Easterly, 2006, p.164) evidence that DA does indeed generate double binds.

Given the frequency of paradox in human communication, and the complex nature of the philosophical structures within which development is conducted, what can we say about the way that the paradoxes in development are turned into double binds? In development important double binds are generated at two levels. The first level consists of the systemic paradoxes contained in the nature of what we are seeking to bring about, which we have identified in the donor-recipient relationship and conditionality; the nature of the free market capitalism that is being globalized; the moral hazard in reverse; the challenge to target aid at the poorest of the poor; the tying of aid; Jevons' paradox of sustainability; and the *Tragedy of the Commons*. The second, at the level below, stems from the way that we go about development that generates paradoxes and their associated double binds. These include the technician/manager dilemma; the sovereignty issue; the employment of expatriates and external change agents; and the learning/accountability dilemma of review and evaluation.

<u>The Donor-Recipient Relationship:</u>

As I argue above, the nature of the classic bind is to present two apparent choices '*develop in your own way*' and '*develop in the way we specify*'. Fukuda-Parr, *et al.* (2002) also drew attention to this particular paradox when they drew attention to the asymmetric donor-recipient relationship that is projected as being between equal partners. As Ellerman (2002, p.45) noted: "*if the doers do X only to satisfy conditionalities and thus receive aid, then the motive will falsify the action, the reforms will not be well implemented,*" and Albert Hirschman maintained that: "*conditional aid is 'fully effective' only when it does not achieve anything*" (quoted in Ellerman 2001, p.3).

This tension between heteronomy versus autonomy in development immediately generates the absurdity that aid can only be '*autonomy-compatible*' when it does not tip the balance of motives in favour of reforms and good policies (Ellerman, *op.cit.*).

However, the doubleness of the bind itself is created by the threat, actual or perceived, to withdraw funds or favours if either choice of the paradox is not achieved, leading recipients to pretend that the donor's objectives are, in fact, what they want for themselves. More importantly, this is usually compounded by preventing the recipient of DA from withdrawing from the bind themselves through the application of various forms of coercion, whilst at the same time prohibiting the recipients from commenting upon the paradoxical behaviour of the donor, or more particularly its agents.

Free-market Capitalism:

As we saw in chapter 8, the various imperatives and contradictions that are at the core of the economic and social system that is free-market capitalism are inimical both to the prosperity of the vast majority of the human population or to the realization of anything beyond a very superficial semblance of democracy. However, it is predominantly the dependency of economic performance under such a system upon market confidence that precludes the open and determined search for workable alternatives. Even today the ruling élite are able to exclude from public debate any discussion of alternatives to the *status quo* which might throw doubt upon the fundamental assumptions of the self-regulated capitalist system (Shutt, 2005). The almost hysterical, dismissive polemics that characterise the knee jerk responses to the recent revival of support for Marxist analysis also contribute to the paradoxes of capitalism being placed beyond discussion. As Mohan (2011, p.56) notes: "*The marketplace of ideas and decline in the quality of public discourse and the triumph of "fear, secrecy, cronyism, and blind faith" has created an environment that is hostile to reason.*"[8]

[8] For example, see some of the responses to George Magnus' article at http://www.bloomberg.com/news/2011-08-29/give-marx-a-chance-to-save-the-world-economy-commentary-by-george-magnus.html
Or the article "*The Man who Hated Britain*" in the Daily Mail, Saturday 14th September, 2013.

Indeed, Sabel and Reddy (2003, p.1) spoke of: "*a straightjacketed conception of the order of things* [which] *diminishes the attainment here and now of human potential, and accentuates the propensity to misapply technology and ideas.*"

Furthermore, those charged with managing development are caught in a double bind of being required to advocate all the trappings of Western plutocracy as the solution to a poverty that is both an inevitable consequence of capitalism's acquisitive imperative and a required condition for its functioning in the first place (Mohan, 2011). As Illich (1978, p.50) noted: "*a profession, …, holds power by concession from an élite whose interests it props up*". They are conductors of a metaphorically crashing train but are seemingly powerless to encourage discussion of actions to avoid the crash or to urge and support countries, communities or individuals to get off before impact.[9] As Rahnema (1997, p.383) noted: "*there is no point in mobilizing spectacular relief for the passengers on the development train. That can only postpone the day of reckoning. If the train continues on the same old tracks, it will result in a disaster that would be beyond the help of such relief operations.*" This leaves development in the *cul-de-sac* of advocating a questionable modernity agenda that mostly benefits the relatively well-off, and then only in the short term.

[9] Indeed, the IFI's quickly and coercively seek to impose the neo-liberal Washington consensus when sovereign countries attempt their own salvation.

The Moral Hazard in Reverse; Targeting aid; and Tying aid:

As I argue in chapter 6, not only are the recipients of aid in danger of becoming dependent upon it but those who dispense assistance are also in a similar, though reverse, moral hazard. Furthermore, as Watzlawick, *et al.* (1967, p.214) pointed out: "*If ... a double bind produces paradoxical behaviour, then this very behaviour in turn double-binds the double-binder.*" The helpers cannot withdraw from helping nor can they comment upon the paradox to which they are party. Thus donors are themselves unable, in many ways, to recognise what is happening let alone take steps to rectify matters.

As we have argued, the imperative of accountability demands the demonstration of progress, but simple cause-and-effect thinking misleads our expectations under the weight of a misplaced sense of agency. The rhetoric that is presented by NGOs and Aid agencies is one of targeting the poorest of the poor, and yet we have seen that in all the helping professions a process of triage has to be undertaken that inevitably requires that there is a trade-off between need and ability to benefit. The challenge that has been the MDGs is part of this process that channels resources in a utilitarian way that has tended to focus on Asia and to allow parts of Africa to fall further behind (Collier & Dollar, 2001).

Furthermore, as part of this moral hazard, aid has been traditionally given first and foremost to friends and used as a means of influencing client states to support the donors' wider policy agenda (Wang, 1999; Schaefer & Kim, 2013)[10]. But it has also been used to promote national economic interests by ensuring that services and products bought with aid money come from the donor country. In the first instance this undermines the establishment of those systems of governance that are supposed to

10 The majority of the history of development aid relations might be construed as a continual search by donors to find ways to maximize their returns on their '*investment*', as judged by them. (Hagen, 2006).

deliver value for money, but it is also a subtle form of corruption that justifies recipient administrators who take the view that looking after your own and your friends' interests (including *clientelism*) is ethically sound. Furthermore, the process of tying aid reinforces the asymmetries of the development '*partnership*'.

To this we must add that by forcing developing countries to receive equipment and consultants that originate in a wide range of donor countries an unnecessary financial and human resource burden is concomitantly being imposed. If we think of the supply of 4x4 vehicles then we can only imagine the range of spares' inventory, tools, and technical know-how that is required to support the fleet. The same is true of IT equipment and technical support, healthcare provision, education equipment and curricula. It is also true of the preparation of bids for funding, subsequent reporting, field missions and analyses, *etc.* which are specialist tasks that are heavily dependent upon scarce public sector expertise, made even more demanding by the different requirements of the plethora of donors[11].

In all these respects the donors, their staff and agents are also caught in the double bind of the moral hazard because, like the recipients of DA, they are themselves dependent upon the continuing dependence of the recipient. Indeed, Lasch (1996, p.100) gave voice to: "*a well-founded suspicion that tax money merely sustains bureaucratic self-aggrandizement.*" Furthermore, as Ellerman (2005b, p.124) noted, in the *Tendler Effect*: "*Without working to generate its own supply of good projects, a development agency would have insufficient 'deal flow' to justify its own budgets.*" In similar vein, the International NGO's are caught up in a process of seeking long term commitments to donate and child sponsorship is a favourite appeal that can yield fungible funds,

---

11 Harmonisation formed one of the focuses of the Paris High Level Forum on Aid Effectiveness, hosted by the French government and organised by the OECD in 2005, and formed one section of the *Paris Declaration*. Progress is being made but damage has already been done.

albeit with associated binds such as the constant need to find suitable children to be sponsored (Dichter, 2003)[12]. However, as Ellerman (2005b, p.281 n.5) argued: "*lump-sum funding of its core budget will more likely sponsor and prolong the self-indulgence of the NGO leadership and staff*".

Indeed, if the recipients were to become truly independent – capable of self-help – then the '*external*' helper would no longer be necessary. This leaves the helpers unable to withdraw from helping or to comment upon the paradox to which they are party. This dependence and all the other ways in which the developed world and the development business are dependent upon the recipients of DA are not included in the analyses of the prevailing situation – and largely remain '*outside*' the deliberations of what can be done to change matters. The fable of the emperor's new suit of clothes is entirely the nature of the double bind in which those providing DA find themselves.

Sustainability and the Tragedy of the Commons:

The supply-side paradox of carbon emissions (otherwise the Jevons' Paradox), so well argued by Sinn (2012), demonstrates that the efforts to address global warming through improving energy efficiency, alternative energy sources and carbon emissions trading are doomed to failure because what inevitably determines carbon dioxide production is the quantity of fossil fuels (oil, coal, and natural gas) brought to the surface, and hence to the market.

This paradox is then turned into a double bind through the impact of any discussions regarding regulating the production quotas on the '*owners*' of the resource. As Sinn (2012, pp.188-189) explained their motivations: "*isn't it better to extract much more in the present, and to safeguard the wealth in financial and*

12 Only a portion of the moneys so donated are likely to go directly to a named child. Some goes to core funding of '*overheads*' and some is channelled through projects that '*help*' the child's community.

real assets … than to leave the resources underground and remain at the mercy of alternative-energy freaks and 'green' politicians?" The end result then becomes the next example of the *Tragedy of the Commons* where, like the *Gerasene swine*[13], the madness from the double bind brings about the very thing which the green lobby are seeking to avoid, followed by the mutual destruction of the hitherto favourable climate, the damage to which common pool resource falls heavily upon the marginalized, who have no voice and are unable to move to more conducive localities.

This then combines with the behaviour of the multi-national manufacturing companies who, rather than pay higher prices for sustainable energy, driven by the imperative of capitalism's profit motive, relocate to take advantage of '*cheaper*' supplies of carbon based energy, such as shale gas from fracking[14], and thereby giving further force to the second contradiction of capitalism. Like slash and burn agriculture, in the longer term they are in danger of running out of undesecrated environments to which they can escape.

The same features surround the population issue. By making it a taboo subject aid agencies are double binded into behaviours that, at the very least, are confusing and inconsistent. The planet's ecosystems that support human existence cannot survive both the myth of the American dream for all and an ever increasing population (Galeano, 1997). Ethically the wealthy must address their over indulgence and reach out in solidarity to the poor. As Francis I (2013, p.99) maintained: "*Solidarity is a spontaneous reaction by those who recognise that the social function of property and the universal destination of goods are realities which come before private property.*"

---

13 Gospel according to Luke 8, 33

14 Incidentally this particular argument is then reversed to claim that not to engage in fracking locally is economic suicide.

The Implementation of Development Assistance:

DA is increasingly promulgated as institutional strengthening or capacity building (Eade 1997; Fukuda-Parr, *et al.*, 2002), frequently undertaken through projects and heavily dependent on training inputs (Swidler & Watkins, 2009). When an organisation or institution is functioning well it invariably takes on the form of a hierarchy. This is in keeping with the division of labour associated with the gradation from strategy to specific action. The managerial approach pursued within this hierarchy may vary from a very autocratic style in which each level and individual is merely charged with carrying out their function, to a very democratic style in which individuals at all levels are engaged in determining organisational direction as well as being charged with carrying out their own functions. Nevertheless, all necessary functions are catered for and each individual has a clearly defined set of functions to perform; and are supported in that performance.

In an organisation that is not performing well there clearly exists the need to take remedial action. This invariably takes the form of an initiative – which for our purposes we may designate as a project. Whether it is undertaken by outsiders or by staff of the organisation, such a project then is unavoidably separated from the organisation or institution, since it is being charged with action (as *Subject*) that will impact upon the Institution (as *Object*). The important issue here is that the project is not a part of the normal functioning of the organisation, but has been set up for a limited time, with limited resources in order to effect change in the organisation itself.

The danger, which emerges from this *Subject/Object* relationship, is that the logical types separated in this way become confused, and a number of paradoxes result. These are then turned into double binds by the project staff being required, or feeling it necessary, to perform actions and take on responsibilities that are the proper function of the organisation itself.

Although this seems obvious it is remarkable how often this is inflicted upon projects. One way is to set up structures that run parallel to the organisation and which draw off resources from the parent structure. This frequently occurs in matched funding projects where a condition of funding support is the provision of local resources, which, since they don't necessarily exist, often get taken away from the recurrent budget of the parent organisation, thus weakening its ability to carry out its previous work load (delivering vital services). The double bind on the project is completed by the unspoken but very real obligation that the project in some way does the work of the parent organisation that those appropriated resources would otherwise have done.[15]

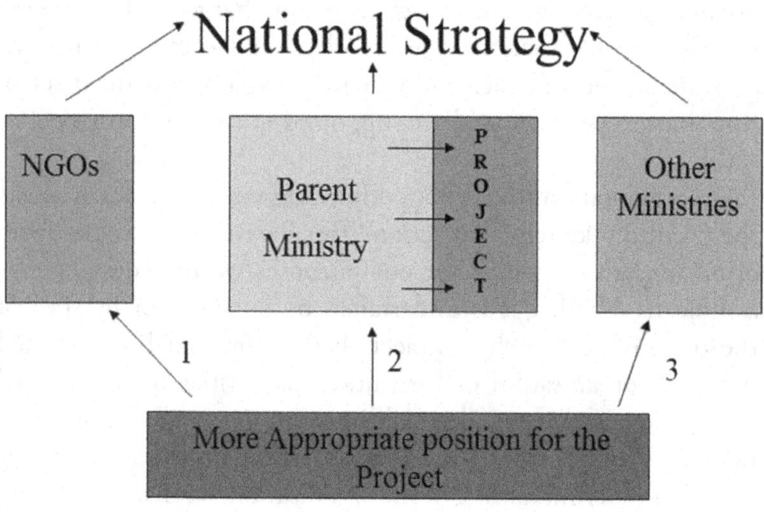
National Strategy
NGOs
Parent
Ministry
PROJECT
Other
Ministries
1
2
3
More Appropriate position for the
Project

Figure 10.2. Positioning of a Project in relation to its Parent Institution; where 1, 2 & 3 are specific actions within the project to support the institutional development of the various stakeholders through generating systems; human capacity; new knowledge; buy-in etc.

15 I recall, with enormous compassion, on arriving for a troubleshooting consultancy, encountering the local project manager of a water and sanitation project in Africa who, experiencing just this double bind, was in a state of nervous exhaustion from which we could hardly rescue him.

This places the project as a more-or-less lateral appendage of the institution, whereas the appropriate position for an institutional strengthening project is *outside* of the institution and *below* it – where it can provide support and not be drawn into taking direct action (see Figure 10.2).

A second way to create a double bind in these circumstances is to draft staff into projects who are primarily qualified technically, with little or no specialist process skills, rather than to find staff with good process skills and only some technical background. The subtext of this metacommunication is that the issues to be faced in the project are really technical, and the result is that the staff concerned get seduced into identifying with the technical actions and activities of the organisation, rather than in promoting the processes of change across the interactions of the personnel that effectively are the organisation. As Beer (1966, 425) warned: "*Since the normal occupation of management is to be expert in using the practical language of the firm's operations, there is the danger that the management will never speak the metalanguage in which its own structure can be discussed.*" The double bind is brought into full effect by the relatively lowly status of project staff who are unable to reject their placement (often a promotion) and yet lack the necessary understanding firstly to appreciate and then to metacommunicate with senior institution staff or the donor's programme managers about the situation in which they find themselves (O'Connor & Kowalski, 2005).

A third contributing bind is contained within the classic form that DA projects or programmes take. These are drawn up and formulated according to the practices of the donor, usually by donor staff or by consultants acting on behalf of the donor, and increasingly using the Logical Framework planning tool. However, the abilities of the draughtsmen (*sic*) and the care with which they approach their task are often inadequate. This is further compounded by the lack of support given to local stakeholders to develop their capacity to operate in such a conceptual minefield.

As outlined in section 2, above, at the very heart of the logframe is an imposed differentiation of logical types into a hierarchy that just invites the creation of paradoxes through the positioning of various objectives in inappropriate places in the structure. An error of this kind that I have frequently encountered is the specification of *Outputs* for the project that are really products of the institution. Thus, even if the project manager is inclined to devote their attention to processes of change, their terms of reference, which are drawn from the project documents, force them to take responsibility for things which are the proper responsibility of the institution (for instance *legislation*) and for which a certain degree of sovereignty is required (thereby further binding paradoxes at the level of implementation as given above).

In particular, dysfunctional institutions frequently lack a strategic plan, and the temptation is to specify that a key *Output* for the project must be such a plan. However, this is a violation of the logical hierarchy, firstly because the creation of a strategy is a *sine qua non* for being able to provide any actions that will strengthen the institution, and secondly the plan cannot be produced by the project, only by the institution. Thus a starting point for any intervention must be the establishment of a strategy for the organisation before any project intervention can be planned. I have facilitated participatory project planning workshops that worked particularly well when the first few days have been spent developing a vision, mission and strategy for the key institution with its staff and stakeholders. On the other hand, experience has shown that the requirement that projects must produce strategic plans invariably leads to a lack of the necessary institutional ownership of the emergent plan[16], resulting in that document literally gathering dust on some shelf.

---

16 Even though the consultants managing the project are usually very comfortable with the task of drawing up a plan for the institution since it falls very much within their technical competence – where changing the institution often does not.

The double bind is then rendered operative by the administrators in the donor organisation insisting that the logic-less framework is adhered to, making it a lock frame (Gasper, 1999), and resisting the application of that degree of flexibility that any process of change management requires. Then the implementers, often wishing to safeguard their reputation for not creating problems so that thcy will win further projects, find themselves unable to robustly challenge the donor's staff.

The Situation of Expatriates and their Counterparts:

There are a number of challenges to expatriate and local counterpart staff many of which have a paradoxical dimension and which can manifest themselves as double binds. Carr, *et al.* (1998) set out the first in the nature of being held responsible for project outcomes. Inevitably expatriate project staff find themselves thrust into positions of responsibility, even though their role is described as advisory. In the case of EU *Twinning* projects, expatriates, recruited as advisers found themselves unable to focus exclusively on their role of providing advice, but almost invariably got coerced or seduced into project management (OMAS Consortium, 2001). Indeed, Carr, *et al.* (*op.cit.*, p.108) noted that: "*Expatriates, as we have seen, are often perceived to be doing too much, and thereby neglecting their core mentoring function.*" This need to interfere beyond their role is often self-generated as well. Because of the relatively well remunerated nature of their employment expatriates often try to compensate by '*working harder*' (Carr *et al.*, *op.cit.*). However, as Ellerman (2005b) has argued, the process of influencing others to achieve change is like pushing on a string. Pushing harder cannot deliver more progress. Indeed it is counter-productive since the work that the expatriate then undertakes is seldom the work of a '*helper*' but is rather that of the '*doer*', who is thereby undermined and incapacitated[17].

[17] Indeed, for agencies, as a collective manifestation of the same phenomenon, Dichter (2003, p.7) asked: "*Why is it, then, that the majority of development assistance organizations continue to 'do' things?*

Secondly, expatriate staff of aid agencies in a country need the best local staff they can find to deliver the agency's programmes. The pay, perks, and prestige of such '*international sector*' jobs are invariably considerably better than what is on offer locally from government, or local NGOs, or similar employers (Ellerman, 2005b). Such opportunities '*remove*' the best people from being able to provide local, quality governance in the public sector, which is one vital aspect of the whole development agenda. It does so in the short term and in the long term, as their network of contacts become a springboard to the next job, or to emigration. As Swidler and Watkins (2009, p. 1191) observed: "[national élites] *learn that it is not only their performance in a particular* [development] *job that will provide for their future, but even more that their network of contacts, their patronage ties, and their good political relations with other members of the elite really determines their future.*" Furthermore Chambers (1997, p.54) noted that: "*Much normal professionalism, ... creates and sustains its own reality. A core magnetic pull draws people inwards towards cities, offices, libraries, laboratories, hospitals, research stations and computers, and then holds them there.*" So that this capable coterie is effectively captured and held by the temptation of a metropolitan and cosmopolitan identity and income and whose services to their communities are to all intents and purposes diverted into the pursuit of an alien agenda (Swidler & Watkins, 2009).

Thirdly, the associated provision of Western vehicles and accommodation of a Western standard, the inescapable quality of apparel and the physical appearance of 30+ years of good nourishment and health care, coupled with the self-esteem conferred by a good education inevitably places the expatriate on a pedestal from which they are unable and often, understandably reluctant to descend and which the local people and partners are even less able to discount. The end result can be a cultural

---

And why do more and more come into existence every day with funding to do still more things?"

distance and deference that makes a listening and facilitatory role extremely difficult (Chambers, 1997; Biggs, Messerschmidt & Gurung, 2005).

These paradoxes are then subject to the balance of power between advisers and implementers, especially if the latter are contractors or donor employees, which precludes the withdrawal of, or any attempts to metacommunicate by the implementer (Fukuda-Parr, Lopes & Malik 2002, p.10-11)[18]. Indeed, Watzlawick, *et al.*, (1967, p.213) warned that: "*A person in a double bind situation is therefore likely to find himself punished (or at least made to feel guilty) for correct perceptions, and defined as 'bad' or 'mad' for even insinuating that there be a discrepancy between what he does see and what he 'should' see.*" As Dewey (1939, p.146) recognised: "*Even today questioning a statement made by a person is often taken as a reflection upon his integrity, and is resented.*" Watzlawick, *et al.* (*op.cit.*, p.218) went on to comment that the avoidance of: "*the real issues becomes all the more plausible if it is remembered that an essential ingredient of a double bind situation is the prohibition to be aware of the contradiction involved.*" To discuss at all the motivations of what Chambers (*op.cit.*) calls '*uppers*' will either be construed as mad (you would destabilize the whole system!) or bad (you are maligning a system whose intention is to do good!). Furthermore, as Fukuda-Parr, *et al.*, (*op.cit.*, p.11) expressed it: "*Consultants … have little incentive to criticize the basic system. If they do, they will soon be replaced by more compliant staff*". The disturbed behaviours of both expatriates and their counterparts that Carr, *et al.* (1998) list are responses that people in double binds frequently make.

Evaluation and the Aid Effectiveness Issue

It might be argued that the primary function of evaluation to bring about change from within an agency otherwise it is in danger

[18] Often referred to as the challenge of speaking truth to power.

of becoming a self-serving, sterile exercise (Binnendijk 1989). However, the whole business of lesson learning and accountability is fraught with difficulties. For example, Michaelowa and Borrmann (2006, p.313) noted that: "*The central problem is that evaluations often serve more than one objective. They are simultaneously used as an instrument of transparency and control, accountability, legitimization, and institutional learning.*" They went on (*op.cit.*, p.328) to conclude that: "*the evaluator's dependency on the acceptance of the results by the principal (i.e., the aid organization), and the potential collusion between the evaluator and the agent (i.e., the project manager), strongly influence the credibility* [and hence usefulness] *of evaluation results.*" and Ellerman (2007, p.154) observed that: "*aside from minor wrist-slapping to show 'independence', evaluators are rarely the bearers of bad news, and project administrators are duly thankful for the 'good job' the evaluators are doing.*"

Furthermore, because of the issues of tying and directing aid to achieve other undeclared, donor agendas, there hardly seems to be any point to evaluations that don't address those objectives as well. In regard to the USA Clements (1995, p.585) observed that: "*initial spending decisions are made in terms of country and regional units and project types. In this context it is perhaps not surprising that the evaluation function in USAID is not taken very seriously.*"

Next there should be serious treatment of the '*compared-to-what?*' question. Evaluations often simply compare initiative impacts against the absence of any actions whatsoever, and as Ellerman (2007, p.155) noted: "*The doctrine of* ***opportunity*** *costs says that the true cost of committing those resources … is the benefit that was forgone by not committing those resources to the best alternative*". Indeed, he commented upon an irony in the World Bank's approach in that, after years of programme failure, the Bank has decided not to compare them with realistic alternatives that could have been undertaken with the same resources, but with '*a hypothetical situation that would occur in the absence of the program*'.

In addition, there is what is referred to as the Micro-Macro Paradox, because it seems that projects are evaluated as having been successful more often and to a greater degree than are the programmes of which they formed a part (Mosely, 1986). Such an observation suggests that it is futile to deliver project outputs without bringing about changes at a higher, systemic level, as embodied in the double binds that we have characterised above. Importantly, in a study of 10 communities in North West Bangladesh that had experienced different rural development programmes (or none), Islam (2002) concluded that it is not the type of initiative which is as important as the impact that the provocation that any and all external contacts have on people's lives.

The double bind of Aid Effectiveness is brought about by the very real reluctance to address these issues. Consequently lessons are continually being re-presented to us because the agenda is driven by inputs (e.g. the OECD target of 0.7% of GDP given as Official Development Assistance) rather than outcomes (e.g. the eight Millennium Development Goals), since '*contribution*' is easier to take responsibility for and demonstrate than '*attribution*'. As Biggs and Smith (2003, p.1747) queried: "*why is it that staff in development agencies appear to repeat the same old mistakes rather than learn from them*"? particularly in view of the emphasis that Project Cycle Management theory places upon lesson learning.

This whole idea of lesson learning will be considered in the next chapter. One response to this challenge would be to adopt an approach that shares responsibility for monitoring amongst those most intimately involved and committed to the project outcomes through a process of action research. Another is to consider more carefully the characteristics and preparation of '*change agents*', and a third is to explore the role and impact of Higher Education.

Chapter 11

Penultimate Essays 2 – Learning and Development

1 Introduction

As we have seen, in a wide variety of contexts effectiveness, efficiency and accountability in the achievement of institutional, organisational and societal change are in many ways synonymous with processes of learning. However, the nexus between learning and development is more deeply registered, and not just in the matter of the seeming impossibility of their contrivance, as discussed in section 2 of chapter 4. The parallels are quite striking, particularly in regard to the ways in which these processes have been, and in many quarters continue to be, similarly misconstrued.

This misapprehension has in no small part been due to an erroneous conception of the nature of causality, on the one hand, and to the reification of '*knowing*' as the nominalization '*knowledge*' on the other. The latter has led to the view that there is one reality that we can all come to know (*objectivism*) and, when combined with the former, results in an approach to teaching that is very didactic and can be summed up in the concept of '*transmission*'[19]. The voices of enlightened educationalist, like Socrates, John Dewey, Paulo Freire, Gilbert Ryle, Carl Rogers, Neil Postman and Charles Weingartner[20], have largely fallen on deaf-ears as the establishment, devoted entirely to support for that unlikely creature *Homo economicus*, has turned an '*education system*' into a '*qualification system*', has sought to commodify our young people and has promoted the absorption and regurgitation of information as the epitome of intellectual achievement.

The contrary view is that learning is very personal and involves making sense of our own experience (*constructivism*), which requires effort and which is continuous and life-long. Indeed, this has been captured by David Kolb in the *Experiential Learning Cycle* as set out in Figure 11.1. Instead of concentrating the learner's resources on making meaning (*abstract conceptualization*), which had become in effect the passive acceptance of the meaning of others based upon vicarious information, this process requires the learner to take ownership of their learning[21] by facilitating them to become self-reflective and active in engaging with the world. One, inevitable consequence of which is the generation of *praxis*, which combines self-formation with the achievement of action in the world (Kemmis, 2009).

---

19 As Zuber-Skerritt & Farquhar (2002, p.106) noted: "*conventional teaching philosophies and practices still predominate.*"

20 The list is not exhaustive but rather represents my own sources of inspiration.

21 Michael Polanyi (1958) stressed the essential component of learning being the knower having a sense of personal possession of what they know, which comes from a sense of having created their own knowledge.

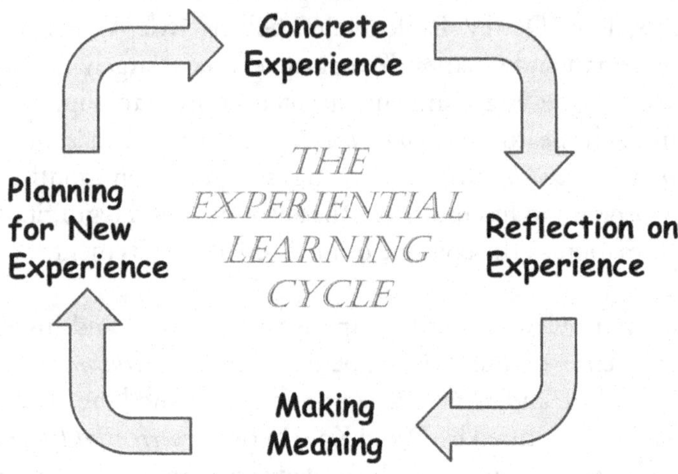
Concrete
Experience
Reflection on
Experience
Making
Meaning
Planning
for New
Experience
THE
EXPERIENTIAL
LEARNING
CYCLE

Figure 11.1 Kolb's Experiential Learning Cycle (Kolb, 1984)

Thus, like development, learning cannot be forced but requires the sensitive facilitation of the most indirect kind. But, like development, this human level engagement does not suit the purposes of those charged with its prosecution, so we deny what we clearly know and behave as if reality is other than what we apprehend it to be. Furthermore, it is evident that knowing is not a simple, individual experience but is naturally a collective enterprise where we may learn less *from* other people but we certainly learn *with* and *through* our engagement with them. Indeed, as Paulo Freire had emphasised, '*critical reflection*' is very much a social act undertaken in a variety of public arenas whose outcome is social and collective empowerment (McLaren & Tadeu da Silva, 1993, pp.54-55). Which is to say that we can neither know nor name our world other than in dialogue with our fellows (as discussed in section 2 of chapter 6). Moreover, the spirit of human emancipation that underpins development, to which Paulo Freire referred, was captured by Lankshear (1993, p.109), who maintained that: "*To reclaim their right to live humanly, marginalized groups must confront, in praxis, those institutions, processes, and ideologies that prevent them from naming their world.*

In praxis they must address, simultaneously, the reality they inhabit ***and*** *their consciousness of it.*" Importantly, Sabel and Reddy (2003, p.2) upheld that: "*The learning centred approach to development avoids the dirigiste pretension that the pathway of development has a clear and pre-determined form.*"

Therefore, we may characterize the development process of the individual human being, or of human beings collectively, as a process of unfolding understanding resulting from reflection on actions taken to achieve a desired state[1]. Now, according to Burns (2004, p.981), Kurt Lewin, a key advocate of planned change, believed that: "*the key to resolving social conflict was to facilitate learning and so enable individuals to understand and restructure their perceptions of the world.*" and this process he termed '*Action Research*' (AR).

2 Action Research

The false dichotomy of theory and practice, which had seen the expropriation of research by institutions of Higher Education, had led to a knowledge generating process that had little impact upon everyday practice, especially in professional endeavours such as teaching, extension and social work. John Dewey was very critical of this divide, as Argyris, Putnam and McLain Smith (1985) noted: "*Dewey was eloquent in his criticism of the traditional separation of knowledge and action, and he articulated a theory of inquiry that was a model both for scientific method and for social practice.*" Indeed, positivist methods and the simple position of the objective observer were clearly perceived to be inappropriate for researching social phenomena. Whereas research carried out in the actual settings of social practice allows any research findings to be seamlessly projected into that practice.

---

1 Gajanayake & Gajanayake (1993) refer to empowerment as implying enabling people to understand the reality of their situation, reflect on the factors shaping that situation and take steps to effect changes to improve it.

Thus AR can be seen as a dialectic process that: "*proceeds in a spiral of steps each of which is composed of a circle of planning, action, and fact finding about the results of the action.*" (Lewin, 1952, p.463) leading to making sense of the results and on-going embellishment of the action plan, as elaborated in Figure 11.2 (Altricher, Kemmis, M^c^Taggart & Zuber-Skerritt, 2002). Indeed, this reinforces the notion that, in so many ways, reflective practice, as embodied in AR, is substantially the process that we call development. As such, reflective practice can be seen as a process oscillating between periods of pre-planned, experiential activities and enhanced understanding which, depending upon context, receives a different appellation. Accordingly, in rural development it might be termed *Participatory Action Research* (Rahman, 1993), in business *Action Science* (Argyris & Schön, 1991), in manufacturing *Total Quality Management* (Drummond, 1992), and in education, health and social welfare *Action Learning* (Zuber-Skerritt, 2002). Although in its original form the action very much took the form of an experiment-like intervention in the most recent manifestations the action phase is very much perceived to be the form that current practice takes (Carr, 2006). Whichever the specific designation we are dealing with, all face the same challenge concerning the ways in which people can be facilitated to take a more systematic approach to analyse and respond to their own circumstances, their desires and the means they have at their disposal. In other circumstances this facilitation might be considered as '*psychotherapy*'[2] (Kowalski, 1999) or as '*psychosynthesis*' (Assagioli, 1999) or as '*process consultation*' (Schein, 1987[3]).

---

2 Indeed, Burnes (2004, p.984) noted that: "*The theoretical foundations of Action Research lie in Gestalt psychology, which stresses that change can only successfully be achieved by helping individuals to reflect on and gain new insights into the totality of their situation.*"

3 Which he described as: "*a set of activities on the part of the consultant that helps the client to perceive, understand and act upon the process events that occur in the client's environment*" (p.34).

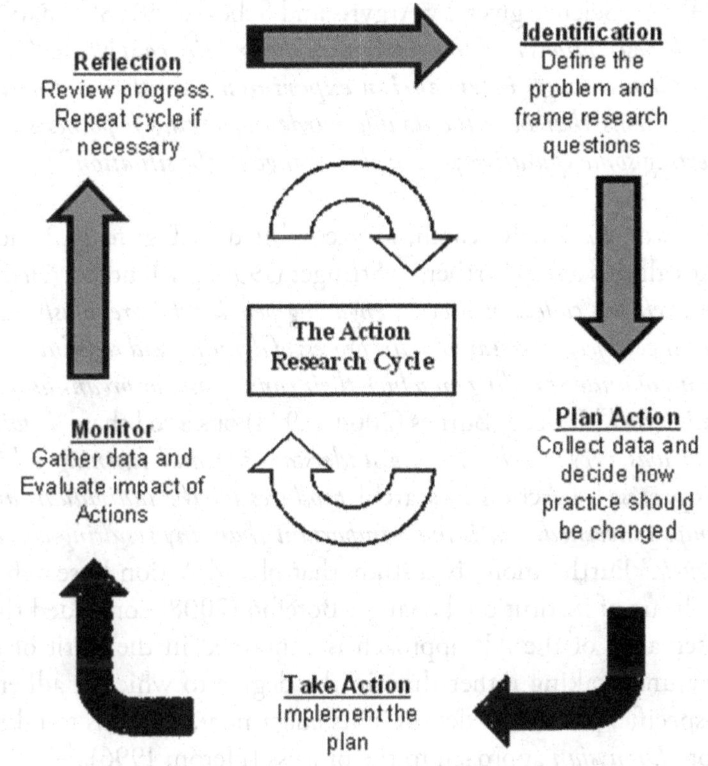
Reflection
Review progress. Repeat cycle if necessary
Identification
Define the problem and frame research questions
The Action Research Cycle
Monitor
Gather data and Evaluate impact of Actions
Plan Action
Collect data and decide how practice should be changed
Take Action
Implement the plan

Figure 11.2 The Action Research Cycle[4] (modified after Paisey & Paisey, 2005, p.2)

Furthermore, Ellerman (2005b, p.49) had suggested that: "*If* [development] *is a matter of 'seeing the light,' then the best approach would be to support a scheme of parallel experimentation by the doers so they could find out for themselves what works.*" He went on (*op. cit.*, p.228) to suggest that: "*Decentralized parallel experimentation with centrally sponsored framing and quality benchmarking followed by peer-to-peer cross-learning in the periphery is a more appropriate model than research at a central facility followed by the teaching, or dissemination, of the results.*" Which chimes well with a description

4 Note the similarity to both Kolb's experiential learning cycle and the project management cycle.

of Action Science given by Argyris and Schön (1991: 86) that: "it *builds descriptions and theories within the practice context itself, and tests them through* ***intervention experiments*** *— that is, through experiments that bear the double burden of testing hypotheses and effecting some (putatively) desirable change in the situation.*"

However, Action Research, as exemplified in Figure 11.2, now takes all this a step further, as Stringer (1996, p.10) noted: "*Action Research is a collective process, engaging people who previously have been the subjects of research in the process of defining and redefining the corpus of understanding on which their community or organisational life is based.*" Indeed, Burnes (2004, p.984) observed that: "*Lewin's view was very much that the understanding and learning which this process* [of Action Research] *produces for the individuals and groups concerned, …, is more important than any resulting change as such.*" Furthermore, in a study that placed Action Research at the heart of institutional change, Botelho (2008) concluded that observance of the AR approach is contained in the spirit of its very undertaking rather than in the degree to which it adheres to specific, prescribed details in its enactment, which is to take a more *Dionysian* approach to the process (Heron, 1996).

In the context of our exploration of the role of paradox in development the observation by Carr and Kemmis (1986, p.184) that: "*The dialectical view of rationality employed by action researchers places particular emphasis on the dialectical relationships between two pairs of terms which are normally thought of as opposed and mutually-exclusive: theory and practice and individual and society.*" is important in helping us to see that systematic reflective practice through Action Research is one significant way to respond to this challenge of paradoxes. However, as Porter (1995, p.72) noted: "*development agents were seen as, and remain, the keys to successful development and styled as linchpins of development, builders of order, catalysts and inducers of economic and social change*", and, as suggested above, the whole process of intentional development seems to involve and indeed require an external agent. Furthermore, we must be ever mindful of the caution that Kaplan (1996, p.3) noted in that: "*the appropriate stance becomes one of facilitation rather than force; nurture rather than imposition; respect rather than arrogant presumption*" and that such agents should be comfortable with the indirect approach in order to foster reflective practice in others. Again, Kaplan (*op.cit.*, pp.9-10) advised that: "*The development practitioner who works without love is like the proverbial bull in a china shop.*"

3 Change Agents

As we noted in chapter 6, the paradox of emancipation is manifested in this involvement of external agents of change, which Aronowitz (1993, p.16) captured as: "*the antinomy of populism and vanguardism*". Indeed, Liddell Hart maintained that:

> *the acceptance and spreading of that* [development] *vision has always depended on another class of men – "leaders" who had to be philosophical strategists, striking a compromise between truth and men's receptivity to it. Their effect has often depended on their own limitations in perceiving the truth as on their practical wisdom in proclaiming it.* (quoted in Nehru, 1951, pp.424-425)

However, Anisur Rahman was critical of any approach that generated a '*consciousness gap*' between revolutionary intellectuals and the '*masses*'. As he maintained, the role of facilitator is a delicate one, for there is always the risk that dedication to principle may fall away and dependency be allowed to re-emerge, or the process may generate alienation rather than the desired self-reliance by being pushed beyond any capacity to be taken up (Rahman, 1993).

Moreover, Chambers (1997, p.230) drew attention to an accompanying dilemma when he asked: "*By what right, with what authority, dare I say what is or what ought to be for others? Is this not contrary to pluralism, doubt and self-critical awareness?*" So what are the desirable characteristics of agents of change, particularly in the face of the paradoxes that we have rehearsed?

Now, the link between development and education and the reason for their susceptibility to paradox lies in the very nature of the learning process that underpins both. It was Gregory Bateson's insight to recognise that the impact of the three levels of communication, identified in chapter 2, would be mirrored in three levels of learning. These are characterised, after Bateson (1972), as:

Learning I (Proto-learning): The simple solution of a specific problem. The manifest content of schooling or instruction.

Learning II (Deutero-learning): Progressive change in the rate of Learning I. Understanding the nature of the context in which the problems posed in Learning I exist; learning the rules of the game. Equivalent to paradigm formation. Often referred to as the '*hidden curriculum*' of schooling (Snyder 1971).

Learning III: An experience which provokes a person to realise the arbitrary nature of their own paradigm, or Learning II, and is enabled to go through a profound reorganization of personal perspectives as a result. One might refer to this reorganisation as Freire's '*conscientizaçao*' – the "*critical consciousness which would result from their intervention in the world as transformers of that world*" (quoted in Shor 1993, p. 26), or as Chambers (1997, p.32) would have it: "*Self-critical epistemological awareness*". Although Ellerman (2001, p.6) has alluded to its rarity when he wrote: "*The roots of intrinsic motivation such as an individual's self-identity … are typically not open to intentional and deliberate choice. One chooses according to who one is, but one does not directly choose who one is.*"

Furthermore, since all adjectives descriptive of character, e.g. fatalistic, superstitious, self-determining, which is to say the interpretations which we derive from the contexts we encounter, (Bateson, 2002) are descriptions of the possible results of *Learning II* (as described above). Therefore, in the context of a purposeful development process it is vital to ask what sort of learning context should we devise in order to inculcate a particular habit of autonomy or free will or solidarity or ability to facilitate others? (Bateson 1972, p.170).

The context of development places both parties (helpers and doers) in situations where they have intentions for change at different levels, and are also communicating about them at different levels, with the evident potential for confusion of logical types in the messages exchanged. The transfer of know-how and the building of human capacity are, in Bateson's terms, *Learning I.* Therefore, what we seem to be about in development when trying to change one set of habits, characterised by context and the process experienced, for a new set denoting the new context and the processes which pertain to it, is to foster *Learning II.* For example, to bring about changes in people's self-confidence or to encourage risk taking and the dawning of entrepreneurial spirit, is to change character. However, these are not the expansion of true autonomy, nor the ability to truly self-help – although *Learning II* is capable of fostering reasonable simulations of these capabilities. True development, like true education, is arguably about giving control over the choice of what habits or characteristics to adopt or change, that is *Learning III.*

Indeed, Kaplan (1996) identified what he considered to be the central intention of the development process as the achievement of a phase of interdependence, which is that stage when a person is secure enough in themselves to be able to accept their, albeit limited, dependence on others. Furthermore, it is such a phase when a person is able to define themselves in and of themselves, and so remain fully engaged with the world around them, and towards others, which I take to be an oblique reference to the importance of *Learning III.* Indeed, Nelson (1949), in speaking of the possibility of education, suggested that fostering a way-of-being in which the individual does not allow their behaviour to be determined by outside influences but judges and acts according to their own insight is the proper *raison d'être* of education i.e. '*rational self-determination*'.

Level of Development	Alternative Approaches in Development	Alternative Tactics	Outcomes
Actions (Behaviour)	• Blue Print Projects • Technical Assistance • Capacity Building • Institutional Strengthening	• Expert advice • In-line work • Agenda setting • Training • Conducting research • Problem setting	***Learning I*** Simple responses Know how *Technē*
Processes (Categories of contextual organization of behaviour[1])	• Top Down • Participatory • Partnership • Direct Budget Support	***Helper*** • Does it; • Facilitates it; • Provokes it; • Mentors it. ***Doer*** • Accepts it; • Informs it; • Directs it; • Controls it	***Learning II*** This is how the world works; characteristics – compliant, fatalistic, resistance, innovative, or self-determining
Systems (Cast of Mind[2])	***That Prevent Outcomes*** • Modernization[3] • Global Reformism[4] • Social Idealism[5] ***That Promote Outcomes*** • Holism[6] • Indigenisation[7] • *Wu-wei*[8]	***Preventing*** • Proscribing • Coercing • Supplying ***Promoting*** • Encouraging • Supporting • Enhancing • Engaging	***Learning III*** Reflection on the variety of ways to respond to any situation – flexibility, debate, prudence *Phronesis*

Table 11.1 A Framework of Logical Types in Development

[1] Bateson (2002, p.126); [2] Sachs (1992, p. 1); [3] Rist (2002, p.93-108); [4] Rist (2002, p.211-237); [5] Rist (2002, p.10); [6] Schumacher (1973, p.168-169) & Hirschman (1984, p.91-93); [7] Hettne (1995, p.75); [8] Rahnema (1997, p.397)

Now, for our purposes development can be stratified into the three levels of *Actions* (simply behaviours), *Processes* (consistent patterns of behaviour) and *Systems* (the broader manifestations of values and beliefs within which the patterns are practised). These can be related to the ultimate ends, as discussed above, via the means we use to achieve them (See Table 11.1). It should be noted that many different kinds of abilities can be learnt by *Learning I*, and there are a wide variety of characteristics (each of which may be portrayed as intrinsically good or intrinsically bad) that can be acquired by *Learning II*. *Learning III*, however, is a single positive outcome, and therefore its acquisition can either be enabled or prevented by any intervention we might make.

The framework of logical types demonstrates that *Actions* lead to *Learning I*; Processes lead to *Learning II*; and Systems lead to or prevent *Learning III*. As is apparent from the framework, *Actions* alone cannot lead to *Learning II*, it is only *Actions* in their wider context (*Processes*) that can do that; nor can *Processes* lead to *Learning III*, but only the experience of *Processes* within a wider, belief *System* that actively seeks to promote it. Indeed, Ellerman (2001) observed that rewards or punishments might induce or purchase compliant behaviours, but there is no way by which they can directly cause changes in the level of intrinsic motivation.

From a consideration of this framework it follows that there needs to be a high degree of congruence between the underpinning value system (or development paradigm), the processes employed and the specific actions taken, if the fullest manifestation of human development (*Learning III*) is to be achieved. Similarly, any incongruence between the way that the different levels are projected, consciously or unconsciously, will be received by all parties as a paradox, and in turn will lay each party open to double binds. This need for congruence emphasises the importance of ensuring that all staff of a DA (or Educational) organisation need to share a common understanding of purpose and process – to pay lip service is effectively to present people with a paradox. Kemmis (2009) capture this in his call for facilitators of the AR process to live the '*philosophical life*' which is a matter of adherence to '*reason*', of adherence to '*acting well*' (avoiding all forms of profligacy and excess), and of adherence to '*ethics*' (right judgment), and which are manifested in *praxis*.

As we saw in Table 4.1, there is often a wide gap between what people say they believe (*espoused theory*) and what determines their actions (*theory-in-use*), which leads us to incongruent behaviours and self-sabotage. We have the *technē* but not the *phronesis*. Thus, and in many ways most importantly, we must address this issue of the need for congruent behaviour and skills of donor staff, consultants and implementing agencies, at all levels. This will require a commitment to training and staff development that far surpasses anything that has gone before. Also, as a mirror image to this initiative, we must commit resources to the capacity building of the personnel of the recipient governments and non-government organisations at all levels (Malik, 2002). This is necessary to provide the local partners with a voice and the potential to understand what is going on and to participate as full partners in the metacommunication necessary to ensure the successful creation of autonomy in a world of paradox. Fundamentally it must cause us to look at the provision of support for fostering the appropriate character of our leaders and change agents, particularly through the formation of Higher Education (HE).

4 The Role of Higher Education

What becomes clear from the outset is that education is at the heart of the epigenic paradox. As Bauman and Donskis (2013, p.142) noted: "*the mission of education, since it was articulated by the Ancients under the name of* ***paidea****, was, remains and probably will remain for the duration the preparation of newcomers to society to life in the society they are preparing to enter.*" Which, in cybernetic terms, is a process of variety reduction. Indeed, Freire (1971) recognised that schooling, which is most people's experience of education, is not about individual development (ability to achieve *Learning III*), but about '*domestication*', developing the ability to conform (through *Learning II*). This contrasts markedly with an alternative, life-affirming view, advocated by Illich (1997, p.97), in that: "*the dynamic underdevelopment that is now taking place is the exact opposite of what I believe education to be: namely, the awakening awareness of new levels of human potential and the use of one's creative powers to foster human life.*" Moreover, as Ira Shor noted:

> *Traditional education orients students to conform, to accept inequality and their places in the status quo, to follow authority. Freirean critical education invites students to question the system they live in and the knowledge being offered them, to discuss what kind of future they want, including their right to elect authority and to remake the school and society they find.* (Shor, 1993, p.28).

Now the HE Sector throughout the world has traditionally viewed itself as an indisputable universal good. The result was the acceptance of a philosophy that valued knowledge for its own sake and gave almost total freedom to academics to define for themselves those aspects of knowledge that were to be pursued as well as promulgated through teaching. This self-serving indulgence drove the HE system into two *cul-de-sacs*; discipline based curricula and separation from its constituencies, thereby laying the foundations for its subversion. This failure to really examine why community resources were being invested in HE came to an end with the economic difficulties of the early 1970's. Criticism mounted, primarily motivated by the concerns of commerce, as Schmitt (1987) lamented the American educational system put little emphasis on the values of the marketplace and focuses mostly on academic values, which emphasise optimum solutions, and Smith (1990) continued this theme when he averred that our educational systems are permeated by a minimalist outlook which is undemanding and, expecting very little of people, is neither surprised nor disappointed when little is achieved. As a result, at least in the UK, there has been a radical re-focusing towards a functional curriculum (Warren-Piper, 1985), as Doring (2002, p.140) noted: "*the higher education system is being encouraged to transfer its allegiance from the academic to the operational*" that primarily serves commercial interests, commodifies students and emphasizes technical knowledge (*technē*) over *phronesis*.

Indeed, there is growing concern about this widespread departure from the essential values of education, as James Hunter and Jennifer Geddes noted:

> *the university seems increasingly the locus of high-level scholarly endeavors, but the structures of university life have led some to wonder whether the academy has rendered "the life of the mind" irrelevant to the larger American society, by turning broad-minded intellectuals into narrowly specialized "technicians," with critical faculties so refined that they often can gain no purchase on the pressing issues facing contemporary society*. (Hunter & Geddes, 2000 p. 5).

Furthermore, as we have marked in section 3 of chapter 10, paradoxes have the ability to bind us in two directions, so it should not surprise us to find an epigenic paradox also embroiling those who provide HE. Perverse incentives create a flawed set of institutions. A key purpose of HE must surely be the provision of '*Self-Contradicting Prophecies*', as Sedlacek (2011, p.64) argued: "*If we are able to anticipate problems and take appropriate measures, they do not have to occur at all.*" But this requires both the ability to speak truth to power and for the power not to shoot the messenger! Neither of which are features of the reward and punishment schemes that prevail in HE. Indeed, Lasch (1996, p.98) commented that the market turns: "*scholarship into professional careerism, social work into the scientific management of poverty.*" Moreover, Geddes (2012, p.2) commenting upon the rise of '*the corporate professor*' noted that: "*professors themselves have bought into or been shaped by the corporate culture of the university and seem strangely inarticulate about the purposes and worth of higher education.*" Indeed, Mohan (2011, p.131) lamented that: "*temples of knowledge and learning have fallen to corporate ethics,*" and leading Bauman (2000, p.56) to observe that: "*For a couple of centuries now academia had no other world to catch in its conceptual nets, to reflect upon, to describe and to interpret, than the one sedimented by the capitalist vision and practice.*" Furthermore, Jennifer Geddes commented that:

> *If professors can't articulate what they do or why it matters in terms not beholden to the market, then who can? What resources are there for re-envisioning and re-articulating the purposes of higher education in a way that responds to the rapid and far-reaching cultural changes taking place in our world today and that resists the commodification of knowledge, scholarship, attention, and reflection?* (Geddes, 2012, p.2).

Leading Doring (2002) to argue that the role of academics has shifted from being agents of change to being victims of change; from being at the heart of '*a centre of learning*' to being just a cog in another '*business organization*'.

This failure of HE to fully explore alternatives to free-market, capitalist economics (as recognized in chapter 8) has been replicated in the concerns over environmental sustainability and ecological illiteracy (as set out in chapter 7) and, in more general development terms, Rahman (1993, p.219) observed that: "*The 'educated' have not proved to be any more 'enlightened' or capable of wise and responsible decisions and conduct than the 'uneducated'.*" Furthermore, HE has been at the forefront of the promotion of *technē* at the expense of *phronesis.*

At the heart of HE's difficulties is a tradition of organizing knowledge into discreet subject areas[5]. As Mohan (2011, p.127) argued: "*The knowledge paradox has deepened the crisis by creating silos of disciplines that do not creatively communicate with each other.*" Such a structure is entirely artificial, smacking of *Objectivism* rather than *Constructivism* (Laurillard, 1993)[6], and has encouraged the dislocation of ways of knowing that hinders a multi-disciplinary attack on the problems of the real world. Indeed, Stafford Beer voiced his own criticism in characteristic polemic:

> *A man who can lay claim to knowledge about some categorized bit of the world, however tiny, which is greater than anyone else's knowledge of that bit, is safe for life: reputation grows, paranoia deepens. The number of papers increases exponentially, knowledge grows by infinitesimals, but understanding of the world actually recedes, because the world really is an interacting system. And since the world, in many of its aspects, is changing at an exponential rate, this kind of scholarship, rooted in the historical search of its own sanctified categories, is in large part unavailing to the needs of mankind.* (Beer, 1980, p. 64).

The appropriate view, as Stacey (2001) suggested is a concept of knowledge as dynamic, ever changing in relation to context, like a chameleon, as meaning continuously reiterated only to be transformed in action. Indeed, McDermott (2000) argued that knowledge is completely different from information and propagating it requires a different approach based upon other concepts and tools. To this end he highlighted six features of knowledge that distinguish it from information:-

---

5 For example, a current university mission statement refers to: "*offering students the full range of disciplines.*"

6 For example, another university claims that: "*The mission of our University is the creation, dissemination and curation of knowledge.*" – begging the question – How could that get past scrutiny by an academic board?

- Knowing is a profoundly human act
- Knowledge is the bounty of thinking
- Knowledge is created in the living present
- Knowledge properly belongs to communities
- Knowledge circulates through such communities in unpredictable ways
- New knowledge is created at the discordant collisions between old ways of knowing.

The representation of knowledge as occurring in discreet disciplines and the behaviours associated with an *objectivist* perspective of knowledge have also contributed to the distancing of HE from its community constituents (including those commercial interests) that is typified by the epithet '*ivory tower*' (Levin & Greenwood, 2001). As Rahman (1993, p.12) expressed it: "*we intellectuals have been educated only to form and to join a class of our own, aspiring for recognition by the international brotherhood of intellectuals, but alien from our own society*". This is also maintained by the traditional approach to research which, contrary to popular perceptions, is not the only, nor even the most sensible, methodology to apply to problem solving. Indeed, Pieterse (1999, p.77) lamented that: "*Interdisciplinary research is more widely applauded than practiced.*"

Here the researcher is effectively neutral (not necessarily objective), off the time-line, able to scan the widest span, though not necessarily the detail, of unfolding events – usually enacted by others – and generating propositional knowledge (*E-theory*) that can be reported and shared, as illustrated in Figure 11.3 below. This may also be captured by the concept of the '*technical rationality*' model that is embedded in the institutional context of professional life and which Donald Schön characterized as:

> *research is institutionally separate from practice, connected to it by carefully defined relationships of exchange. Researchers are supposed to provide the basic and applied science from which to derive techniques*

for diagnosing and solving problems of practice. Practitioners are supposed to furnish researchers with problems for study and with tests of the utility of research results. The researcher's role is distinct from, and usually considered superior to, the role of the practitioner. (Schön 1983, p.26).

Now we must compare this with those circumstances where the practitioner researcher engages with their constituents in action research, as shown in Figure 11.3, being fully associated with the unfolding events, on the time-line, and having to respond and use developing knowledge in the management of the situation in the here and now – and generating more tacit knowledge, more particular knowledge, and more narrative knowledge that others must seek to generalise into their own contexts as seems best to them (*I-theory*[7]), which McNiff and Whitehead (2003, p.22) described as: "*theories which are already located within the practitioner's tacit forms of knowing, and which emerge in practice as personal forms of acting and knowing.*"

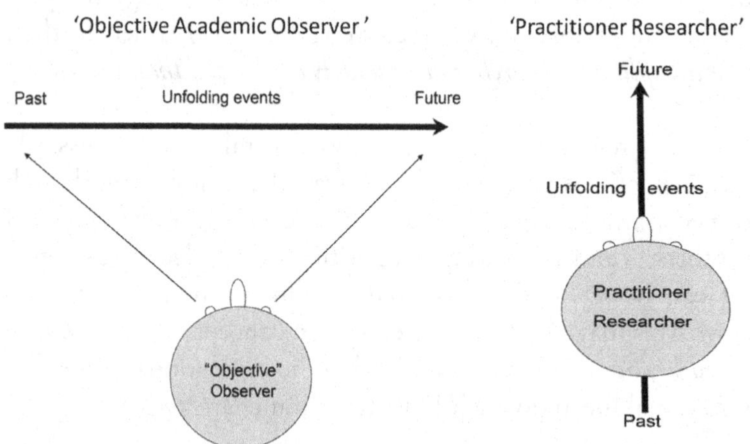
'Objective Academic Observer'
Past
Unfolding events
Future
"Objective" Observer
'Practitioner Researcher'
Future
Unfolding
events
Practitioner Researcher
Past

Figure 11.3 The alternative positions of the '*researcher*'

---

[7] where McNiff and Whitehead (2003, p.22) have describe *I-theory* as: "*a dialectical form of theory, a property of an individual's belief system*".

Again, this is undoubtedly captured in Schön's (1983) concepts of combinations of both '*Reflection-on-Action*' and '*Reflection-in-Action*'. Such reflection has an interrogative function in respect of the assumptions underpinning our '*knowing-in-action*' (Schön, 1987). By thinking critically about the understanding that brought about this difficulty or this opportunity we may reformulate understandings of phenomena, reframe problems or restructure strategies of action. Or as Mezirow (1990, p.12) captured it: "*Critical reflection addresses the question of the justification for the very premises on which problems are posed or defined in the first place.*"

This dichotomy of perspective on generating new knowledge from practice is also mirrored by the distinction in the research process between the creation of the initial research questions ('*the context of discovery*') and the rigorous handling of data ('*the context of justification*') (Lincoln & Guba, 1985), whereby in traditional '*academic research*' the emphasis is placed upon the latter as a process that can be scrutinized for its degree of objectivity and adherence to norms, rather than upon the former which in many respects defies such types of oversight and intrusion. Again, as Schön (1983) noted, professional practice is at least as much about finding the problem as with solving it, and problem setting should be a recognized professional activity.[8]

Finally, as part of this separation process, we must note that many of the models of curriculum development are isomorphic with action research, representing a cycle of analysis, design, implementation and evaluation involving wide stakeholder consultation and involvement. But they, like action research itself, are not widely practiced. Moreover, Levin and Greenwood (2001) were most forthright in their observation that, as institutions given a major share in the responsibility of undertaking the

---

[8] But note that Foucault had argued that to problematize something does not, of necessity, occasion the responsibility for providing a solution (Stacey & Griffin, 2005).

conception and dissemination of knowledge, universities have perversely created a suite of conditions that are inimical to the practice of action research and hence to the proficient fulfillment of their *raison d'être*, thereby divorcing themselves from the very societies they should aspire to serve.

Therefore, we can propose a much more meaningful role for HE in human development. As Hettne (1995, pp.71-72) commented: "*The function of universities in the Third World countries since independence has been in a process of change from an instrument of intellectual reproduction to an instrument of development. Such a function is different not only from the colonial situation, but also from the traditional role of universities in Western countries.*" Surely HE institutions should be operating as hotbeds of problem setting and problem solving that are fully embedded in their communities, acting as conduits of resources and operating as environments for the growth of the sort of change agents discussed in section 3 above. Not just paying passing acknowledgement to the challenge[9] but actually being transformational.

A fundamental part of such a proposal would be the development of appropriate curricula for the preparation of change agents, as Lasch (1996, p.79) noted: "*careerism tends to undermine democracy by divorcing knowledge from practical experience, devaluating the kind of knowledge that is gained from experience, and generating social conditions in which ordinary people are not expected to know anything at all.*" Leading Mohan (2011, p.121) to advocate that: "*Social scientists in general and social work professionals in particular need to develop a coherent program of knowledge-based intervention that will strike at the root of social malaise and human misery – an approach that is inherently preventative, rational and humanistic.*" Such a practice-based approach is underpinned by Gilbert Ryle's identification of the paradox of didactic teaching (quoted in full

9 Another university's mission statement aspires to being: "*a truly international university, which is also a major contributor to the economic, social and cultural transformation of* [our home] *city … and … region.*"

in section 2 of chapter 4) wherein logically the teacher cannot force a pupil into thinking for themselves, nor push them into self-motivation, nor compel them to show initiative, nor urge originality upon them, nor indeed goad them into spontaneity. It is also captured within the concept of '*clinical education*' and is linked to best practice in American law schools. Indeed, the way that we manage, promote, communicate and achieve the potential of HE to lead the development process must be for and through the widest proliferation of *phronesis.* Or, as Kołakowski (1999, p.52) noted: "*true virtue is a natural skill, learnt through our own experience of life and its conflicting demands, and through the society of good and thoughtful people.*" Most importantly, Zygmunt Bauman and Leonidas Donskis queried our ability to form the next generation of European intellectuals and politicians when most young people will no longer enjoy the opportunity to experience a cultured, aspirational, thought-provoking Higher Education: "*where will they learn to recognize and respect freedom of thought and intellectual integrity?*" (Bauman & Donskis, 2013, p.139).

As Beer (2004, p.802) advocated: "*Let us get up and do something in our own shameful mess of a world. It is better than to make excuses; better than to sit on your tenure for 30 years, and hang your hat on a pension.*"

Chapter 12

The Tolerance of Poverty

1 Introduction

Given the foregoing eleven chapters, it seems evident that the concept encapsulated by the term '*development*' is not readily amenable to deliberative, managed endeavour and its associated practices. This is substantially explained by the paradox at the heart of human development interventions by which they inevitably infringe the cardinal ordinance to '*pull ourselves up by our own boot-straps*', supplemented by the occurrence of many other paradoxes within the processes that we have devised as the means to bring about development or the terms that we use to define the end-state to which we are ostensibly striving (Ellerman, 2005b).

I hope that during the course of those preceding chapters I have been successful in demonstrating that the persistence of paradox is the clearest indication that, as yet, we have only an incomplete understanding of the nature of the challenge before us, and that it is this insufficiency of understanding, or our determination to deny what we do know, that brings about our lack of headway. It is also predominantly behind the frequent accusations of hypocrisy levelled at many development endeavours[10], or at the very least our many failures to live up to our rhetoric[11] (Crush, 1995; Severino & Charnoz, 2004).

Nonetheless, as Starbuck (2004, p.1238) argued, when one seeks to construct any theory with the objective of promoting understanding one must always take into account the limitations of people's mental faculties, and that such theories should seek to simplify as well as to represent their realities. Hence, in this process of seeking understanding we are confronted by yet another paradox, attributed to Charles Bonini, which may be expressed as the more realistic any model of reality becomes the more it approximates to the complexity it seeks to represent and so becomes no more comprehensible than reality itself (Starbuck, *op.cit.*).[12]

Indeed, the repercussions presented by such a paradox of rationality were given a further twist by Herbert Simon whose views were paraphrased by Talbot (2005, p.29) as: "*the 'rational utility maximiser' model of humans so beloved of neoclassical economics was fatally flawed on the simple grounds that, paradoxically, humans always had too much information to absorb and yet not enough to really be 'rational utility maximisers'.*"

Let us, therefore, rehearse cautiously the core challenges of development that we have identified as:

- The paradox of control (dirigisme) to produce change;

---

10 For example as one IDS workshop participant commented: "*Partnership is the word used, by far, with the greatest hypocrisy*" (IDS, 2001, p.1).

11 Joseph Conrad (2007, p.29) alluded to development thus: "*It was as unreal as everything else – as the philanthropic pretence of the whole concern, as their talk, as their government, as their show of work.*"

12 The naturalist Lyall Watson is purported to have remarked that if the human brain was simple enough to be understood, human beings wouldn't be smart enough to make sense of it.

- The epigenic paradox of the social reliance of self-centred individualism;
- The paradox of helping to self-help and the toleration of poverty;

before plunging a little more recklessly into prescriptions for future actions.

2 Control versus Change

Since we have observed that development is virtually synonymous with the modernity project we must take note of the observation of Bauman and Donskis (2013, p.30) that: "*Modernity … continues to be obsessed with how to get as much control over the human body and soul as possible without physically exterminating people.*" If anything epitomises the Western mind and culture then it is likely to be the conceit that everything is open to being managed – always remembering that heretofore manage meant coping and has only recently come to mean planning and control (Handy, 1994). Yet, as Goldsmith (1996, p.1433) observed in the context of development, the notion of management, as represented by measurement and control, is arguably the very opposite of what is needed.

Furthermore, Nustad (2004) commented that the concept of development has always been about the creation of that stability and order on which all manner of good things depend – security, justice, schooling, provision of health services, economic enterprise. However, development is also about autonomy, participation and self-determination, which in so many ways are the diametric opposite to that control. For, as Waelchli (1989, p.59), in reference to Ashby's '*Law of Requisite Variety*', argued: "*the practice of management has been the practice of controlling or limiting variety in natural systems, of suppressing entropy so that the remaining natural forces within a system could move it towards man's chosen goals.*" thereby emphasising that intervention and management are largely about thwarting the variety generating tendencies of human interacting. However, in contradistinction, as we have maintained throughout, the state of being developed is argued to be one of increased complexity, variety and freedom (Sen, 1999). Moreover, Mill (1985, p.120) maintained that: "*the free development of individuality is one of the leading essentials of well-being;*". Thus, if to be developed is to be free to fashion our own well-being within our own determination of what that means, then the agenda and methods of development cannot, with integrity, be controlled by an external agency. Yet Stacey (2001) has drawn attention to what he termed '*the paradox of control*' whereby managers are required at all times to be '*in charge*' even though they can never be '*in control*'. Indeed, the power that resides in '*being in charge of development*' has the potential to deny such self-determination and thus to be inimical to the process of development itself (Ellerman, 2002).

Despite this, as Stacey (2007) remarked, in seeking to explain organisations, and put forward ideas about how to manage them we have created a '*fantasy world*' whose real purpose is to preserve the illusion that someone is in control. Consequently, this obdurate paradox of management remains. Indeed, Beckhard (1969) had reported that organizations can still spend considerable money and effort on efforts to improve organizational effectiveness and yet the effectiveness of the organization is only marginally increased, which he attributed to the top management still operating in a generally autocratic and frequently crisis-oriented style, despite the many management books that have advocated the path of M^c^Gregor's 'Y' throughout the intervening years. Since the rest of the organization is not oblivious to this it has as a consequence only limited trust in the '*rhetoric*' from the top. Such a credibility gap encourages people to be cautious, conservative and self-protective and not to buy in to necessary changes, which is an experience with which we are all familiar, to a greater or lesser extent.

Although there could be other motives for such management behaviours, as Erich Fromm commented: "*The pleasure in complete domination over another person … is the very essence of the sadistic drive*" (quoted by Freire, 1971, p.35), this pursuit of control can largely be attributed to fear for, as Espejo (2003) captured it, managers inevitably have lower variety than the workers under their charge which means that they cannot control everything that happens and yet are acutely aware of their responsibility for anything that goes wrong.[1]

Furthermore, in regard to all in one-up positions, Ellerman (2005b) noted that they must be able to show appropriate results in order to be considered to have done their job well. This demand leads to them assuming more and more responsibility and ownership of the results, to the detriment of those who are the real '*doers*' of development. If you can lead a horse to water but are unable to make it drink you cannot improve matters by bringing the horse more swiftly to the water nor by bringing more non-drinking horses to it, nor by consuming the water yourself.

The end result is the asinine behaviour of hindering by meddling, where the desperation to make things happen causes the protagonists to involve themselves at an inappropriate point in the development process, denying autonomy to other players and, as we saw in chapter 10, placing them in double binds (Kowalski, 2004). Therefore, in reference to Table 3.1, there is a need, in partnerships, to understand the interests, resources and roles of all the partners and how they themselves can contaminate the levels below by seeking to force change to happen where they have neither the ability to deliver nor to sustain. As Brunsson (1989) observed, most inconsistencies within an organisation, like a donor, are not necessarily hypocritical, but probably arise from interactions between differently perceiving individuals,

---

1 See the quotation from Espejo (2003, p.19) given in full in section 2 of chapter 3..

protagonists, sections or departments, whose behaviour is otherwise reasonably consistent - like a Maurice Escher print.

Moreover, within the context of development this notion of control and accountability is frequently manifested in the concept of '*attribution*' – the ability to first claim and then demonstrate a linkage between development actions and programme outcomes. However, as Stacey (1992) recognised, we can only claim to have achieved something intentionally if we can show the connections between our actions and the outcomes and that what has happened was not a result of others' actions or indeed a result of chance events[2], a tall order indeed! Furthermore, Gareth Morgan argued that:

> *Though it is often possible to spot an initial 'kick' that sets a system moving in a particular direction, it is important to realize that such kicks are not really the cause of the end result. They merely trigger transformations embedded in the logic of the system.* (Morgan, 1986, p.253).

Thus, development, education and other transformative social processes are really activities to expand variety, and yet they are undertaken by '*helpers*' in a spirit of variety reduction. This demonstrates a profound misunderstanding on the part of those directing these helping processes.

I well recall when, as a young lecturer, I under-went some teacher-training and we were challenged to reflect upon the metaphors that we were using to describe what we were doing in our classes, and thereby revealing our '*theory-in-use*'. Were we shining a light into a dark place? Were we filling an empty vessel? Or gardening? Or leading an expedition into unknown territory? *etc.* In similar fashion, it is helpful for us as development practitioners to explore

2 See Stacey's quotation in full in section 3 of chapter 3.

the metaphors that we are using and gain self-knowledge as a consequence. Figure 12.1 seeks to represent some alternative conceptualisations of that particular relationship.

a.
b.
c.

Figure 12.1 Caricatures of the development relationship a) the protégé; b) the dance partner; c) the sparring partner.

The motivation of many helpers is to re-create their image of themselves and so would like to receive the unquestioning admiration of a protégé. Others seek to engage in a very mutual process but one in which they take the lead to be complemented by the responses of a compliant partner, as in a dance. A third alternative is that of the sparring partner, the engagement and struggle with whom strengthens, and hones the abilities and the resolve of both to their mutual benefit.[3] There are others that you can think of that are equally revealing.

However, from the perspective of the paradox of control, the approach that we must advocate in order to achieve any traction is indirect. In particular, Hart (1941, p.x) emphasised that: "*This idea of the indirect approach is closely related to all problems of the influence of mind upon mind – the most influential factor in*

3 Unlike the version outlined by Ashby (1960, p.234) that: "*it is **the mouse** which teaches the kitten the finer points of how to catch mice.*"

human history." Moreover, Ellerman (2005b) provided extensive arguments to show that only indirect approaches are capable of bringing about changes at the level of attitude. Thus, in my terminology, development can neither be engineered, nor managed but only **contrived,** and contrived in the spirit of *wu-wei*, which is not so much about making minimum effort but rather is **reticent action initiated under *phronesis*.**

3 The epigenic paradox of the social reliance of self-centred individualism

The epigenic paradox, which Hann and Hart (2011, p.51) depicted as: "*Human institutions everywhere are founded on the unity of individual and society, freedom and obligation, self-interest and concern for others.*", and its implications for development, has been explored extensively in chapter 6. Therefore, it just remains for me to set down a few additional remarks. Firstly, as we commented earlier, there continues to be the question regarding how much of human life should be devoted to the individual, and how much to the social? (Mill, 1985) and currently Western culture emphasises the rights of the individual before any collective responsibility. Indeed, Kropotkin (2010, p.122) long since upheld that: "*the theory which maintains that men can, and must, seek their own happiness in a disregard of other people's wants is now triumphant all round in law, in science, in religion.*"[4] Moreover, the emphasis on the self/other boundary is seen as a principle characteristic of Western culture (Holdstock, 1993). Thus we must question the extent to which the problems of development are products of the masculine, materialistic, individualistic, Western culture that has spawned capitalism and from which the majority of development interventions are initiated.

Contrariwise, the individual is firmly dependent for their efficacy upon the goodwill and cooperation of others, and in this regard,

---

4 Indeed, Francis I (2013, p.39) noted that: "*In the prevailing culture, priority is given to the outward, the immediate, the visible, the quick, the superficial and the provisional.*"

Talbot (2005) maintained that if there is a '*human universal*' then it is unquestionably the instinct for cooperation. As Habermas, (1990, p.316) noted: "*Communicative reason is directly implicated in social life processes insofar as acts of mutual understanding take on the role of a mechanism for coordinating action.*" and Bauman and Donskis (2013, p.213) remarked that: "*If you want to know another person, you can aspire to this only through empathy and love*".

Thus we see that, in interactions in social settings of all kinds, it is desirable for each individual to be able to apprehend the feelings of others. Indeed, Adam Smith commented that:

> *By the imagination we place ourselves in his situation, we conceive ourselves enduring all the same torments, we enter as it were into his body, and become in some measure the same person with him, and thence form some idea of his sensations, and even feel something which, though weaker in degree, is not altogether unlike them.* (Smith, 2006, p.3)

and Bateson and Bateson (2005, p.194) noted that: "*The evocation of self-knowledge as a model for understanding another, because of similarities or congruences that make the knowing possible, is properly called sympathy, but the current usage that seems to me to come closest is the term **empathy**.*" where such ability to empathise is a *sine qua non* of being able to function well in human society. Nevertheless we must recognise, with Max Scheller, that: "*sympathy is not a simple fusion of two subjectivities or a return to primal unity, but is, instead, a feeling that can only exist when difference is acknowledged and preserved.*" (Dillard-Wright, 2007, p.7).

Moreover, the inclination to separate ourselves as subjects from others as objects is countered by the natural tendency to fellow feeling[5]. As Fromm (1995, p.67) stated: "*I become one with the*

---

5 Captured in the national motto of France "*Liberté, Egalité, Fraternité*"

object of my concern, but in this process, I experience myself also as subject." and Bauman (2013, p. 85) recognised that: "*Unlike the client-commodity pattern, the human-human relationship is symmetrical; both sides of the relation are 'subjects' and 'objects' at the same time*". Indeed, Smith (*ibid.*) argued that: "*How selfish soever man may be supposed, there are evidently some principles in his nature, which interest him in the fortune of others, and render their happiness necessary to him, though he derives nothing from it, except the pleasure of seeing it.*"

Therefore, it seems to be in our nature to be affected by the circumstances of those around us. Indeed, there is benefit to be gained from the empathetic society of others. In this respect the utilitarian position is that of opposition to any selfish principle and that the good of society is generally to be found in the subordination of individual interests to the general good (Bain, 2006). Furthermore, as Smith (*op.cit.*, p.86) maintained: "*Where the necessary assistance is reciprocally afforded from love, from gratitude, from friendship, and esteem, the society flourishes and is happy.*" Moreover, Fromm (1995, p.66) upheld that: "*Joy, energy, happiness, all this depends on the degree to which we are related, … to which we are in touch with the reality … of other people,*" and More (1996, p.43) asserted that: "[Utopians] *define virtue to be life ordered according to the prescript of nature. But in that that nature doth allure and provoke men to help another to live merrily*". Indeed, as Marley's ghost, in Charles Dickens' *a Christmas Carol*, lamented: "*Mankind was my business. The common welfare was my business; charity, mercy, forbearance, and benevolence, were, all, my business*" (Dickens, 1985, p.62). All of which is to suggest that

– Fraternité; and in Article 1 of *UN Declaration of Human Rights* that: "*All human beings are born free and equal in dignity and rights. They are endowed with reason and conscience and should act towards one another in a spirit of brotherhood.*" But not just brotherhood but particularly the sentiments that sustain brotherhood. Indeed, Francis I (2013, p.53) argued that: "*the way to relate to others which truly heals instead of debilitating us, is a* ***mystical*** *fraternity, a contemplative fraternity.*"

we have an intrinsic interest in the prosperity of others that has implications for our own sense of well-being. Furthermore, it is clear that empathy is deeply embedded in *phronesis*.

Now, in regard to this other pole of the paradox, Kropotkin (2010) argued that his studies demonstrated that a reckless prosecution of personal interests, with no regard to other people's needs, was not the only characteristic observable in modern life. Indeed, hand-in-hand with this tendency which stridently claims leadership in human affairs, could be perceived a battle sustained by both rural and urban communities to reintroduce institutions of mutual aid and support.

And AtKisson (1997, 285) observed that: "*Long before there were corporations or governments or even a market economy, there were self-organized groups of people committed to the betterment of human life.*" Indeed, Polanyi (1998, p.158) maintained that: "*A free society is characterized by the range of public liberties through which individualism performs a social function, and not by the scope of socially ineffective personal liberties.*" Furthermore, Kropotkin (*op.cit.*, p.122), presaged Marcel Mauss' astonishment when he noted that: "*Although the destruction of mutual-aid institutions has been going on in practice and theory, for full three or four hundred years, hundreds of millions of men continue to live under such institutions; they piously maintain them and endeavour to reconstitute them where they have ceased to exist.*"

Thus, try as we might, modernity cannot dispense with the structures or patterns of human relating that make all institutions, including the market, viable. Indeed, the calls of Uphoff (1996) and Chambers (1997) to rehabilitate altruism as a way of promoting development are apposite and coincide with insights from psychology. The intention is to suggest the possibility that it is the altruistic orientation which is fundamental (Brazier, 1993). In essence the view we hold of human nature does not have to be centred on self nor even on self-actualization, but might, more constructively, be based on the idea of a need **to** love rather than a need **for** love. Indeed, it is through altruism that we can integrate the self/other paradox[6], which Talbot (2005, p.60) explained as: "*a single human can have a preference for **both** selfish egotistical acts **and** for apparently unselfish altruistic acts – which perhaps sounds rather paradoxical?*"

Therefore, one response to the natural concern for the welfare of others is what may be described as benevolence. As May (1972, p.109) noted: "*all our lives we get pleasure out of exerting ourselves from time to time for the sake of the other.*" and we can thereby be seduced into adopting a paternalistic attitude to the recipients of our beneficence. In Transactional Analysis parlance (Stewart & Joines, 1987) we relate from our '*Nurturing Parent*'[7] ego state and summon forth the '*Adapted Child*' in the recipient[8]. This paternalism very much underpins the self-justificatory, imperial metaphor of trusteeship, which has continued in different formulations into the present (Cowen & Shenton, 1996), as Nustad (2004, p.21) maintained: "*The form of development therefore implies an idea of trusteeship: that someone who has the necessary vantage point guides the process of development.*"

Importantly, we must recognise that as people relate to each other they inevitably both constrain and enable each other at the same time (Stacey & Griffin, 2005). Transactions are precisely that, an exchange of perceptions, permissions and imperatives. Furthermore, Stacey (2001, p.149) had argued that: "*Power is constraint that excludes some communicative actions and includes others. However, at the same time power enables. The process of*

6 It is interesting to note that, as Josselson (1987, p.170) recognised: "*Boundaries of the self are never as rigid in girls as in boys, and the basic female sense of self is connected with a good deal of fluidity, to the world.*"

7 Or even '*Critical Parent*', since Lasch (1996, p.28) speaks of: "*the venomous hatred that lies not far beneath the smiling face of upper-middle-class benevolence.*"

8 From such ego states it is possible to engage in playing '*games*' one of which allows each party to lay the blame for failure at the door of the other, and another is learned helplessness.

turn-taking/turn-making is both enabling and constraining at the same time" and the whole is governed by patterns and rules[9]. This implies that every social arena is manifested as cooperative and competitive interactions that are effectively moral order (Stacey, *op.cit.*). Indeed, AtKisson (1997, p.289) had argued that: "*Civil society is humanity's conscience.*" suggesting yet again that the meta-language for discussing social development should be ethics. However, Francis I (2013, p.37) warned that: "*Ethics has come to be viewed with a certain scornful derision. It is seen as counterproductive, too human, because it makes money and power relative. It is felt to be a threat, since it condemns the manipulation and debasement of the person.*" Indeed, the threatening nature of ethics was identified by David Korten when he suggested that: "*If* [the wealthy] *were to acknowledge that their own abundance is the cause of the plight of those so deprived, could any person bear the terrible moral burden?*" (Korten, 1996, p.109).

Therefore, in the final analysis, the challenge for development may not be so much to empower the oppressed, although this must remain a guiding principle, but rather to help the powerful to transform the nature of their relationship to power-over so that it ceases to limit the power-to of others and thereby releases the powerful themselves to become more fully human. As Pope Francis maintained:

> *I am interested only in helping those who are in thrall to an individualistic, indifferent and self-centred mentality to be freed from those unworthy chains and to attain a way of living and thinking which is more humane, noble and fruitful, and which will bring dignity to their presence on this earth.* (Francis I, *op.cit.*, pp.106-107).

---

9 See the discussion in chapter 5, section 2, point 7; and the strange law of alternation identified by Godbout and Caillé (2000, p.134) and quoted therein.

4 The paradox of helping to self-help and the toleration of poverty

Now, as we recognise from experience, and the Easterlin paradox, wealth *per se* does not lead to happiness. On the contrary our conscience pricks us into acts of '*benevolence*' [10]. To which we can add the acknowledgement that: "*There is something clearly immoral about sustaining the present levels of poverty.*" (Haq, 2000, p. 79) and the recognition that: "*development assistance has been driven by the question, How can we stand by and allow poverty in our midst?*" (Dichter, 2003, p.5). However, as Illich and Rahnema (1997, p.108) cautioned: "*Social responsibility, we now know, is but the soft underbelly of a weird sense of power through which we think ourselves capable of making the world better. We thus distract ourselves from becoming fully present to those close enough to touch.*" Indeed, Pieterse (1999, p.79) commented that: "*One of the core problems of development is its pretentiousness, the insurmountable arrogance of intervening in other people's lives.*"

Unquestionably, a great challenge in this whole development effort is to manage our fellow-feeling, because it tempts us simply to throw money at the problem, thereby making things worse. Indeed, Rahnema (1997, p.392) argued that: "*development incarnated a false love for an abstract humanity that it ended up by upsetting the lives of millions of living human beings.*" Furthermore, Ellerman (2005b, pp.16-17) recognised that: "*again and again, one finds benevolent aid being defended as "doing good" in the sense of "delivering resources to the poor" without any real recognition as to how this undercuts the incentives for developing self-reliance.*" and Lasch (1996, p.105) argued that: "*The ideology of compassion, however agreeable to our ears, is one of the principle influences, in its own right, on the subversion of civic life, which depends not so much on compassion as on mutual respect.*" Moreover, Rist (2002, p.125) commented that: "*the history of 'development' merges with the*

[10] See Kropotkin (2010) quoted in full in section 4.v of chapter 5.

progressive destruction of self-reliance." Leading Sen (1999, p.283) to note that: "*some argue that dependence on others is not only ethically problematic, it is also practically defeatist in sapping individual initiative and effort, and even self-respect.*" and Dichter (2003, p.154) to lament that: "*the seemingly sound instinct to help the poor of the developing world gets inevitably distorted and eventually corrupted when put into the service of long-term and sustainable development, as opposed, say, to emergency relief.*"

As Dewey and Tufts (1909, p. 304) argued: "*The inherent irony and tragedy of much that passes for a high kind of socialized activity is precisely that it seeks a common good by methods which forbid its being either common or a good.*" Likewise Dichter (*op.cit.*) cautioned that helping people, whether they seek help or not, seems to be morally and psychologically questionable. At best helping is a matter of some delicacy; at worst it puts us on a slippery slope to interference. Most people intuitively sense this and thus feel some hesitancy about helping or being helped.

If we reflect upon our own sentiments concerning our own life and aspirations it becomes clear that an inseparable element in our well-being is a sense of self-efficacy that Henry David Thoreau captured in characteristic terms: "*If I knew for a certainty that a man was coming to my house with the conscious design of doing me good, I should run for fear that I should have some of his good done to me*" (quoted in Ellerman, 2005b, p.283). Furthermore Rahman (1993, p.19) spoke eloquently of finding: "*emotional fulfilment not only in achieving* [one's] *objectives as such but also in the very fact of having achieved them primarily by using one's own resources.*"

It seems clear that development, as opposed to the relief of acute suffering in the face of natural and man-made (*sic*) disasters, undertaken as a process directed towards the goal of helping a particular section of society or humanity to '*catch up*' is not really development. Paulo Freire recognised this when he argued that the solution to the challenge of humanization is not to try to integrate people into the structures of oppression, but to transform those structures so as to enable people to be '*beings for themselves*'[11].

Now, Arnold Toynbee in his epic '*A Study of History*' argues for and documents an interaction between environment and human culture that he termed Challenge-and-Response (Toynbee, 1974), accompanied by its own law of diminishing returns. The essence is that peoples respond to difficulties and problems with creativity, energy and obstinacy. However, where the challenge is weak the incentive to '*bestir oneself*' is also weak, and where the challenge is considerable it can be debilitating. Similarly we can envisage normal human existence as caught between the forces of opportunity and threat, comfort and struggle, and to which we each make the response that our material and psychological resources allow us, as seems best to us at the time. From this struggle to wrest from life both our needs for sustenance and, just as importantly, for growth we obtain our sense of self-efficacy and the blessing of providence. The impact of which, in turn, is the appreciation of self-esteem and the respect of our fellow humans. As Lasch (1996, p.89) commented: "*Respect is what we experience in the presence of admirable achievements, admirably formed characters, natural gifts put to good use. It entails the exercise of discriminating judgment, not indiscriminate acceptance.*"

However, there is a downside to this self-efficacy that is pride and a stubborn self-sufficiency that is portrayed as a certain civility which ostensibly seeks to prevent us being a burden on others but may rather reflect a desire not to be burdened with other people (Sennett, 2002). Indeed, the duplicity of this tacit compact was captured by Bauman (2000) who averred that to refrain from interfering in the lives of other people makes sense as long as they exercise similar self-restraint in return. One important manifestation of '*Liquid Modernity*' is the ephemeral nature that

---

11 See the full quotation from Freire (1971, p.61) in section 4 of chapter 1; see also the Gospel according to Mark 2, v.27.

we afford all but a very few relationships[12], leading Sennett (1998, p.24) to argue that: "*fleeting forms of association are more useful to people than long-term connections.*" This dissolution of bonds of affection and affiliation has been catalysed by urbanization and the expansion of the State. As Kropotkin (2010, p.121) maintained: "*as the obligation towards the State grew in numbers the citizens were evidently relieved from their obligations towards each other.*" Indeed, as we saw in chapter 5, Stirrat and Henkel (1997, p.72) talked about: "*an obligation to give, not an obligation to maintain a social relationship.*" and Benedict XVI (2009, section 9) recognised that, for the most part, modern charity has been reduced to: "*Giving through duty*". Furthermore, the counterpoint to this anodyne charity is manifested in the manipulative means by which charities obtain resources, as Dichter (2003, p.261) commented: "*Private development assistance organizations need to raise money. And given the state of the current market, they also need to make their messages inspirational appeals to love, guilt, and ego.*" On such foundations it is improbable that anything lastingly effective can be built.

As argued in chapter 5, the challenge of this paradox of helping to self-help rests in our ability to differentiate between humanitarian and development assistance. As Ellerman (2007, p.151) noted: "*The international development agencies and organizations were not originally designed to undertake humanitarian relief. … But the difficulties in development assistance … have prompted many agencies to quietly refocus their work towards poverty relief – all the while describing it in developmental terms.*"

Therefore, we may contend that real development requires us to tolerate people struggling, but not those who are drowning. Lasch (1998) argues for the exercise of mutual respect rather than compassion or benevolence, where the place for these last

12 Bauman (2000, p.14) speaks of: "*the friability, the brittleness, the transcience, the until-further-noticeness of human bonds and networks*".

is humanitarian relief to keep body and soul together in the face of insurmountable difficulties. Nevertheless, in arguing for the toleration of poverty I have in mind a very different meaning of tolerance than the one now generally favoured[13]. Kołakowski (1999, p.36) noted that: "*In France brothels used to be called 'houses of tolerance', the name suggesting that while brothels were not on the whole a good thing, it was better, for various reasons, to tolerate them.*" Prudent pragmatism is a better guide to helping behaviour in circumstances where our understanding of the range and nature of our alternatives is woefully inadequate. However, we must take care, as Kołakowski (*ibid.*) warned: "*It is important to notice, however, that when tolerance is enjoined upon us nowadays, it is often in the sense of indifference*:" Indeed, Lasch (1996, p.87) maintained that: "*In the absence of common standards, however, tolerance becomes indifference.*" thereby generating Brij Mohan's '*poverty of culture*' (Mohan, 2011). So, I state unequivocally that in no way am I advocating neglect, but rather a concerned, mutual engagement with the other.

Therefore, when we consider '*tough love*'[14] as an approach to development we must balance the forces of indifference with those of fraternity and solidarity as manifested through the workings of *The Gift* and its associated reciprocity. As John Dewey remarked: "*The gift that pauperizes when proceeding from a philanthropist in his special capacity, is a beneficent acknowledgement of the relationships of the case when it comes from a neighbour or from one who has other interests in common with the one assisted.*" (Dewey & Tufts, 1909, p.390) and Lasch (1996, p.101) commented that: "[populism and

---

13 Once more we are facing a nominalization – toleration – whose meaning as a process (verb) requires clarification.

14 Always remembering as Collier (2013, pp.63-64) noted that: "*the comforting face of benevolence is dependent upon a tough-minded and judgmental minority. Punishment is costly, so people will only be prepared to do it if they have sufficiently internalized not just benevolence, but moral outrage at those who free ride.*"

communitarianism] *reject both the market and the welfare state in pursuit of a third way.*"[15]

Hence, as Dewey and Tufts (*op.cit.*) advocated: "*Whenever conditions require purely direct and personal aid, it is best given when it proceeds from a natural social relationship, and not from a motive of "benevolence" as a separate force.*" Indeed, Kropotkin (2010, p.157) argued that: "*freely giving more than one expects from his neighbours, is proclaimed as being the real principle of morality – a principle superior to mere equivalence, equity, or justice, and more conducive to happiness.*" As such, the approach of *The Gift* is a tonic for people confronted by: "*The great fear we have of becoming fully aware of our powerlessness in situations when nothing can be done.*" (Rahnema, 1997, p.392) and follows the advice of Esteva and Prakash (1997, p.278) who advocated that: "*To make 'a difference', actions should not be grandiosely global but humbly local.*"

It seems that the most prudent approach to contriving development should demand a very human scale to our actions. Engagement through *The Gift* requires a long term commitment to a two-way relationship, and one that may perhaps be best described as '*befriending*'. This fresh nuancing of the development relationship has been tried before through the insistence on partnership, but as Eriksson Baaz (2005, p.6) noted: "*Those few studies that have addressed the question of partnership more specifically conclude that it is often poorly reflected in the practice of development aid.*" and I would argue that it was the lack of reciprocity or mutuality in the partnership that was crucial.

The European Union's response to a failed top-down development process was a promising approach termed '*Twinning*', launched in 1998. The main guideline for management of the Twinning process, the European Commission's Twinning Manual, states

[15] John Paul II (1991, p.52) argued that: "*a society becomes alienated when its forms of social organisation, production and consumption make it more difficult to offer the gift of self and to establish solidarity between people.*"

that: "*Twinning is a joint project. It is not a one-way delivery of Technical Assistance from a Member State to a beneficiary country. It is a close partnership in which the specific commitment of the beneficiary, who is also the driving force behind the changes targeted, is vital*" (EC, 2004, p.5). However, although Twinning brought with it a change in power relations within the Phare programme and a new vocabulary, the actual mechanics of the delivery of assistance essentially remained intact (O'Connor & Kowalski, 2005). Without the deep changes of values and attitudes the paternalistic donor domination of the process remains – primarily because of the scale of inputs which inevitably skews the relationship, but also as a consequence of impatience and inflexibility. It is vital to remember that organic processes of growth and maturation take place at their own pace, which cannot be hurried (Kaplan, 1996).

The '*phenomenon of child sponsorship*' (Dichter, 2003, p.257) is a similar, flawed idea that contains, as a kernel, the human sentiments of solidarity that, with Twinning, point the way towards a variety of creative initiatives that can be taken between one organization, group or individual and another in a complementary situation, not in the spirit of benevolence but of fraternity.

5 In Conclusion

After so many words it seems almost improper to try to pick out a few key points since what you, my reader, have made of the foregoing can only be a matter of respectful sovereignty. Nevertheless, in conformity to my training, I am unable to resist the temptation to try to manage closure of my enterprise and so would like to offer a few valedictory observations.

Firstly, two aphorisms spring to mind. The first is the recognition that '*If I wanted to get to Böchten I wouldn't have started from here!*' and the second is the rule of golf that states '*The ball must be played as it lies*'. Clearly our cultural overemphasis on capitalism and the free market has driven human social development in a direction that is unsustainable and, some would argue, undesirable. Nevertheless, we are where we are and however we are to bring about the humanization project that Mohan (2011) has dubbed '*Enlightenment II*', we have to do so from within that context. As Bateson and Bateson (2005, p.67) maintained: "*If we have taught men to be rascals, we cannot immediately set up a system appropriate to saints because the rascals will take advantage of the change.*"

The argument of this book is that the first step to make development more effective is to look out for and avert paradox whenever possible. A great help in this undertaking are David Ellerman's five themes:

1. Start from where the doers are.
2. See the world through the doers' eyes.
3. Don't override self-help capacity with conditional aid.
4. Don't undercut self-help capacity with benevolent aid.
5. Put the doers in the driver's seat.

(Ellerman, 2002)

But additionally:

1. We need to eliminate double binds.
   To this end a number of measures need to be taken to avoid paradoxes. Principal amongst these are that the logic of the plan set out in the logframe must preclude paradox. Secondly, throughout the development process it is important to emphasise the processes of strategic planning, ensuring that, as far as possible the higher order objectives are discussed and established **before** the detailed actions are planned and carried out. In this matter it is gratifying to see that nation states are developing *Poverty Reduction Strategy Plans* (Hanley, 2001), and that in some cases donors are putting in place their *Country Strategy Plans* thereafter, with donor programmes and projects dovetailing into an existing, locally-owned,

development planning process. This is not to say that development cannot take place at the grassroots, but that even the grassroots need to think strategically on occasion.

Next, it is important to recognise that paradoxes cannot always be avoided. In fact it is likely that paradoxes in development and education will continue to exist and to be created. For example, the asymmetry of the relationships between donors and recipients, between advisers and consultants or contractors, and within the hierarchies of Ministries between staff at various levels will continue to be features of the DA landscape. However, neither reconciliation nor compromise is the proper tenor of successful organisations. Rather, it is the ability to hold opposites as opposites, unreconciled. To treat both as far as possible as true at the same time, or at least as embodying aspects of the truth, until such time as a proper understanding emerges (Kaplan, 1996).

Therefore, it is an absolute priority to prevent turning those unavoidable paradoxes into double binds.

The double bind's requirement that the minor partner should be unable to comment upon any paradox confronting them is a key element. Therefore, the next action to take in this prevention is to deal with the hubris that can arise from the exercise of power by individuals on behalf of donors, or similarly powerful players, by giving a voice to the less powerful partners and participants. This provision of a voice should be taken very much, in the first instance, in terms of enabling people to name their world based upon a Freirian pedagogy that accepts that human emancipation requires that the oppressed's right to be heard is given substance in the behaviour of practitioners (Aronowitz, 1993, p.18). This requires that the primary action of the more powerful partners and their staff is **to listen**, to facilitate speaking.

Importantly, as we saw in chapter 5, giving voice and dealing with hubris should also countenance whistleblowing and gainsaying, particularly when presented in the form of a '*Socratic gadfly*'. This is so important that I reiterate that there is a strong case to be made that this particular aspect of giving voice to balance the asymmetrical donor-recipient relationship is actually a matter of applying good governance. As such the appointment of an Ombudsman (Storm, 1999) for development within all donor agencies to whom all stakeholders can go to seek redress might be an appropriate step to take. In the same vein, the suggestion to try to foster another means of redressing the power balance by strengthening recipients' networks, South to South, and to provide forums in which recipients can talk to each other about the problems of managing unequal relationships should receive serious consideration (Fukuda-Parr, *et al.,* 2002).

2. Separate Humanitarian Assistance from Development Investment.
   The imperative that attends emergency relief is inimical to the slower, more considered pace of the development process. The accompanying focus upon inputs and getting the money out the door provides perverse incentives for most of the protagonists, and the prominence of the state acting on behalf of the tax payer removes the individual citizen from the front line. Therefore, HA can be organized at an appropriate scale – international, regional, national or local – by multilateral agencies, NGOs or even the private sector (commissioned by the others) and can be removed from any accompanying horse trading or Trojan horsing[16].
   Certainly for Development Investment we must change the nature of the donor/recipient relationship from one of benevolence or dominance based upon a power differential and instead, at all levels, take development forward in the spirit of *The Gift* and reciprocity founded upon real human engagement in a long term and truly developmental encounter for both parties. Indeed, recall that Emerson (1983, p. 537)

16 It is alarming to hear of instances where state security services have used aid agencies as a cover for their activities.

said: "*The gift, to be true, must be the flowing of the giver unto me, correspondent to my flowing unto him.*" As John Paul II (1994, p.202) maintained: "*if man does not commit himself to becoming a gift for others, then this freedom* [of individualism] *can become dangerous. It will become freedom to do what I myself consider as good, what brings me a profit or pleasure, even a sublimated pleasure.*"

Over the longer term centrally organized Development Investment must be replaced by less grandiose and more human-scale endeavours. It is evident that small scale, human-sized, groups of people who know and trust one another, are the best place to foster the humanization project (otherwise Enlightenment II) and to eventually change the worlds which they love and care about (Rahnema, 1997), in the words of Margaret Mead: "*Never doubt that a small group of thoughtful, committed, citizens can change the world. Indeed, it is the only thing that ever has.*" (quoted in Sommers & Dineen, 1984, p. 158). What many people need in order to move forward is a vision and the support of a friend standing at their side.

3. Provide Inspirational Leadership

The cultural élites who are best placed to respond to the paradoxes of contriving human development need, as Lasch (1996, p.26) argued, to: "*reassume responsibility for the exacting standards without which civilization is impossible.*" The obligations that come with power and wealth are both a burden[17] and an unparalleled opportunity to demonstrate integrity. Too much in the current situation is urgent and will not brook duplicity. If you seek office then the responsibility for tackling matters is yours. But the answers are to be found in *phronesis*, which regrettably is currently absent from most curricula, and, as Kołakowski (1999, p.48) observed: "*We learn virtues by being brought up in a community where they are practiced.*"

---

17 See the Gospel according to Luke chapter 12 verse 48.

Similarly, we cannot expect business to deliver progress under the force of Corporate Social Responsibility. It is quite evident that in any market-based system there is a selective disadvantage to acts of altruism that would quickly see their disappearance. Indeed, it is also clear that to appeal to people's altruism in the face of such a market-based system is to place them in a cruel double bind (Hardin, 1973). However, if instead of voluntary actions and self-regulation business leaders sought to establish the rules of the game with which all enterprises must conform, and do so with fervour, under the promptings of ETHICS, and then vigorously applied themselves to observe those rules in both form and spirit, and campaign and act to ensure that others do likewise, then that may be all that we can expect from free enterprise and the market. Such ethical and leadership behaviour should produce fair trade, fair employment practices, environmental protection, the disappearance of corruption and the expansion of democratic processes and the rule of law. Nothing proves more offensive to my sensibilities than the thought of the cream of professionals using their intelligence, creativity and time seeking to evade and avoid the rules that systems of governance put in place to promote the well-being of their fellow citizens.

Nonetheless, we do well to remember that change is not a simple linear process that takes us smoothly from where we are to where we want to be. What we learned from our work in Brazil (Botelho, Kowalski & Bartlett, 2013) is that it is not down to the sequence of actions nor even the planning of the change that is most important but, as Kurt Lewin would have recognised, it is the congruent adherence to a set of core values or principles within a flexible framework of action that permits us to achieve our objectives, yet by no means guaranteeing that we will do so.

In all aspects of development, but particularly in the social, economic and environmental dimensions, the meta-language that we should be using to discuss policies, processes and procedures must be *ETHICS* which requires that all of us, and especially those involved professionally, must become proficient in that language. As Francis I (2013, p.37) observed: "*Ethics – a non-ideological ethics – would make it possible to bring about balance and a more humane social order.*" But ethics is about challenging the *status quo*, about stopping and asking, not if we can, but if we should. Again, Pope Francis commented:

> *How many words prove irksome to this system! It is irksome when the question of ethics is raised, when global solidarity is invoked, when the distribution of goods is mentioned, when reference is made to protecting labour and defending the dignity of the powerless, when allusion is made to a God who demands a commitment to justice.* (Francis I, *op.cit.*, p.105).

References

Abel, R. (1976) *Man is the measure.* New York: Free Press.
Ackoff, R.L. (1970) *A Concept of Corporate Planning.* New York: Wiley.
Adler, P.S. & Borys, B. (1996) Two Types of Bureaucracy: Enabling and Coercive. *Administrative Science Quarterly* 41, 61-89.
Adloff, F. & Mau, S. (2006) Giving Social Ties, Reciprocity in Modern Society. *Arch.europ.sociol.*, 47 (1), 93-123.
Al-Bazzaz, S.J. & Grinyer, P.H. (1981) Corporate Planning in the U.K.: The State of the Art in the 70s. *Strategic Management Journal* 2, 155-168.
Alfaro, L., Kalemli-Ozcan, S., and Volosovych, V. (2005) Capital Flows in a Globalized World: The Role of Policies and Institutions, *NBER Working Paper* 11696.
Allen, H. (2007) Finance begins with savings, not loans. In *What's wrong with MICROFINANCE?* Thomas Dichter & Malcolm Harper (eds.). pp.49-59. Rugby: Practical Action Publishing.
Allison, H.E. (1997) We can only act under the idea of freedom. *Proceedings of the American Philosophical Association* 71 (2), 39-50.
Altrichter, H., Kemmis, S., McTaggart, R. & Zuber-Skerritt, O. (2002) The concept of action research. *The Learning Organization* 9 (3), 125-131.
Amabile, I.M. (1983) *The Social Psychology of Creativity.* New York, Springer Verlag.
Amason, A.C. (1996) Distinguishing the Effects of Functional and Dysfunctional Conflict on Strategic Decision Making:

Resolving a Paradox for Top Management Teams. *The Academy of Management Journal*, 39, (1), 123-148.

Amsden, A.H. (2012) Grass Roots War on Poverty. *World Economic Review* 1, 114-131.

Anderson, W.L. (2009) Say's law and the Austrian theory of the business cycle. *The Quarterly Journal of Austrian Economics* 12 (2), 47–59.

Anon (2006) *Mathpages* [online] http://www.mathpages.com/rr/s3-07/3-07.htm

Ansoff, H.I. (1987) *Corporate Strategy*. Revised Edition. London: Harmondsworth.

Apple, M.W. (2001) The Politics of Labeling in a Conservative Age. In G.M. Hudak and P. Kihn (eds.) *Labeling: Pedagogy and Politics.* pp.261- 283. New York: RoutledgeFalmer.

Aras, G. & Crowther, D. (2009) Corporate Sustainability Reporting: A Study in Disingenuity? *Journal of Business Ethics* 87, 279-288.

Archer, M.S. (1995) *Realist social theory: the morphogenetic approach.* Cambridge: Cambridge University Press.

Argyris, C. (1990) *Overcoming Organizational Defenses: Facilitatting Organizational Learning.* Upper saddle River, NJ: Prentice Hall.

Argyris, C. (1992) *On Organizational Learning.* Cambridge, MA: Blackwell Publishers Inc.

Argyris, C,. Putnam, R, & McLain Smith, D. (1985) *Action Science.* San Francisco: Jossey-Bass.

Argyris, C. & Schön, D. (1991) Participatory Action Research and Action Science Compared. In W. F. Whyte (ed.) *Participatory Action Research,* pp.85-97. Newbury Park: Sage.

Armendáriz, B. & Morduch, J. (2007) *The Economics of Microfinance.* Cambridge, MA.: The MIT Press.

Arnstein, S. (1971) Eight rungs on the ladder of citizen participation, reprinted in Cahn, E. & Passett,B. (eds.) *Citizen Participation: effecting community change.* New York: Praeger Publishers.

Aronowitz, S. (1993) Paulo Freire's Radical Democratic Humanism. In P.McLaren & P. Leonard, (eds.), *Paulo Freire : a critical encounter*, pp. 8-24. London: Routledge.
Ashby, W.R. (1960) *Design for a Brain*. New York: John Wiley and Sons.
Assagioli, R. (1999) *The Act of Will*, 2nd ed., Woking: David Platts.
AtKisson, A. (1997) Why Civil Society Will Save the World. In J. Burbidge (ed.) *Beyond Prince and Merchant: Citizen Participation and the Rise of Civil Society*. pp.285-292. New York: Pact Publications.
Bain, A. (2006) *Emotions and Will*. 3rd ed., New York: Cosimo Classics.
Balcerowicz, L. (2013) The Post-socialist Transition in a Comparative Perspective: The Lessons. *19th IFMA Congress* "Transforming agriculture - between policy, science and the consumer" July 21-26, Warsaw, Poland.
Bandler, R. & Grinder, J. (1975) *The Structure of Magic*. Palo Alto, California: Science and Behavior Books, Inc.
Barque, C. (1993) *The End of Economics?* London: Zed Books.
Bateman, M. (2010) *Why Doesn't Microfinance Work? The Destructive Rise of Local Neoliberalism*. London: Zed Books.
Bateman, M. & Chang, H-J. (2012) Microfinance and the Illusion of Development: From Hubris to Nemesis in Thirty Years. *World Economic Review* 1, 13-36.
Bateson, G. (1972) *Steps to an Ecology of Mind*. London: Paladin.
Bateson, G. (2002) *Mind and Nature: a necessary unity*. Cresskill, New Jersey, Hampton Press, Inc.
Bateson, G. & Bateson, M.C. (2005) *Angels Fear: Towards an Epistemology of the Sacred*. Cresskill, NJ: Hampton Press.
Bauer, P. (1991) *The Development Frontier: Essays in Applied Economics*. Cambridge, MA: Harvard University Press.
Bauman, Z. (2000) *Liquid Modernity*. Cambridge: Polity Press.
Bauman, Z. (2001) *Community: Seeking Safety in an Insecure World*. Cambridge: Polity Press.
Bauman, Z. (2013) *Does the Richness of the Few Benefit US All?* Cambridge: Polity.

Bauman, Z. & Donskis, L. (2013) *Moral Blindness: The Loss of Sensitivity in Liquid Modernity.* Cambridge: Polity Press.

Baylies, C. (1995) 'Political Conditionality' and Democratisation. *Review of African Political Economy* 65, 321-337.

Beckert, J. (2011) The Great Transformation of Embeddedness: Karl Polanyi and the New Economic Sociology. In C.Hann & K.Hart (eds.) *Market and Society: The Great Transformation Today.* Pp.38-55. Cambridge: Cambridge University Press.

Beckhard, R. (1969) *Organization Development: Strategies and Models.* Reading, MA: Addison-Wesley.

Beemans, P. (1997) Culture, Spirituality and Economic development- opening a dialogue. *Forest, Trees and People Newsletter* 34, September, 1997.

Beer, S. (1959) *Cybernetics and Management.* New York: John Wiley.

Beer, S. (1966) *Decision and Control.* Chichester: John Wiley & Sons.

Beer, S. (1979) *The Heart of Enterprise.* Chichester: John Wiley & Sons.

Beer, S. (1980) Preface to Autopoiesis: The Organization of the Living. In H. Maturana & F. Varela. 1980 *Autopoiesis: The Organization of the Living.* pp. 63-72. Dordecht: D. Reidel Publishing Company.

Beer, S. (1981) *Brain of the Firm.* Chichester: John Wiley & Sons.

Beer, S. (1986) Recursions of Power. In R. Trappl (ed.) *Power, Autonomy, Utopia: New Approaches towards Complex Systems.* pp.3-17. New York: Plenum Press.

Beer, S. (1989) The Viable System Model: its provenance, development, methodology and pathology. In R.Espejo & R.Harnden (eds.) The Viable Systems Model: Interpretations and Applications of Stafford Beer's VSM. pp. 11-37. Chichester: John Wiley & Sons Ltd.

Beer, S. (1994) *Platform for Change.* Chichester: John Wiley & Sons Ltd.

Beer, S. (2004a) World in Torment: A Time Whose Idea Must Come. *Kybernetes* 33 (3/4), 774-803

Beer, S. (2004b) Man in a garrulous silence. *Kybernetes* 33 (3/4), 809-827.

Beer, S. (2004c) Reflections of a Cybernetician on the Practice of Planning. *Kybernetes*, 33 (3/4), 767-773.

Bell, D. (1970) The cultural contradictions of capitalism. *The Public Interest* 21, 16-43.

Bendell, J. (2000a) Introduction: Working with stakeholder pressure for sustainable development. In J. Bendell (ed.) *Terms for Endearment*. pp.14-29. Sheffield: Greenleaf Publishing Limited.

Bendell, J. (2000b) A No Win-win Situation? GMOs, NGOs and sustainable development. In J. Bendell (ed.) *Terms for Endearment*. pp.96-110. Sheffield: Greenleaf Publishing Limited.

Bendell, J. (2000c) Civil Regulation: A new form of democratic governance for the global economy?. In J. Bendell (ed.) *Terms for Endearment*. pp.239-254. Sheffield: Greenleaf Publishing Limited.

Bendix, R. (1956) *Work and Authority in Industry*. New York: John Wiley & Sons Inc.

Benedict XVI (2009). *Caritas in Veritate*. Encyclical letter. Vatican: Libreria Editrice http://www.vatican.va/holy_father/benedict_xvi/encyclicals/documents/hf_ben-xvi_enc_20090629_caritas-in-veritate_en.html accessed on 8/10/2010

Bennis, W.G. (2006) Foreword to the twenty-fifth anniversary printing. In Douglas McGregor (2006) *The Human Side of Enterprise*. Annotated Edition. pp.xv-xx. London: McGraw-Hill.

Benton, T. (1981) "Objective" Interests and the Sociology of Power. *Sociology* 15 (2), 161-184.

Berger, P.L. & Luckmann, T. (1966) *The Social Construction of Reality: A Treatise in the Sociology of Knowledge*. London: Penguin,

Berman, M. (1981) *The Reenchantment of the World*. Ithaca: Cornell University Press.

Berne, E. (1966) *Transactional Analysis in Psychotherapy*. New York: Grove Press.

Berthélemy, J-C. (2006) Bilateral Donors' Interest vs. Recipients' Development Motives in Aid Allocation: Do All Donors Behave the Same? *Review of Development Economics*, 10 (2), 179-194.

Bhaskar, R. (2002) *From Science to Emancipation: Alienation and the Actuality of Enlightenment.* New Delhi: Sage Publications.
Bichler, S. & Nitzan, J. (2012a) The asymptotes of power. *real-world economics review,* 60, 18-53.
Bichler, S. & Nitzan, J. (2012b) Capital as Power: Toward a New Cosmology of Capitalism, *real-world economics review* 61, 65–84.
Bierhoff, H.W. & Klein, R. (1990) Prosocial Behaviour. In M. Hewstone, W. Stroebe, J. Codol & G.M. Stephenson (eds) *Introduction to Social Psychology: A European Perspective.* pp. 246-262. Oxford: Blackwell.
Biggs, S., Messerschmidt, D. & Gurung B. (2005) Contending Cultures Among Development Actors. In J. Gonsalves, T. Becker, A. Braun, D. Campilan, H. De Chavez, E. Fajber, M. Kapiriri, J. Rivaca-Caminade & R. Vernooy (eds). pp.126-132. *Participatory Research and Development for Sustainable Agriculture and Natural Resource Management: A Sourcebook. Volume 2: Enabling Participatory Research and Development.* Ottawa, Canada: International Potato Center-Users' Perspectives With Agricultural Research and Development, Laguna, Philippines and International Development Research Centre.
Biggs, S. & Smith, S. (2003) A Paradox of Learning in Project Cycle Management and the Role of Organizational Culture. *World Development* 31, (10) 1743–1757.
Billington, R. (1993) *Living Philosophy: an introduction to moral thought.* 2nd ed. London: Routledge & Kegan Paul.
Binnendijk, A. (1989) Rural development: Lessons from experience. *Highlights of the seminar proceedings, A.I.D. Program Evaluation Discussion Paper* N°. 25. Washington, DC: USAID.
Bohm, D. (1951) *Quantum Theory.* London: Prentice-Hall.
Boserup E (1981). *Population and technological change: A study of long term trends.* Chicago, IL: University of Chicago Press.
Botelho M. do Nascimento (2008) *Learning to be an Insider Agent of Change in a Brazilian Rural University.* Unpublished PhD thesis: University of Wolverhampton.

Botelho, M., Kowalski, R. & Bartlett, S. (2013) Kurt Lewin's model of change revisited in a Brazilian Higher Education context. *Educationalfutures* 5 (2), 23-43.

Bourdieu, P. (1992) *The Logic of Practice.* (trans. R.Nice) Cambridge: Polity Press.

Bourland, D.D. (1949) A Linguistic Note: Writing in E-prime. *General Semantics Bulletin* 32, 111.

Brinkerhoff, J.M. (2002) *Partnership for International Development: Rhetoric or Results?* Boulder, CO: Lynne Rienner.

Brunsson, N. (1989) *The Organization of Hypocrisy: Talk, Decisions and Actions in Organizations.* Chichester: John Wiley & Sons.

Buchanan, J. (1977) The Samaritan's Dilemma. In J.Buchanan (ed.) *Freedom in Constitutional Contract*, pp.169-180. College Station: Texas A&M University Press.

Buckingham, S. (2007) Microgeographies and Microruptures: The Politics of Gender in the Theory and Practice of Sustainability. In R. Krueger & D. Gibbs (eds.), *The Sustainable Development Paradox: Urban Political Economy in the United States and Europe.* pp. 66-94. London: The Guildford Press.

Burnes, B. (2004) Kurt Lewin and the Planned Approach to Change: A Re- appraisal. *Journal of Management Studies* 41 (6) 976-1002.

Burns, J. H. (2005) Happiness and Utility: Jeremy Bentham's Equation. *Utilitas* 17 (1), 46-61.

Butler, C.D. (2004) Human carrying capacity and human health. *PLoS Med* 1(3): e55.

Carnegie, D. (1936) *How to Win Friends and Influence People.* New York: Simon and Schuster.

Carney, D. (1998) Implementing the Sustainable Rural Livelihoods Approach. in D.Carney (ed.), *Sustainable Rural Livelihoods: What contribution can we make?*, pp.1-26. London: DFID.

Carr, S., McAuliffe, E. & MacLachlan, M. (1998) *Psychology of Aid.* London: Routledge.

Carr, W. (2006) Philosophy, Methodology and Action Research. *Journal of Philosophy of Education*, 40 (4), 421 – 435.

Carr, W., & Kemmis, S. (1986) *Becoming Critical: Education, Knowledge and Action Research.* Lewes: Falmer Press.

Chamberlain, N.W. (1968) *Enterprise and Environment.* New York: McGraw-Hill.

Chambers, R. (1992) Scientist or resource-poor farmer – whose knowledge counts? in R.W. Gibson & A. Sweetmore (eds.), *Proceedings of a Seminar on Crop Protection for Resource-Poor Farmers*, Chatham: NRI.

Chambers, R. (1997) *Whose reality counts? : putting the first last.* London: Intermediate Technology.

Chang, H-J. (2000) The Hazard of Moral Hazard: Untangling the Asian Crisis. *World Development* 28 (4), 775-788.

Chang, H-J. (2011) *23 Things They Don't Tell You about Capitalism.* London: Penguin Books.

Checkland, P. & Scholes, J. (1999) *Soft Systems Methodology in Action*. Chichester: John Wiley & Sons.

Child, J. (1972) Organization structure, environment and performance: the role of strategic choice. *Sociology* 6, 1-22.

Chomsky, N. (1957) *Syntactic Structures.* The Hague: Mouton.

Clarke, J.G.I. (2006) The Eudemony Index: Toward a methodology for overcoming chronic vulnerability to HIV/AIDS pathology by strengthening 'community immunity' by the amplification of resilience factors. http://www.docstoc.com/docs/48047508/The-Eudemony-Index-Toward-a-methodology-for-overcoming-chronic accessed last on 6 October 2013.

Cleaver, F. (1999). Paradoxes of Participation: Questioning Participatory Approaches to Development. *Journal of International Development* 11, 597-612.

Clegg, S.R., (1989) *Frameworks of Power.* London: Sage Publications.

Clegg, S.R., Cunha, J.V. & Cunha, M.P. (2002) Management Paradoxes: a relational view. *Human Relations*, 55, (5), 483-503.

Clements, P. (1995) A Poverty-Oriented Cost-Benefit Approach to the Analysis of Development Projects. *World Development*, 23 (4), 571-592.

Coale, A.J. & Hoover, E.M. (1958) *Population growth and economic development in low income countries.* Princeton: Princeton University Press.

Cole, K. (2005) The last putting themselves first. *Progress in Development Studies* 5, (1) 45–53.

Cole, K. (2006) The last putting *themselves* first III: progress, intuition and development studies. *Progress in Development Studies* 6, (4) 343–349.

Collier, P. (2013) *Exodus: Immigration and Multiculturalism in the 21st Century.* London: Allen Lane.

Collier, P. & Dollar, D. (2001) Can the World Cut Poverty in Half? How Policy Reform and Effective Aid Can Meet International Development Goals. *World Development* 29(11), 1787-1802.

Collier, P. & Dollar, D. (2002) Aid allocation and poverty reduction. *European Economic Review* 46, 1475-1500.

Commission of the European Communities (2001) *Green paper promoting a European framework for corporate social responsibility*, Brussels: COM.

Contu, A. & Girei, E. (2013) NGOs management and the value of 'partnerships' for equality in international development: What's in a name? *Human Relations* 1-28.

Cook, T.D. & Campbell, D.T. (1979) *Quasi-experimentation: Design and analysis issues for field settings.* Chicago: Rand McNally.

Cooke, B. (1998) Participation, Process and Management: Lessons for Development in the History of Organisation Development, *Journal of International Development* 10 (1), 35-54.

Cooke, W. (2001) The Social Psychological Limits of Participation? In Bill Cooke and Uma Kothari (eds.), *Participation the New Tyranny?* pp. 102-122. London: Zed Books.

Cowen, M.P. & Shenton, R.W. (1996) *Doctrines of Development.* London: Routledge.

Coyle, D. (2011) *The Economics of Enough: How to run the economy as if the future matters.* Princeton: Princeton University Press.

Craib, I. (1992) *Anthony Giddens.* London: Routledge.

Craig, D. & Porter, D. (1997) Framing Participation: Development projects, professionals and organizations. *Development in Practice* 7, (3), 229 – 236.

Craig Smith, N. (2003) Corporate Social Responsibility: Not Whether, But How? *London Business School, Centre for Marketing Working Paper* No. 03-701.

Crewe, E. & Harrison, E. (1998) *Whose Development? An Ethnography of Aid.* London: Zed Books.

Crick, B. (2002) *Democracy: A Very Short Introduction.* Oxford: Oxford University press.

Cruz, I. Stahel, A. & Max-Neef, M. (2009) Towards a systemic development approach: Building on the Human-Scale Development paradigm. *Ecological Economics* 68, 2021–2030

Dagron, A.G. (2005) Communication for Social Change: The New Communicator http://www.geocities.com/agumucio/ArtNewCommunicator.html accessed 6 May 2005.

Dahl, R.A. (1957) The Concept of Power. *Behavioral Science* 2, 201-215.

Dahl, R.A. (1990) *After the Revolution: Authority in a good society.* Revised Edition. New Haven: Yale University Press.

Dahl, R.A. (2000) *On Democracy.* New Haven: Yale University Press.

Dale, R. (2004) *Development Planning: Concepts and Tools for Planners, Managers and Facilitators,* London: Zed Books,

Dalton, G.E. (1988) Is Forward Budgeting Justified? *Farm Management* 6 (12), 505-512.

Daly, H. E. & Cobb, J. B. (1989) *For the common good: redirecting the economy toward community, the environment, and a sustainable future.* Boston: Beacon Press.

Dalyell,T. (2000). "Democracy needs its awkward squads". http://www.theherald.co.uk/perspective/archive/16-8-1999-23-37-35.html accessed 28 April 2003.

Damrosch, D. (2006) Vectors of Change. In C.M. Golde & G.E. Walker (eds.) *Envisioning the Future of Doctoral Education: Preparing Stewards of the Discipline.* Carnegie Essays on the Doctorate (pp. 34-45). San Francisco: Jossey-Bass.

Davidoff, P. & Reiner, T.A. (1973) *A Choice Theory of Planning. In A Reader in Planning Theory.* A. Faludi (ed.) pp. 11-39, Oxford: Pergamon Press.
Dearden P. N. & Kowalski, R. (2003) Programme and Project Cycle Management (PPCM): Lessons from South and North. *Development in Practice* 13(5), 501-514
De Bono, E. (1990) *The Happiness Purpose.* Harmondsworth: Penguin Books.
Deci, E. with Flaste, R. (1995) *Why We Do What We Do.* New York: Penguin Books.
Denison, D.R., Hooijberg, R. & Quinn, R.E. (1995) Paradox and Performance: Towards a Theory of Behavioural Complexity in Managerial Leadership. *Organization Science* 6(5), 524-540.
Dennett, D.C. (2003) *Freedom Evolves.* London: Allen Lane The Penguin Press.
Derrida, J. (1994) *Given Time: 1. Counterfeit Money.* Chicago: Univ. of Chicago Press.
Derrida, J. & Caputo, J.D. (1997) *Deconstruction in a Nutshell.* New York: Fordham University Press.
Dewey, J. (1939) *Freedom and Culture.* New York: Capricorn.
Dewey, J. & Tufts, J. (1909) *Ethics.* London: George Bell and Sons.
DFID (2005) *Partnerships for poverty reduction: rethinking conditionality.* London: DFID.
Diamond, J. (2006) *Collapse: How Societies Choose to Fail or Survive.* London: Penguin Books.
Dichter, T. W. (2003) *Despite Good Intentions: Why Development Assistance to the Third World has Failed.* Amherst & Boston: University of Massachusetts Press.
Dichter, T (2006), *Hype and Hope: The Worrisome State of the Microcredit Movement.* Available from http://www.microfinancegateway.org/p/site/m//template.rc/1.26.9051
Dichter, T. (2007a) Can microcredit make an already slippery slope more slippery: Some lessons from the social meaning of debt. In T. Dichter & M. Harper (eds.) *What's wrong with MICROFINANCE?.* pp.9-17. Rugby: Practical Action Publishing.

Dichter, T. (2007b) The chicken and egg dilemma in microfinance: An historical analysis of the sequence of growth and credit in the economic development of the 'north'. In T. Dichter & M. Harper (eds.) *What's wrong with MICROFINANCE?*. pp.179-192. Rugby: Practical Action Publishing.
Dickens, C. (1985) *A Christmas Carol*. London: Penguin Classics.
Dietz, T. (2005) The Darwinian trope in the drama of the commons: variations on some themes by the Ostroms. *Journal of Economic Behavior & Organization* 57, 205–225.
Dillard-Wright, D. (2007) Sympathy and the Non-human: Max Scheler's Phenomenology of Interrelation. *Indo-Pacific Journal of Phenomenology* 7 (2), 1-9.
Dilman, I. (1999) *Free Will: an historical and philosophical introduction*. London: Routledge.
Dilts, R.B., Epstein, T. & Dilts, R.W. (1991) *Tools for Dreamers: Strategies for Creativity and the Structure of Innovation*. Capitola: Meta Publications Inc.
Dixon, J. (2009) Comparative social welfare: the existential humanist perspective and challenge. *Journal of Comparative Social Welfare* 26 (2-3), 177-187.
Dobb, M. (1973) *Theories of Value and Distribution Since Adam Smith: Ideology and Economic Theory*. Cambridge: University Press.
Donaldson, T. (1982) *Corporations and Morality*. Englewood Cliffs, NJ: Prentice Hall.
Doring, A. (2002) Challenges to the Academic Role of Change Agent. *Journal of Further and Higher Education* 26 (2), 139-148.
Douglas, M. (2002) No free gifts. Forward in Marcel Mauss, (2002) *The Gift: The form and reason for exchange in archaic societies*. pp. ix-xxiii. Abingdon: Routledge
Douthwaite, R. (1999) Is it Possible to Build a Sustainable World? In *Critical Development Theory*, Ronaldo Munck & Denis O'Hearn (eds.). pp.157-177. Dhaka: The University Press.
Dreschler, W. (2004) Natural versus social sciences: on understanding in economics. In, Erik S. Reinert (ed.) *Globalization, Economic Development and Inequality*, pp.71-86. Cheltenham: Edward Elgar.

Dror, Y. (1971) *Ventures in Policy Sciences.* New York: American Elsevier.

Drummond, H. (1992) *The Quality Movement: What Total Quality Management is Really All About!* London: Kogan Page.

Dryden, J. (1742) *The hind and the panther, a poem. In three parts.* London: Reproduced from the British Library, Gale, ECCO.

Duvendack, M., Palmer-Jones, R., Copestake, J.G.,Hooper, L., Loke, Y., & Rao, N. (2011) *What is the evidence of the impact of microfinance on the well-being of poor people?* London: EPPI-Centre, Social Science Research Unit, Institute of Education, University of London.

Eade, D. (1997) *Capacity Building: an approach to People-Centred Development*, Oxford: Oxfam.

Easterlin, R.A. (1974) Does economic growth improve the human lot? Some empirical evidence. In: P.A. David & W.R. Melvin (eds.) *Nations and Households in Economic Growth.* pp. 89–125. New York: Academic Press.

Easterly, W. (2006) *The White Man's Burden: Why the West's efforts to aid the rest have done so much ill and so little good.* Oxford: Oxford University Press.

Ehrlich P. R. (1968). *The population bomb.* New York: Ballantine.

Ehrlich P.R. (2008). *The dominant animal: Human evolution and the environment.* Washington DC: Island Press.

Einstein, A. (1998) Why socialism. Monthly Review May. Retrieved 4 August 2004 from http://www.monthlyreview.org/598mill.htm

Eisenhardt, K.M. (2000) Paradox, spirals, ambivalence: The new language of change and pluralism. *The Academy of Management Review* 25, 703 – 705.

Elias, N. (1991) *The Society of Individuals*, Oxford: Blackwell

Ellerman, D.P. (1995) *Intellectual Trespassing as a Way of Life: Essays in Philosophy, Economics, and Mathematics.* Lanham, Maryland: Rowman & Littlefield Publishers.

Ellerman, D.P. (2001) Helping people help themselves: Towards a theory of Autonomy-compatible help, *World Bank Working paper* 2693. http://econ.worldbank.org/view.php?type=5&id=2513 accessed 28 April 2003.

Ellerman, D. (2002) Autonomy-respecting assistance: Towards new\strategies for capacity-building and development assistance. In *Capacity for Development*, S. Fukuda-Parr, C. Lopes & K. Malik (eds.), pp.43-60. London: Earthscan Publications.

Ellerman, D. (2005a). How do we grow: Jane Jacobs on diversification and specialization. Challenge, 48(3), 50–83.

Ellerman, D. (2005b) *Helping People Help Themselves: From the World Bank to an Alternative Philosophy of Development.* Ann Arbor: The University of Michigan Press.

Ellerman, D. (2007) Microfinance: Some conceptual and methodological problems. In Thomas Dichter and M. Harper (eds.) What's wrong with Microfinance? pp.149-161. Rugby: Intermediate Technology Publications Ltd.

Ellerman, D. (2010) Marxism as a capitalist tool. *The Journal of Socio-Economics* 39, 696-700.

Elsner, W. (2012) Financial Capitalism—at Odds With Democracy: The Trap of an 'Impossible' Profit Rate, *real-world economics review* 62, 132–159.

Emerson, R.W. (1983) Gifts. Essay V, Second Series In Joel Porte (ed.) *Ralph Waldo Emerson; Essays & Lectures.* pp.535-538, Cambridge: The Press Syndicate of the University of Cambridge on behalf of the Library of America.

Engeström, Y. (2007) Putting Vygotsky to work: The Change Laboratory as an application of double stimulation. In H. Daniels, M. Cole, & J. V. Wertsch (eds.), *Cambridge companion to Vygotsky.* Cambridge, England: Cambridge University Press.

Epstein, W.M. (2009) Romanticism, community and social services. *Journal of Comparative Social Welfare* 26 (2-3), 117-136.

Eriksson Baaz, M. (2005) *The Paternalism of Partnership*. London: Zed Books.

Ernst, F. (1971) The OK corral: the grid for get-on-with. *Transactional Analysis Journal*, 1(4): 231 – 240.

Escobar, A. (2004). Development, violence and the new imperial order. *Development*, 47, 15–21.

Esman, M. & Uphoff, N. (1984) *Local Organizations: Intermediaries in Rural Development*. Ithaca: Cornell University Press.

Espejo, R. (2003) *The Viable System Model - A briefing about organisational structure*. Syncho Ltd.: Birmingham.

Espejo, R. (2004) The footprint of complexity: the embodiment of social systems. *Kybernetes* 33 (3/4), 671-700

Esteva, G. (1992) Development, in W.Sachs (ed.), *The Development Dictionary*. pp. 6–25, London: Zed Books Ltd.

Esteva, G. & Prakash, M.S. (1997) From Global Thinking to Local Thinking. In *The Post-Development Reader*. Majid Rahnema with Victoria Bawtree (eds.) pp.277-289. London: Zed Books.

Esteva, G. & Prakash, M.S. (1998) Beyond development, what? *Development in Practice*, 8(3), 280 -296.

European Commission. (2001) Twinning in Action, October. Accessed at http://europa.eu.int/comm/enlargement/pas/twinning/pdf/twinning_en.pdf on 22/11/2004.

Faludi, A. (1973) *Planning Theory*. Oxford: Pergamon Press.

Fan, S. & Chan-Kang, C. (2004) Returns to investment in less-favored areas in developing countries: a synthesis of evidence and implications for Africa. *Food Policy* 29, 431-444.

Ferguson, N. (2008) *The Ascent of Money: A Financial History of the World*. New York: Penguin Press.

Ferré, F. (1998) *Knowing and Value: Towards a Constructive Postmodern Epistemology*. Albany: State University of New York Press.

Finlayson, J.G. (2005). *Habermas: A very short introduction*. Oxford: Oxford University Press.

FitzPatrick, S. (2005) Open-Ended Tangled Hierarchies: Zen Koans and Paradox in Public Administration. *International Journal of Public Administration* 28, 957 – 971.

Flank, L. (2007) *Contradictions of Capitalism: An Introduction to Marxist Economics*. St Petersburg, Florida: Red and Black Publishers.

Flyvbjerg, B. (2001) *Making Social Science Matter: Why social inquiry fails and how it can succeed again*. Cambridge: Cambridge University Press.

Foucault, M. (1981) The Order of Discourse. In R.Young (ed.) *Untying the Text: A Post-structuralist Reader*. p.48-79. London: Routledge, Kegan and Paul.

Francis I (2013) *Evangelii Gaudium – Apostolic Exhortation on the Proclamation of the Gospel in Today's World*. Dublin: Veritas.

Francis, P. (2002) Social Capital, Civil Society and Social Exclusion. In U. Kothari, & M. Minogue, (eds.) *Development theory and practice: critical perspectives*. pp.71-91. Basingstoke: Palgrave.

Frankl, V. (1985) *Man's Search for Meaning*. New York: Washington Square Press.

Freire, P. (1971) *Pedagogy of the oppressed*. Harmondsworth: Penguin.

Freud, S. (1949) *Introductory Lectures on Psycho-Analysis*. Translation by Joan Riviére. London: Allen and Unwin.

Friedman, M. (1962) *Capitalism and Freedom*. Chicago: University of Chicago Press.

Friedman, M. (1970) The Social Responsibility of Business is to Increase its Profits. *The New York Times Magazine* Sept. 13, 1970.

Fritz, R. (1994) *The Path of Least Resistance*. Oxford: Butterworth-Heineman.

Fromm, E. (1995) *The essential Fromm : life between having and being*. London: Constable.

Fukuda-Parr, S., Lopes,C. & Malik, K.(2002) Institutional innovations for capacity development. In *Capacity for Development*, S. Fukuda-Parr, C. Lopes, & K. Malik, (eds.), pp.1-21. London: Earthscan Publications Ltd.

Fulcher, J. (2004) *Capitalism: A Very Short Introduction*. Oxford: Oxford University Press.

Fuller, R. B. (1981) *Critical Path*. New York, NY: St.Martin's Press.

Gajanayake, J. & Gajanayake, S. (1993) Community Empowerment: a participatory training manual on community project development. New York: PACT Publications.

Galbraith, J. K. (1976) *Money: Whence it came' where it went*. New York: Bantam Books.

Galbraith, J. K. (1979) *The Nature of Mass Poverty*. Cambridge, Mass.: Harvard University Press.

Galeano, E. (1997) To Be Like Them. In *The Post-Development Reader*. Majid Rahnema with Victoria Bawtree (eds.) pp.214-222. London: Zed Books.

Gasper, D. (1999) Problems in the Logical Framework Approach and the challenges for Project Cycle Management, *The Courier* (January/February), 75-77.

Gaylin, N.L. (1993) Person Centred Family Therapy. In D.Brazier, (ed.), *Beyond Carl Rogers,* pp.181-200. London: Constable.

Geddes, J. L. (2012) The Corporate Professor. *The Hedgehog Review* 14 (1), 1-2.

George, S. (1992) *The Debt Boomerang: How third world debt harms us all*. London: Pluto Press.

Gergen, K.J. & Gergen, M.M. (1971) International assistance from a psychological perspective. In G.W. Keeton & G. Schwartzenberger (eds.), *Year Book of World Affairs 1971* pp. 87-103. London: Stevens & Sons.

Gergen, K.J. & Gergen, M.M. (1974) Understanding foreign assistance through public opinion. In G.W. Keeton & G. Schwartzenberger (eds), *Year Book of World Affairs 1974* pp. 125-140). London: Stevens & Sons.

Gibbs, D. & Krueger, R. (2007) Containing the Contradictions of Rapid Development? New Economy Spaces and Sustainable Urban Development. In R. Krueger & D. Gibbs (eds.), *The Sustainable Development Paradox: Urban Political Economy in the United States and Europe*. pp. 95-122. London: The Guildford Press.

Gibson, C.C., Andersson, K., Ostrom, E. & Shivakumar, S. (2005) *The Samaritan's Dilemma: The Political Economy of Development Aid*. Oxford: Oxford University Press.

Giddens, A. (1982) *Profiles and critiques in social theory*. Basingstoke: Macmillan.

Giddens, A. (1989) A reply to my critics. In Held, D. & Thompson, J.B. (eds.) *Social theory of modern societies: Antony Giddens and his critics*. pp. 249-301. Cambridge: Cambridge University Press.

Gil, D. G. (2011) Forward, in B. Mohan, *Development, Poverty of Culture, and Social Policy*. pp. ix–x. New York: Palgrave Press.

Gillborn, D. & Youdell, D. (2000) *Rationing Education: policy, practice, reform and equity*. Buckingham: Open University Press.

Godbout, J.T. with Caillé, A. (2000) *The World of the Gift*. Translated by D. Winkler. London: McGill-Queen's University Press.

Goffman, E. (1968) *Stigma: Notes on the Management of Spoiled Identity*. London: Penguin Books.

Goldsmith, A.A. (1996) Strategic Thinking in International Development: Using Management Tools to See the Big Picture. *World Development* 24 (9), 1432 – 1439.

Goleman, D. (1998) *Vital Lies, Simple Truths*, London, Bloomsbury Publishing plc.

Gould, J. (2005) Conclusion: the politics of consultation. In J. Gould (ed.), *The New Conditionality: The politics of poverty reduction strategies*. pp.135-151. London: Zed Books.

Gouldner, A.W. (1960) The Norm of Reciprocity: A preliminary statement. *American Sociological Review* 25 (2), 161-178.

Graham, C. (2012) *Happiness around the world: the paradox of happy peasants and miserable millionaires*. Oxford: Oxford University Press.

Gramsci, A. (1971) *Selections from the Prison Notebooks*. London: Lawrence & Wishart.

Granovetter, M. (1985) Economic Action and Social Structure: The Problem of Embeddedness. *American Journal of Sociology*, 91, 481–510.

Gray, J. (1998) *False Dawn: The Delusions of Global Capitalism*. New York: The New Press.

Greiner, L.E. & Schein, V.E. (1989) *Power and Organization Development : Mobilizing Power to Implement Change*. Reading, MA.: Addison-Wesley.

Grieve, R. H. (2012) The Marginal Productivity Theory of the Price of Capital. An Historical Perspective on the Origins of the Codswallop, *real-world economics review* 60, 138–149.

Gronemeyer, M. (1992) Helping. In W.Sachs (ed.) *The Development Dictionary: A guide to knowledge as power.* pp. 51-69. London: Zed Books.

Grunwald, M. (2009) How Obama is using the science of change. *Time*, April 13: 28-32.

Habermas, J. (1990) *The Philosophical Discourse of Modernity.* Cambridge, MA.: MIT Press.

Hagen, R.J. (2006) Buying Influence: Aid Fungibility in a Strategic Perspective. *Review of Development Economics*, 10 (2), 267-284.

Haji, I. (2003) Determinism and Its Threat to the Moral Sentiments. *The Monist* 86(2), 242-260.

Hall, E.T. (1976) *Beyond Culture.* London: Doubleday.

Hamann, R. & Acutt, N. (2003) How should civil society (and the government) respond to 'corporate social responsibility'? A critique of business motivations and the potential for partnerships. *Development Southern Africa* 20 (2), 255-270.

Hampden-Turner, C. (1990) *Charting the Corporate Mind, from Dilemma to Strategy.* Oxford: Blackwell Publishers.

Hancock, G. (1993) *Lords of Poverty*, London: Mandarin.

Handy, C. (1994) *The Age of Paradox.* Boston: Harvard Business School Press.

Hann, C. & Hart, K. (2011) *Economic Anthropology: History, Ethnography, Critique.* Cambridge: Polity Press.

Hannagan, T. (2002) *Management Concepts & Practices* 3rd ed. Harlow: Prentice Hall.

Hansen, M.J., Buhl, J., Bazazi, S., Simpson, S.J. & Sword, G.A. (2011) Cannibalism in the lifeboat — collective movement in Australian plague locusts. *Behavioural Ecology and Sociobiology* 65:1715–1720.

Haq, M.U. (2000) *Reflections on Human Development.* 2nd Edition. New Dehli: Oxford University Press.

Hardin, G. (1968) The Tragedy of the Commons. *Science* 162, 1243-1248.

Hardin, G. (1973) *Exploring New Ethics for Survival: The Voyage of the Spaceship Beagle.* New York: Pelican Books.

Hardy, C. & Clegg, S.R. (1996) Some Dare Call It Power. In S.R. Clegg, C. Hardy & W.R. Nord (eds.) *Handbook of Organizational Studies*. pp.622-658. London: Sage Publications.

Häring, N. (2013) The veil of deception over money: how central bankers and textbooks distort the nature of banking and central banking, *real-world economics review*, 62, 2-18

Harper, M. (2007) Some final thoughts. In T. Dichter & M. Harper (eds.). *What's wrong with MICROFINANCE?* pp.257-259. Rugby: Practical Action Publishing.

Harré, H.R. (1981) The positivist-empiricist approach and its alternatives. In P. Reason & J. Rowan (eds.) *Human inquiry: a sourcebook of new paradigm research*. pp. 3-17. New York: John Wiley.

Harvey, D. (2011) *The Enigma of Capital and the crises of Capitalism*. London: Profile Books.

Harvey, J.B. (1988) The Abilene Paradox: The Management of Agreement. *Organizational Dynamics* Summer 1988, pp.17-43.

Hayek, F.A. (2007) *The Road to Serfdom: Text and Documents*. The Definitive Edition. B. Caldwell (ed.). Chicago: The University of Chicago Press.

Hefeker, C. (2006) Project Aid or Budget Aid? The Interests of Governments and Financial Institutions. *Review of Development Economics*, 10 (2), 241-252.

Herbert, C. (1991) *Culture and Anomie*. Chicago: University of Chicago Press.

Heron, J. (1996) *Co-operative Inquiry: Research into the Human Condition*. London: Sage.

Herzberg, F. (1974) *Work and the nature of man*. London: Crosby Lockwood Staples,

Hettne, B. (1995) *Development Theory and the Three Worlds: Towards an international political economy of development*. (2nd edition), Harlow: Longman Scientific & Technical.

Hillman, A. & Keim, G. (2001). Shareholder value, stakeholder management, and social issues: what's the bottom line? *Strategic Management Journal*, 22, 125–139.

Hilton, R. (2006) *The Transition from Feudalism to Capitalism.* Delhi: Aakar Books.

Hinchman, L. (1996) Autonomy, Individuality, and Self-Determination. In J. Schmidt (ed.), *What Is Enlightenment: Eighteenth-Century Answers and Twentieth-Century Questions.* pp.488-516. Berkeley: University of California Press.

Hirschman, A.O. (1973) *Journeys towards Progress.* New York: Norton.

Hirschman, A.O. (1992) *Rival Views of Market Society.* Cambridge MA: Harvard University Press.

Hirschman, A.O. & Bird, R.M. (1971) Foreign Aid: A Critique and a Proposal. In Hirschman, A.O. (ed.) *A Bias for Hope* pp. 197-224 New Haven: Yale University Press.

Hodgson, G.M. (2007). Institutions and Individuals: Interaction and Evolution. *Organization Studies* 28 (1), 95 – 116.

Hofstadter, D.R. (2000) *Gődel, Escher, Bach: an Eternal Golden Braid.* 20th Anniversary Edition. London: Penguin Books.

Hofstede, G. (1984) The cultural relativity of the Quality of Life concept. *Academy of Management Review* 9, 389-398.

Holdren, J.P. & Ehrlich, P.R. (1974). Human Population and the global environment. *American Scientist* 62(3), 282–292.

Holdstock, L. (1993) Can We Afford not to Revision the Person-Centred Concept of Self? In D. Brazier, (ed.), *Beyond Carl Rogers,* pp.229-252. London: Constable.

Hudson, M. (2010) The use and abuse of mathematical economics, *real-world economics review,* 55, 2-22.

Hudson, M. (2011) How economic theory came to ignore the role of debt. *real-world economics review* 57, 2-24.

Hudson, M. (2012) *The Bubble and Beyond: Fictitious Capital, Debt Deflation and Global Crisis.* Dresden: ISLET.

Hunter, J. D., & Geddes, J. L. (2000). What's the University for?. *The Hedgehog Review,* 2 (3), 5-6.

IDS (2001) The new dynamics of aid: Power, Procedures and Relationships. *IDS Policy Briefing* 15.

Illich, I. (1978) *The Right to Useful Employment: and its professional enemies.* London: Marion Boyars.

Illich, I. (1997) Development as Planned Poverty. In M. Rahnema with V. Bawtree (eds.) *The Post-Development Reader.* pp.94-101. London: Zed Books.

Illich, I. with Rahnema, M. (1997) Twenty-six Years Later. In M. Rahnema with V. Bawtree (eds.) *The Post-Development Reader.* pp.103-110. London: Zed Books.

IMF. (2011) Technical Assistance. IMF Fact Sheet, http://www.imf.org/external/np/exr/facts/tech.htm accessed on 17 November 2011.

Ingham, G. (2004) *The Nature of Money.* Cambridge: Polity.

Iserson, K. V. & Moskop, J. C. (2007) Triage in Medicine, Part I: Concept, History, and Types. *Annals of Emergency Medicine* 49, 275-281.

Islam, M.M. (2002) *An Analysis of the Role of Extension Methodology on Poverty Reduction: A Comparative Study of Aquaculture Extension Programmes in the Northwest Fisheries Extension Project (NFEP) Command Area, Bangladesh.* Unpublished PhD thesis: the University of Wolverhampton.

Jamieson, K. H. (1995). Beyond the double bind: women and leadership. Oxford: Oxford University Press.

Jamieson, N. (1987) The Paradigmatic Significance of Rapid Rural Appraisal. In Proceedings of the 1985 International Conference on Rapid Rural Appraisal, Thailand, Khon Kaen University.

John Paul II (1994) *Crossing the Threshold of Hope.* London: Random House.

Johnson, S. & Rogaly, B. (1997) *Microfinance and Poverty Reduction*, Oxford and London: Oxfam and ActionAid.

Jones, M. (2003) The Lasa Computanews Guide to Project Management. http://www.lasa.org.uk/it/lcgpm.pdf accessed 17 May 2005

Jung, C.G. (1973) *Synchronicity: an acausal connecting principle.* Translation by R.F.C.Hull. Princeton: Princeton University Press.

Kalecki, M. (2009) *Theory of Economic Dynamics: An Essay on Cyclical and Long-Run Changes in Capitalist Economy*, New York: Monthly Review Press.

Kane, J. & Patapan, H. (2006) In Search of Prudence: The Hidden Problem of Managerial Reform. *Public Administration Review* 66 (5), 711-724.

Kant, I. (1951) *The Moral Law.* (trans. H.J.Paton) London: Hutchinson University Library.

Kant, I. (1964) *Critique of Pure Reason.* (trans. J.M.D. Meiklejohn) London: Dent & Sons Ltd.

Kant, I. (1991) *Kant: Political Writings.* Second, Enlarged Edition. Edited by Hans Reiss and translated by H.B. Nisbet. Cambridge: Cambridge University Press.

Kaplan, A., (1996) *The development practitioner's handbook*, London: Pluto.

Keil, R. (2007) Sustaining Modernity, Modernizing Nature: The Environmental Crisis and the Survival of Capitalism. In R. Krueger & D. Gibbs (eds.), *The Sustainable Development Paradox: Urban Political Economy in the United States and Europe.* pp. 41-65. London: The Guildford Press.

Kelly, G. (1955) *The Psychology of Personal Constructs.* New York: Norton.

Kemmis, S. (2009) Action research as a practice-based practice. *Educational Action Research* 17 (3), 463-474.

Kindleberger, C.P. (1984). *A Financial History of Western Europe.* London: George Allen and Unwin.

Kindleberger, C.P. (1996) *Manias, Panics and Crashes: a history of financial crises.* 3rd Edition. New York: Wiley.

King, M. & Elliott, C. (1997) To the point of farce: A Martian view of the Hardinian taboo – the silence that surrounds population control. BMJ 315, 1441-1443.

Koestler, A. (1964) *The Act of Creation.* New York: the MacMillan Company.

Koestler, A. (1967) *The Ghost in the Machine.* London: Pan Books.

Kołakowski, L. (1999) *Freedom, Fame, Lying and Betrayal: Essays on everyday life.* London: Penguin Books.

Kolb, D. A. (1984) *Experiential learning: experience as the source of learning and development.* London: Prentice-Hall.

Koontz, H. (1958) A preliminary statement of principles of planning and control. *Journal of the Academy of Management* 1, 45 – 61.

Korten, D. C. (1983) Social Development: putting people first. In *Bureaucracy and the Poor: closing the gap*. D.Korten & F.Alfonso (eds.) pp. 201-221, West Hartford: Kumerian

Korten, D. C. (1996) *When Corporations Rule the World*. London: Earthscan Publications.

Korten, D. C. (2006) *The Great Turning: From Empire to Earth Community*. San Francisco: Berrett-Koehler Publishers, Inc.

Korzybski, A. (1933) *Science and Sanity: an introduction to non-aristotellian systems and general semantics*. Lakeville, Connecticut: International Non-aristotelean Library Publishing Co.

Kovel, J. (2002) *The enemy of nature: The end of capitalism or the end of the world?* Nova Scotia: Fernwood.

Kowalski, R. (1994) The teaching of Agricultural Economics, Farm and Agri-business Management in Polish Universities - Quo Vadis? In E. Majewski & G. Entwhistle (eds.), "*Changes in the teaching of Economic subjects in Agricultural Universities*". pp. 26-32. Warsaw: Wydawnictwo SGGW

Kowalski, R. (2004) Development – Paradox, paralysis and praxis. *Protosociology* 20, 390 – 411.

Kowalski, R. (2005) On Terrorism and the Politics of Compulsion. *World Futures* 61(3), 188 – 198.

Kowalski, R. (2006) The Paradoxes of Management with particular reference to the conduct of Development Assistance. *Int. J. Management Concepts and Philosophy* 2 (2), 168-182.

Kowalski, R. (2007). Reflections on the role of logical frameworks in the management of development assistance. *International Journal of Management Practice*, 2 (4), 297 – 305.

Kowalski, R. (2010) The Phenomenology of Development. *Journal of Comparative Social Welfare*. 26 (2-3), 153-164.

Kowalski, R. (2011a) The Gift – Marcel Mauss and International Aid. *Journal of Comparative Social Welfare*. 27 (3), 189-205.

Kowalski, R. (2011b) Brij Mohan: Development, Poverty of Culture, and Social Policy – A Review. *Research on Social Work Practice* 21, 748-751.

Kowalski, R. (2012a) Paradox and Logical Types in Social Enterprises. In Georg Peter & Reuss-Markus Krausse (eds.) *Selbstbeobachtung der modern Gesellschaft und die neuen Grenzen des Sozialen.* pp. 185-201. Wiesbaden: VS Verlag.

Kowalski, R. (2012b) International Development, Paradox and Phronesis. *Protosociology* 29, 183-205.

Kowalski, R. & Kamiński, R. (1999) Business Development Services in Poland – reaching rural areas. *Small Enterprise Development* 10(3), 52 – 59.

Kowalski, R. & Kaškelyte, I. (2005) Project Cycle Management training to empower local communities. *Management in the Public Sector* 1, 93-103.

Kropotkin, P. (2010) *Mutual Aid: A Factor of Evolution.* USA: Digireads.com Publishing.

Krueger, R. & Agyeman, J. (2005) Sustainability schizophrenia or "actually existing sustainabilities?" toward a broader understanding of the politics and promise of local sustainability in the US. *Geoforum* 36, 410-417.

Krueger, R. & Gibbs, D. & (2007) Introduction: Problematizing the Politics of Sustainability. In R. Krueger & D. Gibbs (eds.), *The Sustainable Development Paradox: Urban Political Economy in the United States and Europe.* pp. 1-11. London: The Guildford Press.

Kubose, G. (1973) *Zen Koans.* Chicago: Regnery.

Kuznets S (1967). Population and economic growth in population problems. *Proceedings of the American Philosophical Society.* 3:170 – 93.

Laing, R.D. (1990) *The Divided Self.* Harmondsworth: Penguin.

Lankshear, C. (1993) Functional Literacy from a Freirean Point of View. In McLaren, P. and P. Leonard, (eds.), *Paulo Freire : a critical encounter*, pp. 90-118. London: Routledge.

Lasch, C. (1996) *The Revolt of the Elites and the Betrayal of Democracy.* London: W.W. Norton & Company.

Latouche, S. (2003) Sustainable Development as a paradox. Paper given at a Symposium of the Religion, Science and the Environment Movement on the Baltic Sea, June Retrieved 4 August 2004 from http://www.rsesymposia.org/themedia/File/1151679499-Plenary2_Latouche.pdf

Laurillard, D. (1993) *Rethinking University Teaching: A Framework for the Effective Use of Educational Technology*. London: Routledge.

Lave, J. & Wenger, E. (1991) *Situated Learning: Legitimate Peripheral Participation*. Cambridge: Cambridge University Press.

Lawley, J. (2000) Modelling the structures of binds and double binds. *Rapport* 47, 32 – 35.

Lawn, P. A. (2003) A theoretical foundation to support the Index of Sustainable Economic Welfare (ISEW), Genuine Progress Indicator (GPI), and other related indexes. *Ecological Economics* 44, 105-118.

Lerner, J. (2009) *Boulevard of Broken Dreams: Why Public Efforts to Boost Entrepreneurship and Venture Capital Have Failed – and What to Do About It*. Princeton: Princeton University Press.

Levin, M. & Greenwood, D. (2001) Pragmatic Action Research and the Struggle to Transform Universities into Learning Communities. In Reason, P. & Bradbury, H. (eds.). *Handbook of Action Research*. pp. 102-113. London: Sage.

Lewin, K. (1952) Group decision and social change. In Swanson, G.E., T.M.Newcomb & F.E.Hartley (eds.) *Readings in Social Psychology*. pp.459-473. New York: Henry Holt & Co.

Lewis, M.W. (2000) Exploring paradox: Toward a more comprehensive guide. *Academy of Management Review* 25(4), 760-776.

Lewis, O. (1964) *The Children of Sanchez*. Harmondsworth: Penguin Books.

Lincoln,Y.S. & Guba,E.G. (1985) *Naturalistic Inquiry*. London: Sage Publications.

Lipietz, A. (1995) *Green Hopes: The Future of Political Ecology*. Translated by Malcolm Slater. Cambridge: Polity Press.

Long, N. (2004) Contesting policy ideas from below. In Bøås, M. & D. McNeill (eds.) *Global Institutions and Development: Framing the world?* pp.24-40. London: Routledge.
Long, N. & Villareal, M. (1994) The interweaving of Knowledge and Power in development interfaces. In R. Chambers, I. Scoones & J. Thompson (eds) *Beyond Farmer First: rural people's knowledge, agricultural research and extension practice.* pp.41-52. London: Intermediate Technology.
Lucas, R. (1990) Why Doesn't Capital Flow from Rich to Poor Countries? *American Economic Review*, 80, 92-96.
Lukes, S. (1974) *Power : a radical view.* London: Macmillan.
Machiavelli, N. (2005) *The Prince.* Translated and Edited by Peter Bondanella. Oxford: Oxford University Press.
Marris, P. (1975) *Loss and Change.* New York: Anchor Press/ Doubleday
Martin, S. & Jucker, R. (2005) Educating Earth-literate Leaders. *Journal of Geography in Higher Education* 29 (1), 19 – 29.
Maslow, A.H (1968) *Towards a psychology of being.* New York: D. Van Nostrand Company.
Mauss, M. (2002) *The Gift: The form and reason for exchange in archaic societies.* Abingdon: Routledge.
Max-Neef, M. (1991) *Human Scale Development: Conception, Applications and Further Reflections.* London: The Apex Press.
Max-Neef, M. (1995) Economic growth and quality of life: a threshold hypothesis. *Ecological Economics* 15, 115-118.
May, R. (1974) *Power and Innocence: A search for the sources of violence.* London: Souvenir Press.
Mayers, J. & Vermeulen, S. (2002) *Company-community forestry partnerships: From raw deals to mutual gains?* Instruments for sustainable private sector forestry series. London: International Institute for Environment and Development.
McClelland, D.C. (1987), *Human motivation.* Cambridge: Cambridge University Press.
McDermott, R. (2000) Why Information Technology Inspired but Cannot Deliver Knowledge Management. In E.L. Lesser,

M.A. Fontaine & J.A. Slusher (eds.) *Knowledge and Communities.* pp.21 – 35. Oxford: Butterworth.

M[c]Farlane, C. (2006) Knowledge, learning and development: a post-rationalist approach. *Progress in Development Studies* 6, (4) 287–305.

M[c]Gillivray, M. (1991) The Human Development Index: Yet Another Redundant Composite Development Indicator? *World Development*, 19 (10), 1461-1468.

M[c]Gregor, D. (1960) *The Human Side of Enterprise.* London: M[c]Graw-Hill Book Company.

M[c]Laren, P. & Silva, T.T. da (1993) Decentering Pedagogy: critical literacy, resistance and the politics of memory. In P.M[c]Laren & P. Leonard, (eds.), *Paulo Freire: a critical encounter*, pp. 47-89. London: Routledge.

M[c]Neill, J.R. (2000) *Something New under the Sun: An Environmental History of the Twentieth-Century World.* New York, NY: W.W.Norton.

M[c]Niff, J. & Whitehead, J. (2003). *Action Research: principles and practices.* Second Edition. London: Routledge.

M[c]Whirter, J. (1999) Re-Modelling NLP Part One: Models and Modelling. *Rapport*, 43, 13-16.

M[c]Williams, A., Siegel, D.S. and Wright, P. M. (2006) Guest Editors' Introduction Corporate Social Responsibility: Strategic Implications. *Journal of Management Studies* 43 (1), 1-18.

Mellor, M. (2010) Could the money system be the basis of a sufficiency economy? *real-world economics review* 54, 79-88)

Meppem, A, & Bourke, S. (1999) Different ways of knowing: a communicative turn toward sustainability. *Ecological Economics* 30, 389-404.

Meppem, A. & Gill, R. (1998) Planning for sustainability as a learning concept. *Ecological Economics* 26, 121-137.

Mezirow, J. & Associates (1990) *Fostering critical reflection in adulthood : a guide to transformative and emancipatory learning.* San Francisco: Jossey-Bass Publishers.

Michaelowa, K. & Borrmann, A. (2006) Evaluation Bias and Incentive Structures in Bi- and Multilateral Aid Agencies. *Review of Development Economics* 10(2), 313-329.

Mill, J.S. (1985) *On Liberty*. London: Penguin Books.

Millennium Ecosystem Assessment (2005) Living beyond our means: Natural assets and human well-being. Statement from the Board. http://www.maweb.org/documents/document.429.aspx.pdf accessed on 28 March 2012.

Miller, D. (1990) *The Icarus Paradox: How Exceptional Companies Bring About Their Own Downfall*. New York: Harper Business.

Miller, D. (1993) The Architecture of Simplicity. *Academy of Management Review* 18(1), 116-138.

Miller, S.J., Hickson, D.J. & Wilson, D.C. (1996) Decision-Making in Organizations. In S.R. Clegg, C. Hardy & W.R. Nord (eds.) *Handbook of Organizational Studies*. pp. 291-312. London: Sage Publications.

Mills, S. (2003) *Michel Foucault*. London: Routledge.

Minsky, H. P. (2008) *John Maynard Keynes*. London McGraw-Hill.

Mintzberg, H. (1994) *The rise and fall of strategic planning*. New York: Free Press.

Mintzberg, H., Ahlstrand, B. & Lampel, J. (1998) *Strategy Safari*. London: Prentice Hall.

Mintzberg, H., Raisinghani, D. & Théorêt, A. (1976) The Structure of 'Unstructured' Decision Processes. *Administration Science Quarterly* 21, 246-275.

Mirowski, P. (1991) Post-modernism and the Social Theory of Value. *Journal of Post-Keynesian Economics*. 13, 565-582.

Mischel, T. (1967) Kant and the Possibility of a Science of Psychology. *The Monist* 5, 599-622.

Mohan, B. (2005) New internationalism: Social work's dilemmas, dreams and delusions. *International Social Work*, 48 (3), 237-246.

Mohan, B. (2007) *Fallacies of Development: Crises of Human and Social Development*. New Delhi: Atlantic Publishers & Distributors (P) Ltd.

Mohan, B. (2009) The Politics of Development. 16th ICSD Symposium, Monterrey, Mexico, July 27-31.

Mohan, B. (2011) *Development, Poverty of Culture, and Social Policy.* New York: Palgrave Press.

Morduch, J. (2000) The Microfinance Schism. *World Development* 28 (4), 617-629.

Morgan, J. & Welton, P. (1986) *See what I mean: an introduction to visual communication*. London: Edward Arnold

Morrison, I. (1996) *The Second Curve: Managing the Velocity of Change.* London: Nicholas Brealey Publishing.

Morrow, C.E. & Hull, R.W. (1996) Donor-Initiated Common Pool Resource Institutions: The Case of the Yanesha Forestry Cooperative. *World Development* 24 (10), 1641-1657.

Mosely, P. (1986) Aid Effectiveness: the micro/macro paradox. *Institute of Development Studies Bulletin*, 17, 214-225.

Moskop, J. C. & Iserson, K.V. (2007) Triage in Medicine, Part II: Underlying Values and Principles. *Annals of Emergency Medicine* 49, 282-287.

Mullins, L.J. (2007) Management and Organizational Behaviour. 7th edition, Harlow: Prentice Hall.

Muntz, P. (2004) *Beyond Wittgenstein's Poker: New light on Popper and Wittgenstein*. Aldershot: Ashgate Publishing Ltd.

Murphy, D.F. & Coleman, G. (2000) Thinking partners: business, NGOs and the partnership concept. In J. Bendell (ed.) *Terms for Endearment.* pp.207-215. Sheffield: Greenleaf Publishing Limited.

N'Dione, E.S., Leener, P. de, Perier, J-P., Ndiaye, M. & Jacolin, P. (1997) Reinventing the Present: The Chodak Experience in Senegal. In M. Rahnema with V. Bawtree (eds.) *The Post-Development Reader.* pp.364-376. London: Zed Books.

Nehru, P. (1951) *The Discovery of India*. 3rd ed., London: Meridian Books.

Nelson, L. (1949) *Socratic Method and Critical Philosophy.* Trans. T.K. Brown. New York: Dover.

Nelson, N. & Wright, S. (1995) Participation and Power, in N. Nelson, and S. Wright, (eds.), *Power and participatory development : theory and practice*, pp. 1-18. London: Intermediate Technology.

Neumayer, E. (2001) The human development index and sustainability — a constructive proposal. *Ecological Economics* 39, 101–114.

Newell, P. (2000) Globalisation and the new politics of sustainable development. In J. Bendell (ed.) *Terms for Endearment*. pp.31-39. Sheffield: Greenleaf Publishing Limited.

Nicholson, W. (1999) *Katherine Howard.: A Play*. London: Samuel French.

Nolan, P. (2008) *Capitalism and Freedom: The contradictory character of globalisation*. London: Anthem Press.

North, D. (1981). *Structure and change in economic history*. New York: W.W. Norton.

Nunnenkamp, P. & Thiele, R. (2006) Targeting Aid to the Needy and Deserving: Nothing But Promises? *The World Economy* 29(9),1177 - 1201

Nustad, K.G. (2004) The development discourse in the multilateral system. In Bøås, M. & D. McNeill (eds.) *Global Institutions and Development: Framing the world?* pp.13-23. London: Routledge.

O'Connor, J. (1998) *Natural Causes: Essays in Ecological Marxism*. New York: The Guildford Press.

O'Connor,J. & Seymour,J. (1993) *Introducing Neuro-Linguistic Programming*. London: Mandala.

O'Connor, S. & Kowalski, R. (2005) On Twinning: The Impact of Naming an EU Accession Programme on the Effective Implementation of its Projects. *Public Administration and Development* 25, 437-443.

Offerman, T. (2002) Hurting hurts more than helping helps. *European Economic Review* 46, 1423-1437.

Ollman, B. (1993) *Dialectical investigations*. London: Routledge.

OMAS Consortium (2001) Assessment of the European Union Phare Programmes (Multi-Country) http://europa.eu.int/comm/enlargement/phare_evaluation_pdf/interim_s_zz_eur_01006_fv.pdf Accessed on 20/11/2004.

Orr, D.W. (2004) *Earth in Mind: On Education, Environment, and the Human Prospect*. Washington, D.C.: Island Press.

Osteen, M. (2002) Introduction: Questions of the Gift. In Mark Osteen (ed.) The Questions of the Gift, Essays across Disciplines. pp.1-41. London: Routledge.

Paisey, C., & Paisey, N.J. (2005) Improving accounting education through the use of action research. *Journal of Accounting Education*, 23, 1-19.

Paloni, A. & Zanardi, M. (2006) Development Policy Lending, Conditionality, and Ownership: A Dynamic Agency Model Perspective. *Review of Development Economics,* 10(2), 253–266.

Park, D. & Krishnan, H.A. (2003) Understanding the Stability-Change Paradox: Insights from the Evolutionary, Adaptation, and Institutionalization Perspectives. *International Journal of Management* 20(3), 265-270.

Parguel, B., Benoît-Moreau, F. & Larceneux, F. (2011) How Sustainability Ratings Might Deter "Greenwashing": A Closer Look at Ethical Corporate Communication. *Journal of Business Ethics* 102 (1), 15-28

Paul VI (1967) *Populorum Progressio* Encyclical letter. Vatican: Libreria Editrice. http://www.vatican.va/holy_father/paul_vi/encyclicals/documents/hf_p-vi_enc_26031967_populorum_en.html accessed on 6/9/10

Peetz, D. & Genreith, H. (2011) The financial sector and the real economy. *real-world economics review*, 57, 40-47.

Perrow, C. (1979) *Complex Organizations – a critical essay.* 2nd edition, Glenview, Illonois: Scott, Foresman & Co.

Peters, T. (1988) *Thriving on Chaos.* London: Pan Books.

Peters, T. & Waterman, R.H.Jr. (1982) *In Search of Excellence.* New York: Harper & Row.

Pieterse, J.N. (1999) Critical Holism and the Tao of Development. In *Critical Development Theory,* Ronaldo Munck & Denis O'Hearn (eds). pp.63-88. Dhaka, The University Press.

Pieterse, J.N. (2004) Globalization and Culture: Global melange. Lanham, MD: Rowman & Littlefield.

Pimbert, M. & Pretty, J. (1997) Diversity and Sustainability in Community-based Conservation, paper presented at the

UNESCO-IIPA Regional Workshop on Community-based Conservation.

Pinker, S. (1994) *The Language Instinct: The New Science of Language and Mind.* London: Penguin Science

Plato (1993) *The Republic.* (trans. R Waterfield). Oxford: Oxford University Press.

Polanyi, M. (1958) *Personal Knowledge: towards a post-critical philosophy.* London: Routledge & Kegan Paul.

Polanyi, M. (1998) *The Logic of Liberty: Reflections and Rejoinders.* London: Routledge.

Polimeni, J. M. & Polimeni, R.I. (2006) Jevons' Paradox and the myth of technological liberation. *Ecological Complexity* 3, 344 – 353.

Porter, D. & Onyach-Olaa, M. (1999) Inclusive planning and allocation for rural services. *Development in Practice* 9, 56 – 67.

Porter, D.J. (1995) Scenes from Childhood: The homesickness of Development Discourses. In *Power of Development*, J. Crush (ed.) pp.63-86. London: Routledge.

Postman, N. & Weingartner, C. (1969) *Teaching as a subversive activity.* New York: Delacorte Press.

Presich, R. (1985) Five Stages in My Thinking on Development. In Meier, G. & D. Seers (eds.) *Pioneers in Development.* pp. 175-191. Oxford: Oxford University Press.

Pressfield, S. (2002) *The war of art.* New York, NY: Grand Central Publ.

Pugh, D.S. & Hickson, D.J. (2000) *Great Writers on Organizations.* 2nd Omnibus edition, Aldershot: Ashgate Publishing.

Putnam, R.D. (2000) *Bowling Alone.* New York: Simon & Schuster Paperbacks.

Putz, M. & Raynor, M.E. (2005) Integral Leadership: overcoming the paradox of growth. *Strategy and Leadership* 33 (1), 46-48.

Quine,W.V. (1976) *The Ways of Paradox and Other Essays.* Cambridge: Harvard University Press.

Rabey, G. (2003) The paradox of teamwork. *Industrial and Commercial Training* 35(4), 158 – 162.

Rahman, M.A. (1993) *People's self-development: perspectives on participatory action research.* London: Zed Books.

Rahnema, M. (1992) Participation. In W. Sachs (ed.) *The Development Dictionary: A guide to knowledge as power.* pp. 116-131. London: Zed Books.

Rahnema, M. (1997) Towards Post-development: Searching for Signposts, a New Language and New Paradigms. In M. Rahnema with V. Bawtree (eds.) *The Post-Development Reader.* pp.377-403. London: Zed Books.

Ramus, C. A. & Montiel, I. (2005) When Are Corporate Environmental Policies a Form of Greenwashing? *Business & Society*, 44 (4), 377-414.

Ranson, S., Hinings, R. & Greenwood, R. (1980) The structuring of organizational structure. *Administrative Science Quarterly* 25(1), 1-14.

Ravalion, M. (2012) Troubling tradeoffs in the Human Development Index. *Journal of Development Economics* 99 (2), 201-209.

Reagan, G.M. (1990) An Artist Explores the Concept of Levels in Matter. *Leonardo* 23 (1), 35-40.

Reinhardt, G. Y. (2006) Shortcuts and Signals: An Analysis of the Micro-level Determinants of Aid Allocation, with Case Study Evidence from Brazil. *Review of Development Economics,* 10(2), 297–312.

Reinert, E.S. (2006) German Economics as Development Economics: From the Thirty Years War to World War II. In Jomo, K.S. & E.S. Reinert (eds.) *The Origins of Development Economics,* pp.48-68. New Delhi: Tulika Books.

Reinert, E.S. (2012) Neo-classical economics: A trail of economic destruction since the 1970s. *real-world economics review* 60, 2-17.

Reinert, E.S. (2013) Civilizing capitalism: "good" and "bad" greed from the enlightenment to Thorstein Veblen (1857-1929). *real-world economics review*, 63, 57-72.

Rihani, S. (2002) *Complex Systems Theory and Development Practice: understanding non-linear realities.* London, Zed Books.

Rist, G. (2002) *The History of Development: From Western Origins to Global Faith.* (new edition), London: Zed Books.

Rittel, H.W.J. & Webber, M.M. (1973) Dilemmas in General Theory of Planning. *Policy Sciences* 4(2), 155-169.

Ritzer, G. (2007) The Globalization of Nothing 2. Thousand Oaks, CA: Pine Forge Press.

Rodrik, D. (2011) *The Globalization Paradox: Why global markets, states and democracy can't coexist.* Oxford: Oxford University Press.

Rogers, A. (1993) Adult education and agricultural extension: some comparisons. *International Journal of Lifelong Education* 12, (3) 165-176.

Rogers, E. & Shoemaker, F.F. (1971) *Communication of Innovations: a Cross Cultural Approach.* 2nd ed. New York: The Free Press.

Rosen, R. (1986) The Physics of Complexity. pp.35 -73 In Trappl, R. (ed.) "*Power, Autonomy, Utopia: New Approaches toward Complex Systems*". New York and London: Plenum Press.

Rossi, S. (2007) *Money and Payments in Theory and Practice*, London: Routledge.

Rowlands, J. (1998) *Questioning Empowerment, Working with Women in Honduras*. London: Oxfam.

Roy, A. (1999) *The Cost of Living.* New York: The Modern Library.

The Royal Society (2012) *People and the planet.* The Royal Society Science Policy Centre report. p.134. London: The Royal Society.

Ruffer, T. & Lawson, A. (2002) General Budget Support: Rationale, Characteristics and Experience. Paper for the Rural Livelihoods Advisors' conference, DFID, June 2002.

Russell, B. (1908). Mathematical Logic as based on the Theory of Types. *American Journal of Mathematics* 30, 222-262.

Russell, B. (1993) *Introduction to Mathematical Philosophy.* London: Routledge.

Ryle,G. (1960) *Dilemmas.* Cambridge: The University Press.

Ryle, G. (1967) Teaching and Training. In *The Concept of Education.* R.S.Peters (ed.), pp.105-119. London: Routledge & Kegan Paul.

Sabel, C. & Reddy, S. (2003) Learning to Learn: Undoing the Gordian Knot of Development Today. Mimeo. http://www2.law.columbia.edu/sabel/papers.htm

Sachs, J. (2009) *Common Wealth: Economics for a Crowded Planet.* London: Penguin Books.

Sachs, W. (1992) *The Development Dictionary.* London: Zed Books.

Sachs, W. (1997) The Need for the Home Perspective. In M. Rahnema with V. Bawtree (eds.) *The Post-Development Reader.* pp.290-300. London: Zed Books.

Sahlins, M. (1997) The Original Affluent Society. In M. Rahnema with V. Bawtree (eds.) *The Post-Development Reader.* pp.3-21. London: Zed Books.

Santiso, C. (2003) The Paradox of Governance: Objective or Condition of Multilateral Development Finance. Washington: *SAIS Working paper* WP/03/03 pp.1-30.

Santos, B. de Sousa (1999) On Oppositional Postmodernism. In R. Munck & D. O'Hearn (eds.) *Critical Development Theory.* pp.29-43. Dhaka: The University Press.

Sawyer, G.C. (1983) *Corporate Planning as a Creative Process.* Oxford: OH, Planning Executives Institute.

Say, J.-B. (1971) *A Treatise on Political Economy or the Production, Distribution and Consumption of Wealth.* New York: Augustus M. Kelley.

Schaefer, B. D. & Kim, A. B. (2013) U.N. General Assembly: Foreign Aid Recipients Vote Against the U.S. *Issue Brief* 3862, 1-4. http://report.heritage.org/ib3862 accessed on 22 December 2013.

Schein, E.H. (1987) *Process Consultation (volume 2): Lessons for Managers and Consultants.* Reading, MA.: Addison Wesley.

Schein, E.H. (1996) Kurt Lewin's Change Theory in the Field and in the Classroom: Notes Towards a Model of Managed Learning. *Systems Practice* 9 (1), 27-47.

Schein, E.H., Kahane, A. & Scharmer, C.O. (2001) Humility and Ignorance: What It Takes to Be an Effective Process Consultant. *Reflections* 3 (2), 8-20.

Schmitt, R. (1987) Wanted: Hands-on Engineers. *High Technology Magazine*, Boston

Schoeck, H. (1969) *Envy: a Theory of Social Behaviour.* London: Secker & Warburg.

Schön, D. A. (1983) *The Reflective Practitioner: How professionals think in action*. London: Temple Smith.

Schön, D. (1987) *Educating the Reflective Practitioner: Towards a New Design for Teaching and Learning in the Professions.* San Francisco; Jossey-Bass.

Schopenhauer, A. (1951) *On Human Nature, Essays.* London: Allen and Unwin.

Schumacher, E. F. (1973). *Small is beautiful: Economics as if people mattered.* London: Blond & Briggs. Schumpeter, J.A. (2010) [1943] *Capitalism, Socialism and Democracy.* London: Routledge Classics.

Scitovsky, T. (1976) *The Joyless Economy: An Enquiry into Human Satisfaction and Consumer Dissatisfaction.* Oxford: Oxford University Press.

Scott, J.C. (1998) *Seeing Like a State.* New Haven: Yale University Press.

Scruton, R. (2002) *An intelligent person's guide to Philosophy.* London: Gerald Duckworth & Co. Ltd.

Seabrook, J. (1988) *The Race for Riches: The Human Cost of Wealth.* Basingstoke: Marshall Pickering.

Searle, J.R. (1995) *The Construction of Social Reality.* London: Penguin

Sedlacek, T. (2011) *Economics of Good and Evil: The quest for economic meaning from Gilgamesh to Wall Street.* Oxford: Oxford University Press.

Seely, M., Duong, P.Q. & Trites, R. (2000) The Path to Cybernance. www.pmforum.org/library/papers/2000/pathcybernance.pdf accessed on 22 November 2007.

Seers, D. (1969) The meaning of development. *International Development Review* pp.2-6.

Sen, A. (1999) *Development as Freedom.* Oxford: Oxford University Press.

Senge, P., Scharmer, C.O., Jaworski, J. & Flowers, B.S. (2005) *Presence: Exploring profound change in people, organizations and society.* London: Nicholas Brealey Publishing.

Sennett, R. (1998) *The Corrosion of Character: The Personal Consequences of Work in the New Capitalism.* New York: W.W.Norton & Co.

Sennett, R. (2002) *The Fall of Public Man.* London: Penguin Books.

Servaes, J. (1996) Participatory Communication Research with New Social Movements: a Realistic Utopia. In J. Servaes, T.L. Jacobson, & S. A. White (eds.) *Participatory Communication for Social Change.* pp. 82-108. New Dehli: Sage.

Severino, J. & Charnoz, O. (2004) A Development Paradox. *Revue d'Economie du Développement,* 17: 77-97.

Shelton, C.D. (1999) Quantum Leaps: Seven Skills for Workplace Re-creation. Boston, MA: Butterworth-Heinemann.

Sheldrake, R. (1988) *The Presence of the Past: Morphic Resonance & The Habits of Nature.* Rochester, Vermont: Park Street Press.

Sheth, D.L. (1997) Alternatives from an Indian Grassroots Perspective. In *The Post-Development Reader.* Majid Rahnema with Victoria Bawtree (eds.) pp.329-335. London: Zed Books.

Shor, I. (1993) Education is Politics: Paulo Freire's Critical Pedagogy. In P. McLaren, and P. Leonard, (eds.) *Paulo Freire : a critical encounter,* pp.25-35. London: Routledge.

Shreeves, R. (2004) *Gender Issues In The Development Of Rural Areas In Kazakstan.* Unpublished PhD thesis: University of Wolverhampton.

Shultz, H. & Smith, O.C. (2001) *Starbucks Coffee Company; Corporate Social Responsibility Annual Report.* USA: Starbucks.

Shutt, H. (1999) *The Trouble with Capitalism: an enquiry into the causes of Global Economic Failure.* Dhaka: The University Press.

Shutt, H. (2001) *A New Democracy: Alternatives to a Bankrupt World Order.* London and New York: Zed Books.

Shutt, H. (2005) *The Decline of Capitalism: Can a Self-Regulated Profits System Survive?* London: Zed Books.

Sigelman, L., Sigelman, C.K. & Walkosz, B.J.(1992) The Public and the Paradox of Leadership: An Experimental Analysis. *American Journal of Political Science.* 36 (2), 366-385.

Simmel, G. (1997) Simmel on Culture: Selected Writings. D. Frisby & M. Featherstone (eds.) Thousand Oaks, CA: Sage.

Simon J (1981). *The ultimate resource.* Princeton, NJ: Princeton University Press.

Sinn, H.-W. (2012) *The Green Paradox: A supply-side approach to global warming.* London: The MIT Press.

Skinner, A.S. (1997) Analytical Introduction. In Adam Smith *The Wealth of Nations* Books I-III, p.8-85. Harmondsworth: Penguin Books.

Sklair, L. & Miller, D. (2010) Capitalist globalization, corporate social responsibility and social policy. *Critical Social Policy* 30 (4), 472-495.

Sklar, M. J. (1992) *The United States as a Developing Country.* Cambridge: Cambridge University Press.

Smith, A. (1999a) [1776] *The Wealth of Nations Books I-III.* London: Penguin Classics.

Smith, A. (1999b) [1777] *The Wealth of Nations Books IV-V.* London: Penguin Classics.

Smith, A. (2006 [1759]) *The Theory of Moral Sentiments.* Mineola, New York: Dover Publications.

Smith, D. (1990) Assessment, technology and the quality revolution. (in) Bell, C. & Harris, D. (eds.) *Assessment and Evaluation: World Yearbook of Education 1990.* pp 41-55, London: Kogan Page.

Smith, J. (2003) Patronage, per diems and the "workshop mentality". The practice of family planning programs in Southeastern Nigeria. *World Development* 31 (4), 703-715.

Smith, T.B. (1973) The Policy Implementation Process. *Policy Sciences* 4(2), 197-209.

Snowden, D. (2002) Complex acts of knowing: paradox and descriptive self-awareness. *Journal of Knowledge Management* 6 (2), 100-111

Snyder, B.R. (1971) *The Hidden Curriculum*. Cambridge, MA: MIT Press.
Söderbaum, P. (2012) Democracy and Sustainable Development—Implications for Science and Economics, *real-world economics review* 60, 107–119.
Sorensen, R.A. (2003) *A Brief History of the Paradox*. Oxford: Oxford University Press.
Speth, J.G. & Haas, P.M. (2006) *Global Environmental Governance*. Washington, D.C.: Island Press.
Stacey, R.D. (1992) *Managing the Unknowable: strategic boundaries between order and chaos in organizations*. San Francisco: Jossey-Bass.
Stacey, R. (2001) *Complex Responsive Processes in Organizations: Learning and Knowledge Creation*. London: Routledge.
Stacey, R. (2003) Learning as an Activity of Interdependent People. *The Learning Organization* 10 (6), 1-10.
Stacey, R.D. (2007) *Strategic Management and Organisational Dynamics: The challenge of complexity to ways of thinking about organisations*. 5th ed. Harlow: Prentice Hall/Financial Times.
Stacey, R. & Griffin, D. (2005) *A Complexity Perspective on Researching Organizations*. London: Routledge.
Standing, G. (2011) *The Precariat: The New Dangerous Class*. London: Bloomsbury Academic.
Starbuck, W. (2004) Why I stopped trying to understand the real world. *Organization Studies*, 25(7): 1233-1254.
Steiner, G.A. (1979) *Strategic Planning: What every manager must know*. New York: Free Press.
Steiner, G.A. & Kunin, H.E. (1983) Formal Strategic Planning in the United States Today. *Long Range Planning* 26 (3), 12-17.
Stewart, I. & Joines, V.S. (1987) *TA Today: A new introduction to Transactional Analysis*. Nottingham: Lifespace Publishing.
Stigler, G.J. (1987) Frank Hyneman Knight. In J. Eatwell (ed.) *The New Palgrave: A Dictionary of Economics*, vol. 3, 55-59. New York: Stockton Press.
Stiglitz, J. (2010) *Freefall: Free Markets and the Sinking of the Global Economy*. London: Penguin Books.

Stirrat, R.L. & Henkel, H. (1997) The Development Gift: The Problem of Reciprocity in the NGO World. *Annals of the American Academy of Political and Social Science* (Nov.), 66 – 80.

Storr, A. (1998) *The Essential Jung: Selected Writings.* London: Fontana Press.

Strawson, P.F. (2004) *Subject and Predicate in Logic and Grammar.* 2nd ed. Aldershot: Ashgate Publishing.

Streatfield, P.J. (2001) *The Paradox of Control in Organizations.* London: Routledge.

Stringer, E. (1996) *Action Research: A handbook for practitioners.* London: Sage.

Sullivan, R. & Warner, M. (2004) Introduction. In M. Warner & R. Sullivan (eds.) *Putting Partnerships to Work.* pp.12-23. Sheffield: Greenleaf Publishing Ltd.

Swidler, A. & Watkins, S.C. (2008) "Teach a Man to Fish": The Sustainability Doctrine and the Social Consequences. *World Development* 37(7), 1182-1196.

Sykes, K. (2005) *Arguing with Anthropology: An introduction to critical theories of the gift.* London: Routledge.

Talberth, J., Cobb, C. & Slattery, N. (2007) *The Genuine Progress Indicator 2006: A Tool for Sustainable Development.* Oakland, CA: Redefining Progress

Talbot, C. (2005) *The Paradoxical Primate.* Exeter: Imprint Academic.

Tallis, R.C. (2003) Human Freedom as a Reality-producing Illusion. *Monist* 86 (2), 200 – 219.

Tendler, J. (1975) *Inside Foreign Aid.* London: The John Hopkins University Press.

Thiele, R., Nunnenkamp, P. & Dreher, A. (2007) Do donors target aid in line with the Millennium Development Goals? A sector perspective of aid allocation, *Discussion paper, World Institute for Development Economics Research, Helsinki,* No. 2007,(4), 1-27.

Thomas, A. (2000) What makes good development management? In D. Eade (ed.) *Development and Management.* pp. 40 – 52. Oxford: Oxfam.

Thomas, K. (1976) Conflict and Conflict Management. In M. Dunnette (ed.) *Handbook of Industrial and Organizational Psychology*, pp.889-935. New York: John Wiley & Sons.

Tocqueville, A. de (2002 [1835]) *Democracy in America*. New York: Bantam Dell.

Toynbee, A.J. (1974) *A Study of History*. Abridgement of volumes I-VI by D.C.Somervell,. Oxford: Oxford University Press.

Tsoukas, H. & Chia, R. (2002) On Organizational Becoming: Rethinking Organizational Change. Organization Science, 13, (5), 567-582.

Tucker, V. (1996) Health, Medicine and Development: A Field of Cultural Struggle. In Vincent Tucker (ed.) *Cultural Perspectives on Development*. pp. 110-128 London: Frank Cass.

Turner, A. (2009) Population ageing: what should we worry about? *Philosophical Transactions of the Royal Society B*, 364, 3009 – 3021.

Turner, B.L. (1996) The sustainability principle in global agendas: implications for understanding land use/cover change. *The Geographical Journal*, 163 (2), 133 – 140.

UNDP (1990) *Human Development Report 1990*. New York: Oxford University Press.

UNRISD (United Nations Research Institute for Social Development) (1995) *States of Disarray: The Social Effects of Globalization*. Geneva: UNRISD.

Uphoff, N.T. (1996) *Learning from Gal Oya : Possibilities for Participatory Development and Post-Newtonian Social Science*. London: IT Publications.

Vaihinger, H. (1924) *The Philosophy of "As If."* London: Routledge & Kegan Paul.

Van den Ban, A.W. & Hawkins, H.S. (1996) *Agricultural Extension*. 2nd Edition. Oxford: Blackwell Science.

Vanaerschot, G. (1993) Empathy as Releasing Several Micro-Processes in the Client. In D.Brazier, (ed.), *Beyond Carl Rogers*, pp.47-71. London: Constable.

Visvanathan, S. (1991). Mrs. Brundtland's disenchanted cosmos. *Alternatives*, 16, 377–384.

von Bertalanffy, L. (1968) *General System Theory.* New York: George Braziller.
Waelchli, F. (1989) The VSM and Ashby's Law as illuminants of historical management thought. In R.Espejo & R.Harnden (eds.) *The Viable Systems Model: Interpretations and Applications of Stafford Beer's VSM.* pp. 51-75. Chichester: John Wiley & Sons.
Waggoner, P.F. & Ausubel, J.H. (2002) A framework for sustainability science: a renovated IPAT identity. *Proceedings of the National Academy of Science* 99 (12), 7860-7865.
Wallace,T. (2000) Development management and the aid chain: the case of NGOs. In D. Eade (ed.) *Development and Management.* pp.18-39. Oxford: Oxfam GB.
Wallich, H. (1972) Zero Growth. *Newsweek* 24 January p.62
Walzer, M. (1983) *Spheres of Justice : A Defense of Pluralism and Equality.* New York: Basic Books Inc.
Wang, T. Y. (1999) U.S. Foreign Aid and UN Voting: An Analysis of Important Issues. *International Studies Quarterly.* 43 (1), 199-210.
Warhurst, A. (2005) Future roles of business in society: the expanding boundaries of corporate responsibility and a compelling case for partnership. *Futures* 37, 151-16
Warren-Piper, D. (1985) The changing role and status of post secondary teachers. *Higher Education in Europe*, 10, 6-11.
Watts, M. (1995) A New Deal in Emotions: Theory and practice and the crisis of development. In J. Crush (ed.) *Power of Development*, pp.44-62. London: Routledge.
Watzlawick, P. (1993) *The Language of Change: Elements of Therapeutic Communication.* New York: Norton & Co.
Watzlawick, P., Bavelas, J.B. & Jackson, D.D. (1967) *Pragmatics of Human Communication.* London: W W Norton & Company.
Weber, M. (1947) *The Theory of Social and Economic Organization.* London: Routledge and Kegan Paul.
Webster, A. (1990) *Introduction to the Sociology of Development.* 2nd edition, London: MacMillan.
Weeks, D. (1992) *The Eight Essential Steps to Conflict Resolution.* Los Angeles: J.P.Tarcher.

Weick, K.E. (1990) Cartographic Myths in Organizations. In A.S. Huff (ed.) *Mapping Strategic Thought*. pp.1-10. Chichester: John Wiley and Sons.
Weick, K.E. & Westley, F. (1996) Organizational Learning: Affirming an Oxymoron. In Clegg, S.R., Hardy, C. & Nord, W.R. *Handbook of Organization Studies*. pp.440 – 458. London: Sage.
Wharton, L. (2001) Order Through Chaos. http://www.leader-values.com/content/detailPrint.asp?ContentDetailID=215 (accessed on 25 October 2006).
Whitehead, A.N. (1922) *The Principle of Relativity with Applications to Physical Science*. Cambridge: Cambridge University Press.
Wield, D. (1999) Tools for project development within a public action framework, *Development in Practice* 9(1):33-42.
Wildavsky, A. (1971) Does Planning Work? *Public Interest* 24, 95-104.
Wildavsky, A. (1973) If Planning is Everything, Maybe it's Nothing. *Policy Sciences*, 4(2), 127-153.
Williams, H. (1996) *The essence of managing groups and teams*. London: Prentice Hall.
Wilson, K. (2007) The money lender's dilemma. In *What's wrong with MICROFINANCE?* Thomas Dichter & Malcolm Harper (eds.). pp.97-108. Rugby: Practical Action Publishing.
Wilson, R.A. (1990) *Quantum Psychology*. Tempe, Arizona: New Falcon Publications.
de Wit, R. & Meyer, R. (1999) *Strategy Synthesis: Resolving Strategy Paradoxes to Create Competitive Advantage*. London, Thomson Learning.
World Bank (1989) *Sub-Saharan Africa: From Crisis to Sustainable Growth. A Long-Term Perspective Study*. Washington, D.C. : The World Bank.
World Commission on Environment and Development (WCED) (1987). *Our Common Future*. Oxford: Oxford University Press.
Worthy, J.C. (1959) *Big Business and Free Men*. New York: Harper & Row.

Wotton, K., Amit, H.R., Kalma, S., Hillman, E., Hillman, D., Smith, S.E. & Cosway, N. (1994), *Basic Concepts of International Health*, Ottawa: Canadian University Consortium for Health in Development.

Wright, R. (2001) *Nonzero: History, evolution & human cooperation*. London: Abacus.

Yates, J.J. (2012). Abundance on Trial: The Cultural Significance of "Sustainability". *The Hedgehog Review* 14 (2)

Yolles, M. (2004) Implications for Beer's ontological system/ metasystem dichotomy. *Kybernetes* 33 (3/4), 726-764.

Zan, L. (1987) What's left for formal planning? *Economia Aziendale* 6(2), 187-204.

Zaoual, H. (1997) The Economy and Symbolic Sites of Africa. In M. Rahnema with V. Bawtree (eds.) *The Post-Development Reader*. pp.30-39. London: Zed Books.

Žižek, S. (2002) *Looking awry: An introduction to Jacques Lacan through popular culture*. Cambridge, MA: MIT Press.

Zuber-Skerritt, O. (2002) The concept of action learning. *The Learning Organization* 9 (3), 114-124.

Zuber-Skerritt, O. & Farquhar, M. (2002) Action learning, action research and process management (ALARPM): a personal history. *The Learning Organization* 9 (3), 102-113.

Afterwords:

. . .

Tolling for the searching ones on their speechless seeking trail
For the lonesome hearted lovers with too personal a tale
And for each unharmful, gentle soul misplaced inside a jail
And we gazed upon the chimes of freedom flashing

Bob Dylan

Index

B

C

F

G

H

I

O

P

R

S

T

U

V

W